PERSUASIVE COMMUNICATION

PERSUASIVE
COMMUNICATION

THIRD EDITION

James B. Stiff
Paul A. Mongeau

THE GUILFORD PRESS
New York   London

Copyright © 2016 The Guilford Press
A Division of Guilford Publications, Inc.
370 Seventh Avenue, Suite 1200, New York, NY 10001
www.guilford.com

Printed in the United States of America

This book is printed on acid-free paper.

Last digit is print number: 9   8   7   6   5   4   3   2   1

Library of Congress Cataloging-in-Publication Data is available
from the publisher.

ISBN 978-1-4625-2684-0

To Gerald R. Miller (1931–1993),
a good friend and mentor

Preface

This represents the second edition of *Persuasive Communication* that we have coauthored since Jim wrote the first edition. Those of you who know us understand our long friendship and similar academic pedigrees. We were colleagues in the graduate programs at Arizona State University and Michigan State University, and we have coauthored several publications and convention papers. Consequently, we came to this project with similar perspectives and agreement about changes that were necessary to improve upon for the second edition of the book.

After nearly 40 years, we both remain intrigued by the study of persuasion. While Paul remains steadfast in his commitment to teaching, scholarly research, and service, Jim left academia more than two decades ago for a career in applied persuasion as a jury consultant. The combination of our academic and applied backgrounds provides a unique perspective and a solid foundation for addressing both the history and the current state of affairs of the study of persuasive communication.

The third edition of *Persuasive Communication* carries forward several important traditions established in the book's earlier editions. Most important, while our view of persuasion is broad, we consciously apply several filters that narrow the scope of the theory and research we review. First, we are social scientists and therefore adopt a social science approach to the study of persuasion. For example, we devote the first two chapters of this book to defining the concepts and describing the methods used to study persuasion *empirically*. A key assumption stemming from our scientific training emphasizes the importance of research as a cumulative process in which each set of studies builds upon the preceding ones. Particular hypotheses and theories are frequently tested, retested, and revised as our understanding of a particular area increases. Consequently, most of our reviews are historical in nature. We believe that understanding early foundational work in an area is essential to our critically examining the modern state of theory and research. For example, our Chapter 8 examination of the persuasive effects of fear appeals includes a historical review that begins with Janis and Feshbach (1953). In much the same way, our review of the relationships between attitudes and behaviors (in Chapters 3 and 4) focuses much attention on the evolution of knowledge that began during the Great Depression of the 1930s (LaPiere, 1934). This historical understanding not only informs the current literature, but also highlights the important self-correcting function of social science research. For example, we review the literature on gender effects in persuasion in Chapter 9. Although we have known for decades that women are no more easily persuaded than men, reviewing this literature proves informative because it illustrates how Alice Eagly and her colleagues (Eagly & Carli, 1981; Eagly, Wood, & Chaiken, 1978) used social science research methods to correct an incorrect belief that was based on *common sense* but methodologically flawed research.

Second, early studies of persuasion typically focused on the effects of one or two independent variables on a particular outcome, while more recent studies have become quite complex. Thus, current research is replete with multiple moderator variables and intervening variables requiring sophisticated statistical analyses like structural equation modeling and meta-analysis (see Chapter 1). A review of decades-old studies often provides a more straightforward explanation of effects and a simpler pattern of findings that can be useful in describing the current state of knowledge in the field. Thus, our historical reviews of literature typically focus on conceptual rather than methodological advances. We focus on new methodologies and analyses only to the extent that they help inform our examination of theoretical relationships. The misattribution paradigm described in Chapter 4 is an excellent example of a methodological advancement that informs our understanding of theoretical processes.

Third, we focus this book on theory and research rather than on the practical application of theory in persuasive contexts. We designed this book to provide a fundamental understanding of the theory and research in persuasion. In doing so, we expect students who understand this material will be better prepared to both critically analyze messages and design and execute effective persuasive messages and campaigns themselves. Although we introduce a number of applications of theory and research (what we call boxes) to illustrate various concepts, we do not attempt to translate the theory into a series of "how-to" recommendations for designing persuasive appeals. That is left to readers' imagination and creativity.

Finally, we believe that a well-rounded approach to the study of persuasive communication requires looking across disciplines (primarily communication and social psychology, but also marketing, public health, and political science). A complete understanding of the persuasion process, for example, involves knowledge of both attitudes and psychological processes as well as communication and message production processes. We continue to be dismayed by many scholars' isolationist perspective in communication and social psychology. Some communication scholars have become myopic in their focus on message design and production. On the other hand, some social psychologists have correspondingly limited their inquiry to cognitive and affective processes. This book continues to reflect the view we adopted nearly four decades ago that the study of persuasion requires understanding the mutual influence of cognitive and affective processes, on the one hand, and the production and processing of messages, on the other.

This book continues to be organized into three major sections, the first of which focuses on the *fundamental issues in persuasion research*. This section includes chapters on concepts, definitions, and basic distinctions (Chapter 1); methods of investigating persuasive communication (Chapter 2); the attitude–behavior relationship (Chapter 3); the effects of behavior on attitudes (Chapter 4); and cognitive response models (Chapter 5). Given the influential role of cognitive response models in the modern study of persuasion, Chapter 5 was moved forward from Chapter 10 in the second edition.

The second major section of the book, on *components of persuasive transactions*, breaks persuasion down into its component parts. Specifically, this section includes a discussion of source characteristics in persuasive communication (Chapter 6); message appeals (both rational appeals in Chapter 7, and emotional appeals, in Chapter 8); receiver characteristics (Chapter 9); and the characteristics of persuasive settings (Chapter 10).

The final section of the book focuses on *persuasion models*. Specifically, we examine models of interpersonal compliance (Chapter 11); producing and resisting influence messages (Chapter 12); and persuasive communication campaigns (Chapter 13).

NEW TO THIS EDITION

Each chapter reflects a current review of the research and theoretical perspectives while maintaining the same theoretical perspective as the first two editions. We have created boxes in each chapter and added discussions designed to illustrate the practical application of key concepts. In Chapter 1, we describe the rapid change in attitudes regarding same-sex marriage and have added coverage of Schwarz's Construal Model (2007) as we discuss conceptualizations of the attitude construct. In Chapter 2, we describe an example from a patent infringement lawsuit to illustrate the limits of conventional wisdom and underscore the importance of social science research. In Chapter 3, we have added a discussion of the Integrative Model of Behavioral Prediction (Yzer, 2012) and a figure to differentiate the model from similar frameworks. We also discuss how misperceptions of social norms contribute to dangerous levels of drinking on college campuses.

In Chapter 4, we extend our review of counterattitudinal advocacy research and have added a series of figures to illustrate the evolution of Cognitive Dissonance Theory (Festinger, 1957) and Self-Perception Theory (Bem, 1967). Chapter 6 now includes a discussion of the timing of source credibility information and the use of surrogates to bolster the credibility of message sources. Chapter 7 expands the discussion of affective processes and their effect on behavioral intentions as well as the use of statistical and narrative evidence in political settings. Chapter 8 includes a more detailed discussion of guilt appeals and the emotions they can generate in persuasive targets.

Additions to Chapter 10 examine the special challenges with online persuasion and the use of social media by ISIS and revolutionaries during the Arab Spring. In Chapter 12, we extend the discussion of message planning and use courtroom testimony to illustrate the effects of plan complexity on witness credibility. In Chapter 13, we describe the power that computer technology affords political candidates, who are now capable of tailoring their messages to the specific attitudes and experiences of individual voters.

We hope you enjoy reading the book as much as we did preparing it, and find that our review of persuasion research is relevant, clear, and thorough.

Acknowledgments

We would like to thank the good folks at The Guilford Press, especially C. Deborah Laughton, for their exceptional patience. Our lives' complications interfered with this project and delayed its completion on a number of occasions, and we are grateful that we were afforded the opportunity to complete our work. We would also like to thank Carolyn Webster (a colleague of Jim's at The Focal Point), who prepared the graphics for this edition, and Anna Brackett, our editorial project manager at Guilford, for her outstanding work.

Contents

FUNDAMENTAL ISSUES IN PERSUASION RESEARCH

This first part of the book examines the essential concepts of persuasive communication. Chapter 1 introduces and defines persuasive activity. Chapter 2 reviews the research methods most common to persuasion research; included in this review are the key criteria for evaluating the quality of research investigations. Chapter 3 investigates the relationship between attitudes and behavior and answers the question "Under what conditions do attitudes predict behavior?" Next, Chapter 4 describes the conditions under which changes in behavior actually produce attitude change. Part I concludes with Chapter 5, where we outline the predominant paradigm in persuasion research, namely, cognitive response models.

CHAPTER 1

Concepts, Definitions, and Basic Distinctions

LOOKING AHEAD . . . This chapter introduces the concept of *persuasion* and provides a definition of *persuasive communication*. Next, several related definitions of the *attitude* construct are proffered and analyzed. The chapter concludes with a discussion of functional approaches to studying attitudes as well as the role that attitudes play in the development of theories of persuasion.

As connoisseurs of late-night "junk TV," we routinely subject ourselves to the worst that television advertising has to offer. The number and variety of advertisements that can be aired in a single commercial break often amaze us. Not long ago, Jim watched seven different messages during one commercial break. One ad encouraged viewers to try a new low-fat yogurt that helps regulate the digestive system, another touted the speed of a wireless phone network, and there were two competing commercials for low-cost auto insurance. Of course, there were the ubiquitous fast-food commercials and one for an online dating service.

There were marked differences in the style, substance, and objectives of these TV ads, but they shared one important characteristic: they were all intended to persuade late-night viewers (like ourselves) of *something*. The diverse goals of these motley commercials underscore the variety of functions that persuasive messages can serve.

For example, the yogurt and wireless network commercials were designed to promote new attitudes toward existing products. The fast-food ads were intended to reinforce buying decisions and promote brand loyalty.

3

The auto insurance and dating service ads were targeted to promote specific behaviors—either making a call or going online to inquire about a service. The variety of goals and message characteristics apparent in these TV commercials is evidence of the large number of communicative options available in everyday persuasive transactions. The diversity of this type of communication is also reflected in the variety of academic fields—from communication and social psychology to political science and advertising—that focus on persuasive messages and their effects as phenomena *worth studying*. Given the professional and intellectual diversity of people interested in this process, the term *persuasion* has been assigned a number of different meanings over an extended period of time. Thus, setting forth a clear definition of *persuasive communication* seems a logical way to begin this book. After defining persuasion, we examine the concept of *attitude*, the conceptual cornerstone of many persuasion theories. Finally, we integrate these concepts by examining the functions that attitudes serve in the persuasion process.

As we begin, however, it is important to note that no single, universally accepted, definition of persuasion exists. Instead of presenting *the* definition of persuasion, we present *a* definition that is suggestive of both the breadth and complexity of our focus. Specifically, we begin our discussion by focusing on G. R. Miller's (1980) definition of *persuasive communication*—first, because the term is more specific than persuasion and, second, differentiates the messages that people send to one another (the focus of the communication discipline) from cognitive processes (the focus of psychology). As a consequence, we do not present *objectively the best* definition of persuasive communication (however that could be determined), but rather the one that *works best for us*.

DEFINING PERSUASIVE COMMUNICATION

G. R. Miller (1980) recognized the breadth of communicative activities that are potentially persuasive. To reflect this range, he advocated a definition of persuasion that differs from those typically presented in literature reviews, both in his day and more recently (e.g., Insko, 1967; Kiesler, Collins, & N. Miller, 1969/1983; Petty, Wheeler, & Tormala, 2003; C. W. Sherif, Sherif, & Nebergall, 1965; Triandis, 1971). Working from G. R. Miller (1980) we define persuasive communication as *any message that is intended to shape, reinforce, or change the responses of another, or others.* This definition limits persuasive activity to intentional behavior. This limitation is important, because one can argue that all communication is, by its very nature, persuasive. What is more, many activities that are not designed as persuasive might inadvertently affect others' responses. Given these complications, our discussion of persuasive activity will only consider communicative behaviors that are *intended* to affect others' responses because it focuses our attention on a specific subset of all communication behavior. For example, an informational message may or may not be intended to affect the responses of others, but propaganda messages are more likely persuasive because their intent is to influence others. So, G. R. Miller's definition of persuasive communication as intentional limits the scope of the term when compared to typical definitions.

In another way, however, Miller's (1980) definition is broader than the typical definition. His use of the term *response* reflects his concern that persuasion should consider outcomes beyond attitudes and attitude change. As we explain in Chapter 3, one overriding limitation of prior persuasion research stems from a nearly exclusive emphasis on attitudes. Titles of several important persuasion books, both in Miller's day and more recently, such as *Theories of Attitude Change* (Insko, 1967), *Attitudes and Attitude Change* (Crano & Prislin, 2008; Triandis, 1971), *Attitude Change* (Kiesler et al., 1969/1983), *The Psychology of Attitudes* (Eagly & Chaiken, 1993), and *Attitudes and Opinions* (Oskamp & Schultz, 2005), reflect this focus. However, Miller's use of the term *response* reflects an emphasis on other types of persuasive outcomes such as perceptions of the source, emotions, beliefs, behavioral intentions, and behaviors.

There is a second way that Miller's (1980) definition of persuasive communication is wider than was typical for his (or our) time. Look at the titles of the books we listed in the preceding paragraph. One of the elements common to several titles (and several of the theories we discuss throughout this book) is a focus on attitude *change*. Miller felt that, although changing responses is important (e.g., convincing adolescents to stop using tobacco), it was important to consider other outcomes as well. Specifically, he identified three dimensions of persuasive activity: response shaping, response reinforcing, and response changing. We will consider each of these dimensions in turn.

Response-Shaping Processes

Every 4 years, the American electorate engages in response-shaping processes concerning candidates running for president of the United States. While some candidates are familiar to voters when campaigning begins, others are relatively obscure. In the fall of 2007, relatively few people outside of Illinois were familiar with U.S. Senator Barack Obama; yet, barely a year later, he handily won the presidential election. Some three decades earlier, in January 1976, a Gallup poll indicated that fewer than 5% of

Democratic voters supported Jimmy Carter for their party's presidential nomination (Gallup, 1977). Some 10 months later, however, he was elected president of the United States.

Like most political campaigns, the campaigns supporting Barack Obama and Jimmy Carter were designed to create media images that would foster positive responses to a new stimulus object—the candidate. In each instance, voters were relatively unfamiliar with the candidate, and the campaigns initially focused on a *response-shaping process* to aid in creating favorable beliefs, images, and (eventually) attitudes where none previously existed.

BOX 1.1. The Rise and Fall of Herman Cain

In May 2011 a businessman named Herman Cain announced his candidacy for the Republican party nomination for president of the United States. Although Cain was a former chairman of the Federal Reserve Bank in Kansas City, chief executive officer of Godfather's Pizza, and head of the National Restaurant Association, he was totally unknown to most voters. According to the Pew Research Center, after 4 months of his debating and campaigning, only 15% of Republican and Republican-leaning independent poll respondents mentioned Herman Cain's name when asked to list the candidates running for the party's nomination (Pew Research Center, 2011). By the end of 2011, however, Herman Cain was a household name. By late October 2011, he was the leading candidate in several opinion polls and had garnered considerable press attention as the front-runner for the nomination. Around the same time, reports surfaced alleging that several women had accused Cain of engaging in sexual misconduct over a period of several years. The subsequent media scrutiny and decline in his popularity caused Herman Cain to end his candidacy in early December.

One remarkable aspect of Herman Cain's short-lived run for the presidency of the United States was the fact that he rose from relative obscurity to lead all other candidates in early public opinion polls within a matter of a few months. Indeed, Cain's rise and fall received more media attention during the final quarter of 2011 than did any other political candidate. Pew Research reported that 5.7% of all news stories during that period focused on Herman Cain. By way of comparison, President Obama and his administration accounted for only 6.9% of the news stories during the same period. Clearly, the dramatic increase in the number of news organizations and bloggers has made it much more difficult for candidates like Herman Cain to manage the 24-hour-a-day news cycle. In this case, the huge explosion in media coverage was the key cause of both Herman Cain's meteoric rise and precipitous fall in public opinion.

G. R. Miller (1980) argued that response shaping is important because we are routinely exposed to new objects, people, and issues that require us to form new attitudes. For example, at the time of Watson and Crick's discovery of the structure of the DNA molecule in 1953 (Watson, 1968), the concept of *cloning* was well beyond the two scientists' wildest dreams. Over time, however, people developed both favorable and unfavorable opinions about how to use cloning technology appropriately from the many messages received on the subject. As a result, scientists today are almost routinely cloning mammals such as sheep, cows, and even household pets, while controversy still abounds as to the medical, moral, and ethical issues surrounding the cloning of human beings.

Response-shaping processes are also important for people entering new professions. Large corporations develop extensive socialization and training programs designed to shape new employees' desired values, goals, and objectives (Cooper-Thomas & Anderson, 2002; Ellis, Bauer, & Erdogan, 2014). Though less formalized, socialization processes are also prevalent in smaller businesses as well as religious and social organizations.

Much as with socialization in general, response-shaping processes predominantly take place through social learning (see Bandura, 1977, 1986, 2011; Burgoon, Burgoon, Miller, & Sunnafrank, 1981). Social learning theories describe how people form responses to stimuli by modeling others' behavior after observing the positive and negative outcomes associated with that behavior (see Chapter 13 for an extended discussion). Successfully resisting a friend's attempt to get you to drink alcohol, for example, might well be facilitated by observing how others have done it (Hecht, Corman, & Miller-Rassulo, 1993).

Response-shaping processes are also typical in many everyday settings. We routinely develop impressions about people we meet and form opinions about new products. Many of these impressions are formed on the basis of intentional behaviors (e.g., ones designed to impress a job interviewer). Although they are typically not included in traditional change-based (and attitude change-based) definitions of persuasion, response-shaping processes are a prominent feature of human social influence.

Response-Reinforcing Processes

Although the exact number is difficult to determine (owing, in part, to the number of online groups), more than 500,000–750,000 self-help groups in the United States offer support to people coping with crises, role transitions, or problems (A. Katz, 1993). Many of the 15 million Americans attending these self-help groups are recovering alcoholics and drug addicts who meet across the country in church basements and community centers. For many people, these weekly meetings provide the only meaningful encouragement they receive as they struggle to maintain their sobriety (Groh, Jason, & Keys, 2008).

Like many self-help groups, Alcoholics Anonymous strives to reinforce the sobriety of alcoholics and assists them on their road to recovery. For most alcoholics, the decision to stop drinking is just the first step in the recovery process. Self-help groups provide social support and reinforce an individual's decision to remain sober (Groh et al., 2008). Because these support activities are designed to maintain and strengthen existing behaviors, they reflect the *response-reinforcing* dimension of Miller's (1980) definition of persuasive communication.

Response-reinforcing processes are also the mainstay of the advertising industry. Although some advertising campaigns introduce new products and services, most advertising dollars are spent maintaining *brand loyalty* (Hong-Youl, Joby, Swinder, & Siva, 2011). Whether promoting L'Oreal hair coloring products, Dunkin' Donuts fast food, or Google search services, developing brand loyalty is the *bread and butter* of traditional advertising (Jackall & Hirota, 2000). In a similar vein, Tellis (1987) concluded that "advertising is more effective in increasing the volume purchased by loyal buyers than in winning new buyers" (p. 22). Recognizing that repeat customers are critical to their success, advertisers fill the media with jingles and slogans that increase the salience of products ranging from toothpaste to Cadillacs. Airline commercials promote frequent flyer programs that offer substantial rewards for repeat customers. These commercials are an excellent example of the response-reinforcement dimension of persuasion.

Similarly, politicians recognize the importance of reinforcing the opinions and values of their constituents. As campaigns near election day, politicians spend a disproportionate amount of their time in precincts and districts where they already enjoy widespread support. Returning home to friendly districts, political candidates reinforce existing political opinions and motivate their committed supporters to go to the polls on election day. Response-reinforcing processes extend well beyond self-help groups and advertising campaigns: they also play a central role in the maintenance of our social, political, and religious institutions. Most religious services, for example, are designed to reinforce belief in a prescribed doctrine and to maintain lifestyles consistent with that doctrine. Elementary and high school curricula in the United States reinforce the positive attributes of capitalism while describing socialist and communist economic and political systems much less favorably.

Much like the response-shaping function, the response-reinforcing dimension of persuasion has not been emphasized in traditional definitions of persuasion. Response reinforcing is difficult to observe (as it does not involve a change), and so most persuasion research focuses on response-changing or -shaping processes. However, G. R. Miller (1980) emphasized the importance of response-reinforcing processes in his more broad-based definition of persuasive communication.

Response-Changing Processes

> After breaking up with her boyfriend, Debbie left home on the East Coast to start summer school at a college in California. She was optimistic, if also a bit apprehensive, about her upcoming adventure. Her parents expected her to do well in the school environment, as she had dealt quite successfully with high school and the first year in a local college. Before summer school began, though, she was befriended by a group of youths who suggested that she get to know members of their informal organization dedicated to promoting "social ecology and world peace." Within a month she was spending all her spare time with the group. Only at this point did they tell her that the group was associated with a small religious cult with an elaborate and arcane theology. She was asked by the group's leader to adopt its idiosyncratic beliefs and leave school. Interestingly, she agreed to all of this without hesitation, and began to devote herself full time to raising funds for the cult. For the next three months her parents could not locate her. In the midst of their anxiety, they could offer no explanation as to why she "threw away" the family's values and her own stake in her future. Five years later Debbie described the period as a difficult but meaningful time, and the friends she made there as the best she ever had. (Galanter, 1999, p. 2)

Debbie's story is just one illustration of the dramatic changes in personal and religious values that often coincide with cult indoctrination. Each year, thousands of adolescents and young adults abandon their traditional values along with their family and friends to become members of religious and political cults. According to the International Cultic Studies Association (2012), there are currently more than 4,000 active cults in the United States. Most of these groups are small (i.e., have fewer than 100 members), while others have tens of thousands of members, controlling substantial financial and social resources.

More recently, law enforcement officials have been concerned about the use of social media sites by ISIS to recruit young men and women to join its cause. During the first half of 2015, dozens of Americans were arrested and most of them charged with supporting ISIS. Early converts had become radicalized on their own by watching ISIS propaganda videos on the Internet. But once those initial Western recruits arrived overseas, taking up residence within the self-declared ISIS caliphate that spanned portions of Syria and Iraq, they started to entice friends and other contacts back home via social media to join them (Perez, 2015).

Whether in joining a religious cult or ISIS, new members experience changes that clearly reflect the *response-changing* dimension of persuasion as their existing attitudes, beliefs, values, and behaviors are exchanged for new ones. Although indoctrination into cults and cult-like organizations is often extreme, marking a critical event in a person's life history, the changes involved reflect the same basic processes of response changes that underpin more mundane interactions.

Reliance on a charismatic leader, manipulation, and coercion are some of the persuasive characteristics that distinguish cults from other highly cohesive groups and organizations (MacHovec, 1989). Though perhaps more extreme, the persuasive strategies employed by cults are often reflected in mainstream political and religious communication as well. For example, both politicians and cult leaders are often described as "charismatic." Like cult leaders, politicians and mainstream clergy have been known to use coercive strategies to achieve their goals. Although significant differences distinguish the latter from cult leaders, it is worth considering the similarities of many of their underlying persuasive strategies.

Although some response-alteration experiences are sudden and extreme, most response-changing processes evolve slowly over time. Consider, for example, the traditional opposition to gay men and lesbians serving in the military. During the 1992 presidential campaign, Bill Clinton promised to end the ban on gays serving in the military. Following the election, he faced considerable opposition to lifting the ban from military leaders—this, despite a 1993 Rand Corporation study that concluded that sexual orientation was "not germane" to military readiness. Although the Rand Corporation study recommended "characterizing the issue as one of conduct rather than orientation" (Rostker, Hosek, & Vaiana, 2011, p. 1), the report was shelved, and in 1993 a compromise solution—Don't Ask, Don't Tell—was reached. The compromise permitted gay men and lesbians to serve in the military so long as they did not disclose their sexual orientation, while at the same time military authorities were prohibited from asking questions about their sexual orientation. At that time, Don't Ask, Don't Tell was perceived as a progressive challenge to the military establishment.

During the ensuing two decades, however, attitudes toward gay men and lesbians changed dramatically. Gay men and lesbians became much more visible in American society as television shows incorporated gay and lesbian characters, gay-talk show hosts enjoyed popular success and large television audiences, and nearly everyone became familiar with at least one colleague who was openly gay. Indeed, the percentage of people who reported "that they know someone who is gay or lesbian increased from 42 percent in 1993 to 77 percent in 2010" (Rostker et al., 2011, p. 1). When the Defense of Marriage Act was passed in 1996, only 25% of Americans supported same-sex marriage. By 2011, however, several national polls found that more than half of all Americans supported same-sex marriage (e.g., Gallup Organization, 2011). When we first began revising this text-book a few years ago, only a handful of states legally recognized same-sex marriage. Each time we edited this chapter, the number had increased—such that by 2014 some 18 states and the District of Columbia recognized it as a legal right. Finally, on July 3, 2015, the U.S. Supreme Court established same-sex marriage as a constitutionally guaranteed right.

Over time, as attitudes changed, the Don't Ask, Don't Tell policy—which, as already noted, was originally considered a progressive solution to an intractable problem—became a symbol of discriminatory and repressive government policies against gay men and lesbians. Finally, in 2010 politi-cal and military leaders realized that they were lagging behind a several decades-long attitudinal transformation. Congress repealed the ban on gays and lesbians serving in the military soon afterward, and the ban was formally lifted in September 2011. Like many response-changing processes, the shift in attitudes about gay men and lesbians serving in the military was motivated by new information and messages from a variety of sources that caused people to reexamine and eventually abandon their previously held beliefs. Many persuasive theories, including Information Integration Theory (Anderson, 1971, 1981) and Social Judgment Theory (M. Sherif & Hovland, 1961), help explain these response-changing processes that have been the central focus of traditional persuasion research.

Response-shaping processes are similar to response-changing pro-cesses because both involve a change in responses from one position to another. They differ, of course, because in response shaping the change is from *no* response to *some* response, while in response changing it is from *one* (existing) position to *another* (different) position. This is an impor-tant distinction because research on some theories that presumably focus on attitude change (e.g., the Elaboration Likelihood Model; see Chapter 5) actually focus on issues that are *new* to message recipients. This is so because it is generally easier to create a new response than to change an existing one, especially when that existing response is well entrenched. Thus, in reality these theories actually focus on response-shaping rather than response-changing processes.

Related Issues

The response-shaping, -reinforcing, and -changing processes described above reflect the variety of outcomes that fall under G. R. Miller's (1980) definition of persuasive communication. For example, presidential cam-paigns reflect a concern with voters' beliefs, attitudes, and behaviors. Vot-ing behavior is the eventual desired outcome to be affected, but attitude and belief formation are critical initial components in the persuasion process. Organizational socialization, another response-shaping process, emphasizes the development of employee values. Response-reinforcing processes apparent in such self-help groups as Alcoholics Anonymous often emphasize maintaining desirable behaviors. Advertising campaigns that promote brand loyalty are also geared toward reinforcing targeted behaviors. Finally, the example of Debbie's experience with the religious cult reflects a response-changing process that targets a person's values and beliefs. In short, the broader definition of persuasion offered by Miller is consistent with the wide range of cognitive, emotional, and behavioral outcomes that are normally associated with persuasive communication.

Finally, although some scholars distinguish persuasion from manipulation and coercion (see, e.g., D. J. O'Keefe, 2015), Miller does not draw any conceptual distinctions among these related terms. Attempts to differentiate persuasion from coercion typically center on the receiver's free will (as with O'Keefe). The distinction typically goes like this: in persuasion the receiver has the ability to accept or reject the persuasive attempt, whereas in coercion the receiver's ability to refuse is compromised. Although this might be a minority opinion, G. R. Miller (1980) argued that differentiating persuasion from coercion based upon free will, however, is rarely satisfactory for two reasons. First, it is difficult to separate these constructs because "much persuasive discourse is *indirectly* coercive" (p. 12, emphasis in original). For example, a parent might threaten to cut off his or her child's allowance if the son or daughter does not improve his or her grades. This persuasive attempt is indirectly coercive because a punishment is promised if the child does not conform. Another reason why it is difficult to separate persuasion from coercion is that there can be disagreement on the degree of free will the receiver actually has in the situation. In our previous example, the teen might consider that he or she has no choice but to study more, while the parent might believe that the child has all the choice in the world.

Although you might not consider an armed robber's request to "hand over your wallet" as an instance of *persuasive communication*, studies of interpersonal compliance examine almost equally coercive messages that somehow fall under that same wide rubric. Again, in summary, persuasive communication represents *any message that is intended to shape, reinforce, or change the responses of another, or others.*

CONSIDERING THE ATTITUDE CONSTRUCT

A variety of responses are consistent with Miller's (1980) definition of persuasion (e.g., attitudes, behaviors, behavioral intentions, values, beliefs, moods, and emotions). Although affective and emotional responses fit under Miller's response concept, attitudes and, to a lesser extent, behaviors have been the focus of most prior persuasion research. Over the course of more than 80 years, attitudes have remained a central component of many persuasive communication theories. Consequently, a historical review of the major models of attitude change is crucial to understanding theories of persuasive communication.

There are important differences between attitudes and behaviors. *Behavioral responses* (e.g., donating to a charity or buying a particular product) are relatively concrete and as such are often directly observable by researchers. Cognitive responses such as *attitudes*, however, are more abstract and relatively difficult to observe directly. Given the important roles that attitudes play in persuasion theories and their hidden nature, it is important that we spend some time discussing various definitions of the attitude concept and the functions that attitudes serve.

The attitude construct initially gained prominence through the writings of Gordon Allport (1935), who used it to help understand and explain human behavior. An attitude is a theoretical construct created by social scientists to explain why people react differently to similar objects or situations. Unlike behaviors, attitudes are not directly observable and hence are more difficult to measure. Nevertheless, the explanatory power of the attitude construct has helped lay the foundation for modern persuasion research.

The attitude construct in an old one. Thurstone (1928, 1931) and Allport (1935) were influential in early views of how attitudes should be conceptualized and measured. Specifically, Allport defined attitude as "a mental and neural state of readiness, organized through experience, exerting a directive or dynamic influence upon the individual's response to all objects and situations with which it is related" (Allport, 1935, p. 810). Thus, according to Allport (and many who followed), the utility of the attitude construct depends on its ability to predict behaviors. During the ensuing decades, the construct has evolved as various ways of thinking about attitudes developed (Eagly & Chaiken, 1993; Gawronski, 2007; Schwarz, 2007; Zanna & Rempel, 1988). As with definitions of persuasion, no single definition of attitude has received universal acceptance. Of course, a comprehensive review of this literature is beyond the scope of this book. Nevertheless, we consider four approaches to defining attitudes because these warrant attention and reflect the evolution of scholarly thinking in this area. Specifically, we wish to discuss in some detail the Tripartite Model (Rokeach, 1968), the Attitude toward Behavior Model (Fishbein & Ajzen, 1975), the Single-Factor Model (Zanna & Rempel, 1988), and the Construal Model (Schwarz, 2007).

Rokeach's Tripartite Model of Attitudes

One of the most straightforward definitions of *attitude* was provided by Rokeach (1968), who defined it as "a relatively enduring organization of beliefs around an object or situation predisposing one to respond in some preferential manner" (p. 112). There are several important implications of Rokeach's definition. First, *attitudes are relatively enduring.* Most scholars agree that attitudes represent more than a fleeting thought about, or a momentary evaluation of, an object. Attitudes are developed over a long period of time, and some are reinforced frequently. As such, they are relatively stable and can be difficult to change. This does not imply that attitudes are not susceptible to sudden and dramatic shifts—only that such changes are exceptional.

The second implication of Rokeach's definition is that *an attitude is an organization of beliefs.* Rather than regarding an attitude as a single element within a person's cognitive or mental framework, Rokeach conceptualizes an attitude as a cluster, or combination, of several related elements. These cognitive elements are defined as beliefs that cluster around a central attitude object, and the entire cluster of beliefs represents one's attitude about that object.

A *belief* is a single proposition (or statement) about an object or a situation. The content of a belief usually describes the object as something that is correct or incorrect, good or bad, moral or immoral, or the like. Rokeach (1968) identified three types of beliefs, namely, descriptive, prescriptive, and evaluative.

Descriptive beliefs are verifiable statements about people, objects, or situations. Like factual statements, descriptive beliefs are objective statements that, in principle, can be shown to be correct or incorrect. For example, the statement "*Saturday Night Live* is a television comedy show" is a descriptive belief, because its validity can be established.

Prescriptive beliefs are statements about the appropriateness of a position or activity in a given situation. These subjective statements reflect the values, morals, or ethics of the person(s) advocating them. For example, agreement with the statement "*Saturday Night Live* promotes immoral behavior" may reflect beliefs about the role of the media in reinforcing cultural, moral, and ethical standards. Beliefs like these cannot be demonstrated as objectively incorrect, as they reflect subjective assessments of the attitude object.

Evaluative beliefs, according to Rokeach, are statements that reflect a general evaluation of an attitude object—for example, "*Saturday Night Live* is entertaining." Evaluative beliefs are very similar to the general view of attitudes, and, like prescriptive beliefs, they cannot be shown to be objectively correct or incorrect.

The third implication of Rokeach's (1968) definition reflects the behavioral component of beliefs. An attitude, as a combination of beliefs about an object or situation, represents a *predisposition to respond*. Once established, this predisposition guides our behavior as we encounter situations relevant to the object of the attitude. For example, if you have a negative attitude toward recreational drug use, you are likely to refuse a friend's offer of the drug ecstasy at a party. You might also be motivated to join a community organization that promotes drug resistance when you see their booth around campus.

Rokeach's definition, like many others, presumes that attitudes have affective, behavioral, and cognitive components. Because these approaches depict attitudes as having three components, they are referred to as

---

BOX 1.2. How Are Attitudes Measured?

Traditional approaches to attitude measurement evolved from the early work of Thurstone (1928). To assess a person's attitude toward an object, researchers have relied primarily on explicit measures that ask people to respond to verbal statements about the attitude object. Two of the most popular attitude measures are Likert scales and semantic differentials.

Attitude measurements using *Likert scales* contain a number of positive and negative opinion statements. Each statement is accompanied by a set of response scales, typically ranging from "strongly disagree" to "strongly agree." Assume that we are using two Likert-type scales to measure attitudes toward *Saturday Night Live*. In a questionnaire, we might use the two items provided in the upper half of Figure 1.1.

In a Likert scale, respondents indicate the response that most clearly matches their opinion on each statement. The numbers below each response represent the score assigned to an individual for each response. (These numbers would *not* appear in the actual survey.) In this example, high scores reflect positive attitudes and low scores represent negative attitudes.* The scoring is reversed in the second Likert item because the wording of the statement is opposite to that of the first item. A person with a very positive attitude would likely mark "strongly agree" on the first statement and "strongly disagree" on the second.

(continued)

---

*Likert items could also be scored with values ranging from −2 to +2. While this scoring more clearly reflects the evaluative component of the attitude underlying the response, it is functionally equivalent to the 1–5 scoring schema we discuss.

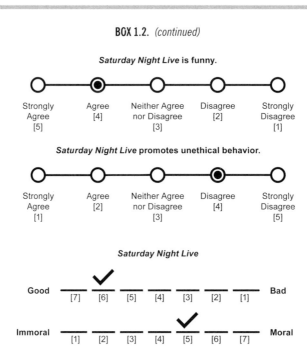

FIGURE 1.1. Likert scale (at top) and semantic differential scale (at bottom) measures of attitudes toward *Saturday Night Live*.

Semantic differential scales appear as an attitude object accompanied by a number of bipolar (i.e., opposite) adjective pairs (e.g., good–bad). These opposites are typically separated by seven segmented response options. To indicate one's attitudes, the respondents mark the response option that most clearly matches their opinion. Two semantic differential attitude scales assessing *Saturday Night Live* are provided at the bottom of Figure 1.1.

Using these semantic differential scales, a person with a very positive attitude would likely check a response close to the "good" and "moral" ends of the two scales. The numbers associated with each option represent the score that particular response would generate (and would not be provided in the questionnaire) such that, again, high scores would represent positive attitudes.

"tripartite" models of attitudes (Zanna & Rempel, 1988). The cognitive component of attitudes represents the beliefs (particularly descriptive beliefs) that a person has about an attitude object. The affective component of attitudes represents people's positive, negative, or neutral evaluations of attitude objects. Rokeach's evaluative beliefs are a good example of the affective components of attitudes. Finally, attitudes have a behavioral component because they are considered as closely linked to behaviors. This is best represented by Rokeach's view that attitudes are "predispositions to respond" (1968, p. 112; see also Eagly & Chaiken, 2007).

While Rokeach's Tripartite Model of attitude is popular, it is not without its problems (Zanna & Rempel, 1988). The principal concern with such traditional conceptualizations was the absence of a strong relationship between attitudes and behaviors. Wicker (1969) reviewed much of the early research examining the predictive utility of attitudes and concluded that there was scant evidence of a robust relationship between attitudes and behaviors. He argued that if attitudes were conceptualized as *predispositions to respond* and yet the research suggested that there was no systematic relationship between attitudes and behaviors, then perhaps it was time to rethink how we conceptualize the attitude construct.

In Chapter 3 we closely examine the research describing the relationship between attitudes and behaviors. For now, we will focus on how concerns about the relationship between attitudes and behaviors led scholars to reexamine the definition of an attitude.

Zanna and Rempel's Single-Factor Model

Zanna and Rempel (1988) note that the most important problem with the tripartite model is that it presumes that attitudes, by definition, are related to behaviors. Rather than automatically assume an attitude–behavior relationship, they defined *attitude* "as the categorization of a stimulus object along an evaluative dimension based upon, or generated from, three general classes of information: (1) cognitive information, (2) affective/emotional information, and/or (3) information concerning past behaviors or behavioral intentions" (p. 319). This definition differs from Rokeach's view in two important ways. First, while Zanna and Rempel argue that attitudes can be based on one's past behavior, they do not assume that attitudes, by definition, predict behavior. Second, in their view, attitudes are composed of a *single* evaluative dimension (e.g., good–bad) rather than three. This single-factor conceptualization allows for Rokeach's three components, but it considers them as sources of information upon which the key evaluative judgment is based.

Fishbein and Ajzen's Attitude toward the Behavior Model

In response to concerns about whether attitudes are a "predisposition to respond," Fishbein and Ajzen (1975) developed the concept of *attitude toward the behavior*, which is a more narrow construction of the attitude–behavior relationship. Extending Rokeach's (1968) view, Fishbein and Ajzen (1975) provided a more precise description of the influence of individual beliefs on people's attitudes and how they relate to behavioral intentions. Specifically, they argued that an attitude toward a behavior was a function of the perceived consequences of performing the behavior and an evaluation of those consequences. This relationship is represented by the equation

$$A_B = \Sigma(b_i \times e_i) \tag{1.1}$$

where A_B is the attitude toward performing behavior B; b_i is the belief that performing behavior B leads to the outcome specified in belief statement i (where i represents each belief statement; i.e., the first, second, third, all the way to the last one); and e_i is the person's evaluation of the outcome specified in belief statement i. To estimate a person's attitude toward performing a particular behavior, numbers ranging from 0 to +3 are assigned to the belief (b) component. A zero indicates that the individual considers it highly unlikely that the behavior would lead to the particular outcome, while a +3 would indicate that the outcome is seen as a highly likely result of the behavior. The evaluation (e) component for each belief statement (i) is measured using a –3 (extremely negative evaluation of the outcome) to a +3 (extremely positive evaluation of the outcome) scale. The product of the belief and evaluation values ($b_i \times e_i$) for each belief statement (i) are summed (Σ) to produce a single value representing the attitude toward performing behavior B (Fishbein & Ajzen, 1975, p. 301).

To understand the contribution of beliefs and their evaluation to a person's attitude, let's consider an example. In this example, the behavior in question is advocating tighter border security along the border between the United States and Mexico (see Table 1.1).[1] Consider the beliefs and evaluations of Candidate A, who advocates much tighter border security, and Candidate B, who does not.

Our two candidates disagree on many beliefs, even though they agree on the evaluation of those belief statements. For example, both candidates assign a very positive evaluation to the concept of reducing crime (+3), but they have different beliefs about whether enhanced border security will reduce crime. Candidate A strongly believes that tighter border security will reduce crime (+3), while Candidate B believes that border security will have only a limited effect on reducing crime (+1). Similarly, both candidates

TABLE 1.1. Hypothetical Beliefs about Promoting Border Security

Belief statement	Candidate A		Candidate B	
	b	*e*	*b*	*e*
Restricting immigration will reduce crime.	+3	+3	+1	+3
Restricting immigration will reduce U.S. unemployment.	+2	+3	0	+3
Promoting border security will increase discrimination against Hispanic citizens.	0	−1	+3	−3
Restricting immigration will reduce health care costs for U.S. citizens.	+2	+3	0	+2
	$\Sigma(b \times e) = +21$		$\Sigma(b \times e) = -6$	

Note. b represents belief in the statement (ranging from 0 to +3), and *e* represents evaluation of the belief statement (ranging from −3 to +3).

assign a very positive evaluation to reducing unemployment (+3), but they differ in their belief about whether tighter border security will influence employment rates. Candidate A believes that fewer immigrants will mean there are more jobs for U.S. citizens, while Candidate B believes that restricting immigration will have no effect on the employment rate of U.S. citizens (0).

Our two candidates also disagree on the evaluation of some belief elements. For example, Candidate B is very much opposed to discrimination against Hispanic citizens (−3), while Candidate A is less concerned about discrimination (−1). Moreover, the two candidates have very different views about whether promoting border security will lead to greater discrimination. Candidate B is convinced that efforts to restrict immigration lead to greater discrimination (+3), while Candidate A rejects the suggestion that enhancing border security will promote discrimination (0). The differing attitudes of the two candidates are reflected in the different beliefs and the differing evaluations they assign to those beliefs.

The attitude of Candidate A can be estimated with Fishbein and Ajzen's (1975) formula. To do this, first multiply the belief and evaluation score for each belief statement, then add these products together. In this example, the products ($b \times e$) of Candidate A's views on the four belief statements are +9, +6, 0, and +6, respectively. The sum of these products is +21, and this number represents Candidate A's strongly held attitude about promoting tighter border security. Conversely, the products of Candidate B's views on each of the four belief statements are +3, 0, –9, and 0, respectively. Adding these four products produces an estimate of –6, which represents a negative attitude about promoting greater border security.

This definition permits a precise, quantitative estimate of a person's attitude about a particular behavior. However, such estimates only become meaningful when they are compared with other attitude estimates. In the example, Candidate A's rating (+21) is difficult to interpret by itself. However, compared with the value of Candidate B (–6), Candidate A's attitude is 27 units more positive than Candidate B's attitude. Indeed, this model provides an estimate of both the valence (positive or negative) and strength of a person's attitude. Specifically, the sign (+ or –) associated with the final score indicates the valence of an attitude. The strength of the attitude is indicated by the absolute value of the final score. Strong attitudes differ substantially from zero, while weak attitudes cluster close to zero.

When plotting these values over time, one can also use this approach to track changes in a person's attitude toward a particular behavior. For example, if Candidate A is confronted by angry protesters on the campaign trail, he or she may come to believe that promoting border security will lead to some discrimination against Hispanic citizens and may begin to view such discrimination more negatively. Thus, Candidate A's belief that promoting border security will increase discrimination may change from a 0 to a +2, and the evaluation of that belief may change from –1 to –2. This belief change would result in a slightly less favorable attitude about promoting border security, that is, from +21 to +17.

In this example, the different attitudes held by the two candidates are due to differences in their belief systems and how they value those beliefs. It is easy to understand how people who hold different beliefs will form different attitudes about a behavior. However, it is possible for people to hold the *same* beliefs about a particular object or situation and yet maintain different attitudes toward it because they have different evaluations of those beliefs. In this regard, Fishbein and Ajzen's (1975) Attitude toward Behavior Model highlights the important contributions of beliefs and evaluations of those beliefs in attitude formation.

Schwarz's Construal Model

The most recent approach to defining attitude was developed by scholars who argue that attitudes are a context-sensitive automatic evaluation (Gawronski & Bodenhausen, 2007). This approach has been labeled "construal" because it assumes that evaluations of attitude objects are created as we need them, based primarily on situational or contextual inputs. Schwarz (2007) and others adopting this perspective reject the idea that attitudes are enduring representations of an object that create a predisposition to respond. Instead, "construal models conceptualize attitudes as evaluative judgments, formed on the spot" (Schwarz, 2007, p. 649). Accordingly, people do not "have" attitudes that they carry with them from one situation or context to another.

Many theories in communication and social psychology presume that our behavior is determined in important ways by the specific situation we find ourselves in (Baxter & Montgomery, 1996; Kelley & Thibaut, 1978; Mischel, 1968). For example, a person's behavior at a bar on a Saturday night is likely to be quite different from his or her behavior in church the next morning. Consistent with this notion, the Construal Model posits that those same contextual or situational factors also determine attitudes.[2] For example, continuing with our example on immigration reform, a businessman might express a strong attitude about securing the U.S.–Mexico border at a luncheon sponsored by the Chamber of Commerce. However, that same businessman might reflect a somewhat more tolerant attitude when addressing a college class about the economic and social effects of immigrant workers. Viewed from the Construal Model's perspective, there is no radical change in attitude between these two situations, nor is there necessarily any need to retain either perspective exclusively over time. Instead, one's evaluations of proper ongoing immigration controls may differ or evolve owing to changing circumstances.

It remains to be seen whether, given its recent development, the Construal Model will continue to be useful for persuasion scholars focused on studying the production and effects of persuasive messages. However, this approach renders moot the assumption that evaluations of an attitude object necessarily endure over time. Indeed, advocates of the Construal Model suggest that situational and contextual factors "can specify the conditions of evaluation-behavior consistency, without assuming and enduring disposition" (Schwarz, 2007, pp. 650–651).

Comparing Definitions of Attitudes

These four conceptual definitions of attitude share some important similarities but also exhibit differences (see Table 1.2). Both the Tripartite Model (Rokeach, 1968) and the Attitude toward Behavior Model (Fishbein & Ajzen, 1975) conceptualize an attitude as a relatively enduring combination of beliefs about a particular object, situation, or behavior. However, while both approaches allow for some beliefs to be more meaningful than others in determining the overall attitude, Fishbein and Ajzen (1975) are more precise in their description of how individual beliefs affect one's overall attitude.

TABLE 1.2. Characteristics of Four Major Attitude Models

Underlying assumptions	Tripartite Model	Attitude toward Behavior Model	Single-Factor Model	Construal Model
Relatively enduring	Yes	Yes	Yes	No
Organization of beliefs	Yes	Yes	No	No
Derived from cognitive, affective, and behavioral information	Yes	Yes	Yes	No
Attitudes cause behaviors	Yes	Yes	No	No

Moreover, both the Tripartite Model and the Attitude toward Behavior Model are consistent with Hovland, Janis, and Kelley's (1953) assertion that attitude change is dependent upon the addition to, or alteration of, a person's belief system over time. For Rokeach, adding to and/or restructuring a person's belief system concerning an attitude object is the best way to accomplish attitude change. Fishbein and Ajzen argue that attitude change is accomplished through the addition of new belief statements or by altering a person's evaluation or belief in existing belief statements. The more strongly one's beliefs contribute to the attitude, the more difficult it will likely be to change that attitude.

The traditional Tripartite Model (Rokeach, 1968) and Attitude toward Behavior Model (Fishbein & Ajzen, 1975) differ from the Single-Factor Model (Zanna & Rempel, 1988) on the question of whether an attitude is a combination of beliefs (Tripartite Model and Attitude Toward Behavior Model) or a single evaluation of an attitude object that is informed by various kinds of information (i.e., cognitive, affective/emotional, and information concerning past behaviors; Single-Factor Model). However, the key distinction between the Single-Factor Model and the more traditional approaches is whether or not an attitude is assumed to predict (i.e., cause) behavior. Zanna and Rempel posit that one's attitudes are informed by behavioral experiences but that they do not necessarily cause an individual to behave in a particular way.

The Construal Model (Schwarz, 2007) differs strongly from these more traditional conceptualizations. First, the Construal Model rejects the notion that attitudes are relatively enduring. Instead, the Construal Model posits that attitudes (or evaluations of an attitude object) are formed on the spot and are determined mostly by situational or contextual factors. Thus, attitudes are not a function of beliefs, nor are they a function of one's past behavior. In addition, attitudes do not *cause* behaviors. The two phenomena should be correlated because they reflect the same situational variables, but there is no direct causal link between attitudes and behaviors.

While each of these four conceptualizations of attitudes has something to offer scholars of persuasion, they are not all created equal. The utility of the Single-Factor Model and the Construal Model has yet to be empirically demonstrated. Thus, while an important discussion about the conceptualization of the attitude construct continues, we adopt the traditional conceptualizations reflected in the Tripartite Model (Rokeach, 1968) and the Attitude toward Behavior Model (Fishbein & Ajzen, 1975). We believe that these two models offer the greatest utility for the study of persuasive communication.

THE ROLE OF ATTITUDE IN PERSUASION RESEARCH

Attitudes have become a central focus of many persuasion theories because social scientists believe that attitudes guide and direct human behavior. The attitude construct was originally introduced to explain why people respond differently to similar stimuli (Allport, 1935). One approach that emphasizes the predictive and explanatory power of an attitude is labeled the *functional approach.*

Functional Approaches to Studying Attitudes

Why do people hold particular attitudes? What functions do attitudes serve? Questions like these led to the development of the functional approach to studying attitudes. "Functional approaches attempt to identify the various psychological benefits that people can and do derive from forming, expressing, and changing their attitudes" (Lavine & Snyder, 2000, p. 98). The functional approach was developed during the 1950s primarily through the work of D. Katz (1960) and Smith, Bruner, and White (1956). These researchers studied attitudes by examining the psychological functions they serve.

D. Katz (1960) identified four psychological functions that attitudes serve: (1) an *instrumental, adjustive, or utilitarian* function; (2) an *ego-defensive* function; (3) a *knowledge* function; and (4) a *value-expressive* function. Each of these functions reflects implicit goals that people try to reach by embracing attitudes.

For example, people may want to experience a pleasant state of existence and are motivated to pursue pleasant states by maximizing rewarding experiences and minimizing negative ones. Consequently, Katz suggests that the *instrumental* function is reflected in the positive attitudes people develop toward objects or situations that are rewarding and the negative attitudes they associate with situations producing unfavorable outcomes. For example, college students often develop a special affinity for the specialty courses in their chosen major and are apt to be less enthusiastic about the general studies courses because they view the in-major courses as most relevant to their future goals.

Second, as in psychoanalytic theory, the *ego-defensive* function serves to protect people from basic truths about themselves and their environment that they prefer not to even deal with or even face (D. Katz, 1960; Sarnoff, 1960). People's attitudes toward objects or situations sometimes enable them to insulate themselves from insecurities or emotional conflicts. Attitudes reflecting prejudice often serve this function. Overly negative evaluations of people from different ethnic and racial groups allow bigoted people to maintain the belief that they are superior to *outgroup* members who threaten their egos.

Third, attitudes also serve a *knowledge* function. They enable us to organize information and structure our evaluation of novel stimuli. In situations where we don't have a lot of information on a topic, attitudes can fill the information gap and permit us to interpret and categorize the new information into preestablished categories. This process, referred to as *stimulus generalization,* involves stereotyping new people or stimulus objects into existing categories based on perceived similarities. For example, the knowledge function of attitudes is reflected in the generalizations people make about strangers during their initial interactions with them. Car salesmen, for example, immediately try to "size up" potential customers in the showroom to try to determine how serious they are about purchasing a car. The salesperson might form a positive attitude toward a well-dressed couple carrying an automobile pricing guidebook because he or she judges them to be serious prospective customers. Conversely, the salesperson might form a negative impression about an individual dressed in blue jeans and a sweatshirt because he or she might seem to be more likely a mere window shopper. In an effort to categorize people who enter their showroom, auto salespeople rely on well-established but sometimes erroneous attitudes about the appearance and behavior of potential customers. Salespeople who pay little or no attention to those dressed in blue jeans and a sweatshirt may end up forgoing opportunities to sell cars to qualified but casually dressed potential customers.

Finally, the *value-expressive* function of attitudes is conceptualized as a means of establishing and maintaining norms of social appropriateness. D. Katz (1960) argued that social forces exerted through interaction mold self-concepts. Attitudes serve as reminders of the values and preferred orientations of various groups and organizations. When people identify with a particular reference group, they adopt the values and orientations of that group. For example, a person who serves as a Court Appointed Special Advocate for abused and neglected children may well believe that the government should expand Medicaid access for children in the foster care system.

Among researchers also adopting a functional perspective, Smith and colleagues (1956) provided a list of attitude functions similar to that subsequently proposed by Katz (1960). Though important conceptual differences exist between the two lists, functional theorists are not interested in articulating an exhaustive list of such functions. Indeed, social scientists may never be able to present a truly exhaustive list of functions served by different attitudes.

The initial work undertaken by Smith et al. and Katz provided scholars with a finite number of functions that attitudes might serve; however, these researchers did not describe how the functions might best be measured. As a consequence, research based on the functional perspective languished (Eagly & Chaiken, 1993; Maio & Olson, 2000a). During the past two decades, however, both conceptual and measurement advances have spurred a strong resurgence in functional approaches to attitudes (Maio & Olson, 2000b; Carpenter, Boster, & Andrews, 2013).

More recent work on functional theory has identified several additional functions and created a number of terms to describe similar functions (Carpenter et al., 2013; Maio & Olson, 2000b). This functional research seeks to understand the psychological foundations underlying attitudes and to identify specific persuasive strategies that may facilitate changes in those attitudes.

Understanding attitude functions is important for persuasion practitioners. For example, a politician may favor racial segregation because it expresses a closely held set of beliefs (value-expressive function) or because most of the politician's constituents live in racially segregated neighborhoods (utilitarian function). These two functions have very different implications for his or her attitude change. If the politician's attitude reflects the individual's values, then persuasive messages designed to change the attitude must address his or her prescriptive beliefs about segregation. If, on the other hand, the politician's attitude reflects a utilitarian function, then persuasive messages (if successful) must convince the politician that, although his or her constituents live in segregated neighborhoods, they should nonetheless support programs that encourage racial integration. It is important to match the persuasive appeal to the function(s) that the attitude serves for the particular receivers (Carpenter et al., 2013; Lavine & Snyder, 2000). One particularly interesting application of the functional approach focuses on attitudes toward gay men and lesbians, bisexuals, transgender individuals, and queers (or questioning; i.e., GLBTQ).

Functions of Attitudes toward GLBTQ Individuals

Many people maintain latent (or blatant) prejudicial attitudes toward people from diverse ethnic, religious, or racial backgrounds; people of the other sex; and people with divergent sexual orientations. Although some prejudicial attitudes remain subconscious and undetected, others surface in the form of obvious discriminatory behavior and physical abuse (Herek, 2009).

Homophobia (literally, "fear of homosexuals") is a term commonly used to describe negative attitudes toward gay men and lesbians. Herek (1984a, 1984b, 1987, 1988) was among the first to apply a functional approach to the study of homophobia by focusing on the experiential, ego-defensive, and symbolic functions of attitudes toward gay men and lesbians. In one critically important element of this research, Herek (1988) developed a Likert measure of attitudes toward gay and lesbian individuals (see Table 1.3). More recently, this line of research has been expanded to focus on attitudes toward transgender individuals as well (Hill & Willoughby, 2005).

Herek's (1988, 2000) concept of an *experiential attitude* is consistent with the knowledge function identified by Katz (1960). According to Herek (1984b, 1987), experiential attitudes are formed whenever affect and cognitions associated with specific interpersonal interactions are generalized to all GLBTQ individuals. People with mostly positive experiences will form positive attitudes, whereas those with mostly negative experiences will form negative attitudes. Because face-to-face interactions are more informative than stereotypical information, such interactions will serve to refute stereotypes and reduce ignorance (Herek, 1984b, p. 8). Consistent with this argument is the finding that heterosexuals with GLBTQ friends can more readily recognize inaccurate stereotypes and express more tolerant attitudes (Herek, 1984a). A poll conducted in the early 1990s indicated that only 43% of U.S. adults knew someone who was openly gay and only 20% worked with someone they knew was gay (Wilson, 1992). However, by 2010, 77% of U.S. adults reported knowing someone who was openly gay or lesbian and 57% of Americans reported that "homosexuality is an acceptable alternative lifestyle" (Rostker et al., 2011, p. 1). As more people have become increasingly familiar with GLBTQ individuals, negative stereotypes are giving way to more accepting and supportive attitudes about their sexual orientation.

Herek's concept of *defensive attitudes* is consistent with Katz's ego-defensive function. Defensive attitudes result from insecurity about one's sexual identity and sexual orientation. Herek (1984b, 1987) argues that protection of insecure sexual identities and the perceived threat of homosexuality are the primary functions of defensive attitudes toward GLBTQ individuals. Herek (1984b) argues that insecure heterosexuals should feel more threatened by similar homosexual men. Consistent with this argument, San Miguel and Millham (1976) reported that men with anti-gay attitudes were more punitive toward gay men who were described as being similar to themselves than they were to gay men who were described as being different from themselves.

TABLE 1.3. Herek's (1988) Measure of Attitudes toward Lesbians and Gay Men (ATLG Scale)

Attitudes toward Lesbians (ATL) subscale

1. Lesbians just can't fit into our society. (Short-form item)
2. A woman's homosexuality should *not* be a cause for job discrimination in any situation. (R)
3. Female homosexuality is detrimental to society because it breaks down the natural divisions between the sexes.
4. State laws regarding private, consenting lesbian behavior should be loosened. (R) (Short-form item)
5. Female homosexuality is a sin. (Short-form item)
6. The growing number of lesbians indicates a decline in American morals.
7. Female homosexuality in itself is no problem, but what society makes of it can be a problem. (R) (Short-form item)
8. Female homosexuality is a threat to many of our basic social institutions.
9. Female homosexuality is an inferior form of sexuality.
10. Lesbians are sick. (Short-form item)

Attitudes toward Gay Men (ATG) subscale

11. Male homosexual couples should be allowed to adopt children the same as heterosexual couples. (R)
12. I think male homosexuals are disgusting. (Short-form item)
13. Male homosexuals should *not* be allowed to teach school.
14. Male homosexuality is a perversion. (Short-form item)
15. Just as in other species, male homosexuality is a natural expression of sexuality in human men. (R) (Short-form item)
16. If a man has homosexual feelings, he should do everything he can to overcome them.
17. I would *not* be too upset if I learned my son was a homosexual. (R)
18. Homosexual behavior between two men is just plain wrong. (Short-form item)
19. The idea of male homosexual marriages seems ridiculous to me.
20. Male homosexuality is merely a different kind of lifestyle that should *not* be condemned. (R) (Short-form item)

Note. Scoring for items followed by an (R) should be reversed. People's attitudes about lesbians often differ from their attitudes about gay men. Herek recommends using separate subscales for measuring attitudes about lesbians and gay men. Items used in the short version of each subscale are indicated. From "Heterosexuals' attitudes toward lesbians and gay men: Correlates and gender differences" by G. Herek, 1988, *Journal of Sex Research*, 25, 451–477. Copyright 1988 by Taylor & Francis. Reprinted by permission.

Researchers often separate measures of attitudes about gay men from measures of attitudes about lesbians. The reason for this separation is that heterosexual women tend to hold more negative attitudes toward lesbians than toward gay males, whereas heterosexual men tend to hold more negative attitudes toward gay males than toward lesbians (Herek, 1988). This distinction is further evidence of the defensive function that attitudes toward gay men and lesbians serve.

Herek's *symbolic attitudes* are similar to Katz's (1960) value-expressive function because both represent values and beliefs that are reinforced by important reference groups. Herek (1984b, 1987) argues that sexual attitudes often symbolize a person's larger ideologies, a claim consistent with research findings that correlate negative attitudes toward gay men with positive attitudes toward authoritarianism and religiosity and negative attitudes about pornography and erotic material (Herek, 1988). Not surprisingly, people with negative attitudes toward GLBTQ individuals also tend to be less tolerant of other minority groups.

To reflect these experiential, defensive, and symbolic functions of attitudes toward gay men and lesbians, Herek (1987) developed and validated the Attitude Functions Inventory (AFI) to measure the psychological foundations of attitudes (see Table 1.4). Three dimensions of the AFI, experiential-schematic, defensive, and value-expressive (symbolic), reflect Herek's three original functions of attitudes toward lesbians and gay men. An additional function, social-expressive, emphasizes the role of attitudes in the maintenance of social norms. Herek emphasizes that the AFI is a general measure of attitude functions and can be modified when used in different attitude domains.

More recently, Hall and La France (2007) focused on a social-adjustment function of attitudes when conducting a study of homophobia among fraternity men. Specifically, they suggested that a social-adjustment function of attitudes "predicts that members of any given group will adopt attitudes that are in accordance with the identity and goals of the entire group" (p. 41). For example, fraternity members may perceive that the inclusion of gay members may prevent the level of brotherhood, affinity, and cohesion that is a core value of the organization. Others may perceive that homosexual members would hurt recruitment of new members, particularly if the fraternity became known as the "gay house." Still others might believe that gay members would interfere with the development of social relationships with sorority women. After all, as Hall and La France point out, fraternities are social organizations created predominately for heterosexual social purposes. Hall and La France found that the more negative the attitudes that fraternity members held toward gay men, the more that they perceived that the presence of gay fraternity members would reduce trust and cohesiveness within the fraternity, hamper member recruitment, and damage relationships with sororities (p. 52).

It bears mentioning that functional approaches have not been limited to the study of attitudes toward GLBTQ individuals. For example, Lavine and Snyder (2000) examined the role of attitude functions in the study of political behavior, and Hullett (2004, 2006) used a functional approach to attitudes to examine the effectiveness of messages that promote HIV testing.

TABLE 1.4. Herek's (1987) Attitude Functions Inventory (AFI)

Experiential–schematic function

1. My opinions about gay men and lesbians mainly are based on whether or not someone I care about is gay.
2. My opinions about gay men and lesbians mainly are based on my personal experiences with specific gay persons.
3. My opinions about gay men and lesbians mainly are based on my judgments of how likely it is that I will interact with gay people in a significant way.
4. My opinions about gay men and lesbians mainly are based on my personal experiences with people whose family members or friends are gay.

Defensive function

5. My opinions about gay men and lesbians mainly are based on the fact that I would rather not think about homosexuality or gay people.
6. My opinions about gay men and lesbians mainly are based on my personal feeling of discomfort or revulsion at homosexuality.

Value–expressive (symbolic) function

7. My opinions about gay men and lesbians mainly are based on my concern that we safeguard the civil liberties of all people in our society.
8. My opinions about gay men and lesbians mainly are based on my beliefs about how things should be.

Social–expressive function

9. My opinions about gay men and lesbians are based on my perceptions of how the people I care about have responded to gay people as a group.
10. My opinions about gay men and lesbians mainly are based on learning how gay people are viewed by the people whose opinions I most respect.

Note. Participants respond to each item on a scale of "Strongly disagree" to "Strongly agree." The AFI is not a measure of attitudes toward gay men and lesbians. Rather, it is a measure of the psychological functions served by such attitudes. The value–expressive dimension of the AFI is most similar to the symbolic function described by Herek. From "Can functions be measured?: A new perspective on the functional approach to attitudes" by G. Herek, 1987, *Social Psychology Quarterly, 50,* 285–303. Copyright 1987 by the American Sociological Association. Reprinted by permission.

SUMMARY

This chapter began with a definition of persuasion. Persuasion was defined as involving response-shaping, response-reinforcing, and response-changing processes. Examples of each process were provided along with a discussion of their implications. Following this, attitudes were defined by detailing the definitions proposed by Rokeach (1968) and Fishbein and Ajzen (1975). Rokeach defined an attitude as a combination of beliefs centered around an attitude object. Fishbein and Ajzen's definition was then presented as an extension of Rokeach's. They provided a formula for measuring an attitude, arguing that a person's attitude about performing a particular behavior is a function of his or her salient beliefs and evaluation of those beliefs. Alternative definitions proffered by Zanna and Rempel (1988) and Schwarz (2007) were also examined. Finally, Katz's functional approach to studying attitudes was discussed. Herek's description of the psychological foundations of prejudiced attitudes toward lesbians and gay men exemplified the merits of this approach.

NOTES

1. See Fishbein and Ajzen (1975) for a more extensive discussion of their model. For the sake of simplicity, we include only four beliefs in this example. Fishbein and Ajzen, however, emphasize that attitudes are determined by all the salient beliefs a person may hold about a particular attitude object. In many instances, there are likely to be a large number of relevant beliefs that contribute to an attitude.

2. Given this view, attitudes and behaviors should be fairly strongly correlated—but only because they are both caused by the same set of situational factors. In other words, an imputed correlation between ongoing attitudes and subsequent behaviors is regarded as spurious. Therefore, the Construal Model suggests that attitudes definitely do not "cause" behaviors.

CHAPTER 2

Methods of Investigating Persuasive Communication

LOOKING AHEAD . . . This chapter examines the scientific approach to studying persuasive communication. It begins by distinguishing between commonsense observation and social science and continues with a discussion of the scientific methods employed in individual investigations of persuasive communication. This discussion emphasizes the research design types and observational procedures most frequently employed in persuasion research. The chapter ends with a discussion of the narrative and meta-analytic procedures for cumulating the findings of individual studies.

In the preceding chapter, we voiced our belief that the scientific method can be used fruitfully to increase our knowledge of persuasive communication. In this chapter, we explain how and why this is the case. Before proceeding further, however, we need to ask, "What is science?" Rather than regarding science as the accumulated body of knowledge, we prefer to view it as a systematic way of knowing, or learning about the world around us.

Students frequently challenge the value of academic research in attempting to understand the process of persuasion. They question the usefulness of investigations that end up confirming commonsense conclusions: "Why conduct an experiment that produces findings that everyone already knows to be true?" Responding to this direct challenge is an excellent way to introduce the concepts of scientific inquiry. This chapter discusses the superiority of scientific inquiry over so-called commonsense methods for generating knowledge about persuasion. The characteristics of scientific investigations of persuasion are examined in some detail, and the proper criteria for evaluating and cumulating findings across research investigations are also discussed.

COMMONSENSE VERSUS SOCIAL SCIENCE THEORIES

Persuasion is the primary function of many communicative transactions. The social systems we live in are predicated on the development and maintenance of normative behavior. As active participants in these social systems, we are routinely involved in the process of shaping, maintaining, and changing the thoughts and behaviors of those around us. Whether implicitly or explicitly, we communicate with one another in order to create, reinforce, or change behavior.

Commonsense Theories

Through frequent involvement in persuasive transactions, we develop commonsense or "implicit" theories about the strategies and tactics that help us to achieve desired outcomes. For example, children quickly learn that shrewd timing of a request is essential to gaining compliance from a parent: predicting that a parent's foul mood would likely produce a negative response, a child may wait for a better opportunity to ask whether a friend can spend the night. As children develop cognitively, they become more effective persuaders (Bartsch, Wright, & Estes, 2010; Delia, Kline, & Burleson, 1979; Marshall, 2000). Meanwhile, parents learn through trial and error which rewards and punishments will likely influence their children's behavior. Moreover, they learn that what is rewarding for one child may not be rewarding for another.

Over time, we come to view ourselves as social influence experts. Armed with years of personal experience and countless opportunities for testing and validating our implicit theories, we gain confidence in our understanding of the persuasion process. We develop and maintain these implicit theories because they help us to explain the world around us. They enable us to describe, explain, and predict what will happen in many persuasive exchanges. Indeed, we become so strongly attached to these implicit theories that we develop routine patterns of social influence. Salespeople, for example, can describe the precise sequence and timing of the compliance strategies that they believe are most effective. Expert teachers know when to apply sanctions for noncompliance and when to provide rewards to reinforce behavior. Politicians have discovered that 10-second sound bites are more persuasive than 30-minute speeches. However, while often insightful and frequently correct, these implicit theories are more likely to be inadequate representations of human behavior (Kerlinger & Lee, 2000).

Social Science Theories

Social scientists are also interested in theories; however, they adopt a more public, systematic, and disciplined approach to developing and testing theories of human behavior. Social science theories attempt to describe, explain, and predict human behavior (for a detailed discussion of theory construction, see K. I. Miller, 2005).

For example, Inoculation Theory (McGuire, 1961a, 1961b, 1964) was developed to explain the effectiveness of techniques designed to build resistance to persuasion. Using a biological metaphor, McGuire described how weak attack messages act like a vaccine (or inoculation) to help message receivers build their resistance to stronger ones.

For over 40 years, persuasion scholars studied Inoculation Theory, tested its propositions, and offered modifications that expanded the theory's applications and refined its predictions (Banas & Rains, 2010; Compton, 2013; Compton & Pfau, 2009; McGuire, 1999). In Chapter 13 we discuss the evolution and application of Inoculation Theory. For now, we simply identify the theory as but one example of social science theory construction.

Comparing Social Science and "Implicit" Theories

Compared to the explanations derived from implicit theories of persuasion, social scientific inquiry has several important advantages. First, social science theories are explicit and publicly stated. For example, William McGuire did not develop Inoculation Theory and then keep it to himself. Rather, he published several articles and research studies testing the theory and its propositions (McGuire, 1961a, 1961b, 1964). The public nature of social science research enables other scholars to scrutinize the theory and assess its validity. In contrast, implicit theories are rarely articulated publicly, let alone receive such independent scrutiny.

Second, implicit theories are not objective. Because they are derived from repeated personal experiences, commonsense observations are inextricably woven into the observer's biases. For example, a woman who had been sexually harassed by a former employer might respond suspiciously to a new employer's request to work late to complete an important project, whereas one who had not had a similar experience might be less suspicious. Workers' different experiences would likely generate different theories to account for the supervisor's request. In this example, one implicit theory might be that the supervisor is seeking out amorous relationships, while a competing implicit theory might be that the request reflects confidence in the subordinate's ability to work effectively under a deadline. Clearly, the two employees' different experiences produce dramatically different explanations for the same behavior. In this respect, implicit theories likely reflect the biases of the people developing them.

In contrast, social science strives to make objective observations about phenomena that are not influenced by the biases and experiences of the people making them. For example, since McGuire first described it during the early 1960s, Inoculation Theory and its boundary conditions have been subjected to repeated tests by many scholars in a variety of contexts (see Chapter 13 and Banas & Rains, 2010).

Third, implicit theories are not derived from systematic observation. Instead, they rely on everyday observation that is less likely to recognize or explore counterexamples and alternative explanations. Though many useful theories are intuitively obvious, some are not. For example, Dissonance Theory (Festinger, 1957) offered a counterintuitive prediction about the amount of attitude change people experience after advocating a position they do not believe (see Chapter 4). Over the years, Dissonance Theory has been one of the most influential and provocative theories of attitude change. However, without systematic observation it is unlikely that Dissonance Theory would ever have been developed.

Finally, although commonsense and social science explanations are both fallible, only science has a built-in self-correcting mechanism (M. R. Cohen, 1949; Kerlinger & Lee, 2000). Scientists are human and, as such, are prone to the same biases as everyone else (Gould, 1983). Through replication by various investigators, however, social science explanations are frequently reexamined. Over time, errors caused by biases and other factors are detected. When necessary, theories are modified and even discarded.

In contrast, as commonsense explanations become reified through repeated experience, errors in reasoning become more difficult to change. Although many commonsense observations may be accurate, people often cling tenaciously to beliefs derived from incorrect commonsense observations. For example, traditionally in the past, many people believed that women were more easily persuadable than men (and many probably still cling to this belief). Indeed, countless scholars of persuasion subscribed to this belief until careful investigations by Alice Eagly and her colleagues (Eagly, 1978; Eagly & Carli, 1981) refuted that belief (see Chapter 9).

Formal distinctions between science and commonsense observation are often based on Charles Sanders Peirce's perspective on the scientific method (see Kerlinger & Lee, 2000). Peirce believed that it is important to separate observations from biases and prior personal experiences because objectivity is a key underlying objective of science. Specifically, Peirce asserted that "the method must be such that the ultimate conclusion of every man shall be the same. Such is the method of science" (quoted in Kerlinger & Lee, 2000, p. 7).

BOX 2.1. Conventional Wisdom on Trial

Several years ago, Jim consulted on an important patent infringement case. Jim's client was a small technology company that held a revolutionary patent that was being used, without permission, by several large corporations. One of these corporations learned in advance of the impending patent infringement lawsuit, and therefore it decided to strike first, filing a lawsuit alleging that the small technology company had perpetrated a fraud by withholding information from the Patent and Trademark Office when it applied for the patent. In response, the technology company filed a patent infringement claim against the large corporation, alleging that its patented technology was illegally embedded in a variety of the latter's products.

When companies are about to be sued, there is sometimes a "race to the courthouse," because the party filing first generally is best positioned as the plaintiff (i.e., the party doing the suing). The commonsense understanding among lawyers is that being the plaintiff creates significant advantages at trial because that party makes the first opening statement, presents its case first, makes the first closing argument, and is also permitted to respond to the defendant's closing argument.

Armed with their commonsense theory, the attorneys for the small technology company were planning to file a motion requesting the judge to recast the small technology company as the plaintiff and the large technology company as the defendant. Jim's firm suggested that they consider the benefits of being the defendant before filing the motion with the judge. Given the case's predominant theme—a David versus Goliath matchup—Jim argued that the small company might be better positioned as the defendant so that jurors would perceive the large corporation as picking a fight with a smaller, weaker, foe.

This recommendation admittedly was a tough sell because trial lawyers have long believed that the plaintiff has a decided tactical advantage at trial. Although the lawyers firmly believed in their commonsense theory, they allowed Jim's firm to put their belief to a test. Specifically, they conducted two mock trials to test whether the small technology company would be better off as the plaintiff or defendant at trial. The first mock trial had the large corporation positioned as the plaintiff and the small company as the defendant (as Jim preferred). In the second mock trial, the roles were reversed: the small technology company was the plaintiff and the large corporation was the defendant (as the lawyers preferred). Care was taken to match the two samples of "jurors" and to present the same arguments, documents, and witness testimony in both mock trials.

(continued)

BOX 2.1. *(continued)*

The findings were remarkable. When the small technology company was presented as the defendant (i.e., the party being sued), the jurors were significantly more likely to reach a verdict favoring the small company and awarded it significantly more damages. In this scenario, the jurors viewed the large company as the aggressor, attempting to crush the small company. In contrast, when the small company was the plaintiff (i.e., the party doing the suing), the jurors perceived it as the aggressor (because it had initiated the lawsuit) and were less likely to view it as the underdog (in a David vs. Goliath confrontation). The findings were so compelling that the lawyers set aside their commonsense beliefs in favor of the social science findings, abandoning their efforts to recast the parties to the suit.

Although Peirce's definition allows for only one approach to scientific inquiry, scientists have developed a variety of methods consistent with his approach to avoid the deficiencies of commonsense observation (Kerlinger & Lee, 2000, pp. 7–8). At the level of the individual investigation, the scientific approach provides specific standards for making systematic and objective observations that are capable of producing counterintuitive findings. However, scientific discovery involves more than careful attention to the design and conduct of specific investigations. It also suggests that scientists work within a community of scholars, replicating and cumulating findings over time. This self-correcting function requires different methods than those used to generate primary research findings.

We believe that scientific inquiry is superior to common sense as a way of learning about persuasive communication. Therefore, we consider it important to spend some time discussing the nature of that inquiry. As a consequence, we will spend the rest of this chapter discussing several topics relevant to how scientific investigations of persuasion are performed. We begin with a discussion of the characteristics and component parts of single studies. Following this, two procedures for cumulating findings from individual studies are examined.

SCIENTIFIC METHODS OF PERSUASIVE COMMUNICATION INQUIRY

The vast majority of the studies we discuss in this book are, in one way or another, experiments. Over the past 60 years, a variety of research designs have been employed to test theoretical hypotheses about persuasive communication (Campbell & Stanley, 1966; Cook & Campbell, 1979; Shadish, Cook, & Campbell, 2002). These research designs serve three scientific functions: (1) structuring the investigator's observations; (2) providing a logical rationale for making comparisons among observations; and (3) establishing a procedural record for other scholars who wish to examine or replicate a study's findings.

Designing Scientific Investigations

Too many elements go into designing a scientific investigation for us to describe them all in a single chapter. Our goal, however, is to describe the *essential* elements of persuasive communication experiments. We begin by discussing the concept of variable and the common types of variables used in persuasion studies. We then turn our attention to the three types of research designs (experimental, quasi-experimental, and nonexperimental) and the ways that they are commonly carried out. We conclude the section with a discussion of the nature of causality, which is a critical concept in persuasive communication theory.

Variables

Variables are a vital component in social science theory and research. Put simply, a variable is anything that can take on more than one level (i.e., anything that is not a constant). Sex, race, source credibility, and argument quality (among many others) are all variables because they can take on at least two levels. Sex, for instance, is a variable because people are either male or female.

In persuasion research, there are four common types of variables: independent, dependent, intervening, and moderator variables. First, the *independent variable* is a variable that is hypothesized by the researcher to cause changes in some other variable. As we will discuss shortly, Janis and Feshbach (1953) were interested in the persuasive impact of fear-arousing message content on behavior change. They manipulated fear by creating three messages that varied in the amount of fear-arousing content they contained. The amount of fear in the message, then, was the independent variable.

The second type of variable in an experiment is the *dependent variable*. Most often, the independent variable is the hypothesized cause while the dependent variable is the hypothesized effect. Janis and Feshbach (1953) were interested in the persuasive impact of fear-arousing message content (the independent variable) on behavior change. Since behavior change is what the messages were supposed to influence, they represented the dependent variable (or effect) in that study.

All studies that test causal relationships have at least one independent variable and at least one dependent variable. Many times, research (e.g., Janis & Feshbach, 1953) begins by investigating how one independent variable influences a single dependent variable. As time goes on and more studies are conducted, explanations become more complicated. These more complicated explanations frequently require the addition of either or both of two other types of variables: intervening variables and moderator variables.

An *intervening variable* (sometimes called a *mediating variable*) is a variable that comes between the hypothesized cause (i.e., the independent variable) and effect (i.e., the dependent variable) in a causal relationship, often affecting the *strength* of the relationship between them (see Figure 2.1). For example, one of the explanations for the persuasive effects of fear appeals is that they cause physiological arousal. When an experimenter manipulates the fear-arousing content of a message (by showing driver education students photographs of accident victims), it creates variable levels of physiological arousal in audience members. Physiological arousal, in turn, influences how much students are persuaded by these messages. In a causal sense, the fear appeal (the manipulated independent variable) influences physiological arousal (the intervening variable), which in turn influences attitude and behavior change (the dependent variable).

The fourth variable type is a *moderator variable*. A moderator variable is any variable that affects the *nature* (direction or strength) of the relationship between an independent and dependent variable but doesn't necessarily come between them (as with an intervening variable). In Chapter 5 we discuss the relationship between the quality of message arguments and attitude change. It turns out that this relationship is more complex than one might expect. For example, research indicates that one's involvement with the topic moderates the relationship between the quality of arguments in a message and attitude change. When message receivers are personally involved with the topic, stronger arguments are more persuasive than weaker ones. However, when message receivers are uninvolved with the

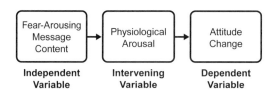

FIGURE 2.1. Causal diagram of independent, intervening, and dependent variables.

topic, the quality of the arguments in the message has little effect on the receivers' attitudes. In this case, issue involvement serves as a moderator variable because it determines whether or not the quality of arguments in a message affects one's attitudes. It is important to note that issue involvement is *not* an intervening variable in that it does not come between the quality of message arguments and attitude change. As we move through our review of persuasion research, we will spend considerable time examining *intervening and moderator variables* that help us to better understand persuasive communication.

Research Design Categories

Now that we have defined the four most common types of variables found in persuasive communication studies, it is time to consider the ways in which studies are performed. There are three basic research design categories: experimental, quasi-experimental, and nonexperimental (Campbell & Stanley, 1966). Two design characteristics distinguish these categories. Experimental and quasi-experimental investigations control (or manipulate) at least one independent variable (hypothesized to be the cause) in order to determine its influence on one or more dependent variables (hypothesized to be influenced by the independent variables). Nonexperimental designs involve no such control. Instead, investigators measure one or more independent variables and assess their influence on one or more dependent variables. In short, if a study involves the *experimental control* of an independent variable, then it is classified as an experimental or quasi-experimental investigation.

The difference between an experiment and a quasi experiment rests on the use of *random assignment* of research participants to experimental conditions. Random assignment means that every research participant has an equal chance of being placed in each of the experimental conditions. In some investigations, it is possible to perform this sort of random assignment. This procedure allows investigators to assume that participants assigned to different experimental conditions are similar when the study begins. This assumption is useful in assessing the effects of experimental treatments (manipulations) on research participants. If there are no systematic differences among participants assigned to different experimental conditions before the experiment, then any differences arising after the experiment can be attributed to the experimental treatment (manipulation) because everything else besides the independent variable is assumed to be constant across conditions.[1]

In many investigations, however, random assignment is just not possible. Instead, participants are assigned to treatment conditions on the basis of membership in some preexisting group. For example, a field experiment on the effectiveness of two different television advertising campaigns may be conducted in separate but similar cities. In these cases, while the communities may be randomly assigned to treatment conditions, the researchers, of course, cannot randomly assign people to live in one city or the other. There may be important differences in the characteristics of people in various cities. Thus, the effectiveness of the two campaigns can only be compared after differences between the two treatment groups are measured and statistically controlled. For example, if socioeconomic status (SES) is considered an important factor in the campaign's effectiveness, then comparisons must statistically control for differences in SES across the two communities—in which case, statistical control replaces random assignment as a means of equating the two treatment groups.

Thus, experimental control and random assignment of research participants are two factors that determine the nature of a research design. These factors are summarized in the decision tree shown in Figure 2.2.

In addition to the differences among experimental, quasi-experimental, and nonexperimental designs, design characteristics also vary in important ways within each general category. The studies described below highlight these differences and reflect the variety of ways that researchers can

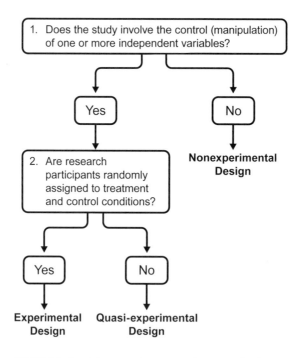

FIGURE 2.2. Decision tree for categorizing study designs.

investigate persuasive communication. Specifically, we use three experimental studies to help us distinguish between single-factor, factorial, and repeated-measures designs. Following this discussion, two investigations are presented as examples of quasi-experimental and nonexperimental research designs.

SINGLE-FACTOR EXPERIMENTAL DESIGNS

The most basic experimental design involves the control (manipulation) of a single independent variable (or factor) and the assessment of its influence on a dependent variable. As we noted above, Janis and Feshbach (1953) were interested in the effects of a single independent variable, *fear-arousing message content*, on a dependent variable, *adherence to message recommendations*, and used such a design.

To study this relationship, Janis and Feshbach (1953) varied the amount of fear-arousing content in three persuasive messages. High school students were randomly assigned to one of three message (experimental) conditions or a control group. In the strong fear condition, students heard a lecture on dental hygiene that emphasized "the painful consequences of tooth decay, diseased gums, and other dangers that can result from improper dental hygiene" (p. 79). The moderate fear-arousing message contained a milder and more factual presentation of these issues, and the minimal fear message "rarely alluded to the consequences of tooth neglect" (p. 79). Each of these messages was accompanied by a number of slides designed to match the verbal message's fear-arousing content. Participants in the no-treatment control group heard a factual lecture about the functions of the eye that was similar in intensity to the minimal fear message.

One week prior to the experiment, every student completed a survey of personal dental hygiene practices (e.g., brushing strokes used and amount of time spent brushing teeth). Students also reported on these practices 1 week following their exposure to the message. Comparing the two sets of surveys revealed that some students changed their dental hygiene practices. The difference between the percentage of students who adopted better dental hygiene and those who became worse represented the "net effect" of the message on behavior.

Results indicated that the minimal fear-arousing message was most effective in changing participants' behavior. The net behavior change was +36% in the minimal fear condition (i.e., 36% more students improved as compared to those who became worse), +22% in the moderate fear condition, and +8% in the strong fear condition. There was no net change in the control condition. To explain these unanticipated findings, Janis and Feshbach (1953) speculated that "when fear is strongly aroused but is not fully relieved by the reassurances contained in the mass communication,

BOX 2.2. Evaluating Experimental Treatments

Although experimental treatments are often referred to as "manipulations," we don't really "manipulate" people in our research. Rather, we manipulate the levels of independent variables and assess the effects of these treatments on relevant attitudes and behaviors. *Manipulation checks* are often used to evaluate the quality and strength of an experimental treatment. For example, many studies of fear appeals manipulate the amount of fear-arousing content in persuasive messages. To check the quality of the experimental treatment—that is, the amount of fear-arousing content in a message—a researcher might ask participants to indicate how fearful the message made them feel. If participants exposed to the "high-fear" message perceived substantially more fear than those exposed to the "low-fear" message, then evidence exists for the quality of the experimental treatment.

An important limitation of persuasion research stems from the often weak correlation between the intended and the actual effects of experimental treatments. For example, reviews of fear-appeal literature found only a moderate correlation average between manipulated and perceived fear (Boster & Mongeau, 1984; Witte & Allen, 2000).

When low-quality treatments are employed, it is very difficult to examine the hypothesis that fear appeals cause changes in attitudes and behaviors. Moreover, problems with experimental treatments raise questions about the conceptual development of the variable itself. That is, researchers may have difficulty creating effective fear-appeal treatments because they do not clearly understand what message factors arouse fear in message receivers. For example, Dillard, Plotnick, Godbold, Freimuth, and Edgar (1996) investigated the emotional reactions created by fear appeals used in public service announcements (PSAs) about AIDS. They found that, in addition to arousing fear, AIDS PSAs affected a host of other emotions in receivers, including surprise, puzzlement, anger, happiness, and sadness. Thus, as you consider the research in later chapters, bear in mind that experimental manipulations of independent variables are imperfect and may trigger unexpected effects that may amplify, mask, or weaken observed relationships among the variables being investigated.

the audience will become motivated to ignore or minimize the importance of the threat" (p. 90).

The independent variable manipulated by these investigators was the amount of fear-arousing information presented in the three persuasive messages. By randomly assigning participants to experimental conditions, and by holding constant all other features of the message, Janis and Feshbach were able to argue that differences in the changes in participants' hygiene practices across the three experimental conditions were attributable to differences in the fear-arousing content of the persuasive messages. While there may be alternative causal explanations for their results, the experimental design renders these explanations unlikely. This allowed Janis and Feshbach to conclude that the most likely explanation was that the independent variable caused the dependent variable.

The Janis and Feshbach (1953) experiment also included a no-treatment control condition. Participants assigned to this condition completed the pretest and posttest surveys of dental hygiene practices. Thus, in addition to estimating the *relative* effectiveness of the three experimental messages, Janis and Feshbach were also able to compare results in each experimental condition with those in the control condition to estimate the *absolute* effectiveness of the three experimental messages. It should be noted that, although some single-factor experiments contain a no-treatment control condition, this feature is not a requirement of the design. Investigators who are only concerned with the relative effects of various experimental treatments need only include the various treatment groups in the design.

Janis and Feshbach employed a single-factor experimental design because they were only concerned with assessing the persuasive effect of a single independent variable. Researchers soon became interested, however, in estimating the separate and combined effects of two or more independent variables on a dependent variable. Factorial designs were developed to accomplish this objective. For example, if one wanted to determine if fear appeals are more persuasive when they come from highly credible sources, a factorial design that manipulates both the amount of fear-arousing information and the credibility of the source would be useful. Agricultural researchers first employed factorial designs in the late 19th century, and they were popularized by Fisher (1935) during the 1930s. By the 1960s, they had become a prominent tool of persuasion scholars.

FACTORIAL EXPERIMENTAL DESIGNS

Often researchers are interested in investigating the separate and joint effects of two or more independent variables in a single study. Factorial designs satisfy the demands of such an investigation.

The basic requirement of a factorial design is that two or more independent variables must be crossed with one another. An experimental design is said to be "completely crossed" when a separate condition is created for every possible combination of all the levels of all the independent variables. For example, if one independent variable (A) has three levels (A_1, A_2, and A_3) and another (B) has two levels (B_1 and B_2), then a completely crossed design will have six experimental conditions or cells (A_1B_1, A_2B_1, A_3B_1, A_1B_2, A_2B_2, and A_3B_2; see Figure 2.3). This particular design is called a 3 × 2 (read as "three-by-two") factorial design because the first independent variable has three levels and the second independent variable has two levels.

Factorial designs enable researchers to identify both separate and combined impacts of the independent variables on dependent variables. The separate effects of the independent variables are called *main effects,* while the combined impact of two or more independent variables is called *interaction effects.* An interaction effect occurs when a moderator variable influences the relationship between the independent and dependent variables.

Petty, Cacioppo, and Goldman (1981) employed a factorial experimental design to test the combined effects of source credibility, argument quality, and involvement on attitude change. As we further elaborate in Chapter 5, they argued that when messages are highly involving (i.e., personally relevant), message receivers are motivated to scrutinize the quality of the message's arguments. When the message topics have little relevance to them, the message receivers are unwilling to think carefully about the issue and instead base their attitudes on more superficial cues such as a source's expertise. Thus, Petty and colleagues hypothesized that when persuasive messages are personally relevant for receivers (i.e., high involvement), argument quality should have an important influence on attitudes. Conversely, when persuasive messages lack personal relevance for receivers (i.e., low involvement), the source's expertise should be more important in changing attitudes. Stated differently, they hypothesized two interaction effects: one specified that the level of personal relevance would "interact" with argument quality to influence attitudes, and the other specified that

FIGURE 2.3. Diagram of a 3 × 2 factorial design.

personal relevance would "interact" with source credibility to influence attitudes.

These hypotheses specified that certain combinations of involvement and argument quality or involvement and source credibility would produce attitude change and that other combinations would produce little or no attitude change. Hence, a three-way factorial design (i.e., an experimental design with three fully crossed independent variables), which completely crossed high and low levels of involvement, argument quality, and source credibility, was employed to test these hypotheses.

Two levels of involvement (high, low), two levels of argument quality (strong, weak), and two levels of source expertise (expert, inexpert) were completely crossed to create an experimental design with eight conditions (see Table 2.1). Petty, Cacioppo, et al. (1981) then created eight experimental messages on the topic of comprehensive exams, one for each condition. For example, students in one condition heard a high-involvement message containing strong arguments that was attributed to an expert source. Students in another condition heard a high-involvement message containing strong arguments that was attributed to an inexpert source, and so on.

Participants were randomly assigned to one of the eight experimental conditions, listened to a recorded message, and then completed an attitude scale (among other measures). The use of random assignment permitted the assumption that the participants' attitudes were similar across the eight experimental conditions prior to hearing the message. Hence, any differences across conditions *after* the message presentation could be attributed to the message presentation itself.

Petty, Cacioppo, et al. (1981) observed their hypothesized effects. As Table 2.2 reveals, participants hearing the high-involvement message were influenced primarily by the quality of the message arguments and not by the source's expertise. Specifically, on the left side of Table 2.2 (i.e., high involvement), average scores are higher in the upper two cells (corresponding to the strong arguments) when compared with the lower two cells (i.e., weak arguments). Participants hearing the low-involvement message were influenced primarily by the source's expertise and were relatively unaffected

TABLE 2.1. Three-Way Factorial Design from the Petty, Cacioppo, and Goldman (1981) Study

	High involvement		Low involvement	
	Expert source	Nonexpert source	Expert source	Nonexpert source
Strong arguments				
Weak arguments				

TABLE 2.2. Findings from the Petty, Cacioppo, and Goldman (1981) Study

	High involvement		Low involvement	
	Expert source	Nonexpert source	Expert source	Nonexpert source
Strong arguments	.64	.61	.40	−.12
Weak arguments	−.38	−.58	.25	−.64

Note. Numbers are standardized attitude scores for participants in the experimental conditions. The score for participants in a no-message control condition was .18. From "Personal involvement as a determinant of argument-based persuasion" by R. E. Petty, J. T. Cacioppo, & R. Goldman, 1981, *Journal of Personality and Social Psychology, 41,* 847–855. Copyright 1981 by the American Psychological Association. Reprinted by permission.

by the quality of message arguments. In the right-hand portion of Table 2.2 (i.e., low involvement), the left-hand-most cells (i.e., expert source) have higher means than the right-hand-most cells (i.e., nonexpert source).

The factorial design was critical for the Petty, Cacioppo, et al.'s (1981) experiment. The design systematically varied the levels of involvement, argument quality, and source expertise, and it assessed the separate and combined influence of these independent variables on the attitudes of message receivers. Without a factorial design, it would have been very difficult to assess the combined (interaction) effects of these variables. Because researchers are frequently interested in both the separate (i.e., main) and combined (i.e., interaction) effects of two or more independent variables, factorial designs have become a critical tool of experimental persuasion research.

Though research designs have become more sophisticated over the past 60 years, one important feature of many early persuasion experiments has been lost in contemporary persuasion research. Specifically, early researchers were frequently interested in both the immediate and long-term effects of persuasive communication. Present-day theorists, in contrast, demonstrate relatively little concern for the persistence of persuasive effects even though persistence remains an important theoretical concern. As a result, designs that assess persuasive effects over time (i.e., repeated-measures designs) remain an important, though underutilized, tool of modern persuasion research.

REPEATED-MEASURES EXPERIMENTAL DESIGNS

The critical feature of repeated-measures designs is the use of multiple assessments (or measurements) of the dependent variable. Repeated measures can be used in conjunction with both single-factor and factorial designs. Whereas the terms *single-factor* and *factorial* describe the structure of the experimental treatments (i.e., manipulations), the term *repeated measures* refers to the assessment (or measurement) of a dependent variable at multiple points in time. Thus, both single-factor experiments and factorial designs can incorporate repeated measures of the dependent variable. For example, if Petty, Cacioppo, et al. (1981) had been interested in the persisting effects of argument quality and source credibility, they would have measured attitudes again a few weeks later to determine the extent to which attitudes remained the same or decayed over time.

Investigations of the "sleeper effect" have relied on repeated-measures designs. Hovland, Lumsdaine, and Sheffield (1949) first observed the sleeper effect when they found that messages presented by low-credibility sources were not immediately accepted but became more influential over time. Hovland and his colleagues speculated that the negative effects of the source's credibility may initially offset the positive effects of a persuasive message but that over time the source becomes disassociated from the message—that is, people remember the message content but not its source. Because the message content is persuasive, attitude change at a later point in time is more positive than immediately following the message's presentation.

As part of a larger study, Kelman and Hovland (1953) tested this explanation for the sleeper effect. They exposed students to a persuasive message advocating lenient treatment of juvenile delinquents from either a positive or a negative communicator. The positive communicator was described as a judge who had written several books on juvenile delinquency and was well known for his views on the integration of the delinquent into society. The negative communicator was described as a "man on the street" who gave the impression of being obnoxious and self-centered and indicated he got into several "scrapes" as a youngster.

Before the experiment, participants in both groups had similar opinions about the treatment of juvenile delinquents. Immediately following the message presentation, participants listening to the positive communicator demonstrated significantly more agreement with the communicator ($M = 46.70$) than participants exposed to the same message attributed to a negative communicator ($M = 42.75$). After 3 weeks, participants were once again asked to indicate their opinions about the treatment of juvenile delinquents. Opinions decreased significantly ($M = -3.22$) among participants exposed to the positive communicator, while the opinions of participants exposed to the negative communicator became slightly more positive ($M = +0.65$). Together, these changes represented a convergence of opinions at the second attitude measurement. This finding is consistent with the general sleeper effect pattern: that is, over time, attitude change produced by the positive communicator declines considerably while attitude change produced by the negative communicator increases slightly.

Relatively few recent studies have focused on the immediate and delayed effects of persuasive messages on attitudes and behaviors. Nevertheless, investigators who are interested in the persistence of change in attitudes and behaviors over time typically employ a repeated-measures design.

QUASI-EXPERIMENTAL DESIGNS

For many investigations, it is possible to experimentally control one or more of the independent variables under consideration but impossible to randomly assign participants to experimental conditions. Field studies, for example, often involve the use of intact groups. Reliance on intact groups negates the advantages of random assignment and represents a hallmark of quasi-experimental designs. Because quasi experiments do not involve random assignment of participants to treatment conditions, they cannot assume that participants in different treatment groups are similar when the study begins. To alleviate this problem, statistical techniques (i.e., analysis of covariance) are used by researchers to statistically control for preexisting differences between treatment groups.

With the exception of assigning participants to treatment conditions, quasi-experimental and experimental designs are identical. Hence, one could conduct a quasi experiment by using a single-factor or a factorial design with single or repeated measures of the dependent variables. Though random assignment of participants to treatment conditions is desirable, field investigations do not always afford researchers this luxury. For example, a study of the effectiveness of a drug resistance program for high school students would be difficult to conduct with an experimental design. Most likely, a quasi-experimental design would be used, and intact classes (or schools) would be assigned to the treatment and control conditions. In this instance, it would be impractical (and perhaps undesirable) to randomly assign students within the same classes (or school) to different conditions. Nevertheless, because field settings often prove to be more realistic arenas for persuasion research, quasi-experimental designs are an attractive alternative for scholars.

Hecht and colleagues (1993) utilized a quasi-experimental design to test the effectiveness of their drug resistance skills training program. This program was designed to provide high school students the persuasive skills they need to resist others' attempts to get them to use illegal drugs. They tested the effectiveness of their program in a high school in the southwestern United States using a factorial design that fully crossed two independent variables. An approximately 30-minute skills training presentation titled "Killing Time" was presented either live or on film. Following the presentation, a follow-up discussion was conducted with some groups but not for others. Still another group was not exposed to the training program at all. In all, Hecht and colleagues created five experimental conditions: live presentation with discussion, live presentation without discussion, film presentation with discussion, film presentation without discussion, and a control (i.e., exposed to neither the presentation nor the discussion). A variety of variables, including drug use, attitudes toward drug use, and confidence in refusing drug offers, were measured 1 month before, immediately after, and 1 month following the presentations. Because of restrictions created by the school setting, they could assign classrooms, but not participants, to the five conditions. This was the characteristic that made their research a quasi-experimental rather than experimental design.

Results of the Hecht and colleagues (1993) investigation indicated that 1 month following the program students in all of the conditions except live performance without discussion exhibited less drug use as compared to control students. Moreover, when compared with control conditions, both discussion conditions created more negative attitudes toward drug use, perceptions that fewer of their peers were using drugs, and increased confidence in refusing future drug offers.

Although not particularly strong, findings from the Hecht and colleagues (1993) investigation indicate that a single anti-drug presentation can produce changes in various attitude, belief, and behavioral outcomes. Moreover, given the restrictions of the research setting (i.e., a high school), an experimental design was not possible. In such cases, researchers have no choice but to use a quasi-experimental design.

Though experimental and quasi-experimental designs have several desirable features, in many situations it is impossible or impractical for investigators to control or manipulate the theoretical variables of interest. In these situations, researchers rely on nonexperimental procedures for testing hypotheses. Though a variety of procedures exist, the study described below illustrates the utility of nonexperimental procedures for persuasion research.

NONEXPERIMENTAL DESIGNS

For over 70 years, persuasion scholars have devoted considerable research effort to examining the relationship between attitudes and behaviors. One popular strategy has been to identify moderator variables that influence the strength of the attitude–behavior relationship. For example, Sivacek and Crano (1982) hypothesized that *vested interest*—the extent to which the message topic influences a person's life—would moderate the strength of this relationship. They argued that when people had a vested interest in a given issue, their attitude about it would more likely correspond with their behavior (i.e., the attitude–behavior correlation would be strong), and, conversely, that there would be a weak attitude–behavior association when people had no vested interest in the issue.

To test this hypothesis, Sivacek and Crano (1982, Study 1) asked college students to complete an attitude survey that included questions on a number of issues, including a state ballot initiative to raise the legal drinking age from 18 to 21 years. Most of the students (80%) reported a negative attitude toward the proposal. About a week later, the students were contacted by a different person and asked if they were willing to work to defeat the proposal to raise the drinking age. The amount of time that the students volunteered to work was the researchers' behavior measure (actually of behavioral *intention*, as the students did not actually participate in a campaign against the proposal).

Readily available demographic data enabled the researchers to classify the students into three distinct groups. Those who would be unaffected by the proposal (i.e., those who would be 21 when the law was enacted) were placed in the low-vested-interest group. Students who would be legally prevented from drinking for at least 2 years (i.e., the 18- and 19-year-olds) were placed in a high-vested-interest group. Finally, a few students were placed in a moderate-vested-interest group because the new law would affect them, but for less than 2 years. Notice that this categorization scheme produced three groups of participants who were analytically equivalent to participants in three experimental conditions without randomly assigning the participants to groups.

Ultimately Sivacek and Crano (1982) reported that the attitude–behavioral intention relationship was strongest for students in the high-vested-interest group ($r = .61$), followed by those in the moderate-vested-interest group ($r = .40$), and then by those in the low-vested-interest group ($r = .16$).[2] Thus, without having to engage in a formal experimental treatment, Sivacek and Crano were nonetheless able to statistically create three groups representing varying levels of vested interest and estimate the effect of vested interest on the attitude–behavior relationship. While these procedures may appear to be similar to those used in experimental investigations, the Sivacek and Crano study did not involve an experimental control or the manipulation of independent variables. Nevertheless, the statistical controls employed by Sivacek and Crano permitted a scientific examination of the relationship between attitudes and behaviors.

Critics of nonexperimental investigations sometimes engage in fallacious reasoning, arguing that one cannot draw causal inferences by using only correlational data. Causal inferences, they assert, can only be properly derived from experimental investigations. Such claims, however, reflect a basic misunderstanding of causal inference and experimental design.

John Stuart Mill identified three requirements for inferring causation: time ordering, covariation, and the elimination of alternative interpretations for the relationship. In sum, before variable *A* can be inferred to cause variable *B*, *A* must precede *B* in time, *A* and *B* must be conceptually and empirically related, and all alternative explanations for the relationship between *A* and *B* must be examined and discredited (Cook & Campbell, 1979, pp. 18–19). For example, if attitudes are hypothesized to cause behaviors, then the attitudes must be formed before the behavior occurs, they must be conceptually and empirically related to the behaviors, and all competing explanations for the attitude–behavior relationship must be eliminated.

Notice, however, that Mill's criteria suggest nothing about the method of observation to be used in gathering the necessary information for causal inference. Individual experiments or quasi-experiments are helpful in meeting the first two criteria, time ordering and covariation, but by themselves they cannot rule out all rival explanations for the hypothesized causal relationship. Nonexperimental observations can also be used to establish temporal ordering and covariation. Statistical procedures such as causal modeling and time-series analyses are effective substitutes for experimental control. Once again, however, the application of these techniques in a *single investigation* is inadequate for eliminating rival explanations. Thus, regardless of its design, no single study is capable of meeting all three of Mill's criteria for inferring a causal relationship. Instead, the process of causal inference occurs over time and with converging evidence generated from many different observations made by a variety of researchers. Clearly, the observation of a correlation between two variables is inadequate for drawing a causal inference, no matter how the study was performed. Instead, careful procedures must be employed to meet all three of Mill's criteria.

CUMULATING THE FINDINGS OF INDIVIDUAL INVESTIGATIONS

To this point in the chapter, we have focused on the generation and interpretation of scientific data from single studies. However, the generation of effects is only part of the scientific process. Once numerous studies have investigated the same phenomenon, scholars face the task of combining findings from individual studies and integrating them with a larger body of persuasion literature. This section discusses two methods for combining or cumulating the findings of individual investigations.

As we just noted, the most difficult requirement for drawing causal inferences is the elimination of rival explanations for the findings of an individual investigation. Many rival explanations can be routinely discounted through careful design and analysis of the observations recorded (Campbell & Stanley, 1966). Alternative explanations that may derive from rival theories, however, often require the development and conducting of several investigations before scholars can confidently choose among them. As further discussed in Chapter 4, for example, Bem's (1967, 1972) Self-Perception Theory provided a plausible rival account for the findings from earlier tests of Dissonance Theory. After many studies pitted the two competing explanations against each other over the course of a decade, researchers concluded that both explanations may be correct but that each is applicable to different circumstances (Fazio, Zanna, & Cooper, 1977).

The continuous nature of scientific inquiry indicates that through replication and extension of prior investigations scientists accumulate knowledge about phenomena of interest. Knowledge generated by many investigations is then organized in reviews of the literature. Two types of reviews—narrative summaries and meta-analysis—appear frequently in the persuasion literature and are described below.

Narrative Summaries

Traditional reviews of the persuasion literature consist of narrative descriptions of studies investigating the same phenomenon. These summaries critically evaluate individual investigations, highlight conceptual differences among them, and organize their findings along unifying dimensions.

Ajzen and Fishbein's (1977) review of the attitude–behavior literature exemplifies the narrative review. They described, and attempted to reconcile, the contradictory conclusions of studies investigating the relationship between people's attitudes and their behaviors. As further elaborated in Chapter 3, these two researchers developed several conceptual and empirical explanations that helped other scholars understand, and investigate, these apparent discrepancies.

Eagly's (1978) review of studies investigating the effects of gender on persuadability (see Chapter 9) is another good example of a narrative review. In addition to evaluating the individual studies' conceptual and methodological characteristics, Eagly counted the number of investigations that found women to be more easily persuaded, less easily persuaded, and equally persuaded as men. This counting procedure allowed her to draw inferences about the relationship between gender and influenceability based on a large number of investigations.

Although such counting procedures can be insightful, they provide only rough estimates of the actual strength of the relationship among variables. Given that shortcoming, narrative reviews may provide more erroneous conclusions than meta-analytic reviews.

Meta-Analytic Summaries

Meta-analytic procedures were developed during the 1980s to provide more quantitative literature reviews (Card, 2012; Glass, McGaw, & Smith,

1981; Hunter & Schmidt, 1990; Rosenthal, 1991). Like narrative reviews, meta-analytic reviews typically begin with a critical assessment of the quality of individual investigations and the conceptual differences among them. Once important study features have been identified, the empirical part of the review unfolds in two stages. The first stage involves estimating, for each study, the strength of the relationship among the variables of interest. This estimation is called a *study effect size* (e.g., a correlation). In the second stage, effect sizes are averaged across studies to provide statistics that summarize the entire body of literature.

Meta-analysis has a number of advantages over traditional counting procedures. Counting procedures rarely consider the strength of the relationship among variables of interest—hence, a small but significant effect is counted the same as a very strong effect. Meta-analysis, on the other hand, is predicated on estimating the *size* of relationships among variables. In addition, "Hunterian" meta-analysis (Hunter & Schmidt, 1990; Hunter, Schmidt, & Jackson, 1982) provides formulas for correcting these estimates for a variety of factors. For example, measurement error always reduces the size of the observed relationship among variables (Hunter et al., 1982). Correcting individual study estimates for measurement error (and other factors) produces a more accurate (and larger) estimate of the relationship between variables. Finally, although counting procedures weigh all studies equally, the procedures developed by Hunter and colleagues place more emphasis on the findings of studies with large samples than on those with smaller samples.

In addition to its statistical prowess, meta-analysis has the added advantage of giving consideration to every study included in the review. Narrative reviews are sometimes biased by the findings of one or two studies published in prominent journals. To correct this problem, meta-analysis requires the analysis of every investigation that meets the inclusion criteria. With meta-analysis, an investigation conducted by the most prominent persuasion scholar and published in a high-quality journal receives the same attention as—but no more than—one conducted by a little-known scholar that appears in an obscure journal.

Meta-analyses enable researchers to draw much more specific conclusions from a body of studies than is possible with narrative reviews. As a consequence, we use them liberally throughout this book. For example, in Chapter 9 we discuss Eagly and Carli's (1981) meta-analysis of the same studies as those included in Eagly's (1978) narrative review. After meta-analyzing the studies, Eagly and Carli were able to make much more precise statements about the issue of gender differences in persuadability. In Chapter 3, we discuss Kim and Hunter's (1993a, 1993b) meta-analysis of the research literature on the relationship between attitudes and behaviors. Estimates of the correlation between attitudes and behaviors in this meta-analysis were more precise than those available in narrative reviews and larger than most scholars would have expected.

Because they sometimes run counter to prevailing wisdom or the conclusions of prior narrative reviews, some meta-analytic reviews are controversial. For example, two meta-analytic reviews (Johnson & Eagly, 1989; Stiff, 1986) that produced findings questioning the validity of the Elaboration Likelihood Model of persuasion (see Chapter 5) soon after publication encountered intense criticism from the developers of the model (Petty & Cacioppo, 1990; Petty, Kasmer, Haugtvedt, & Cacioppo, 1987). Critiques such as the latter often question the appropriateness and utility of meta-analytic techniques. As these exchanges indicate, meta-analytic reviews are subject to the same reinterpretation and scrutiny as original investigations of persuasive communication. Moreover, as with narrative reviews, the validity of a meta-analysis is dependent on the quality of the individual investigations included in the review. Though procedures for correcting some limitations exist, other problems in primary research often degrade the quality of the conclusions emerging from these reviews.

SUMMARY

This chapter began with a discussion of the differences between scientific and commonsense observation. We argued that scientific observations are a superior method for generating knowledge because they are systematic and strive for objectivity, are capable of producing counterintuitive findings, and have a self-correcting function. Consistent with the scientific method, several experimental, quasi-experimental, and nonexperimental research designs were described. These designs reflect strategies for structuring observations about persuasive phenomena. The chapter concluded with a discussion of narrative and meta-analytic methods for cumulating the findings of individual investigations in a review of the literature.

NOTES

1. There are several important issues related to this brief discussion of random assignment (see Campbell & Stanley, 1966; Cook & Campbell, 1979; and Shadish et al., 2002, for thorough reviews). Random assignment is supposed to create identical groups or conditions. However, while it reduces systematic differences among experimental conditions, random assignment does not *guarantee* equivalence. Moreover, the results of almost any experiment can be challenged on a variety of grounds. Therefore, researchers strive to minimize such challenges by attempting to replicate their findings through multiple investigations conducted with different samples and procedures (and, ideally, investigators).

Only after completing multiple studies and achieving consistent results should researchers be confident of the findings they report.

2. The letter r stands for a statistic called the Pearson product–moment correlation coefficient (or, more simply, the correlation). The correlation coefficient measures the linear association between two variables. Correlations range from –1.00 (a perfect linear association between variables where, as one variable increases, the other variable decreases) to +1.00 (a perfect linear association between variables where, as one variable increases, the other variable increases). A correlation of 0.00 indicates that there is no linear relationship between the two variables at all. The larger the correlation (either positive or negative), the more accurately one can predict scores on the dependent variable given scores on the independent variable.

CHAPTER 3

Examining
the Attitude–Behavior Relationship

LOOKING AHEAD . . . This chapter examines the attitude–behavior literature with an eye toward establishing the boundary conditions under which attitudes predict behavior. It begins with a description of the first classic investigation of the relationship between attitudes and behaviors. Next, comes a discussion of Ajzen and Fishbein's (1977) review of this literature, which serves as a framework for assessing this relationship. The Theory of Reasoned Action (Fishbein & Ajzen, 1980) and the Theory of Planned Behavior (Ajzen, 1985) are then presented to elucidate the relationships among attitudes, intentions, and behavior. Finally, the chapter closes with a discussion of several factors that affect the strength of the attitude–behavior relationship.

Persuasion scholars have traditionally focused their attention on assessing persuasive effects by predicting attitudes and attitude change, generally exhibiting relatively little concern for studying behavioral responses. As G. R. Miller and M. Burgoon (1978) noted, "So pervasive has been the tendency of persuasion researchers to employ attitude change as their principal measure of persuasive effect that the terms 'persuasion' and 'attitude change' are virtually synonymous" (p. 34). Although there has been some progress in the study of behaviors in recent years, Miller and Burgoon's critique is as valid today as it was when it was proffered in 1978.

As we pointed out in Chapter 1, the attitude construct was purposively created by social scientists who sought an intervening process to explain behavioral reactions to stimuli. Both the Tripartite (Rokeach, 1968) and Attitude toward Behavior (Fishbein & Ajzen, 1975) views of attitudes discussed in Chapter 1 highlight the close conceptual link between attitudes and behaviors. As a consequence, the utility of the attitude construct rests largely on its ability to predict and explain behavior. If attitudes do not predict behaviors, there may be no rationale for keeping intact the attitude concept.

If the relationship between attitudes and behaviors is consistently strong, then reliance on attitudes as a sole measure of persuasive effect permits us to predict consequent behaviors. Unfortunately, this key relationship has been a point of considerable concern and contention. Since the early 1930s, investigations of this relationship have produced mixed findings and stimulated considerable debate about the utility of the attitude construct.

THE LaPIERE STUDY

LaPiere (1934) performed one of the first investigations of the relationship between people's attitudes and their corresponding behavior. He was intrigued by earlier research suggesting that people's attitudes on racial issues were not closely allied with their overt behaviors. In addition, he questioned the utility of questionnaires (which at that time were a relatively new development) as a valid way of measuring attitudes. To investigate these issues, LaPiere traveled around the West Coast for some 2 years with a Chinese couple. During their travels together, they would stay in hotels and roadside campgrounds as well as eat in cafés and restaurants that ran the gamut in terms of quality. LaPiere generally had the Chinese couple enter the service establishments on their own first to ask for service, while on some occasions they all entered together. Sometimes the trio was well dressed, at other times they dressed casually, and occasionally they were dusty from the road.

LaPiere kept a diary of the group's interactions with the people they encountered. He noted that, of the 251 hotels, campgrounds, restaurants, and cafés they patronized, at only one were they refused service. Moreover, LaPiere found that the overall quality of service they received was quite good and that there was no pattern of discriminatory service in the establishments they visited.

Several months after they completed their travels, LaPiere sent questionnaires to the establishments they had visited and several that they had not visited. The questionnaires inquired whether the establishment would provide service to a Chinese couple. Surprisingly enough, responses from 92% of the restaurants and cafés and 91% of the hotels and campgrounds that they had patronized indicated that the establishment would *not* provide service to Chinese individuals.

Clearly, the attitudes reflected in the questionnaire responses were incompatible with the patterns of behavior LaPiere had observed while traveling with the couple. Though this investigation is not without its methodological limitations,[1] the findings are generally considered to be indisputable: the attitudes reflected in the questionnaire responses were inconsistent with—indeed, the opposite of—the behaviors LaPiere had observed. The LaPiere investigation raised questions about the validity of self-report attitude measures the relationship between attitudes and behavior.

A subsequent study by Corey (1937) produced similar findings. Corey measured college students' attitudes toward cheating and correlated them with actual cheating behavior. Students were asked to grade their own quizzes that had been completed and turned in during a prior class period. Unbeknownst to them, however, the papers had actually been graded before being handed back to the students for self-grading. Thus, this process provided a direct measure of cheating behavior that was then correlated with attitudes toward cheating. As with the LaPiere (1934) study, Corey found that respondents' stated attitudes toward cheating were unrelated to their actual cheating behavior.

Over the next several decades, various investigations added to the controversy over the usefulness of the attitude construct, as results on the attitude–behavior relationship were hopelessly inconsistent. Some studies found strong relationships, while others found no relationship at all. Early optimistic assessments of the importance of attitudes (e.g., Allport, 1935) faded into critical evaluations of the attitude construct. By the 1960s, contradictory findings from many investigations caused some scholars to seriously question the viability of the attitude construct for predicting behavior (Festinger, 1964; Wicker, 1969). Wicker (1969) went so far as to suggest that if strong relationships between attitudes and behaviors were not found more consistently, then one possibility was "to abandon the attitude concept in favor of directly studying overt behavior" (p. 75).

By 1970, things were looking grim for the attitude construct. Persuasion scholars, however, were unwilling to let go of attitudes as an explanatory construct. In response to Wicker's (1969) call to abandon attitudes, scholars developed two separate streams of research (Greenwald, 1989). First, one set of researchers (Ajzen & Fishbein, 1977; Fishbein & Ajzen, 1975) emphasized methodological explanations for the contradictory findings from prior studies. In the other stream of research, scholars began to investigate moderator variables that affect the strength of the attitude–behavior relationship (Fazio & Zanna, 1981; D. J. O'Keefe & Delia, 1981; Sivacek & Crano, 1982). These efforts are examined in the following sections of this chapter.

CHARACTERISTICS OF ATTITUDES AND BEHAVIORS

Ajzen and Fishbein's (1977) review of the attitude–behavior literature emphasized the conceptual and operational characteristics of attitudes and behaviors. Essentially, they argued that the weak attitude–behavior relationship found in prior research was the result of a lack of specificity in both the conceptual definitions and the measures of attitudes and behaviors.

In an effort to improve the conceptual grounding of both attitudes and behaviors, the two researchers described them in terms of their action and target components. They began by arguing that "a given action is always performed with respect to a given target" (p. 889). All behaviors, then, have both an action and a target component—the action component representing the behavior being performed and the target component, the object toward which the action is directed. For example, the behavior of "going to church" has both target (i.e., the church) and action (i.e., attendance) components. To predict a particular behavior maximally well, Ajzen and Fishbein argued that the measures of the attitudes must contain exactly the same action and target components as those represented in the behavior.[2] While this argument seems quite simple, many early studies investigating the attitude–behavior relationship had frequently used general attitude measures (e.g., religiosity) to predict specific behaviors (e.g. attending religious services). Such general attitude measures contained neither the target (religious services) nor the action (attendance) component of the behavior. Given such a mismatch, it is not surprising that such "attitudes" would not correlate strongly with behaviors. Indeed, most of us know people who consider themselves to be very religious but yet do not attend formal religious services.

Ajzen and Fishbein (1977), in the Attitude toward Behavior Model discussed in Chapter 1, argued that a strong attitude–behavior relationship should be expected only when there is a high degree of correspondence between the attitude measure and the behavior. An attitude measure is said to correspond to the behavior if two conditions are met. First, the attitude and behavior must correspond to the extent that the action component contained in the attitude measure matches the behavior. Second, the attitude and behavior correspond to the extent that the target component of the attitude measure is similar to the target of the behavior. For example, measuring attitudes toward charitable organizations and using those measured attitudes to predict contributions to the American Red Cross would constitute a low degree of attitude–behavior correspondence because it contains neither the action component (donating money) nor the target (the *particular* charity in question) of the behavior.

Relying on this conceptual framework, Ajzen and Fishbein (1977) reviewed prior attitude–behavior studies. They categorized each study as having low, partial, or high correspondence between the attitude measure and the behavior. Low-correspondence studies were defined as those that lacked correspondence on both the action and the target components (e.g., attitudes toward relief organizations to predict contributions to the Red Cross). Partial-correspondence studies exhibited correspondence on either the action or the target components but not both. For example, using attitudes toward the Red Cross to predict Red Cross contributions establishes correspondence between the target component (Red Cross) but not the action component (contributions) of a behavior. Finally, studies in the high-correspondence group had correspondence on both the action and the target components of the attitude and behavior (e.g., measuring attitudes toward contributing to the Red Cross to predict subsequent Red Cross contributions).

If Fishbein and Ajzen's explanation is correct, then studies with low correspondence should exhibit a weak attitude–behavior relationship, studies with partial correspondence should exhibit a moderate one and studies with high correspondence should exhibit a strong attitude–behavior relationship. Ajzen and Fishbein's (1977) findings were consistent with this analysis (see Table 3.1). Of the 27 studies classified as having low correspondence, 26 produced an attitude–behavior correlation that was not significantly different from zero (i.e., were very small), and only 1 study produced a small to moderate attitude–behavior correlation. Among the 71 studies in the partial-correspondence category, 20 found nonsignificant (i.e., very small) attitude–behavior correlations, 47 found small to moderate correlations, and 4 studies exhibited a strong relationship. Finally, among the 44 studies with high correspondence, 9 found a small to moderate

TABLE 3.1. Studies Exhibiting the Relationship between Attitude–Behavior Correspondence and the Strength of the Attitude–Behavior Relationship

Degree of correspondence	Size of the attitude–behavior relationship		
	Strong	Small to moderate	Nonsignificant
High	35	9	0
Partial	4	47	20
Low	0	1	26

Note. Numbers reflect the number of studies that fell within each of these categories. From "Attitude–behavior relations: A theoretical analysis and review of empirical research" by I. Ajzen & M. Fishbein, 1977, Psychological Bulletin, 84, 888–918. Copyright 1977 by the American Psychological Association. Adapted by permission.

attitude–behavior correlation, and 35 found strong attitude–behavior cor-relations.[3] This pattern was clear and supported the importance of corre-spondence in determining the relationship between attitudes and behaviors.

In addition, a meta-analytic review of the attitude–behavior literature reported a pattern consistent with the Ajzen and Fishbein analysis (Kim & Hunter, 1993a). In a review of over 100 studies, the strength of the attitude–behavior relationship was a function of the match (correspondence) between the attitude measure and the corresponding behavior. Studies with a strong match (or correspondence) exhibited an average attitude–behavior intention correlation that was larger (average r = .69) than studies in which match (or correspondence) was moderate (.62) or low (.46). In addition, this review underscored the effects of measurement problems on the estimation of the attitude–behavior relationship. Once statistical corrections for these mea-surement problems were applied, the corrected correlations for the high-, moderate-, and low-relevance studies increased dramatically (average r = .90, .82, and .70, respectively)[4] (Kim & Hunter, 1993a).

In summary, the findings of these reviews (Ajzen & Fishbein, 1977; Kim & Hunter, 1993a) are consistent with earlier speculation that the weak attitude–behavior relationship found in many studies is due in part to conceptual ambiguity and measurement problems in the attitude and behavior measures (G. R. Miller, 1967; Wicker, 1969). Many prior studies lacked correspondence because they measured general attitudes (or even broader personality characteristics) and used these to predict behaviors toward specific people or situations—for example, by using a measure of attitudes toward environmental issues to predict attendance at a rally to promote a particular piece of environmental legislation. Essentially, these reviews indicate that conceptual and measurement problems attenuated the strength of the attitude–behavior relationship in prior research.

Thus, the viability of the attitude–behavior relationship (and, as a consequence, the attitude construct itself) was reasserted in the Ajzen and Fishbein (1977) review and reinforced in the Kim and Hunter (1993a) meta-analysis. However, two issues remain. First, the specific nature of this relationship remained unexamined. The next section reviews a math-ematical model of the attitude–behavior relationship. Second, there are also factors that change the strength of the attitude–behavior relationship. The final section in the chapter discusses several moderator variables that affect the size and strength of this relationship.

AJZEN AND FISHBEIN'S REASONED ACTION THEORIES

By the late 1960s, researchers had focused considerable attention on under-standing the specific nature of the relationship between attitudes and behaviors. Perhaps the most widely investigated models to emerge from these efforts became known as the Theory of Reasoned Action (Ajzen & Fishbein, 1980) and the Theory of Planned Behavior (Ajzen, 1985). Examination of these theories (called collectively "Reasoned Action Theories") and the research that tested them provides a clearer understanding of the relationship between attitudes and behaviors (see Fishbein & Ajzen, 2010, and Yzer, 2013, for recent reviews).

Examining the Reasoned Action Theories

Extending Dulany's (1961, 1968) Theory of Propositional Control, Fishbein (1967) argued that the best predictor of behavior (*B*) was not attitudes, but instead an individual's intention to perform a particular behavior (*BI*). Hence, the Theory of Reasoned Action (Ajzen & Fishbein, 1980) was initially designed to predict behavioral intentions toward specific objects or situations (see Figure 3.1, A). Over time, this theory was extended and became known as the Theory of Planned Behavior. To understand this latter theory, we begin by examining the specific components that affect behavioral intentions and then apply them to the example from Chapter 1 regarding voting for a pro-immigration reform politician.

The Theory of Planned Behavior (see Figure 3.1, B) specifies a model where three theoretical components—the individual's attitude toward performing the particular behavior (*AB*), existing subjective norms (*SN*), and perceived behavioral control (*PC*)—combine additively to determine a person's behavioral intention (*BI*). Specifically, the model holds that a behavioral intention (*BI*) is a function (*f*) of the importance (W_1) of an individual's attitude (*AB*), plus the importance (W_2) of subjective norms (*SN*), plus the importance (W_3) of the perceived behavioral control (*PC*). The model is represented in the following mathematical equation:

$$BI = f(W_1 AB + W_2 SN + W_3 PC) \qquad (3.1)$$

As we discussed in Chapter 1, a person's attitude toward performing a particular behavior (*AB*) is determined by the sum of his or her particular beliefs about performing the behavior and the evaluations those beliefs receive.[5] Recall the examples used to describe attitudes about promoting border security (see Table 1.1). That example described how beliefs about the consequences of performing particular behaviors and evaluations assigned to those beliefs combine to determine an individual's attitude toward performing a behavior. This relationship is represented in the following equation[6]:

$$AB = \Sigma(b_i e_i) \qquad (3.2)$$

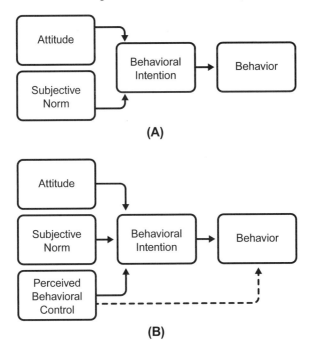

FIGURE 3.1. Comparison of the Theory of Reasoned Action (A) and the Theory of Planned Behavior (B). From "A comparison of the theory of planned behavior and the theory of reasoned action" by T. J. Madden, P. S. Ellen, & I. Ajzen, 1992, *Personality and Social Psychology Bulletin, 18,* 3–9. Copyright 1992 by Sage Publications. Reprinted by permission.

The second predictor of behavioral intentions, the subjective norm (*SN*), has not been discussed previously. It can be defined as the influences that the social world (i.e., specific other people and general social norms) has on a person's behavioral intentions. Although it is likely that attitudes guide behavioral intentions, Ajzen and Fishbein (1980) argued that the opinions and attitudes of a person's reference group (e.g., friends, family, coworkers, religious and political leaders) can also influence behavioral intentions. Hence, the subjective norm represents an individual's perceptions of the social support for performing a particular behavior. Mathematically, the subjective norm is defined by the following equation:

$$SN = \Sigma(b_i m_i) \tag{3.3}$$

where *SN* represents the subjective norm, b_i represents normative beliefs, and m_i represents one's motivation to comply with those beliefs. Normative beliefs (b_i) are simply the attitudes that reference group members have about one's performing the behavior, whereas the motivation to comply (m_i) represents the extent to which one wishes to comply with the reference group members' desires or preferences. Evaluations of normative beliefs and motivations to comply are separately computed for each reference group member. Then the products are added together to form the subjective norm.

Consider the example from Chapter 1 that described a person's attitude about voting for political candidates with varying views about enhancing security along the U.S.–Mexico border. We know that voting intentions are likely to be influenced by the person's individual attitude and by the beliefs of his or her reference group. Who is likely to have an influence on voting decisions? Assume that the relevant reference group in our hypothetical example contains four people: one's neighbor, boss, coworker, and relational partner. (We realize that there are likely more than four people in most reference groups, but we are trying to keep the example simple.) Table 3.2 reflects hypothetical beliefs (b) about each of these reference group members concerning the consequences of voting for the candidate promoting more border security. Because these beliefs are from members of one's reference group, they set a standard or norm for beliefs about the candidate. The beliefs of some reference group members, however, are more influential than others. Thus, the importance of each reference group member's belief is reflected in the motivation to comply (m).

Normative beliefs are typically measured by using a 7-point scale ranging from +3 (very positive) to –3 (very negative), where 0 is neutral. Motivation to comply, on the other hand, is typically measured on a 0 (unconcerned with how the other person feels) to +3 (very concerned). Referring to the hypothetical reference group in Table 3.2, the normative belief of the neighbor (–3) is more negative than for the relational partner (+2). The person in our example, however, feels less motivation to comply with the

TABLE 3.2. Subjective Norm (*SN*) of a Hypothetical Reference Group

Reference group member	Belief about voting for candidate (*b*)	Motivation to comply (*m*)	Normative influence (*bm*)
Neighbor	–3	+1	–3
Boss	–1	+2	–2
Coworker	+1	+1	+1
Relational partner	+2	+3	+6
			$SN = \Sigma(bm) = +2$

Note. Belief about voting for the candidate (*b*) scores range from –3 to +3, and motivation to comply (*m*) scores range from 0 to +3.

neighbor position (+1) than with the relational partner's position (+3). The normative influence of each reference group member is determined by multiplying the value for the normative belief (*b*) by the value for the motivation to comply (*m*). The resulting value (*bm*) reveals that the influence of the neighbor's belief is somewhat negative (–3) but that the influence of the relational partner's belief is strongly positive (+6). These products (*bm*) can then be added across reference group members to obtain the subjective norm (*SN*) for the entire reference group (in this case, +2).

The third determinant of behavioral intention, *perceived behavioral control*, was added by Ajzen (1985) to improve the prediction of behavioral intentions and behaviors. Perceived behavioral control, or the belief that one can perform the behavior in question, may influence behavioral intentions and subsequent behavior (Ajzen, 1985; Yzer, 2013). Consistent with earlier research on *self-efficacy* (Bandura, 1982; Bandura, Adams, Hardy, & Howells, 1980; see Chapter 13), Ajzen (1985) argued that people's intentions to perform a behavior are often thwarted by a lack of confidence in their ability to perform that behavior. Behavioral control likely varies widely across behaviors. People may perceive greater behavioral control over taking daily vitamins than they do over getting a good night's sleep (see Madden, Ellen, & Ajzen, 1992). Thus, in Figure 3.1(B), the line from TPB to intentions is dotted.

As with one's attitude toward the behavior and subjective norms, perceived behavioral control is a product of two separate judgments. Mathematically, perceived behavioral control is defined by the following equation:

$$PC = \Sigma(c_i p_i) \tag{3.4}$$

where *PC* represents perceived behavioral control, c_i represents control beliefs, and p_i represents perceived power beliefs. Control beliefs (c_i) represent the extent to which you believe that you have the resources available to perform the behavior. Power beliefs (p_i) represent the extent to which control over the behavior is sufficient to overcome barriers to behavioral performance.

Consider, for example, someone who smokes but wants to quit. The smoker might understand the dangers of smoking (i.e., have a negative attitude toward smoking), have strong social support for his or her efforts to quit smoking (i.e., a positive subjective norm), and *intend* to quit smoking, but he or she may also believe that smoking is an addiction and that therefore he or she cannot actually perform the behavior (i.e., low perceived behavioral control). As a consequence, a person may continue to smoke, believing that he or she is powerless over the addiction—that even though he or she has a negative attitude toward smoking and that subjective norms support quitting, nonetheless that person has very low perceived control. This component suggests that persuasive message appeals should focus not only on one's attitudes and subjective norms but also on convincing the target that he or she has the ability to engage in particular behavior and that doing so will produce the desired outcome. For example, taking medication to lower one's blood pressure depends in part on one's believing that the medicine will be effective in reducing it but equally that the target can remember to take the medication per the prescribed regimen.

The addition of perceived behavioral control (in the Theory of Planned Behavior) explained people's behavioral intentions and behavior significantly better than the Theory of Reasoned Action (Cooke & French, 2008; Madden et al., 1992). In addition, the predictive value of perceived behavioral control was greater for behaviors that lacked perceived control than for those where perceived control was high. In other words, when most people are certain that they can perform the behavior in question (e.g., take a daily vitamin), perceived behavioral control is not related to behavior. However, when people vary greatly in their ability to perform the behavior in question (e.g., get a good night's sleep), perceived behavioral control is an important predictor of their behavior. People who have high behavioral control will in this instance be more likely to engage in the behavior than people who lack it.

Included in the equation of the entire model that we started with (Equation 3.1) are three weights (W_1, W_2, and W_3) that reflect the relative importance of the attitude (AB), subjective norm (SN), and perceived behavioral control (PC) in determining the behavioral intention (I). In situations where a person's own attitude is the primary determinant of the behavior intention, the weight assigned to the attitude component is larger than the weight assigned to the subjective norm component and perceived behavioral control. In these instances, a person is more concerned with acting in accordance with personal beliefs than with conforming to the beliefs of others. When the subjective norm is more influential than the attitude, the weight assigned to the subjective norm is larger than the weight assigned to the attitude and perceived behavioral control. In such instances, behavioral intentions are determined more by the influence of others than by one's personal beliefs. When the three components contribute equally to behavioral intention, their weights are equal.

Evaluating the Reasoned Action Theories

The Theory of Reasoned Action and the Theory of Planned Behavior have been tested extensively across a variety of behavioral situations. Fishbein and Ajzen (2010) described many investigations that successfully employed their models to predict behavior and intentions (Figure 3.1). A meta-analytic review of these investigations found that the attitude, subjective norm, and behavioral control components explained much of the variance in behavioral intentions ($R \approx .63$)[7] and that behavioral intentions explained much of the variance in actual behavior (average $r \approx .50$) (Armitage & Conner, 2001; Yzer, 2013). What is more, meta-analytic data verified that, by adding perceived behavioral control, the Theory of Planned Behavior explains significantly more variation in behavioral intentions and behaviors than does the Theory of Reasoned Action (which only included attitudes toward the behavior and subjective norms). These findings suggest that the Theory of Planned Behavior is an excellent device for predicting and understanding behavior.

However, Armitage and Conner's (2001) meta-analytic data suggest that the attitude component was a much stronger predictor of behavioral intentions than the subjective norm component. Combined with the fact that these two components tend to be positively correlated with each other, this finding has caused some researchers (Conner & Armitage, 1998) to question the predictive utility of the subjective norm component of the model.

The accumulated evidence suggests that subjective norms predict intentions in some contexts better than in others (Yzer, 2013). Specifically, the importance of subjective norms differs across behaviors, cultures, and people. First, the importance of subjective norms depends on the nature of the behavior involved. One reason why subjective norms do not correlate well with behavior is that many tests of Reasoned Action Theories have focused on predicting individual behaviors in relatively private settings. For example, many studies have focused on behaviors such as physical activity (Hagger, Chatzisarantis, & Biddle, 2002), dietary choices (Armitage & Conner, 1999), and engaging in a health screening (e.g., for breast or prostate cancer; Cooke & French, 2008). Given that such behaviors are individual rather than social, it is not surprising that personal attitudes predict behavioral intentions more strongly than do subjective norms in these contexts.

David Trafimow and his associates performed a number of studies to investigate this notion (see Trafimow, 2000, for a review). Specifically, Trafimow and Fishbein (1994) claimed that some behavior is "normatively controlled" (i.e., influenced more by subjective norms than by attitudes toward the behavior). For example, they found (in Study 1) that intentions concerning "going to a Korean restaurant *alone*" were influenced more by attitudes toward the behavior, while intentions concerning "going to a Korean restaurant *with a date*" were influenced more strongly by the others' opinions than by one's own attitude. Additionally, Trafimow and Finlay (1996) subsequently investigated the relationships between subjective norms, attitudes toward the behavior, and behavioral intentions across

30 behaviors. In the vast majority of these cases, attitudes were a better predictor of behavioral intentions than were subjective norms; however, the importance of subjective norms varied radically across the behaviors. For the most part, subjective norms exerted a stronger impact on the prediction of social (as opposed to individual) behaviors. Social behaviors are those where others' opinions are more highly valued (e.g., "marry someone my parents would approve of") or where others are directly involved (e.g., "use condoms if I have sex") (Trafimow & Finlay, 1996).

Consistent with this line of thinking, a meta-analytic review of studies investigating condom use during sexual intercourse (Albarracín, Johnson, Fishbein, & Muellerleile, 2001) found that the average correlation between subjective norms and behavioral intentions was substantial (average r = .39). Although intentions to use a condom were more strongly related to attitudes toward the behavior (average r = .58), the results of this review support the contention that subjective norms are a more important determinant of social behaviors than of individual behaviors.

In addition, the importance of subjective norms might differ across cultures. Lee and Green (1991), for example, performed a study that compared attitudes toward the behavior (buying sneakers) and subjective norms among college students in the United States (an individualist culture) and South Korea (a collectivist culture). They found that in the United States students' attitudes toward the behavior were a much stronger predictor of behavior intentions than were subjective norms. On the other hand, among the Korean students the pattern was reversed: subjective norms exerted a considerably stronger influence over purchase intentions than did attitudes toward the behavior (for a contrasting view, however, see Trafimow, Clayton, Sheeran, Darwish, & Brown, 2010).

Finally, scholars have also observed that subjective norms influence the behavior of some people more than others. Investigating a wide variety of behaviors, Trafimow and Finlay (1996) found that 20% of the respondents in their study based their behavioral intentions more on the subjective norms of others than on their own attitudes toward the behavior. The two researchers asserted that individuals whose behavioral intentions are primarily determined by subjective norms tend to think about themselves in terms of how they relate to other people.

Most recently, the theories of Reasoned Action and Planned Behavior have been integrated into a combined model (Fishbein & Ajzen, 2010; Yzer, 2012, 2013) that seeks to improve predictive utility by examining factors that moderate the relationship between behavioral intentions and actual behaviors. The integrated model posits that *actual control* includes skills and environmental constraints (see Figure 3.2)—that is, that people often have behavioral intentions but are unable to act on those intentions because they lack the required skills or are restrained by environmental factors. For

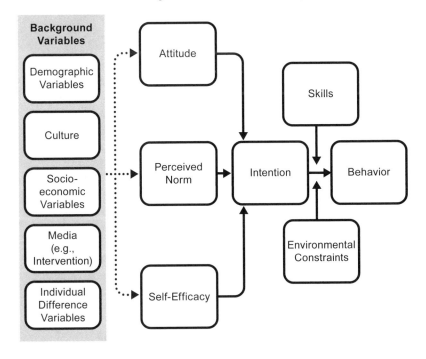

FIGURE 3.2. The Integrative Model of Behavioral Prediction. From "Reasoned Action Theory: Persuasion as Belief-Based Behavior Change" by M. Yzer, 2013. In J. P. Dillard & L. Shen (Eds.), *The SAGE Handbook of Persuasion: Developments in Theory and Practice* (2nd ed., pp. 120–136). Copyright 2013 by Sage Publications. Reprinted by permission.

example, a college student may intend to use a condom when having sex but because of alcohol consumption (an environmental constraint) may be unable to follow through on using one. In much the same way, a student may volunteer to canvass a neighborhood to promote a political candidate, but shyness or lack of confidence may prevent that person from acting on those intentions. Research by Yzer (2012, 2013) and others has demonstrated that when *actual control* is included in the model it helps to explain situations where behavioral intentions do not predict behaviors and understanding these factors improves the overall predictive utility of the model.

Subjective Norms and Social Influence

Work by Trafimow (2000) on subjective norms is consistent with several normative theories of social influence (Aronson, 1999; Deutsch & Gerard, 1955; Festinger, 1954; Kelley, 1952) that describe the effects of social norms

BOX 3.1. Behavioral Norms and College Drinking Behavior

One context where norms play an important role in people's intentions and behaviors is alcohol consumption in college. Reasoned Action Theories typically refer to subjective (sometimes called injunctive) norms, or how important others feel about an individual engaging in a behavior. The college drinking literature, however, focuses more on behavioral norms or perceptions of what other people actually do. Behavioral norms are important in this context because college students typically overestimate the amount that their peers drink. That is, they think their peers drink a lot more than their peers actually drink. The danger behind this misperception is that students might increase their drinking, particularly dangerous binge drinking, to fit in with what they see as the campus norm.

To fight this misperception and to reduce levels of dangerous drinking, many campuses across the United States have instituted social norms-based persuasion campaigns. These campaigns initially survey students about their actual drinking behavior (using questions such as "How many times in the past week have you consumed five or more drinks in a sitting?"). After compiling the results, colleges advertise the true behavioral norm in a number of ways (flyers on campus, ads in the campus newspaper and radio station, etc.). The thinking is that providing accurate normative information will inform students that their behavior is more typical than they thought it was. This information should reduce the social pressure students feel to increase their drinking behavior in order to "fit in."

The effectiveness of norms-based campus drinking campaigns, however, has been mixed. Sometimes these campaigns were quite effective, reducing the frequency and amount that students drink; sometimes they made no difference; and in some cases they actually led to an increase in drinking. Research suggests that a combination of behavioral norms (how much and how frequently people actually drink) and subjective norms (how fellow students actually feel about binge drinking) would be more effective to use than descriptive norms alone. Other research suggests that the nature of the comparison group is critically important to a successful campaign. The closer the comparison is to the person, the more influence normative information will have. So, using a comparison group that students perceive as similar to themselves (e.g., their friends) will be more effective than a comparison group of students in general or students at another university.

on conformity to group (i.e., social) behavior. People often find themselves performing certain behaviors in order to get along with group members and avoid group conflict. In addition, people rely on social norms to interpret ambiguous situations. Such influences stimulated research on *bystander intervention* (Latané & Darley, 1968, 1970; Latané & Rodin, 1969). In several investigations, Latané and his colleagues observed people's reactions to a variety of emergency situations. They consistently found that when more than one person was around to observe the situation no one was likely to offer assistance. However, if only a single person observed the situation, he or she was more likely to offer assistance. One explanation for this curious finding was the hypothesis that when others do not respond immediately to an apparent emergency a nonintervention norm is thereby established. Again, in ambiguous situations people look to the behavior of others to determine whether providing assistance is necessary and appropriate. Bringing this example back to the Theory of Reasoned Action, in situations like these the influence of subjective norms on behavioral intentions may be considerably stronger than the influence of individual attitudes.

Normative influences likely dictated personal behavior in LaPiere's (1934) investigation of attitudes and behavior toward a Chinese couple. Recall that respondents to the questionnaire reported strong prejudicial attitudes, but LaPiere found no evidence of actual prejudicial behavior. Providing or denying service to customers is a social, rather than an individual, behavior. As a consequence, perceptions of social norms (i.e., community values opposing racial discrimination) may have prevented people from behaving in accordance with their personal attitudes.

Together, the Theory of Reasoned Action and the Theory of Planned Behavior provide strong support for the proposition that attitudes, subjective norms, and perceived behavioral control are important predictors of a person's behavior. Although the subjective norm and perceived behavioral control components are not always essential, these theories helped to reestablish an important role for attitudes in the prediction of behavior. Indeed, by the early 1990s, these theories replaced speculation about the existence of an attitude–behavior relationship.

FACTORS MODERATING THE ATTITUDE–BEHAVIOR RELATIONSHIP

As we noted earlier, during the late 1960s and through the 1970s, there was a great deal of concern about people's attitudes' ability to predict behavior (e.g., Wicker, 1969). As a result of this concern, a second group of researchers studying the attitude–behavior relationship focused on the inconsistencies among prior research findings. These scholars assumed that one of the reasons for inconsistent findings was that the strength of the association between attitudes and behaviors varied across situations and across people. In short, these scholars hypothesized that there were a number of moderator variables that influenced the strength of the attitude–behavior relationship. As we noted in Chapter 2, a moderator variable is any variable that influences the direction and/or strength of relationship between two variables of interest. In the present context, the two variables of interest are attitude and behavior. So, the question now is what variables might influence the direction and/or strength of the relationship between these two variables? While a large number of moderators have been identified, we will discuss two factors related to the process of attitude formation, *direct experience* and *vested interest*, and two factors related to cognitive processing, *cognitive differentiation* and *attitude accessibility*, as moderators of the attitude–behavior relationship.

Moderators Related to Attitude Formation

In a review of the attitude literature, Fazio and Zanna (1981) suggested that *direct experience* with the attitude object might influence the strength of the attitude–behavior relationship. According to this hypothesis, attitudes formed through personal experience with an object or situation will be more strongly related to subsequent behaviors than attitudes formed through more indirect experiences. For example, children who play a musical instrument form attitudes about music education and performance based on their direct experience with the activity, whereas children who do not play an instrument form their attitudes indirectly, through discussions with others or perhaps by watching videos online. In this case, Fazio and Zanna hypothesized that children with favorable or unfavorable attitudes formed through direct experience were more likely to act in accordance with those attitudes than children whose attitudes were formed through indirect experience.

Support for this proposition came from a study of college student attitudes about a campus housing shortage (Regan & Fazio, 1977). Participants in this study were Cornell University students who were experiencing an acute housing shortage. As a result, many freshmen spent the first few weeks of the fall semester sleeping on cots in the lounge and common areas of campus dormitories. Questionnaires were sent to students who received permanent housing accommodations (i.e., a dorm room) and to those who were assigned temporary accommodations (i.e., in lounges and common areas). Almost every student was aware of the housing shortage, and most had formed negative attitudes about the university's response to the crisis. However, the manner in which these attitudes were formed differed between students assigned immediately to permanent housing and those assigned to temporary housing accommodations. Students assigned to the temporary housing formed their attitudes about the housing shortage through direct personal experience, whereas those assigned to permanent housing formed them after talking with friends and reading articles in the student newspaper.

In addition to measuring attitudes, Regan and Fazio invited the students to take a series of actions in response to the crisis. They were given a list of six behaviors and asked which they intended to perform:

1. Sign a petition urging the university to solve the problem.
2. Encourage other students to sign the petition.
3. Agree to attend a future meeting to discuss potential solutions.
4. Indicate interest in joining a committee to investigate the problem.
5. Develop a written list of recommendations for solving the problem.
6. Write a letter expressing opinions about the shortage that would be forwarded to the campus housing office.

The researchers then calculated the relationship between student attitudes and behavioral intentions toward the housing crisis. As anticipated, they found that students whose attitudes were formed through direct experience exhibited significantly stronger attitude–behavior correlations than those whose attitudes were formed through indirect experience. In other words, students who formed negative attitudes because they were living in the temporary quarters were more willing to act on their attitudes than students who formed negative attitudes based on a friend's experience or by reading articles in the newspaper.

Although Regan and Fazio's (1977) findings are consistent with the argument that direct experience moderates (i.e., either lessens or *intensifies*) the size of the attitude–behavior correlation, the method employed by the researchers to assign students to the direct and indirect experience conditions confounded the concept of direct experience with a number of other (though related) variables. For example, students in these two groups likely also differed in the amount of their vested interest in the situation. Students assigned to the temporary housing conditions likely had more of a vested interest, or personal stake, in potential solutions to the housing shortage than students assigned to the permanent housing conditions. Thus, it is difficult to determine whether direct experience, vested interest, or both factors accounted for differences in the strength of the attitude–behavior relationship.

To test the hypothesis that vested interest moderates the attitude–behavior relationship, Sivacek and Crano (1982) assessed attitudes of Michigan State University students about proposed changes in the legal drinking age (also discussed in Chapter 2). During the course of the investigation,

Michigan voters were considering a ballot proposition to increase the age for legal consumption of alcohol from 18 to 21 years of age. As part of an attitude survey on a variety of topics, students provided their opinions about the proposition. Students were then contacted by phone 7–10 days after completing the opinion survey and asked if they would volunteer time to phone local residents to argue against the proposition. Their willingness to participate and the number of phone calls they were willing to make served as measures of the students' behavioral intentions.

Sivacek and Crano reasoned that all students formed attitudes about drinking and the ballot initiative through similar experiences. After all, the great majority of students were at least 18 and had some direct experience with alcohol consumption. Thus, for this topic, direct experience was likely a constant across the whole sample of participants. Vested interest, however, varied considerably among the students. Vested interest was higher among the youngest students, who would not be able to drink legally for 2 years or more, and lowest among those who would already be 21 years old when the law took effect. A third group, those who would not be able to drink legally for less than 2 years, fell between the low- and high-vested-interest groups. As a result, the proposition to increase the legal drinking age provided three natural levels of vested interest while controlling for (i.e., keeping constant) the effects of direct experience.

As we noted in Chapter 2, the researchers' findings were consistent with the vested-interest hypothesis. Students in the high-vested-interest group volunteered more time and exhibited a stronger attitude–behavior correlation ($r = .61$) than students in the moderate- ($r = .40$) and low- ($r = .16$) vested-interest groups.

Sivacek and Crano (1982) also conducted a second study in which they assessed attitudes and behaviors toward a proposal to institute comprehensive exams as a graduation requirement for undergraduate students. Students who expected to graduate before the proposal was enacted were placed in the low-vested-interest group, whereas those who would be required to complete the exams were placed in the high-vested-interest group. Once again, the attitude–behavior correlation was significantly higher among students with a high vested interest ($r = .82$) than among students with low vested interest ($r = .52$).

Taken together, the housing shortage, drinking age, and comprehensive examination studies show that the manner in which attitudes are formed influences the relationship between attitudes and behaviors. These studies are not without their limitations, however. In the housing study, the concept of direct experience was confounded with the concept of vested interest. Moreover, the effect of direct experience was held constant in the drinking age and comprehensive examination studies. Thus, although Sivacek and Crano (1982) documented the importance of vested interest,

---

BOX 3.2. Vested Interest Motivates Behavior

There are countless practical examples of situations where people with a vested interest are more likely to act on their attitudes than those who hold similar viewpoints but do not perceive any vested interest. Following the nomination of Elena Kagan to the U.S. Supreme Court in August 2010, the National Rifle Association mounted an intense campaign to oppose her nomination because its leaders perceived that Justice Kagan would likely favor legislation restricting gun ownership (Crabtree, 2010). Similarly, the Susan G. Komen Foundation's decision in early 2012 to stop providing funding to Planned Parenthood for breast cancer screening set off a firestorm of criticism from women's groups and led to a sharp increase in public donations to Planned Parenthood (Sun & Kliff, 2012).

In both of these examples, people with strongly held but dormant attitudes became mobilized to oppose a decision (the nomination of Justice Kagan or the cessation of funding to Planned Parenthood). In each case, people who had long-held and firmly entrenched attitudes were motivated to act on those attitudes once they perceived that the outcome of the debate had significant implications for their own lives. These examples are consistent with the proposition that a strong attitude–behavior relationship exists in situations where the target of a persuasive message has a vested interest in the outcome of the persuasive appeal (Sivacek & Crano, 1982).

---

they were unable to estimate the effects attributable to direct experience. Notwithstanding their limitations, these investigations suggest that vested interest and perhaps direct experience influence the extent to which people act in accordance with their attitudes. These findings suggest that people design their persuasive messages to appeal to the experiences and personal interests of message recipients. The more that message receivers perceive an appeal to be consistent with their personal experience and interests, the more effective it is likely to be.

Factors Related to Cognitive Processes

During the past 40 years or so, a number of cognitive style constructs have been developed to describe differences in the ways people process information. One measure of cognitive style, *construct differentiation*, has been investigated extensively as a moderator of the attitude–behavior relationship.

Delia and his colleagues (Delia & Crockett, 1973; B. J. O'Keefe & Delia, 1978; D. J. O'Keefe & Delia, 1981) have argued that construct differentiation is a significant element in a person's cognitive style. *Construct differentiation* refers to the number of different dimensions along which people judge objects and situations. People with highly sophisticated construct systems cite a greater variety of attributes when describing a person, object, event, or situation than do those with less developed construct systems.

Construct differentiation is typically measured by asking respondents to write a short paragraph describing both a positive and negative person, event, object, or situation. For example, respondents may be asked to describe, first, someone they like and then someone they dislike. These descriptions are then analyzed to determine the number of dimensions or attributes the person used to describe the two persons. Though other coding procedures may also be used, evaluation of these responses usually involves counting the number of unique descriptions (i.e., constructs) included in the paragraphs. Constructs are typically reflected in the use of adjectives and adverbs. The greater the number of unique constructs, the more differentiated the construct system.[8] For example, a person with a less differentiated construct system might describe a well-liked friend as someone who was "fun" and "easy to talk with" (two constructs). Conversely, a person with a highly developed construct category system might describe the same well-liked person as a "thoughtful, compassionate, and empathic" person who is "quite entertaining" and "fun to be with" (five constructs).

D. J. O'Keefe and Delia (1981) argued that people with more developed construct systems should demonstrate lower attitude–behavior intention correlations than those with less developed systems. They reasoned that people with less developed systems are more likely to be guided by a concern for cognitive consistency and hence are more likely to demonstrate a strong relationship between attitudes and behavioral intentions. People with well-developed construct systems, on the other hand, are more likely to tolerate apparent discrepancies between attitudes and behavioral intentions, because they are better able to more precisely differentiate the characteristics of an attitude object from the characteristics of related behavior. By drawing precise conceptual distinctions, people with highly differentiated construct systems are able to logically behave in a manner that might seemingly be inconsistent with the related attitude.

To test their hypotheses, D. J. O'Keefe and Delia (1981) asked students in five small classes to write a short paragraph describing a person they liked and another paragraph describing someone they disliked. After coding, these descriptions represented the measure of construct differentiation. Much later in the semester, the same participants were asked to write a description of the classmate toward whom they had developed the strongest feelings (either positive or negative). Participants also completed rating scales evaluating the person in question (the attitude measure) and also indicated their willingness to act as a *social partner* with the person in a variety of social and work situations (the intention measure).

The results of this investigation were consistent with the two researchers' predictions regarding the moderating role of construct differentiation on attitude and behavior consistency. First, low-differentiation participants showed more consistency in the description of their classmate (either mostly positive or mostly negative), whereas high-differentiation participants tended to provide a mixture of positive and negative characteristics in their descriptions. Compared to the high-differentiation participants, low-differentiation participants also exhibited more consistency between the attitude rankings on the survey and the attitudes reflected in their written descriptions.

Low-differentiation participants also demonstrated more consistency between the attitude and behavioral intention rankings than high-differentiation participants. On eight of the nine hypothetical situations, and for the composite measure of behavioral intentions, correlations between attitudes and behavioral intentions were higher for low-differentiation subjects (average $r = .88$) than for high-differentiation subjects (average $r = .65$).[9]

Consistent with D. J. O'Keefe and Delia's reasoning, these findings suggest that one's cognitive style may influence one's concerns about his or her attitude–behavior consistency. While it may be reasonable to expect that people desire consistency in their attitudes and actions, these findings suggest that people with highly developed cognitive systems are better equipped to tolerate seeming cognitive inconsistencies than those whose cognitive systems are less complex.

Attitude accessibility is another cognitive variable that has been hypothesized to moderate the relationship between attitudes and behaviors. Attitude accessibility refers to the extent to which an attitude is activated automatically from memory. Fazio and his colleagues (Fazio, Chen, McDonel, & Sherman, 1982; Powell & Fazio, 1984) have demonstrated that when a person repeatedly expresses an attitude toward an object or situation, it becomes chronically accessible. Once an attitude has become chronically accessible, it can be activated automatically from memory, and less time is required to use the attitude in response to future encounters with the object or situation (Fazio, Sanbonmatsu, Powell, & Kardes, 1986). Thus, the more frequently an attitude is expressed, the more readily it is recalled from memory. For example, a person who actively works to promote legislation regarding abortion rights is likely to express pro-choice opinions more frequently than someone who holds an identical attitude but who is less actively involved in the issue. Though both people may possess similar attitudes about abortion rights, the person who frequently expresses his or her opinion will have a more accessible attitude and will respond more rapidly to issue-relevant stimuli. A highly accessible attitude is like a "favorites" phone number on your iPhone, or a bookmarked address on your web browser, that enables you to more quickly access the information (see Roskos-Ewoldsen, Apran-Ralstin, & St. Pierre, 2002, for a review of the accessibility construct).

To test the influence of attitude accessibility on the attitude–behavior relationship, Fazio and Williams (1986) examined attitudes toward President Ronald Reagan and Democratic challenger Walter Mondale during the 1984 presidential campaign. Attitude accessibility was assessed by measuring the response latency (the amount of time that elapsed between the end of a question and the beginning of a response) associated with attitudes toward Reagan and Mondale. Some months later, Fazio and Williams measured voting behavior in a postelection interview with the same respondents. Consistent with their hypothesis, Fazio and Williams found that, independent of attitude intensity, people in the high-attitude-accessibility group were more likely to have voted in accordance with their attitudes than those with less accessible attitudes.

A study of attitudes toward a variety of consumer products produced similar results. Kokkinaki and Lunt (1997) found that attitude accessibility was a strong predictor of the strength of the attitude–behavior relationship; participants with highly accessible beliefs demonstrated the strongest attitude–behavior relationship, whereas those with relatively inaccessible beliefs exhibited the weakest attitude–behavior relationship.

These findings suggest that attitude accessibility affects the extent to which attitudes predict behavior. For instance, two people may hold similar attitudes on a political issue such as immigration but differ in their expression of this attitude. For example, one person might frequently discuss the need for immigration legislation, whereas another person with the same attitude may rarely discuss (or even think about) the issue. Research on attitude accessibility suggests that, although these two hypothetical people share the same attitude, the person who routinely discusses illegal immigration is likely to have the more accessible attitude and thus be more likely to act (e.g., vote or circulate a petition to promote immigration legislation).

It bears mentioning that attitude accessibility is conceptually distinct from both attitude extremity (or polarization) and issue-relevant involvement. Though accessibility and extremity are statistically related (Powell & Fazio, 1984), they remain separate constructs. That is, attitudes can vary simultaneously along an extremity dimension and along an accessibility dimension. In addition, Kokkinaki and Lunt (1997) found that accessibility is related to involvement but that these two factors exert separate moderating impacts of the attitude–behavior relationship. The findings of Fazio and his colleagues (Fazio et al., 1982; Powell & Fazio, 1984) suggest that highly accessible attitudes affect the perception of attitude-relevant information and moderate the strength of the attitude–behavior relationship.

Together, construct differentiation and attitude accessibility appear to be two important cognitive factors that influence the relationship between attitudes and behaviors. Given the cognitive nature of the attitude definition presented in Chapter 1 of this volume, it is not surprising that cognitive processes can influence the predictive utility of the attitude construct.

SUMMARY

Several conclusions emerge from prior investigations of the attitude–behavior relationship. First, the attitude–behavior "problem," which emerged during the early 1960s, appears to have been created by sloppy conceptual definitions and poor investigative procedures. Though their work was regarded as a theoretical review of the literature, Ajzen and Fishbein (1977) focused primarily on the conceptual and operational limitations of earlier studies. Most scholars agree that—so long as precise and correct conceptual and operational definitions are employed—attitudes predict related behavior. The results of two meta-analyses (Kim & Hunter, 1993a, 1993b) reinforce the strong relationships among attitudes, behavioral intentions, and behaviors.

The Reasoned Action Theories provide compelling evidence that attitudes, subjective norms, and perceptions of behavioral control are three important factors that predict behavioral intentions. To date, the Theory of Planned Behavior is the best description of the relationship between attitudes and behaviors (Fishbein & Ajzen, 2010; Yzer, 2012, 2013).

Researchers have also examined moderator variables that influence the strength of the relationship between attitudes and behaviors. Research on attitude formation suggests that two factors, direct experience and vested interest, affect the strength of this relationship. Given the sheer number of attitudes that people hold about a variety of issues, it is unrealistic to expect that they will always behave in accordance with all of their attitudes. Instead, people are most likely to act in accordance with their attitudes when the issue is central to their lives.

Investigations of cognitive processing revealed two additional factors that influence the predictive utility of attitudes. D. J. O'Keefe and Delia's (1981) investigations of construct differentiation found that people possessing complex cognitive systems tolerate apparent inconsistencies by drawing precise distinctions between attitudes and related behavior. In addition, research by Fazio and his colleagues demonstrated the importance of attitude accessibility in determining the extent to which attitudes guide behavior (Fazio et al., 1982; Powell & Fazio, 1984).

Today, the controversy about the relationship between attitudes and behaviors has been pretty much laid to rest. Thus, although we can safely conclude that attitudes predict behaviors, Allport's (1935) assertion that attitudes exert a directive influence on all objects with which they come into contact (p. 810) is an overstatement. Over the past 70 years or so, we have learned that, when properly defined and measured, personal attitudes guide individual behavior, but the strength of this directive influence varies across people and situations.

NOTES

1. Many scholars have criticized LaPiere's (1934) study on a variety of grounds (e.g., Petty & Cacioppo, 1981). For example, the measure of attitudes used in this study (i.e., "Will you accept members of the Chinese race as guests in your establishment?") seems more like a measure of behavioral intention than of attitude. Given this and other criticisms, the LaPiere study may not be relevant to our discussion of the relationship between attitudes and behaviors. We include this seminal study chiefly because of its historical relevance to the attitude–behavior "problem."

2. Ajzen and Fishbein (1977) went even further, emphasizing that any given behavior occurs in a *specified* context and at a *particular* time. In our church example, the context component would be the particular church, while the time component would be the particular day and service (e.g., attending the 7:45 A.M. service at the Ebenezer Baptist Church in Atlanta, Georgia, on a particular Sunday).

3. Actually, studies with high correspondence were divided into two groups: those that used reliable measures and those that didn't. Of the 18 studies with unreliable attitude and behavior measures, 9 reported small to moderate correlations, and 9 reported strong attitude–behavior correlations. Of the 26 studies that used reliable measures, all 26 exhibited a strong attitude–behavior correlation. Reliability, which is one assessment of a measure's quality, is a function of the internal consistency of the items in a measure (e.g., are people responding to all of the questions in a similar manner?) and the stability of the measure (e.g., does the measure produce consistent results over time?).

4. As we pointed out in note 2 in the preceding chapter, r is a statistic called the *correlation coefficient*, which measures the strength of the linear association between two variables. The closer the correlation is to 1.00 (or –1.00), the more accurately a dependent variable can be predicted, given knowledge of the independent variable. A correlation of 0.00 would indicate that knowledge of the independent variable would be of no help whatsoever in predicting the dependent variable. In the present context, as correlation coefficients between attitudes and behaviors approach 1.00, behaviors can be predicted very accurately, given knowledge of an individual's attitudes.

5. As we noted in Chapter 1, by specifying attitude *toward a particular behavior,* Fishbein and Ajzen (1975) narrowed the attitude construct. What is more, this shift ensured that both the action and target components would be included in their attitude measurement. Thus, by definition, attitudes should be closely connected to behaviors.

6. Equation 3.2 is a simplified version of the same equation (i.e., Equation 1.1) presented in Chapter 1.

7. The symbol *R* represents the *multiple* correlation coefficient, which is the correlation between more than one predictor variable (in this case, attitude toward the behavior, subjective norms, and the perceived behavioral control) and a single outcome variable (i.e., behavioral intentions).

8. Considerable controversy surrounds the measures employed by Delia and his colleagues (Delia & Crockett, 1973; B. J. O'Keefe & Delia, 1978; D. J. O'Keefe & Delia, 1981). Some critics have argued that the cognitive differentiation measure is confounded with a person's verbosity and lexical diversity: the greater a person's command of the language (and not cognitive complexity), the more constructs he or she is likely to include in a description (Allen, Mabry, Banski, Stoneman, & Carter, 1990; Beatty, 1987; Beatty & Payne, 1984, 1985; Powers, Jordan, & Street, 1979). Such criticisms have not gone unnoticed by constructivist researchers who, for their part, have attempted to demonstrate that lexical diversity and verbosity are unrelated to properly measured cognitive differentiation (Burleson, Applegate, & Newwirth, 1981; Burleson, Waltman, & Samter, 1987).

9. One limitation of the D. J. O'Keefe and Delia (1981) study stems from the measure of behavior intention, which could be little more than another measure of the participant's attitude toward his or her classmate. If this criticism is valid, then analysis of the situational, descriptive, and questionnaire measures of attitude demonstrated that attitudinal consistency was greater among subjects with lower cognitive differentiation scores. Though consistent with the researchers' reasoning, such a conclusion would not be informative about the relationship between attitudes and behaviors.

CHAPTER 4

The Effects of Behavior on Attitudes

LOOKING AHEAD . . . Although in the preceding chapter attitudes were viewed as the causal antecedents to behavior, it is equally plausible that behaviors influence people's attitudes. This chapter investigates the causal impacts of behavior on subsequent attitude change. This discussion begins with a review of Cognitive Dissonance Theory and the counterattitudinal advocacy research paradigm. Following this, several modifications to the original theory and alternative explanations for research findings are discussed. As previously noted, one rival explanation, Self-Perception Theory, has been particularly troublesome for Dissonance Theory advocates. Theoretical differences between these rival explanations and the corresponding investigations of these explanations are reviewed. Finally, we discuss some practical applications of Cognitive Dissonance Theory that have recently been developed to deal with issues such as condom use.

In Chapter 3, we presented several theories that assume attitudes cause behaviors. In this chapter, we turn the question around: Can changes in behavior affect subsequent attitudes? The answer to this question is most definitely "Yes, under certain circumstances." Advertisers have long recognized the role of behavior in the formation and reinforcement of attitudes. Automobile salespeople encourage potential customers to test-drive a particular car early in the sales process. Some car buyers are also given an opportunity to take a car home for a weekend to *see how it feels* before making a decision. The 1970s advertising tagline for a breakfast cereal "Try it, you'll like it" echoed similar convictions. Religious leaders encourage their followers to regularly participate in ceremonies that both reinforce their beliefs and strengthen their commitment. Indeed, very few persuasion scholars would dispute the assertion that behavior influences the formation and reinforcement of attitudes. However, the causal link between behavior and subsequent attitude *change* is less straightforward.

Studies that investigate the effects of behavior on attitude change typically employ counterattitudinal advocacy (CAA) procedures that require people to advocate a position that is inconsistent with their existing attitude. In most cases, attitudes and behaviors mutually influence one another, making it difficult to determine a precise causal relationship. CAA procedures create a context where it is possible to observe the influence of specific behaviors on subsequent attitudes, permitting close examination of a causal relationship. This research paradigm was initially developed during the early 1950s and employed in several investigations of active and passive persuasive message processing (Janis & King, 1954; King & Janis, 1956). By a decade later, it had become a staple in attitude change research (for reviews, see Cooper, 2007, 2012).

THE CAA RESEARCH PARADIGM

The CAA research procedure is relatively straightforward. First, investigators must know in advance participants' attitudes toward a particular issue, object, or situation. Sometimes investigators will conduct attitude pretests several weeks prior to the experiment; or, more frequently, an issue is selected about which most of the participants are known to hold similar attitudes. For example, among most evangelical Christians, the concept of religious freedom is a fundamental belief, and it would be counterattitudinal for them to advocate restricting religious expression. Similarly, college students are almost uniformly opposed to tuition increases, and thus, for most students, advocating a tuition increase would represent CAA.

Once a topic has been selected, investigators ask the research participants to advocate a position *opposite* to that they actually hold. To engage in CAA, the participants might be asked to write an essay, present a speech, or talk with another person. Thus, on the tuition increase issue, CAA might involve the respondent's writing an essay justifying a tuition increase. CAA poses an interesting dilemma in that the people engaging in CAA knowingly articulate a position that is inconsistent with their personal beliefs and convictions: they believe x but advocate *not-x*, and this inconsistency should create a certain amount of cognitive dissonance in them.

What effect does such advocacy have on a person's attitude toward an issue? For example, if the president of a campus evangelical Christian organization advocated limits on the expression of religious beliefs in public schools, would this CAA influence his or her attitude toward freedom of religious expression? Although the answer to such questions is somewhat complicated, we can offer a qualified generalization: CAA will produce attitude change in the direction of the position advocated, provided that certain situational conditions are present. It bears mentioning that CAA emphasizes attitude change in the advocate, him- or herself; it does not produce attitude change in passive audience members (in the way that traditional persuasive appeals do). That is, CAA is a technique for inducing *self*-persuasion, not for persuading others.

The amount of attitude change that advocates experience following CAA depends on several situational factors, including perceived justification, freedom of choice, and the consequences of the CAA. It is relatively uncommon for people in actual interactions to freely engage in CAA without some external justification. Thus, the practical ability of CAA to actually induce attitude change may be rather limited. The studies and theories discussed in this chapter represent a good example of how researchers address *theoretical* issues (i.e., basic, as opposed to applied, science) with a variety of research designs. We conclude this chapter, however, by reviewing some recent practical applications of the CAA paradigm. Despite these qualifications, the CAA paradigm has important theoretical implications for persuasion because it enables researchers to distinguish attitude-reinforcement and attitude-formation processes from attitude-change processes.

There has been little disagreement about CAA's effectiveness in changing an advocate's position. However, considerable controversy has surrounded several theoretical explanations of this effect. The most extensively investigated explanation is Cognitive Dissonance Theory (Festinger, 1957). The original theory, along with its subsequent modifications and extensions, is discussed in the next section, followed by several alternative explanations of the CAA effect.

A THEORY OF COGNITIVE DISSONANCE

In 1957, Leon Festinger postulated his Theory of Cognitive Dissonance (or, more simply, Dissonance Theory), which became the most widely investigated social psychological theory of its era. Evolving from basic consistency principles (e.g., Heider, 1946; Newcomb, 1953), Dissonance Theory postulated three basic assumptions about human cognition: (1) people have a need for cognitive consistency; (2) when cognitive inconsistency exists, we experience psychological discomfort; and (3) psychological discomfort motivates us to resolve the inconsistency and restore cognitive balance.

While it can be placed in a larger family of consistency theories, Dissonance Theory differs from the others by virtue of its being a *postdecisional* theory. Festinger was interested in explaining how people resolve the internal psychological conflict they often experience after making an important decision.

Basic Components of Dissonance Theory

Festinger (1957) argued that not all cognitive elements (e.g., thoughts, ideas, values) are relevant to one another. For example, the belief that one is an honest person is probably unrelated to one's preference for the color blue. Hence, Festinger stipulated that his theory only explained cognitions that were perceived to be relevant, or related to one another, by the attitude holder. He then proposed two cognitive states to describe the relations among relevant cognitive elements. Though he employed somewhat different language, Festinger argued that a state of *consonance* was said to exist when two or more cognitions were consistent with one another. An example might be a person who is a registered Democrat and who voted for Barack Obama in the 2012 presidential election. The cognitive elements in this case, one's party affiliation and voting behavior, are consistent with each other. A state of *dissonance* exists when two or more related cognitions are inconsistent with one another. For example, a politician who has strong environmental beliefs might experience dissonance after voting for legislation that permits oil exploration in protected wetlands.

Dissonance occurs to varying extents. Some cognitive elements may be highly inconsistent with one another and yet produce only a negligible amount of dissonance. For example, if a person believes in the merits of recycling but yet disposes of a used soft drink can in a wastepaper basket instead of recycling it, he or she might well experience cognitive dissonance. However, the extent of the dissonance and the person's subsequent motivation to reduce it would likely be quite small. If this same person failed to vote for legislation instituting a local recycling program and the proposition was defeated by a single vote, however, the magnitude of the resulting cognitive dissonance would likely be considerably larger.

Festinger (1957) stated that dissonance is an aversive state, that is, something that we try to avoid. He also argued that dissonance creates so much psychological discomfort that we try to reduce it whenever it occurs. The greater the dissonance, the greater the psychological discomfort and the greater the motivation to reduce it. The magnitude of dissonance is determined by (1) the importance of the dissonant elements and (2) the proportion of consonant to dissonant relations among the relevant elements in the cognitive system.

Implications of Cognitive Dissonance

Because decisions involve choosing one option over another, dissonance is an inevitable consequence of making decisions. When people must choose among two or more competing alternatives, the amount of dissonance (and thus psychological discomfort) experienced depends on both the importance of the decision and the relative attractiveness of the foregone alternative(s).

Each year, college seniors interview for jobs in their chosen career fields. The fortunate ones receive multiple offers and are placed in the enviable position of having the freedom to choose among alternative employment opportunities. If the alternatives are quite dissimilar—for example, a choice between a $35,000-a-year job in Otis, Kansas, and a $60,000-a-year job in Minneapolis—the amount of dissonance produced by the decision should be minimal because one option is likely to be evaluated much more positively than the other. However, if the alternatives are equally attractive—for example, the choice between a $60,000-a-year job in Minneapolis and a $57,000-a-year job in Chicago—the amount of dissonance created by making the choice may be substantial (no matter which option is chosen), and the decision maker will inevitably try to reduce it once the choice is made.

Festinger (1957) described three ways a person can reduce his or her cognitive dissonance following an important decision. First, the person can change the *cognitive element related to the behavior.* Assume that our college senior decided to accept the job in Minneapolis instead of the initially equally attractive position in Chicago. The theory predicts that the decision will produce cognitive dissonance. In an effort to reduce that dissonance, our college senior could attempt to change the decision. However, a more likely response would be to change the cognitive elements related to the decision by, for example, distorting information about the decision or denying that there was much of a choice to begin with. For example, the person might conclude, "I made the best decision, given the information I had available to me at the time."

A second method of reducing dissonance is to change the *cognitive element(s) related to the attitude.* That is, if the decision is inconsistent with the person's existing attitude, a common way to reduce the dissonance is to modify the attitude. Indeed, most studies of the theory have employed attitude change measures to document the existence and reduction of cognitive dissonance. Thus, another way for the college senior to reduce dissonance stemming from his or her decision to accept the job in Minneapolis is to form a more negative attitude about living or working in Chicago, a more positive attitude about living or working in Minneapolis, or both.

Finally, Festinger (1957) specified that *adding new cognitive elements* may reduce dissonance. Selective exposure to new information (Freedman & Sears, 1965; Hart et al., 2009) often occurs after a decision has been made. People intentionally expose themselves to information that reinforces the merits of their decision and intentionally avoid information that would cast doubt on the decision. This new information, by realigning cognitive elements, reduces dissonance. Extending the job offer example a bit further, the college senior might reduce dissonance after making the decision by paying special attention to reports that favorably compare Minneapolis to Chicago. For example, our student might read a recent news article rating Minneapolis as "one of the 10 most desirable cities for young professionals."

The Festinger and Carlsmith Study

Festinger and Carlsmith (1959) conducted the initial test of Dissonance Theory. In this study, participants arrived one at a time at the experimental laboratory and were asked to turn pegs on a board for a long period of time. After completing this task, which was excruciatingly dull, participants were told that the experiment was designed to examine the effects of expectations on performance. The participants were told that they were in a control condition where there were no prior expectations and that other participants would be in a condition where they would be told that the task was very exciting and interesting. Then the experimenter indicated that the student who had been hired to provide positive expectations for subjects had just called in sick for that day. The experimenter then asked the subject if he or she would be willing to introduce the experiment to the next research participant and to be on call for performing this task in the future. The experimenter indicated that the participant had to describe the study as fun and exciting. What is more, the experimenter would be paying either $1 or $20 (depending on the experimental condition) for creating the expectation. Once the participant agreed to serve as the assistant, he or she was asked to introduce the experiment to the next participant (actually a confederate who played the role of a subject). The participant introduced the task and described it as fun and exciting.

After positively introducing the experiment, the participant engaged in a previously arranged interview with another psychology researcher who was conducting a separate survey on research performed in the department. Respondents were told that the survey was being administered to all participants in any department-sponsored research project. They were then asked how much they liked the experiment they had just participated in, how much they had learned from it, and how likely they would be to participate in similar projects. Actually, this interview was created to assess the participants' reactions to the original experimental task (which represented the study's dependent variables).

The Creation of Cognitive Dissonance

Because the procedure was dull and uninteresting, Festinger and Carlsmith (1959) hypothesized that people would experience dissonance after introducing the study as interesting and exciting. Because the participants had clearly been deceptive when introducing the study, it was difficult for them to deny or distort their CAA behavior. Moreover, it was unlikely that they could anticipate seeing the confederate again, either to alter the consequences of their decision or to provide an explanation for their behavior. There were also no sources of external information about the experiment readily available to participants, meaning that selective exposure to information was an unlikely possibility.

Thus, these procedures largely eliminated two of the three methods outlined by Festinger (1957) for reducing dissonance—that is, changing cognitive elements related to the behavior or adding new cognitive elements. Hence, the easiest method for reducing dissonance created by the CAA was changing one's attitude (see Figure 4.1).

Effects of Cognitive Dissonance

To the extent that their procedures led to cognitive dissonance, Festinger and Carlsmith (1959) hypothesized that participants would change their attitudes, because the other methods of reducing dissonance had been effectively blocked. Recall, however, that there were two payment conditions in the study. Some participants received $1 and others were paid $20 for their CAA introduction of the experiment (roughly equivalent to $8 and $160 in current dollars). The payment might serve as a justification for the CAA. Participants receiving $1 had little external justification for their behavior, whereas those receiving $20 could easily justify their CAA. Participants receiving $20 could easily say to themselves, "Why did I say the task was interesting? Because I received $20 for it." Because the participants' CAA

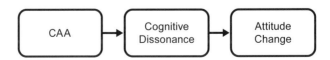

FIGURE 4.1. A Theory of Cognitive Dissonance (Festinger, 1957). CAA = counterattitudinal advocacy.

in the $20 condition was easily justified, it is unlikely that cognitive dissonance and subsequent attitude change would occur. In the $1 condition, however, participants had little external justification for their behavior and hence would likely experience greater dissonance. Thus, Festinger and Carlsmith hypothesized that to reduce the attendant dissonance those who received only $1 (low justification) would have to change their attitudes toward the experimental task more radically than would those paid $20 (high justification).

The findings were consistent with these expectations. The participants in the $1 condition reported attitudes indicating that the experimental task was significantly more enjoyable than did those in the $20 condition. However, there were no differences between these two groups on the questions regarding the scientific or educational value of the experiment or the desire to participate in similar experiments. Festinger and Carlsmith (1959) concluded that the difference between the attitudes of participants in the low and the high justification conditions "strongly corroborated the theory that was tested" (p. 210).

Although there was reason to question the strength of their convictions at the time they drew this conclusion, the attitude results from the Festinger and Carlsmith (1959) study have been replicated in many subsequent investigations of Dissonance Theory (for reviews, see Cooper, 2007; Greenwald & Ronis, 1978; Harmon-Jones, Amodio, & Harmon-Jones, 2009; Harmon-Jones & Mills, 1999; G. R. Miller, 1973). Today, there remains little doubt about the persuasive effects of CAA. The correct theoretical explanation of these effects, however, remains a source of considerable controversy over a half-century later.

Limitations of Cognitive Dissonance Theory

Although many investigations have provided support for Dissonance Theory, it is difficult to imagine a set of research findings that could not be explained by Festinger's original explication of Dissonance Theory. Festinger's writing was conceptually vague and sufficiently general to prevent falsification of the theory. That is to say, in order for one to have confidence in the validity of a theory, the theory must be subjected to tests that attempt to prove it false. If rigorous tests fail to disprove a theory, then scholars gain confidence that the theory must be valid. However, when a theory is conceptually ambiguous—so as to impede rigorous attempts at falsification—then one cannot have confidence in the validity of the theory (K. I. Miller, 2005).

For example, Dissonance Theory fails to articulate when people will likely use each of the three methods for reducing cognitive dissonance. Instead, Festinger opined that dissonance is reduced by modifying the cognitive element that is *least resistant to change.* Because Festinger did not explain how the resistance of cognitive elements could be assessed, it is difficult to predict *a priori* whether dissonance will produce behavior change, attitude change, or selective exposure to new information. In particular, the notion of adding new cognitive elements is vague and nearly impossible to assess.

The considerable ambiguity present in Cognitive Dissonance Theory is important because, following CAA, a person may exhibit no observable signs of psychological discomfort or dissonance reduction—and yet dissonance and its subsequent reduction may have occurred. Because thinking about the topic at hand fits within the category of adding new cognitive elements, a person may reduce dissonance by generating new thoughts or by recalling information stored in memory. Consider the earlier example of an evangelical Christian who publicly advocates limits on religious expression in public schools. Though no observable signs of dissonance reduction may occur, our evangelical friend may internally rationalize the counter-attitudinal behavior by recalling positions held by some religious leaders who are careful not to impose their religious views on others for fear that it might result in having the religious views of others imposed on him- or herself. Though investigators may never have access to this private internal rationalization, dissonance and its subsequent reduction may nevertheless have occurred.

Because two of the three methods for reducing dissonance—namely, attitude change and adding new cognitive elements—are not directly observable, the original version of Dissonance Theory was virtually impossible to disprove. If observable changes follow CAA, Dissonance Theory may be able to account for these changes. However, the absence of observable change might mean that dissonance did occur and was subsequently reduced internally. It simply means that researchers did not observe dissonance reduction if it occurred. In an effort to resolve this limitation, researchers have suggested several modifications and extensions of the original theory. For the most part, these suggestions were intended to limit the scope of the theory.

Modifications and Extensions of Cognitive Dissonance Theory

The evolution of Cognitive Dissonance Theory has been impressive. Harmon-Jones and Mills (1999) summarized several modifications that have been suggested to clarify Festinger's original articulation of the theory, and we discuss many of those modifications, along with a theoretical challenge to Cognitive Dissonance Theory that was posed by Self-Perception Theory (Bem, 1967). As we discuss these developments, we provide a number of figures to depict the theoretical modifications to the original theory.

Two of the earliest modifications were suggested by Brehm and A. R. Cohen (1962), who conducted a series of investigations testing the theory. First, Brehm and Cohen introduced the notion of *commitment* to Dissonance Theory. Though Festinger originally argued that dissonance resulted from any decision making, Brehm and Cohen argued that dissonance should occur only when people experience a state of psychological commitment to their decision. In essence, if a decision can be easily reversed, then the decision maker should experience little dissonance. If the decision is not (or not easily) reversible, then cognitive dissonance should occur, with the extent of this dissonance being a function of the importance of the decision and the relative attractiveness of the unchosen alternative.

In other words if a customer decides to purchase a car for a particular price but doesn't say anything about it, little dissonance is likely produced. It is only when the commitment is made (i.e., he or she signs the contract and/or agrees to the price verbally with the salesperson) that it can later create dissonance.

The importance of Brehm and Cohen's suggestion is apparent in consumer purchasing decisions. For example, would cognitive dissonance occur if you spent $1,000 on clothes at the mall? According to Festinger's version of the theory, the answer is "Yes," and the amount of dissonance would be a function of how dear $1,000 is to you and your evaluation of the alternative uses you might have for that money. If we consider as authoritative Brehm and Cohen's notion of commitment, however, dissonance will occur only if you feel psychologically committed to your purchase. Because most clothing stores permit shoppers to return unwanted merchandise, often there is no *legal* commitment to the purchase. However, the act of returning clothes is easier psychologically for some people than for others. In earlier times, when Jim was growing up, one of his sisters would routinely purchase clothes and then return them a week later, being little committed to her initial purchase decisions. Conversely, Jim feels highly uncomfortable when returning anything he buys, even if it is totally unsatisfactory in practice. That is, he experiences much more psychological commitment to personal purchase decisions than does his sister.

Obviously, marketers understand the force of psychological commitment. Television ads invariably promise a 30-day money-back guarantee on any of their products. Such guarantees serve to temporarily reduce the level of actual commitment consumers experience when they call to purchase a product. Once the product arrives, however, perceptions of commitment to the purchase largely return, the 30-day period passes, and the decision then becomes no longer reversible. Such guarantees underscore the importance of psychological commitment in the postdecisional dissonance reduction process.

BOX 4.1. Psychological Commitment in Relation to the Low-Ball Technique

The role of psychological commitment is evident in research on the *low-ball technique* (see also Chapter 11 for additional details). This technique is often used by salespeople whose initial goal is to get a customer to make a psychological commitment (e.g., by accepting as reasonable a particular price for a product or service). Following the initial agreement, the salesperson effectively raises the price (Cialdini, Cacioppo, Bassett, & Miller, 1978). For example, a customer might accept a price for a new automobile only to have the salesperson subsequently reduce his or her offer on the trade-in vehicle, effectively increasing the cost of the transaction to the customer. Research has long demonstrated that when targets commit to accepting an initial offer they are more likely to accept the less attractive second offer—but the commitment must be public (i.e., stated orally or communicated to others) in order for the effect to occur (Burger & Cornelius, 2003).

In a second modification of the theory suggested by Brehm and A. R. Cohen (1962), they argued that *volition* (free choice) is essential to the onset of cognitive dissonance. If people perceive that their options were restricted or that someone else heavily influenced them, they may feel as though they had little choice in their decision (see Figure 4.2). If people do not feel *personal* responsibility for a decision, dissonance should not occur (Wicklund & Brehm, 1976).

The concept of volition highlights a major criticism of what became known as the "forced-compliance research paradigm." If student participants in these research studies engaged in CAA mainly because doing so was a requirement for receiving extra credit in their introductory psychology course, then they may have felt that they were being forced to comply with the request to engage in CAA. Thus, if they believed that they had little choice but to engage in the CAA, they may not have experienced much cognitive dissonance. Thus, *forced-compliance* may be one explanation for

FIGURE 4.2. The role of volition and commitment (Brehm & A. R. Cohen, 1962). CAA = counterattitudinal advocacy.

the limited effects found in early CAA research (e.g., J. R. Cohen, Brehm, & Fleming, 1958; Festinger & Carlsmith, 1959; see Chapanis & Chapanis, 1964).

In addition to the stipulations offered by Brehm and A. R. Cohen (1962), Aronson (1968) offered another modification of the original theory (see Aronson, 1992, for an interesting review). Aronson's version of the theory argued that the source of dissonance following CAA was not the knowledge that cognitions were inconsistent with one another but rather one's belief that he or she is sensible but yet behaved in an *unsensible* manner. Aronson (1992) observed that "dissonance is greatest and clearest when it involves not just any two cognitions but, rather, a cognition about the self and a piece of our behavior that violates that self-concept" (p. 305).

Sometimes referred to as Later Dissonance Theory, Aronson's (1968) modification casts the inconsistency at a higher level of abstraction that underscores the role of personality factors (particularly the self-concept) in characterizing cognitive dissonance (see Aronson, 1992). More recently, Cialdini and colleagues (Cialdini, Trost, & Newsome, 1995) examined individual differences in the need for consistency (see Table 4.1 for a useful measure) and their effect on attitude change following counterattitudinal advocacy (for a review, see Guadagno & Cialdini, 2010).

Aronson argued that people with positive self-concepts should experience greater dissonance following willful CAA than those with negative self-concepts. Cialdini and his colleagues additionally found that people with a high need for consistency experience greater attitude change (because they experience proportionally higher levels of cognitive dissonance) than do people with a low need for consistency. Presumably, for people with more positive self-concepts and a high need for consistency, the CAA presents itself as highly inconsistent with their perception that the self is honest. Since people with negative self-concepts do not have the expectation that they will always be honest, they will experience more limited dissonance when their behavior is inconsistent with their attitude (e.g., when writing a CAA essay). The key to the perspectives introduced by Brehm and A. R. Cohen (1962), Aronson (1968, 1992), and Cialdini and colleagues (1995) is the realization that not all people experience the same levels of dissonance even though they might engage in the same counterattitudinal behavior (see Figure 4.3).

Together, the modifications suggested by Brehm and A. R. Cohen (1962; see Cooper, 2007, for a review) and Aronson (1968; see also Brehm, 2007) produced versions of Dissonance Theory that were more precise but narrower in scope. The most serious challenge to Cognitive Dissonance Theory, however, came from Darryl Bem's (1965, 1967) Self-Perception Theory, which we take up next.

TABLE 4.1. Cialdini, Trost, and Newsome's (1995) Preference for Consistency Scale

1. I prefer to be around people whose reactions I can anticipate.
2. It is important to me that my actions are consistent with my beliefs.
3. Even if my attitudes and actions seemed consistent with one another to me, it would bother me if they did not seem consistent in the eyes of others.
4. It is important to me that those who know me can predict what I will do.
5. I want to be described by others as a stable, predictable person.
6. Admirable people are consistent and predictable.
7. The appearance of consistency is an important part of the image I present to the world.
8. It bothers me when someone I depend on is unpredictable.
9. I don't like to appear as if I am inconsistent.
10. I get uncomfortable when I find my behavior contradicts my beliefs.
11. An important requirement for any friend of mine is personal consistency.
12. I typically prefer to do things the same way.
13. I dislike people who are constantly changing their opinions.
14. I want my close friends to be predictable.
15. It is important to me that others view me as a stable person.
16. I make an effort to appear consistent to others.
17. I'm uncomfortable holding two beliefs that are inconsistent.
18. It doesn't bother me much if my actions are inconsistent.

Note. A Likert scale can be used to solicit responses. Statement 18 is reverse-coded. From "Preference for consistency: The development of a valid measure and the discovery of surprising behavioral implications" by R. B. Cialdini, M. R. Trost, & J. T. Newsome, 1995, *Journal of Personality and Social Psychology, 69,* 318–328. Copyright 1995 by the American Psychological Association. Reprinted by permission.

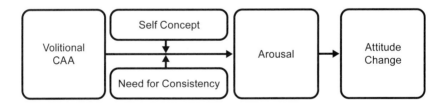

FIGURE 4.3. Moderating effects of self-concept (Aronson, 1968) and need for consistency (Cialdini, Trost, & Newsome, 1995). CAA = counterattitudinal advocacy.

BOX 4.2. Self-Perception and Fish Camp

Colleges and universities around the country routinely have orientation programs for incoming freshmen that range from informational sessions on campus to off-campus retreats. At Texas A&M University, *Fish Camp* is a 4-day off-campus orientation program that is designed to "offer a smooth transition for incoming freshmen and build a support system for their college experience at Texas A&M. The focus is on teaching *traditions*, building the Aggie family and spirit, and forming bonds through an unconditionally accepting environment" (*http://fish-camp.tamu.edu*). There are approximately 40 Fish Camps every year, each one named for a faculty or staff member who has made an important contribution to the university. At these gatherings, attendees bond with one another, learn about the many university traditions, and practice the "yells" (cheers) that are used at sporting events.

Fish Camp is an excellent example of the application of Self-Perception Theory. Students who attend Fish Camp learn and practice Aggie traditions. As they observe themselves behaving like Aggies and performing common traditions, they become more committed to perpetuating these traditions. This self-perception process serves to create and reinforce cultural values and commitment to the university.

SELF-PERCEPTION THEORY

When Dissonance Theory was initially developed, the predominant social science paradigm of the day was behaviorism (Skinner, 1938), which posits that only observable behaviors can be studied scientifically and that consideration of cognitions has no value. Dissonance Theory dramatically strayed from this paradigm by highlighting the importance of cognitions (thoughts) in human behavior. Firing back from the behaviorist paradigm, Daryl Bem (1965, 1967) introduced Self-Perception Theory, which rejects Dissonance Theory's cognitive assumptions and underpinnings. In doing so, Self-Perception Theory provides a compelling alternative explanation for research findings from Dissonance Theory experiments. In a short time, Self-Perception Theory emerged as a major theoretical roadblock for dissonance theorists. In the decade that followed, an intense rivalry evolved between the proponents of these two competing theories. At stake was not only the theoretical superiority but also the relative prominence of the behaviorist versus cognitive ways of looking at the world. The basic assumption of Self-Perception Theory is that individuals come to know their own attitudes, emotions, and other internal states partially from inferring them from observations of their own overt behavior and/or circumstances in which this behavior occurs. Thus, to the extent that external cues are weak, ambiguous, or uninterpretable, the individual is functionally in the same position as an outside observer, an observer who must rely upon those same external cues to infer the individual's internal states. (Bem, 1972, p. 2)

In short, there are circumstances when a person is forced to infer his or her own attitudes in the same way that others' attitudes are inferred—that is, from overt behavior. Bem (1972) reported findings from several studies that corroborated his assumptions about the inference-making process. In each of these investigations, people's evaluations of experimental stimuli were guided by their overt behavior toward the stimuli.

Explaining Attitude Change Following Decisions

Bem (1972) employed this self-perception process to explain attitude change following CAA. Absent any external justification, Bem argued, people modify their attitudes following CAA because they have observed a change in their own overt behavior (see Figure 4.4). Applied to the Festinger and Carlsmith (1959) experiment, Bem's explanation holds that participants receiving $1 for their CAA changed their attitudes because they observed a change in their overt behavior, namely, the advocacy itself. What is more, the $1 that participants received was not sufficient remuneration to be considered an external justification for changing their behavior. On the other hand, participants who received $20 for their CAA underwent less attitude change because the monetary reward itself served as an external justification for their behavior. The $20 payment made moot the inference-making process, providing a compelling rationale for their change in behavior. Thus, Bem's alternative explanation accounted for the findings of Festinger and Carlsmith's (1959) seminal study without its being necessary to invoke the constructs of cognitive dissonance or psychological discomfort.

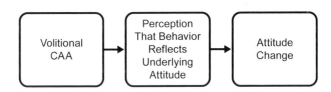

FIGURE 4.4. Self-Perception Theory (Bem, 1967). CAA = counterattitudinal advocacy.

The concepts of volition and justification are equally important to Bem's self-perception explanation of attitude change as they were to Cognitive Dissonance Theory. According to Self-Perception Theory, CAA will not produce attitude change when people perceive that their behavior was not volitional or when they conclude that some external justification better explains their behavior. In those instances, people conclude that observation of their own behavior is not a valid indicator of their underlying attitude.

Self-Perception Theory versus Cognitive Dissonance Theory

Although both Cognitive Dissonance Theory and Self-Perception Theory account for the findings from CAA studies, there are important theoretical differences between the two. The fundamental disagreement between these two explanations centers upon the underlying *causes* of attitude change. According to Dissonance Theory, CAA creates a feeling of psychological discomfort, which motivates people to reduce their cognitive inconsistency, including (in some cases) changing their attitudes. In contrast, Bem makes no mention of internal motivational pressures such as discomfort or arousal. Instead, Self-Perception Theory postulates that attitude change following CAA is produced by an attempt to explain the counterattitudinal behavior (i.e., the advocacy). When behavior is inconsistent with prior attitudes, and when no external justification is available to explain the behavior, people conclude that the underlying attitude must have produced the behavior. In these cases, people base attitude judgments on what information is available to them (Bem, 1967).

Because the fundamental difference between these two theoretical processes is not directly observable, early tests of the relative merits of these theories produced equivocal findings (Greenwald, 1975). In an effort to differentiate these theories, by the mid-1970s most dissonance theorists had redefined Festinger's concept of psychological discomfort to mean *physiological arousal*. Arousal is manifested in increases in heart rate, blood pressure, respiration rate, and/or sweating. Because discomfort or arousal was the most important element of Cognitive Dissonance Theory that was absent in Self-Perception Theory, subsequent critical tests between these two competing explanations focused on the emergence of arousal following CAA.

AROUSAL, CAA, AND ATTITUDE CHANGE

Because arousal plays an important role in Cognitive Dissonance Theory but not in Self-Perception Theory, several studies investigated the precise role of arousal in the attitude-change processes predicted by both theories. For the most part, studies investigating the effects of CAA on arousal and subsequent attitude change have employed a *misattribution* research procedure developed by Schachter and Singer (1962). This procedure does not involve the direct measurement of arousal, but it provides research participants with an external cue (e.g., taking a stimulant) to explain any arousal they might experience. While the external cue is not the actual cause of the arousal, its presence allows people to misattribute the arousal as being created by the external cue rather than the CAA.

Applied in dissonance experiments, an external cue provides a clear explanation for the arousal that participants experience following CAA. If arousal is misattributed to the external cue instead of being attributed to the CAA, then little or no attitude change should result. On the other hand, participants who experience arousal in the absence of an external cue should attribute their arousal to the CAA and subsequently change their attitude in order to reduce it (see Figure 4.5).

The Zanna and Cooper Study

Zanna and Cooper (1974) used a misattribution procedure to determine whether arousal associated with CAA was sufficient to produce attitude change. Participants in the study either volunteered (free choice, dissonance aroused) or were induced to comply (forced choice, no dissonance) with a request to write a counterattitudinal essay. Recall that Brehm and A. R. Cohen (1962) argued that free choice (volition) was necessary to produce dissonance following CAA.

In addition to the free-choice versus forced-choice manipulation, Zanna and Cooper (1974) gave all participants in their study a placebo (i.e., a pill that had no actual physiological effects). Half of the participants in the free-choice and forced-choice conditions were told that the placebo was a mild tranquilizer and that it would have a relaxing effect on them. The remaining participants in each condition were told that the placebo was a stimulant that would generate physiological arousal.

As expected, participants in the forced-choice (no dissonance) conditions exhibited little attitude change after writing their CAA essay. Among

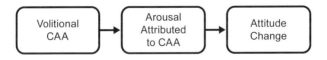

FIGURE 4.5. The role of arousal (Zanna & Cooper, 1974; Cooper, Zanna, & Taves, 1978). CAA = counterattitudinal advocacy.

participants who freely chose to write the CAA essay (dissonance condition), those who were told that the placebo was a stimulant exhibited little attitude change. Presumably, these participants attributed their arousal to the drug, not to the CAA. Thus, attitude change was unnecessary since the source of their arousal was not a mystery. Conversely, participants in the free-choice condition who were told that they had received a tranquilizer exhibited significant attitude change. These participants had no external cue to explain their arousal. Presumably, these participants attributed their arousal to the CAA and changed their attitude in an effort to reduce it.

Thus, in conditions where the arousal following CAA can be misattributed to an external cue (i.e., the alleged stimulant), no attitude change is necessary to reduce arousal. When arousal is attributed to CAA, attitude change presumably occurs to reduce arousal. Although actual arousal was not measured in this study, the results suggest that arousal attributed to CAA is sufficient to produce attitude change but that attributed to external factors does not produce attitude change.

The Cooper, Zanna, and Taves Study

The conclusion that arousal is sufficient for attitude change does not imply that arousal is necessary for attitude change following CAA. To investigate this issue, Cooper, Zanna, and Taves (1978) conducted another study using the misattribution research procedure.

In this study, however, all participants were told that they had been placed in the placebo condition and that the pill they were to ingest would have no effect on them. Although this was true for one-third of the participants, one-third were actually given a tranquilizer that had a relaxing effect, and one-third were given an amphetamine that stimulated their physiological arousal. Participants wrote CAA essays about Richard Nixon. Half of the participants were in the high-choice (dissonance) condition, and half were in the low-choice (no dissonance) condition.

By manipulating arousal physiologically, the experimenters were able to influence participants' attributions for their physiological arousal. Participants experiencing heightened arousal had no external cue to explain their arousal and would likely attribute it to the CAA. Moreover, participants in the high-choice tranquilizer condition probably did not experience the arousal that they normally would because the drug physiologically relaxed them.

The attitudes of research participants after writing the counterattitudinal essay are summarized in Table 4.2. Inspection of this table reveals a number of interesting findings. First, attitudes toward Nixon were more favorable in the high-choice placebo condition than in the low-choice placebo condition. This difference represents the classic dissonance effect

TABLE 4.2. Summary of Attitudes in the Cooper, Zanna, and Taves (1978) Study

	Type of drug administered		
	Tranquilizer	Placebo	Amphetamine
High-choice CAA (dissonance)	8.6	14.7	20.2
Low-choice CAA (no dissonance)	8.0	8.3	13.9

Note. Larger numbers reflect favorable attitudes toward Richard Nixon after writing the counterattitudinal essay. From "Arousal as a necessary condition for attitude change following induced compliance" by J. Cooper, M. P. Zanna, & P. A. Taves, 1978, *Journal of Personality and Social Psychology, 36*, 1101–1106. Copyright 1978 by the American Psychological Association. Reprinted by permission.

found in prior research. Moreover, the attitudes of participants in the three high-choice (dissonance) conditions suggest that as arousal increases attitude change increases. This finding is consistent with Dissonance Theory's assertion that arousal motivates attitude change following CAA. There was no difference in attitudes between the high-choice and low-choice tranquilizer conditions. The relaxing effects of the tranquilizer most likely offset heightened arousal that might have been associated with volitional CAA. As a result, participants in the high-choice tranquilizer condition exhibited little attitude change. Thus, volitional CAA was not sufficient to produce attitude change; it must be associated with a heightened level of arousal. This finding suggests that arousal may be necessary for attitude change following CAA.

The difference between the attitudes of the low-choice placebo and amphetamine conditions suggests that physiological arousal is sufficient to produce attitude change if it is misattributed to the CAA. In the low-choice amphetamine condition, individuals probably misattributed the cause of their arousal to the CAA. Individuals in this condition, after experiencing an unexplained high level of arousal, may have perceived that they had more of a free choice than they actually did when they wrote the CAA essay. In fact, analysis of the measures of *perceived choice* in writing the CAA revealed that participants in the low-choice amphetamine condition reported significantly higher perceived choice than participants in the other two low-choice conditions and had perceptions of choice similar to participants in the three high-choice conditions. If individuals in the low-choice amphetamine condition attributed their arousal to the CAA—and there is good evidence to suggest that they did—then we would expect the same levels of attitude change as we observed in the high-choice placebo condition. This, in fact, was the case. After feeling aroused, the participants apparently deduced that they were in some way responsible for writing the CAA essay.

The Croyle and Cooper Studies

One limitation of the Zanna and Cooper (1974) and the Cooper et al. (1978) experiments is their reliance on misattribution procedures to make inferences about the role of arousal following CAA. Although these studies provided compelling support for Dissonance Theory (and were inconsistent with Self-Perception Theory), they employed indirect assessments of physiological arousal.

To address this limitation, Croyle and Cooper (1983) conducted two experiments that demonstrated the effects of CAA on attitudes and directly measured levels of physiological arousal induced by CAA. In the first experiment they found the traditional pattern of attitude change predicted by Dissonance Theory. Participants in the high-choice condition reported significantly more attitude change after writing a counterattitudinal essay than participants in the low-choice condition.

The second experiment employed the same design and used physiological measures to directly record participants' arousal after they wrote the counterattitudinal essay. Consistent with Dissonance Theory, participants in the high-choice CAA condition exhibited significantly greater levels of physiological arousal than participants in the low-choice CAA condition.[1] Taken together, these studies provide strong support for the dissonance arousal explanation for attitude change following CAA. The first study demonstrated the effects of CAA on attitude change, and the second study demonstrated that willful CAA heightened physiological arousal, which is the hypothesized cause of the attitude change in Cognitive Dissonance Theory.

Summary of Arousal Studies

Findings from the arousal studies provide clear and compelling evidence for Later Dissonance Theory explanations of attitude change following CAA. Investigations using either the misattribution research procedure or direct measurement of arousal provide consistent evidence linking CAA to arousal and, in turn, linking arousal to attitude change. Therefore, two specific conclusions can be drawn from this research.

First, CAA is not sufficient to produce attitude change. For attitude change to occur, CAA must be both volitional and associated with physiological arousal. Cooper and Fazio (1984) argued that people must perceive that their counterattitudinal behavior will produce negative consequences before they experience physiological arousal. If no negative consequences are anticipated, then dissonance arousal will not occur (though see Harmon-Jones, 2002, for another view). Zanna and Cooper (1974) and Cooper et al. (1978) provided support for this conclusion when they demonstrated that arousal attributed to CAA is necessary for attitude change. When arousal following CAA was misattributed to another source, attitude change did not occur.

Second, the amount of physiological arousal experienced following CAA appears to determine the extent of attitude change. Croyle and Cooper (1983) provided a direct link between physiological arousal and attitude change, while Cooper and colleagues (1978) found that the amount of arousal attributed to CAA was positively related to the amount of attitude change exhibited by participants.

During the past decade, research on arousal has focused on neurophysiological indicators (cortical brain activity) of cognitive dissonance and dissonance reduction during and after CAA (for a review, see Harmon-Jones et al., 2009). This research indicates that dissonance and its reduction are clearly related to different centers of brain activity and melds nicely with more than 50 years of psychological research on CAA. From a practical communication perspective, however, the relevance of this phenomenon to the relationship between attitudes and behaviors is unclear.

INTEGRATING COGNITIVE DISSONANCE AND SELF-PERCEPTION THEORIES

Research examining the physiological arousal associated with CAA provides strong support for dissonance explanations of attitude change. Research establishing a link between arousal and attitude change is clearly incompatible with Self-Perception Theory. But does this research invalidate the self-perception explanation?

In an effort to reconcile the different theoretical positions advanced by self-perception and dissonance theorists, Fazio and his colleagues proposed that perhaps both theories were correct explanations of attitude change following CAA but that each theory had its own domain (Fazio et al., 1977). That is, Fazio and his colleagues (1977) suggested that, once the *scope* of each theory is clearly defined by specifying its boundary conditions, the apparent contradiction between dissonance and self-perception explanations of attitude change following CAA can be resolved.

Fazio and his colleagues argued that the important distinction between attitudes and behaviors is not that they are consistent or inconsistent but rather that they are consistent or inconsistent *to some degree*. That is, some behaviors can be counterattitudinal but only marginally discrepant from a person's attitude, whereas other counterattitudinal behaviors are greatly discrepant from the relevant attitude. For example, if a student who was opposed to tuition increases wrote an essay advocating a 20% increase in tuition, the CAA would be greatly discrepant from the student's position on the issue. However, if the student wrote an essay advocating only a 2% increase in tuition, the CAA would be only slightly discrepant from the student's position.

Fazio et al. (1977) proposed boundary conditions to identify the scope of each theory. Specifically, the researchers argued that when the discrepancy between a person's attitude and a counterattitudinal behavior is relatively small there should be little physiological arousal. When the discrepancy is quite large, however, physiological arousal should occur. In short, they proposed that because there is little or no arousal with mildly discrepant CAA, Self-Perception Theory could explain subsequent attitude change. However, when the attitude–behavior discrepancy is quite large, physiological arousal is likely to occur and Dissonance Theory is needed to explain the subsequent attitude change (Fazio et al., 1977). Put another way, Self-Perception Theory explains attitude change following mildly discrepant CAA, and Cognitive Dissonance Theory explains attitude change following highly discrepant CAA (see Figure 4.6)

To test this explanation, Fazio and colleagues (1977) conducted an experiment in which participants were given the option of writing a counterattitudinal essay (high-choice condition) or were told to write the essay (low-choice condition). Based on the results of an attitude pretest, the counterattitudinal position was slightly discrepant or greatly discrepant from participants' position on the issue. In addition, the high-choice participants were asked to write their essays in a small soundproof booth during the experiment. They were told that the booths were new and that the psychology department was interested in people's reactions to them. Half of the high-choice participants were then asked if the booth made them feel tense or uncomfortable. This induction provided them with an external cue to misattribute any arousal they might experience to the booth instead of to

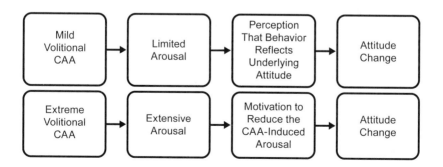

FIGURE 4.6. Integration of Dissonance Theory and Self-Perception Theory (Fazio, Zanna, & Cooper, 1977). CAA = counterattitudinal advocacy.

writing the counterattitudinal essay. The other half of the high-choice participants were not asked about their reactions to the booth, and thus were not provided with a misattribution cue.

Both the Self-Perception Theory and the Dissonance Theory predict no attitude change in the low-choice conditions (see Table 4.3). In the high-choice, no-misattribution-cue conditions, attitude change was expected to occur. In fact, attitudes in these two conditions were predicted to be significantly more favorable than attitudes in the two no-choice conditions. Thus far, the hypotheses were consistent with both traditional dissonance and self-perception experiments.

The high-choice, misattribution-cue conditions provided the critical test of the study. According to the theoretical integration proposed by Fazio and his colleagues (1977), participants in the high-choice, misattribution-cue condition who wrote a highly discrepant counterattitudinal essay were likely to experience dissonance-induced arousal. However, the presence of the misattribution cue would lead these participants to attribute their arousal to the booth and not to writing the counterattitudinal essay. Because their arousal would not be associated with the CAA, Dissonance Theory would predict no attitude change. Conversely, participants in the high-choice, misattribution-cue condition who wrote counterattitudinal essays that were less discrepant should not have experienced arousal and would not have used the booth as a misattribution cue. Nevertheless, these participants should have observed a discrepancy between their behavior and their attitude, and according to Self-Perception Theory should have adjusted their attitudes to match their behavior. If this occurred, then the attitude change of participants who wrote the slightly discrepant counterattitudinal essays in the high-choice, misattribution-cue condition would mirror the attitude change of participants writing slightly discrepant counterattitudinal essays in the high-choice, no-misattribution-cue condition. Moreover, the attitude change of participants who wrote the mildly discrepant essays in the misattribution-cue condition would be greater than the attitude change of those who wrote the highly discrepant essays in the

TABLE 4.3. Predicted Pattern of Attitude Change in the Fazio, Zanna, and Cooper (1977) Study

Discrepancy level of CAA	Low choice	High choice, no misattribution cue	High choice, misattribution cue
Small	No attitude change	Attitude change	Attitude change
Large	No attitude change	Attitude change	No attitude change

Note. Summary of data from Fazio, Zanna, and Cooper (1977).

misattribution-cue condition. This predicted pattern of attitude change in this study is reflected in Table 4.3.

The findings in this study were generally consistent with the predicted pattern of attitudes and hence consistent with the boundary conditions that Fazio and his colleagues (1977) proposed. Given their proposed boundaries, both Self-Perception Theory and Dissonance Theory are viable accounts of attitude change following CAA. When CAA is only mildly discrepant and does not heighten arousal, Self-Perception Theory can explain subsequent attitude change. When CAA is highly discrepant and heightens a person's physiological arousal, Dissonance Theory can explain subsequent attitude change.

Although Fazio and colleagues' (1977) integration of dissonance and self-perception processes is compelling, it remains at odds with research findings that arousal is both necessary and sufficient for attitude change to occur following CAA (Cooper et al., 1978; Zanna & Cooper, 1974). However, neither of the latter studies examined the effect of the level of discrepancy in the counterattitudinal message or measured its influence on arousal. Thus, although arousal remains an important factor in the explanation of attitude change following CAA, it is possible that many of the counterattitudinal behaviors we engage in are only minimally discrepant from our position on an issue and unlikely to induce arousal. In these cases, Self-Perception Theory appears to be the better theoretical explanation for attitude change.

Finally, Fazio (1987) argued that the Self-Perception Theory is a better explanation for *attitude formation* than it is for *attitude change*. Working from the functional perspective of attitudes (as elaborated in Chapter 1), Fazio argued that when people are forced to create an attitude they look to their own past relevant behavior to determine what their attitude should be. The new attitudes serve to organize information that the individual has about the attitude object (i.e., serve the knowledge function of attitudes). However, when attitudes already exist (particularly when *strong* attitudes exist), the consideration of past behavior may be a relatively unimportant determinant of attitude change.

APPLICATIONS OF COGNITIVE DISSONANCE THEORY

Social scientific theories typically have a short shelf life. There tends to be a relatively brief time period between a theory's development and when it is abandoned for a newer theory. Bucking this trend, Cognitive Dissonance Theory continues to drive research nearly 60 years after its inception, in part fueled by several theoretical modifications suggested by a number of scholars (see Cooper, 2007, 2012; Eagly & Chaiken, 1993; Harmon-Jones et al., 2009; and Harmon-Jones & Mills, 1999, for detailed recent reviews).

While much of the research discussed in this chapter is basic research that tested a theoretical concept or perspective, several recent studies have attempted to place Cognitive Dissonance Theory in a more applied context (see Stone & Fernandez, 2008, for a review). For example, Stone, Aronson, Crain, Winslow, and Fried (1994) investigated the extent to which cognitive dissonance could influence college students' purchases of condoms. Half of the participants in this experiment wrote a persuasive speech advocating condom use and presented it before a video camera. These participants were told that the best of these speeches would be shown to local high school students as part of a safe-sex campaign (i.e., a high commitment to the position). The remaining students simply wrote a message but did not present it (i.e., low commitment). Crossed with this commitment manipulation was a mindfulness manipulation. Half of the students in the high- and low-commitment conditions were asked to recall and explain the circumstances where they engaged in intercourse without using a condom (i.e., high mindfulness). The other half of the participants were not asked to recall these circumstances.

Participants who had publicly committed to a position advocating condom use *and* who had recalled their past unsafe sexual behavior were in what the researchers labeled the "hypocrisy condition," because they advocated a position that was inconsistent with their past behavior. This hypocrisy created cognitive dissonance "because although their public commitment about the importance of safe sex was consistent with their beliefs, the advocacy was inconsistent with their past risky sexual behavior" (Stone et al., 1994, pp. 121–122). After the study was over, participants were given an opportunity to purchase condoms with the money they had earned for participating in the experiment. Participants in the hypocrisy condition were more likely to purchase condoms and bought more condoms than participants in the other conditions. Stone and colleagues concluded that those in the hypocrisy condition experienced dissonance and that, as a means of reducing that dissonance, engaged in behaviors that would allow them to perform more consistent safe-sex practices (i.e., the purchase of condoms).

More recent research on the hypocrisy paradigm has more clearly placed this phenomenon under the umbrella of Cognitive Dissonance Theory (see Stone & Fernandez, 2008). Thus, not only does the Stone and colleagues (1994) study provide an applied use for Cognitive Dissonance Theory, it shows how cognitive dissonance can be created even if a message is pro-attitudinal. In this case it was the pro-attitudinal message combined with the recall of the counterattitudinal behavior that caused the dissonance.

SUMMARY

Chapter 3 examined the attitude–behavior relationship and concluded that under certain circumstances attitude change will result in behavior change. The present chapter examined the effects of behavior change on attitude change. Most studies investigating the behavior–attitude relationship have employed a CAA research paradigm. Although relatively few people willfully engage in CAA that differs strongly from their attitude without some external justification for doing so, the CAA research paradigm has proven effective in investigating the effects of behavior change on subsequent attitude change.

Several theories have been proposed to explain the effects of CAA on subsequent attitudes. Among them, Dissonance Theory has received the most attention. While its original version (Festinger, 1957) was sufficiently vague to prevent falsification, the theory has since undergone a remarkable evolution (Cooper, 2007; Greenwald & Ronis, 1978; Harmon-Jones et al., 2009; Harmon-Jones & Mills, 1999) and continues to receive considerable scholarly attention. Instead of its original description as "psychological discomfort," cognitive dissonance is presently defined as a state of physiological arousal and neurological activation. Physiological arousal associated with CAA has been linked to attitude change in several investigations.

Self-Perception Theory (Bem, 1967) posed a serious challenge to Dissonance Theory. Many studies attempted to examine the relative merits of each theory. Although research linking physiological arousal to highly discrepant counterattitudinal behavior is incompatible with Self-Perception Theory, other research has shown that minimally discrepant counterattitudinal behaviors are likely to produce little arousal. In these cases, Self-Perception Theory remains a viable explanation of attitude change and perhaps an even better explanation of attitude formation.

Collectively, the studies reviewed in this chapter provide strong evidence that behavior change can produce attitude change. Although there is some debate about the best theoretical explanation for this effect, the relationship between behaviors and subsequent attitudes is clear. Although the scope of Dissonance Theory has been narrowed over the years, the theory remains a viable tool for persuasion in a variety of influence situations (Harmon-Jones & Mills, 1999; Wicklund & Brehm, 1976).

Dissonance Theory also provides a good example of how theories work in the social sciences. Rather than remaining the property of their developers, theories belong to all interested scholars. These scholars, in turn, can use the theory (and in many cases extend or expand it) to increase understanding of the particular phenomenon under consideration. In the case of Dissonance Theory (and many other theories in this book), it is the sustained inquiry undertaken by countless scholars over the course of decades that increases our understanding of persuasive communication.

NOTE

1. There was no difference across conditions in the amount of attitude change in Study 2, but Croyle and Cooper (1983) attributed this finding to a misattribution of arousal. Participants in the high-choice condition could easily have attributed their heightened arousal to the equipment that was used to measure arousal. If this misattribution occurred, then attitude change would be unlikely for these participants.

CHAPTER 5

Cognitive Response Models
of Persuasion

LOOKING AHEAD . . . In this chapter, we discuss the all-important cognitive response models of persuasion, which over the past few decades have become the dominant conceptual framework for studying persuasion. Recall that in Chapter 3 we discussed the Theories of Reasoned Action and the Theory of Planned Behavior, which emphasize the role that cognitions (perceptions and attitudes toward a behavior) play in determining behavioral intentions and behavior. These theories focus on the effects of cognitions *about* behavior (e.g., beliefs about one's ability to perform a behavior, the consequences of performing the behavior, and social evaluations of the behavior). In Chapter 4 we discussed Cognitive Dissonance Theory and Self-Perception Theory, which describe the effects that cognitions about behavioral inconsistency have on subsequent attitude change. In this chapter, we maintain our focus on the role of cognitive processes in persuasion, but we shift gears and more closely examine the effects of message receivers' thoughts about the content of persuasive messages on their attitudes.

The models described in this chapter presume that the *cognitive responses* that people generate in response to persuasive messages—that is, what receivers think about during and following a message presentation— ultimately determine how persuasive the message is. This chapter begins with a discussion of cognitive processing in persuasive situations as a foundation and then moves to a description and evaluation of two important cognitive response models: the Elaboration Likelihood Model of persuasion (ELM) and the Heuristic–Systematic Model (HSM) of persuasion.

Early persuasion research typically examined the influence of source and message factors on message recipients' attitudes and behaviors. The traditional *message effects* research did not focus on how people processed persuasive messages but instead investigated characteristics of the message (and source) and examined how those variables influenced attitudes and behaviors. Early conceptions of persuasion adopted a Hypodermic Needle or Magic Bullet Model (Berger, 1995), with the implicit assumption that persuasive messages would be processed the same way by all message recipients in all contexts. Over time, however, it became clear that this was not the case. Scholars of persuasive communication realized that there are important differences among people and across contexts in the ways that persuasive messages are processed and understood. The emergence of cognitive models of persuasion represented a paradigm shift that focused on characteristics of the message receivers and how (and how much) they think about the content and presentation of persuasive appeals. This chapter focuses on the role of message receivers, particularly their cognitive processing of messages, in the study of persuasion.

One of the early efforts to consider the importance of message receivers in the attitude change process was Inoculation Theory (McGuire, 1964, 1999; Szabo & Pfau, 2002). As we discussed in Chapter 2, Inoculation Theory described a technique for increasing people's resistance to future persuasive attempts by providing them with counterarguments (see also Hovland et al., 1949). Having already processed the counterarguments, people are somewhat more effective at resisting a subsequent persuasive appeal. This focus on individual responses to persuasive appeals became more pronounced by the late 1960s (e.g., McGuire, 1968), became dominant during the early 1980s (e.g., Chaiken, 1980; Petty & Cacioppo, 1981), and has since evolved into present-day cognitive theories of persuasion.

The primary assumption of many cognitive theories of persuasion is that message receivers can (and often do) play an active role in forming, reinforcing, and changing their own attitudes and behaviors. According to this approach, when exposed to a persuasive message, people attempt to integrate the message appeal with their existing attitudes and knowledge about the topic. During this integration process, message recipients may generate additional arguments and information that support or oppose the message recommendation. These self-generated thoughts and arguments contribute to the success or failure of the message in important ways. If the communication evokes favorable thoughts in message recipients, those cognitions should enhance the effectiveness of the persuasive appeal. If, however, the communication inclines the recipients toward counterarguments their cognitive responses are likely to inhibit the appeal's persuasiveness.

Two empirical issues are fundamental to the utility of this perspective. First, research must document that people generate both favorable and unfavorable thoughts about the attitude object or recommendation as they process persuasive messages and that these self-generated thoughts influence their subsequent attitudes about the message recommendation. Second, research must identify the characteristics of the persuasive situations that affect the production and character of these cognitive responses.

This first issue was the focus of a program of research by Abraham Tesser and his colleagues (Sadler & Tesser, 1973; Tesser, 1978; Tesser & Conlee, 1975), who established a link between cognitive processes and attitudes. More recently, the ELM (Petty & Briñol, 2012; Petty & Cacioppo, 1981, 1986; Petty & Wegener, 1998) and the HSM (Chaiken, 1987; Chaiken & Ledgerwood, 2012; Chen & Chaiken, 1999) have sought to address the second issue by identifying factors that motivate and guide the generation of these cognitive processes. Details of these research programs are presented in the following sections of the chapter.

THE PERSUASIVE EFFECTS OF "MERE THOUGHT"

A basic assumption of cognitive models of persuasion is that people are capable of recalling and evaluating previously held information about a particular issue as they process persuasive messages. These self-generated cognitions (thoughts) combine with message content, message source, and persuasive context to affect a receiver's ongoing evaluation of the message recommendation. To demonstrate the existence and influence of these self-generated thoughts on subsequent evaluation of a stimulus object, Tesser and his colleagues conducted a series of investigations of the effects of "mere thought" on attitudes (Clarkson, Tormala, & Leone, 2011; Sadler & Tesser, 1973; Tesser, 1978; Tesser & Conlee, 1975; Tesser, Martin, & Mendolia, 1995).

In the first study, research participants were told that they were participating in a study of "first impressions" (Sadler & Tesser, 1973). Specifically, they were informed they were being matched with another person in an adjoining cubicle and then were asked to briefly introduce themselves through a self-description. After composing these individually, the participants listened to a *simulated* self-description of their partner via a recorded message. Half of the participants heard the description of a likable person, while the other half heard a less favorable description. Following these introductions, half of the participants were asked to think about the person who had just been described, and the other half were asked to complete an irrelevant task. The irrelevant task was designed to distract participants from thinking about the description they had just heard. Following the relevant or irrelevant thinking task, participants next evaluated their partner.

As expected, participants evaluated the likable partner more positively than the unlikable partner. More important, these differences were most pronounced among the participants who were given time to think about their partner before offering their impressions. That is, when offered a chance to think about their partner, people's reactions became more extreme, in either a positive or a negative direction, depending on the valence of the initial introduction (Sadler & Tesser, 1973).

Tesser and colleagues (Tesser, 1978; Tesser et al., 1995) argued that the persuasive effects of "mere thought" were guided by how people organize information in memory. Cognitive schemas (i.e., knowledge structures) influence thinking by directing attention toward certain information and away from other information and by providing rules for making inferences about the stimuli under evaluation. In the case of the Sadler and Tesser (1973) study, the likable (or unlikable) introduction served to activate favorable (or unfavorable) cognitive structures that guided the generation of thoughts about the stimulus object. These cognitive structures generated *biased processing* by affecting the favorableness (or unfavorableness) of self-generated thoughts and information recall. For example, thinking about an individual as "outgoing" (a positive trait) is likely to produce other positively evaluated trait descriptions (e.g., sociable, fun to be around, socially attractive). Thus, when given time to think about an issue (or particular person), people who evaluate it favorably are likely to generate mostly favorable thoughts about it. On the other hand, people with unfavorable evaluations are likely to generate mostly unfavorable thoughts. In this regard, the thoughts that are generated and recalled about the person are biased in favor of the positive (or negative) stimulus that prompted the additional thinking. Combined with research on cognitive schemas, Tesser's investigations of the "mere thought" phenomenon established an important link between individual cognitive responses toward a stimulus object and evaluations of that object.

Subsequent research on the "mere thought" phenomenon focused on the role of a person's *need for cognition* (A. Cohen, Stotland, & Wolfe, 1955; Petty, Briñol, Loersch, & McCaslin, 2009). Need for cognition reflects the extent to which individuals "need to engage in and enjoy effortful cognitive endeavors" (Petty & Cacioppo, 1986, p. 48). Leone (1994) hypothesized that people who have a high need for cognition are likely to consider both the pros and cons of an issue when they are engaged in mere thought. By contrast, people with a low need for cognition are less likely to consider both sides of an issue, being more likely to generate only thoughts that are consistent with their attitude on the issue.

As a result, Leone (1994) predicted and found that people who have a low need for cognition are likely to experience more attitude change after thinking about an issue because their thinking will be biased—they are only likely to generate additional thoughts that support their attitude. People with a high need for cognition, however, are likely to generate thoughts on both sides of an issue and, consequently, experience less attitude change. In this regard, the mere thought phenomenon appears to be moderated by an individual's need for cognition (Petty et al., 2009).

Research has also examined the effects of the amount of time spent thinking about a political issue on one's evaluation of that issue. In two experiments, Tesser and Conlee (1975) found a direct positive relationship between the amount of time participants spent thinking about an issue and the polarization of their attitudes about the issue. It is likely, however, that this positive linear relationship does not extend indefinitely. For example, Tesser (1978) found that the positive relationship between self-reported thought and attitude polarization diminished after a period of several minutes. As he noted, "Thoughtful people simply don't walk around with more and more extreme attitudes" (p. 301). To be sure, there appear to be practical limits to the persuasive effects of the "mere thought" phenomenon. Indeed, Clarkson and colleagues (2011) found that increasing the time for thinking after people have exhausted the pool of favorable thoughts can become counterproductive—as if to say, "I can't think of anything more favorable about this matter."

BOX 5.1. Mere Thought and Performance Evaluations

Students are quite familiar with the effects of "mere thought." When Jim was a young professor, he developed a tendency in reviewing students' papers to write comments on them whenever he identified shortcomings. This tendency of his to focus on problem issues led to more negative evaluations than Jim's students were accustomed to receiving. Over time, though, Jim made it a point to comment on not just the negative but also the positive attributes of his students' papers. Although it is hard to know for sure whether attention to the positive as well as negative aspects of each paper caused Jim to assign more favorable grades, his students were clearly more pleased with the process and perceived it to be fairer.

This same phenomenon can occur in performance evaluations. A supervisor who likes a subordinate may naturally develop a tendency to overlook the employee's limitations during evaluations, while one who dislikes an employee might focus greater attention on negative aspects of the employee's job performance. In both grading and performance appraisal situations, one's explicit awareness of the mere thought phenomenon can lead to more balanced evaluations.

Nevertheless, these studies document the influence of self-generated thoughts on the evaluation of stimulus objects. Whether the object under consideration is a political issue or another person, the opportunity to think about the stimulus object is likely to make favorable evaluations more favorable and unfavorable evaluations more unfavorable. This attitude polarization process is similar to the group polarization effects discussed later in Chapter 9. In the present case, however, biased processing (i.e., recalling either primarily favorable or primarily unfavorable thoughts) appears to be limited to people with low need for cognition and is the result of individual cognitive processes rather than of group interaction.

More recently, researchers have investigated the effects of meta-cognition (thinking about one's thoughts) on the confidence with which beliefs are held (see Petty, Briñol, Tormala, & Wegener, 2007). Researchers have found that emotional states also increase confidence in beliefs that are held, with people exhibiting more confidence in their thoughts when they are happy than when they are sad (Tiedens & Linton, 2001). The *self-validation hypothesis* suggests that the more confidence people have in their thoughts, the greater the effect of those thoughts on attitudes (Petty, Briñol, & Tormala, 2002; Clarkson et al., 2011). Thus, mere thought about an attitude object not only causes a more favorable (or unfavorable) attitude about the object but also increases the confidence with which one holds those thoughts (and that increased confidence also affects one's attitude).

Applied to persuasive transactions, this body of research suggests that message recipients' thought processes play a significant role in determining the effectiveness of a persuasive message. Investigations of several different persuasive phenomena have established that people are capable of generating their own arguments to support a message recommendation (Vinokur & Burnstein, 1974) or to oppose it (M. Burgoon, M. Cohen, M. D. Miller, & Montgomery, 1978; McGuire, 1961b; G. R. Miller & M. Burgoon, 1978). For example, Hample (1978) argued that if a persuasive message contained no evidence supporting the claim, receivers would add the missing information from what they have in memory. Given the potential persuasive influence of self-generated arguments, researchers have focused attention on the processes that guide the generation of these cognitive responses and determine their persuasive effects.

During the early 1980s, two contemporaneous programs of research emerged that attempted to model factors that affect the production of cognitive responses to persuasive messages and explain their influence on individual attitudes. The ELM (Petty & Cacioppo, 1981, 1986) has received the most attention from persuasion scholars and is most closely associated with traditional cognitive response approaches to persuasion (see Petty, Ostrom, & Brock, 1981). A second model, the HSM (Chaiken, 1987), is more firmly rooted in theories of social cognition. Although the two models are similar in many respects, there are also important differences between them. Because their differences are more subtle than their obvious similarities, students of persuasion often discuss these models as though their conceptual components are interchangeable. However, the theoretical differences between these two programs of research necessitate a separate discussion of the respective models.

THE ELM

The ELM evolved from dissatisfaction with the contradictory findings of various theoretical approaches to studying persuasive communication. Petty and Cacioppo (1981) argued that many of the theoretical approaches they uncovered in their review of the persuasion research reflected one of two distinct routes to persuasion. The *central route* to persuasion is an active and mindful process marked by a careful scrutiny of message content and posits that attitude change is a function of message content and

---

BOX 5.2. Johnnie Cochran and the Peripheral Route to Persuasion

Many years ago, Jim was consulting with an oil and gas company that was involved in litigation over the calculation of royalty rates for oil produced from land owned by the state of California and leased to the oil company. The trial involved a considerable amount of technical testimony about the low quality of California crude oil and the cost of processing the oil in accordance with environmental regulations. The long trial also had a few interesting side notes, including a visit to the courtroom by Johnnie Cochran. Johnnie Cochran was a famous Los Angeles attorney who in 1995 successfully defended O. J. Simpson in a nationally televised trial after he was charged with murdering his former wife, Nicole Brown, and Ronald Goldman.

   One day, as Jim was entering the courthouse with the trial team for the oil royalty case, a police officer told the lead trial lawyer that "your friend" was also in the courthouse that day. The trial lawyer, who was white, requested that the officer ask Cochran to "stop by" when he had a chance. A few hours later, just as everyone was leaving the courtroom for a lunch break, Cochran entered the courtroom and shook hands with the lead trial lawyer. Several members of the predominantly black jury saw the interaction, and there was little doubt that their affinity to Cochran enhanced the credibility of the lead trial lawyer. While this interaction was definitely not central to the issues in the trial, it is nonetheless an excellent example of the *peripheral route* to persuasion.

recipients' self-generated thoughts (what Petty & Cacioppo [1981, 1986] called "elaboration"). A second general approach, the *peripheral route*, reflects a less effortful attitude change process determined by the association of message recommendations with positive or negative cues in the message environment (Petty & Cacioppo, 1981, 1986).

The ELM posits that when message receivers engage in central processing, the characteristics of persuasive messages (particularly a variable called *argument quality*) determine the extent and direction of attitude change. When people engage in peripheral processing, the persuasive cues that are not directly related to the quality of the message content (e.g., the expertise, trustworthiness, and attractiveness of the source as well as the message length) determine the extent and direction of attitude change.

Distinguishing between Central and Peripheral Processing

Given the distinction between central and peripheral routes to persuasion, the primary goal of the ELM is to identify the conditions under which message receivers engage in each form of processing. The ELM's first two postulates were derived to assist in this endeavor. This model's primary postulate is that people are motivated to hold *correct* attitudes. Referring to Festinger's (1954) Social Comparison Theory, Petty and Cacioppo (1986) argued that "incorrect or improper attitudes are generally maladaptive and can have deleterious behavioral, affective, and cognitive consequences" (p. 6). As a result, people are often motivated to actively process persuasive messages in an effort to adopt an appropriate or correct attitude about message recommendations. However, the ELM's second postulate recognizes that, although people are often motivated to maintain correct attitudes, they simply cannot actively process every persuasive message that comes their way. As a consequence, the ELM posits that the amount of cognitive effort people are willing or able to engage in to process persuasive appeals varies widely across people and situations (Petty & Cacioppo, 1986, p. 6).

To represent the range of processing activity available to message receivers, Petty and Cacioppo (1986) introduced the concept of an *elaboration likelihood continuum*. One end of this continuum represents highly active cognitive processing, in which message receivers generate their own cognitive responses in an effort to scrutinize message content. According to the ELM, when conditions are ripe for this type of message processing, elaboration likelihood is high and the central route to persuasion is most probable. In such conditions, issue-relevant thoughts generated by receivers affect attitude change and help determine the overall effectiveness of the message. If these thoughts are favorable toward the message recommendation, acceptance of the message recommendation is more likely.

Conversely, thoughts opposing the message recommendation are likely to decrease acceptance.

The other end of the continuum represents processes that require very little cognitive effort. Instead of paying careful attention to message content, receivers rely on persuasive cues in the message environment to make decisions about message recommendations. When conditions are ripe for this type of processing, elaboration likelihood is low and the peripheral route to persuasion is most probable. When receivers use a peripheral route to persuasion, positive persuasion cues in the message environment (e.g., a highly attractive source) increase message acceptance, whereas negative persuasion cues (e.g., an unattractive source) decrease message acceptance.

Predicting Message Elaboration

The ELM's second postulate suggests that cognitive elaboration of persuasive messages varies widely across people and situations. Thus, the crux of this model is identifying the conditions under which message elaboration is likely (and unlikely) to occur. A large variety of situational and personal characteristics may affect elaboration likelihood. For the most part, these characteristics have been subsumed by two factors—*motivation* and ability—that have received considerable attention from ELM researchers.

Motivation

According to the ELM, message receivers must be motivated to engage in effortful cognitive elaboration of a persuasive message before they can actually carry it out. One factor that influences a message recipient's level of motivation is involvement with the issue. Accordingly, receivers who perceive a high degree of issue involvement (i.e., personal relevance of the message topic) should be motivated to carefully scrutinize message content in hopes of making the correct decision about the message recommendation. Though a variety of other factors, such as need for social approval and self-monitoring, may also affect a person's motivation to scrutinize a message, issue involvement has been used most often to influence receiver motivation in prior ELM research (see Petty & Briñol, 2012; Petty & Cacioppo, 1986; Petty & Wegener, 1998).

As discussed earlier in this chapter, one individual difference characteristic that affects a person's motivation, and perhaps his or her ability, to elaborate message content is the person's need for cognition (A. Cohen et al., 1955; Petty & Cacioppo, 1986). Although this factor has been considered mainly to reflect a person's motivation to scrutinize persuasive messages, it may also reflect his or her ability to do so. If you have a high need for cognition and routinely scrutinize persuasive message content, you are likely to develop the cognitive skills necessary to effectively scrutinize even very difficult messages. Thus, people with a strong need for cognition are probably more adept at scrutinizing message content than are those with relatively little need for it.

Ability

A second factor that affects message elaboration is cognitive ability. According to the ELM, recipients must be both willing and able to cognitively elaborate message content in order for central processing to occur. ELM researchers have largely ignored this factor, although investigations of message comprehension underscore the importance of this variable. For example, distracting stimuli (Buller, 1986), message distortion (Eagly, 1974; Eagly & Warren, 1976), and message difficulty (Chaiken & Eagly, 1976) have all been found to reduce message learning and comprehension. As such, these variables should affect cognitive evaluation of message content. Thus, even though message recipients have the cognitive ability to elaborate message content, message presentations that are difficult to understand are less likely to result in cognitive elaboration.

In summary, the ELM posits that receivers must be willing and able to cognitively elaborate messages in order to travel the central route to persuasion. Issue involvement is one factor that reflects motivation, message comprehensibility is one factor that affects ability, and need for cognition is an individual factor that probably affects both motivation and ability to scrutinize message content.

Message Elaboration and Attitude Change

The ELM's predictions regarding message processing are straightforward: "As motivation and/or ability to process arguments is decreased, peripheral cues become relatively more important determinants of persuasion. Conversely, as argument scrutiny is increased, peripheral cues become relatively less important determinants of persuasion" (Petty & Cacioppo, 1986, p. 5). That is, when central processing occurs, the quality of message arguments (i.e., argument quality) will influence attitudes more than persuasive cues (e.g., source credibility). However, when peripheral processing is predominant, message arguments are relatively unimportant and external persuasion cues affect attitude change.

An impressive number of experiments have examined the validity of the ELM, and for the most part they have employed the same experimental procedure (see Petty & Briñol, 2012, for a review). This general procedure evolved from the original model tests that we discussed in Chapter 2 (e.g.,

Petty, Cacioppo, et al., 1981). This procedure involves creating two persuasive messages that advocate the same position (typically a tuition increase or requiring comprehensive exams for undergraduates). One message contains strong arguments supporting the message recommendation, and the other contains weak arguments. When these messages are presented to research participants (usually college students), they are typically attributed either to an expert or to a less authoritative source. Thus four message categories are created: strong arguments from an authoritative source, weak arguments from an authoritative source, strong arguments from a less authoritative source, weak arguments from a less authoritative source.

To control the motivation factor, the experimenters usually tell half of the message recipients that the message is personally relevant to them and tell the remaining participants that the message has little relevance to them. For example, when messages advocate a tuition increase or comprehensive exams, half of the student participants are told that the advocated action will begin the following year, while the remaining participants are told that the recommended action is not scheduled to occur for several years (or will occur at another university). When the recommended action is proposed for several years in the future (and/or at another school), the message has low outcomes relevant involvement for message recipients.

The three variables manipulated with this procedure reflect three important components of the ELM. Although a number of variables have played this role (Petty & Briñol, 2012; Petty & Cacioppo, 1986; Petty & Wegener, 1998), the receiver's motivation to scrutinize message content is typically manipulated by varying levels of issue involvement. Argument quality typically represents a central cue that may or may not be scrutinized by message recipients, and source expertise typically represents a peripheral cue that is external to the message content.[1]

Consistent with ELM predictions, Petty and colleagues have repeatedly found that, under conditions of high issue involvement, argument quality has a stronger effect on attitudes than does source expertise. When receiver involvement is low, the source expertise manipulation routinely has a much stronger effect on attitudes than the argument quality manipulation (see Petty & Cacioppo, 1986). In statistical terms, two two-way interactions provide support for the ELM. In the first interaction, issue involvement and argument quality combine to affect attitudes (see Figure 5.1). In this case, argument quality has a stronger impact on attitudes when issue involvement is high, compared to when issue involvement is low. The second interaction reflects the combined effects of issue involvement and source expertise on attitudes (see Figure 5.2). Specifically, source credibility will have a stronger impact on attitudes when issue involvement is low (compared to when it is high).

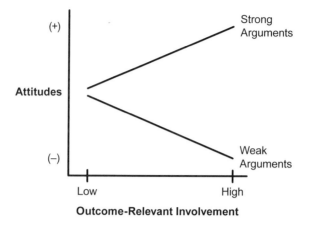

FIGURE 5.1. Combined effect of outcome-relevant involvement and argument quality on attitudes.

Evaluating the Utility of the ELM

The ELM is an important theory of persuasion. The metaphor of the central and peripheral routes of persuasion and the corresponding prediction that different variables likely influence responses at different points along the elaboration likelihood continuum are powerful ideas. For example, until the ELM came along (as we will discuss in Chapter 7), reviewers found it difficult to explain inconsistencies in the persuasive impact of evidence.

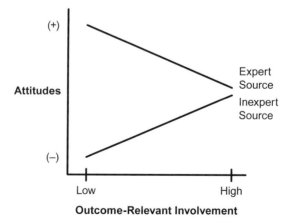

FIGURE 5.2. Combined effect of outcome-relevant involvement and source expertise on attitudes.

More recent reviews all conclude that evidence most influences attitude change when receivers actively cognitively process the message (e.g., Reinard, 1988; Reynolds & Reynolds, 2002).

Although Petty and Cacioppo, and their colleagues, have marshaled considerable evidence in support of the ELM, several investigations have raised numerous concerns about the logical validity and practical utility of this model. These concerns stem from the theoretical specificity of, and the quality of empirical support for, the model. We dedicate considerable space to this discussion because the ELM was a dominant model of persuasion research for over 30 years, and (as with our discussion of Dissonance Theory in Chapter 4), examination of the evolution of this model informs our current understanding of cognitive response approaches to persuasion. This review also serves as an excellent foundation for our discussion of the Heuristic-Systematic Model of persuasion (Chaiken, 1987).

Theoretical Limitations of the ELM

In the first published critique of the ELM, Jim questioned the extent to which it accurately reflected human information processing capacities (Stiff, 1986). Specifically, he argued that the ELM depicted humans as single-channel information processors who can deal with only one stream of information at a time. Jim argued that this view was inconsistent with theories of information processing that maintain that humans are capable of parallel information processing (i.e., capable of dealing with two simultaneous streams of data; see Kahneman, 1973; Stiff, 1986). At issue is whether people are able to engage in both central and peripheral processing of persuasive messages simultaneously. If message content and peripheral cues can be processed in parallel, then both types of information may simultaneously affect attitudes. However, as articulated by Petty and Cacioppo (1986), the ELM postulates "a trade-off between argument elaboration and the operation of peripheral cues" (p. 21). This postulate led to an interpretation of the ELM as a single-channel processing model (Stiff, 1986).

The practical implication of this debate centers on the persuasive effects of variables that are processed centrally and peripherally. That is, in many persuasive situations (but not all of them; see Petty & Briñol, 2012; Petty & Wegener, 1998), message arguments are processed centrally and persuasive cues (e.g., source characteristics) are processed peripherally. However, in circumstances where source characteristics like physical attractiveness are relevant to the message argument (e.g., an attractive model promoting hair shampoo), the source characteristics can also be centrally processed as though they are part of the message argument (Trampe, Stapel, Siero, & Mulder, 2010). In these situations, single-channel processing models would predict that *either* message arguments or persuasive cues (*but not both*) are processed and subsequently influence attitudes. Conversely, parallel processing models predict the simultaneous evaluation of both message and source characteristics and specify that *both* types of processing may contribute independently or together to influence attitude change. Specifically, parallel processing models allow for equal contributions from both types of processing, a clear departure from the processing trade-off initially described by Petty and Cacioppo (1986, p. 21).

To reflect the persuasive effects of parallel processing, Jim (Stiff, 1986) proposed an alternative persuasion model derived from Kahneman's (1973) Elastic Capacity Model (ECM) of human information processing. The ECM posits that the amount of cognitive capacity expands and contracts, depending on the importance of the issue. Applied to persuasion settings, the ECM posits that message receivers are capable of parallel processing and specifies the conditions under which they engage in central and/or peripheral processing. Specifically, the ECM predicts that, under conditions of low issue involvement, receivers engage in *neither* central nor peripheral processing, because they are unmotivated to do so. At moderate levels of involvement, receivers are sufficiently motivated to engage in *both* central and peripheral (i.e., parallel) processing. And at high levels of involvement, while parallel processing is possible under the ECM, receivers will most likely focus their attention on a single processing task. Given the importance of holding the correct attitude on a personally relevant issue, Jim hypothesized, receivers would engage primarily in central message processing (Stiff, 1986).

The predictive differences between the ELM and Jim's application of the ECM are apparent. The ELM predicts a negative relationship between a person's level of involvement and the influence of peripheral processing on attitudes and a positive relationship between involvement and the influence of central processing on attitudes (see Figure 5.3). Conversely, applied to the same persuasive settings, the ECM predicts a curvilinear (inverted-U-shaped) relationship between receiver involvement and the influence of peripheral processing on attitudes. Similar to the ELM, however, the ECM predicts a positive linear relationship between receiver involvement and the influence of central processing on attitudes (see Figure 5.4).

Jim tested the competing predictions from the ECM and ELM in a meta-analytic review of persuasion research that examined the effects of source credibility and message evidence on attitudes (Stiff, 1986). Results of the meta-analysis regarding the effects of message evidence (i.e., central processing) were consistent with both the ELM and the ECM. Specifically, Stiff reported a positive linear relationship between issue involvement and the effects of supporting information on attitudes. In short, as involvement increased, evidence had greater influence on attitudes.

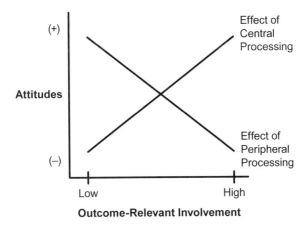

FIGURE 5.3. Effects of central and peripheral processing on attitudes across levels of outcome-relevant involvement as predicted by the ELM.

Jim's meta-analytic review also found a curvilinear relationship between receiver involvement and the effects of source credibility on attitudes (Stiff, 1986). Source credibility influenced attitude change most strongly at moderate (as compared with both low and high) issue involvement. Assuming that source credibility effects reflected peripheral processing, this latter finding is consistent with the ECM and incompatible with the ELM.

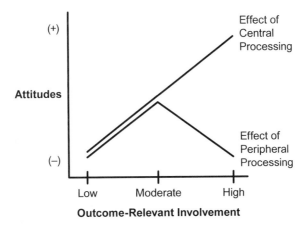

FIGURE 5.4. Effects of central and peripheral processing on attitudes across levels of outcome-relevant involvement as predicted by the ECM.

Petty and his associates have, over time, changed their view of how involvement and persuasive cues (i.e., source credibility) influence attitudes. In their initial response to Jim's research findings, Petty and his colleagues criticized the characterization of the ELM as a single-channel processing model. Specifically, Petty et al. (1987) waffled in saying that their view of the ELM "does not mean that people are incapable of processing *both* arguments and cues" (p. 238, emphasis in original). More recently, Petty and his colleagues' views have become more consistent with what Jim argued (Stiff, 1986). For example, Petty and Wegener (1999) argued that the relationship between peripheral processing (e.g., source credibility) and attitude change is curvilinear. Specifically, they noted that:

> when one is going from extremely low levels of elaboration likelihood to moderately low levels of elaboration likelihood, the impact of some peripheral processes . . . might be increased. Once one is past the minimal point on the continuum necessary to invoke the process, however, moving higher along the continuum should reduce the impact of the process on attitudes. (p. 67)

Given this claim, as involvement shifts from low to moderate, the persuasive influence of both argument quality and persuasive cues (e.g., source credibility) increases. This strongly suggests that people have the ability to process both arguments and persuasive cues simultaneously (see Figure 5.4). More recently, Petty and Briñol (2012) have posited that parallel processing is typical, noting that "much of the time, persuasion is determined by a mixture of these [i.e., central and peripheral] processes" (p. 226).

A second theoretical limitation of the ELM is its inability to specify *a priori* the conditions under which particular variables play a particular role. Original ELM investigations uniformly associated message content cues (e.g., argument quality) with central processing and persuasion cues (e.g., source expertise and attractiveness) with peripheral processing (Petty & Cacioppo, 1981). That is, under conditions of high receiver involvement, the positive relationship between argument quality and attitudes was interpreted as evidence of central processing. Under conditions of low receiver involvement, the positive relationship between source expertise and attitudes was interpreted as evidence of peripheral processing (Petty, Cacioppo, et al., 1981). By 1986, however, Petty and Cacioppo (1986) indicated that the same variable could serve multiple persuasive roles. Expanding on the notion later on, Petty and Wegener (1999) postulated that "a variable can influence attitudes in four ways: (1) by serving as an argument, (2) by serving as a cue, (3) by determining the extent of elaboration, and (4) by producing a bias in elaboration" (p. 51). For example, the beautiful scenery depicted in a vacation resort advertisement is likely a peripheral cue if the recipient is not thinking about the scenery very much. As elaboration likelihood increases, however, that same scenery can act as a message argument because the scenery is relevant to the recipient's evaluation of the resort's quality (Petty & Wegener, 1999). If the same scenery appeared in an advertisement for an automobile, on the other hand, it is likely to be processed peripherally no matter how much elaboration occurs. As M. Burgoon (1989) noted, classification of these cues is often

> derived from inferring antecedents from consequents, or a teleological method of explanation. Thus, *if* specific outcomes occur (e.g., attitude change), then certain kinds of intrapsychic message processing had to have occurred. Such an explanatory mechanism is relatively unproductive for people interested in the social effects of strategy choices. The more appropriate approach is to specify *a priori* how message variables affect the persuasive process. (p. 157)

In other words, this conceptual flexibility clearly identifies the ELM as "primarily a descriptive, rather than explanatory, theory of persuasion" (Eagly & Chaiken, 1993, p. 321). According to the ELM, whether a recipient engages in central or peripheral processing depends on where he or she is on the elaboration likelihood continuum. "The actual placement of an individual along the continuum, of course, cannot be known until after the message or attitude object has been processed" (Petty & Wegener, 1999, p. 66). As a consequence, rather than predicting *a priori* whether central or peripheral processing will occur, the ELM looks at attitude and other study data to determine, after the fact, what persuasive process must have occurred. Such practice "allows the ELM to explain all possible outcomes of an experimental study without predicting which will occur," making it practically impossible to falsify (Stiff & Boster, 1987, p. 251). If a theory is not falsifiable, it can explain all experimental results but not predict when each will occur. As we mentioned in our critique of Dissonance Theory (Chapter 4), from a scientific perspective, if a theory is not falsifiable, then we have no confidence about the validity of the theory (K. I. Miller, 2005).

Empirical Limitations of the ELM

In addition to pointing out the ELM's theoretical shortcomings, literature reviews have challenged the legitimacy of empirical support for the model. Perhaps the most important revelation emerged from a meta-analysis of the involvement literature (Johnson & Eagly, 1989) that we will discuss in detail in Chapter 9. When cumulating the effects of issue involvement (what they called outcome-relevant involvement) on attitudes, Johnson and Eagly (1989) found evidence of an involvement by argument quality interaction, as predicted by the ELM. They noted, however, that there was considerable variation among individual studies' findings. Some studies found large interaction effects, while others found none at all. Johnson and Eagly found one interesting moderator variable that helped explain that variation, namely, *who* performed the study. Specifically, studies authored by Petty, Cacioppo, their students, or their colleagues found the predicted interaction between argument quality and involvement. Studies performed by researchers not affiliated with Petty or Cacioppo found either weak or no evidence of this same interaction (Johnson & Eagly, 1989, p. 304). That is, studies conducted by Petty, Cacioppo, and their colleagues consistently found the involvement by argument quality interaction predicted by the ELM, but no one else could.[2]

One possible explanation for this curious result stems from the operational definition of argument quality (i.e., how strong and weak arguments are supposed to be created). Petty and Cacioppo (1986) defined a strong argument as information that, when scrutinized by message receivers, generates at least 65% favorable or supportive cognitions and 35% or less unfavorable cognitions. They defined a weak argument as information that, when scrutinized by message receivers, produces only 35% (or less) favorable cognitions (pp. 54–55).

This view of argument quality has several important implications for the study of persuasion. First, although the variable is called *argument quality*, we (Mongeau & Stiff, 1993) argued that the variable being manipulated has little to do with actual message arguments. Thus, we questioned the validity of the ELM's argument quality construct. In an important clarification, Petty, Wegener, Fabrigar, Priester, and Cacioppo (1994) responded that we misunderstood the intended purpose of the argument quality manipulation. Specifically, they asserted: "The ELM has never attempted to provide a theory of argument quality, cogency, or quality per se. Instead, argument strength [quality] manipulations have been used as a methodological tool for indexing the level of argument-based processing underlying postcommunication attitudes" (p. 350).

In short, the argument quality manipulation, as defined in the ELM, is designed to influence the valence (i.e., positive or negative nature) of recipients' cognitions *if they actively process the message*. The argument quality variable in the ELM says nothing about the actual quality or strength of an argument (Petty & Cacioppo, 1986; Petty & Wegener, 1999) as it is typically discussed by communication scholars (Reinard, 1988; Toulmin, 1964). Thus, the practical value of the argument quality variable (and the entire ELM) is very limited. For example, the ELM can provide no useful advice as to how to construct a persuasive message (apart from recommending producing a message that generates as many positive cognitions as possible).

The final implication of Petty and Cacioppo's (1986) operational definition of argument quality is that it may be the reason why they could consistently produce the interaction between argument quality and involvement that eluded so many other researchers (Johnson & Eagly, 1989). The *proper* way of manipulating argument quality was not explicated until nearly a decade after ELM-like studies were initially performed (i.e., Petty & Cacioppo, 1986). Studies conducted by scholars other than Petty, Cacioppo, and colleagues employed more traditional definitions of argument quality—for example, based on their structure or logical validity (cf. Reinard, 1988; Toulmin, 1964) rather than the pattern of cognitions they produced. Consequently, the failure to replicate the argument quality–involvement interaction may stem from the use of a different way of manipulating argument quality. Careful examination of these methodological differences may eventually resolve the conflicting findings of early experiments conducted by Petty, Cacioppo, and their associates versus those conducted by other researchers.

Although several important questions remain, the ELM has provided evidence of two types of message processing and has established an important relationship between receiver motivation, message scrutiny, cognitive responses, and attitudes (Petty & Wegener, 1998; Petty & Briñol, 2012). In addition, the ELM has spawned considerable research and renewed interest in the study of persuasive message processing. This research has helped to clarify the previously inconsistent research on several constructs—including message evidence and source credibility—that are reviewed in the next few chapters.

A second cognitive model of persuasion, the HSM (Chaiken, 1987; Chaiken & Ledgerwood, 2012; Chen & Chaiken, 1999), was developed concurrently with the ELM. Although the two models share a number of conceptual similarities, they differ in several significant ways.

THE HSM

Although Chaiken's (1987) HSM has received considerably less attention from persuasion scholars than the ELM, the HSM provides an attractive alternative to persuasion researchers seeking a cognitive model of persuasion (see Chen & Chaiken, 1999, and Chaiken & Ledgerwood, 2012, for reviews). Like the ELM, the HSM posits that two distinct cognitive processes guide the evaluation of persuasive messages. One process, labeled *systematic processing*, involves the careful scrutiny of message content and is similar to Petty and Cacioppo's concept of central processing. A second type of processing, labeled "heuristic processing," involves very little cognitive effort by message receivers.

Although Chaiken's (1987) *systematic processing* is similar to Petty and Cacioppo's (1986) *central processing*, the concepts of *heuristic processing* and *peripheral processing* are distinct. Petty and Cacioppo's peripheral processing reflects a wide variety of theoretical processes such as Reactance Theory (Brehm, 1966), identification processes (Kelman, 1961), and models of classical conditioning (Staats & Staats, 1957), among others. Thus, Chaiken (1987) claims that peripheral processing features a wide variety of motivational orientations, while heuristic processing typically reflects only one. Specifically, in heuristic processing, receivers employ cognitive heuristics to assess the validity of a persuasive message. *Heuristics* are simple decision rules that allow people to evaluate message recommendations in a simple and easy fashion. For example, using the heuristic that "experts are generally correct" permits receivers to make a decision about a message recommendation based only on a quick assessment of the source's expertise and the position that he or she advocates. Thus, peripheral processing in the ELM reflects a variety of psychological motivations that associate a speaker's position with rewarding or unrewarding persuasive cues. Conversely, heuristic processing in the HSM reflects a single motivation, that is, evaluation of the message recommendation through simple decision rules.[3]

The centerpiece of the HSM is the explicit recognition that people are typically minimalist information processors (i.e., cognitive misers; Fiske & Taylor, 1991) who are unwilling to engage in highly active, conscious processing of persuasive message content unless it is really necessary. Applying prior investigations of cognitive heuristics (Kahneman & Frederick, 2002; Kahneman & Tversky, 1973; Tversky & Kahneman, 1974, 1982), Chaiken (1987, p. 4) argued that many persuasion cues are processed with simple schemas or decision rules that are learned through experience and observation. For example, many people hold the conviction that "taxes are bad," which leads to a simple decision rule that messages advocating tax increases should be rejected. Indeed, the political effectiveness (at least temporarily if not ultimately) of George H. W. Bush's now famous 1988 campaign pledge, "Read my lips . . . no new taxes" was derived from the assumption that voters would employ this simple heuristic, hopefully increasing the likelihood they would vote for him.

Other, more general, heuristics may guide the processing of many persuasive messages. For example, the heuristic that *experts are generally correct* is a decision rule that evolves over time as receivers note that sources with expertise are likely to advocate the correct positions on issues. Once established, this heuristic is available for use in evaluating messages from both expert and inexpert sources. Applied to persuasion settings, this heuristic may lead message receivers to accept the recommendations of an expert source (or to reject recommendations of inexpert sources) without the need for carefully examining the reasons supporting the recommendation that

---

BOX 5.3. Assessing the Credibility of Witness Testimony

Jim routinely uses the HSM when helping lawyers to prepare their expert witnesses for trial testimony. In complex cases, expert witness testimony is often so technical that jurors cannot readily understand it. However well one presents graphs, charts, and other visuals, the fact is that many jurors will struggle to grasp the expert's testimony. As a consequence, jurors often rely on *heuristics* to make judgments about the testimony provided. Consequently, Jim instructs his clients to provide simple decision rules that jurors can use to make judgments about the complex testimony.

The influence of heuristic processing was apparent in a lawsuit alleging that an accounting firm was negligent because, when performing its annual audit, one of its auditors failed to detect corporate fraud. When it came time for the accountant who performed the audit to provide his testimony, the lawyers spent a considerable amount of time reviewing the accountant's credentials, Generally Accepted Auditing Standards (GAAS), and evidence that the accountant followed those standards. Next, jurors were able to view the original audit records, which revealed all the intricate details, including check marks and notes made by the accountant. The jurors later indicated that, although they were unable to follow the technical accounting issues, they concluded that the accountant was well qualified, that he followed appropriate standards, and that he carefully performed the audit. Consequently, they found that he was not at fault for failing to detect the fraud perpetrated by the client's corporate executives.

---

the source is making. In much the same fashion, the heuristic "long messages are strong messages" may produce greater acceptance of a message containing four supporting arguments than one containing a single argument. In this case, the sheer number of arguments (regardless of how good they are) is the critical factor for attitude change.

Unlike the careful scrutiny of message content, cognitive heuristics require little cognitive effort. In general, all that is required is the proper application of an available heuristic in an appropriate situation. If the message characteristics match a general prototypical example of the heuristic (i.e., if it is appropriate), then the decision rule is likely to guide the evaluation of the persuasive appeal. Thus, the heuristic "Experts are generally correct" or "People I like usually have correct opinions" may guide the evaluation of a speaker's recommendation, once the level of the speaker's expertise or likability has been established (Chaiken, 1987; Cialdini, 2009). In much the same way, the consensus heuristic "If other people believe it, then it is probably true" can often substitute for careful scrutiny of message content, particularly in social settings (Axsom, Yates, & Chaiken, 1987). Once devised, these heuristics are available for use by message receivers. The successful application of these heuristics depends on both their relevance to the particular persuasive context and how frequently they have been used in the past (Fiske & Taylor, 1991; Higgins, 1996, 2012; Wyer & Srull, 1981). Higgins, King, and Mavin (1982) note that cognitive constructs (e.g., heuristics) that people frequently use to evaluate others are likely to become chronically accessible. Bargh and Pratto (1986) observed that the "frequency of use of a cognitive process results in its becoming more efficient, and eventually in its automation" (pp. 295–296; see also our discussion of the automatic nature of attitudes in Chapter 3). Thus, cognitive heuristics allow many persuasive cues to be processed with comparatively little real cognitive effort on the part of message receivers.

Predicting Systematic and Heuristic Processing

While the HSM is a cognitive model of persuasion, it does not emphasize message receivers' cognitive *responses*. Instead, Chaiken (1987) describes how cognitive processes permit message receivers to evaluate persuasive messages without much cognitive activity or even conscious control. As cognitive misers (Fiske & Taylor, 1991), people generally seek to minimize their cognitive activity, preferring less effortful methods of information processing. Thus, although systematic processing is one method of message evaluation, it is employed less often than cognitive heuristics.

The central focus of the HSM is to describe the conditions that determine when message receivers will rely on cognitive heuristics and when they will engage in systematic processing to evaluate persuasive messages. In doing so, a critical assumption underlying the HSM is that "heuristic and systematic processing of persuasion cues represent parallel, rather than mutually exclusive, modes of message processing" (Chaiken, 1987, p. 11). Thus, whereas the ELM initially posited that central and peripheral processing do not occur at the same time, the HSM has always maintained the view that systematic and heuristic processing "co-occur and even interact" (Chaiken & Ledgerwood, 2012).

Given the minimal cognitive load required for heuristic processing, people with relatively low motivation to scrutinize a message can form judgments about the message by using simple decision rules. Systematic evaluation of persuasive messages, on the other hand, is predicated on the receiver's ability to comprehend the message and motivation to exert the cognitive effort required for systematic processing (Chaiken, 1987; Chaiken & Ledgerwood, 2012; Chen & Chaiken, 1999). Thus, although they are derived from different theoretical perspectives, the HSM and the ELM hypothesize similar roles for motivation and ability in determining the extent of systematic (central) processing. As a result, the situational and individual difference factors that affect receiver ability and motivation are equally relevant to the HSM as to the ELM.

Because it reflected a bold attempt to integrate the conflicting predictions and findings from a wide variety of different persuasion theories, the ELM has received considerably more attention from persuasion scholars than the HSM. However, the HSM offers an attractive alternative to researchers and practitioners who have concerns about the ELM's theoretical and empirical limitations.

Perhaps the single greatest asset of the HSM is its derivation from a single theoretical perspective: a social-cognitive approach to information processing. In contrast, the ELM is based on the premise that "many theories of attitude change could be roughly placed along an elaboration likelihood continuum" (Petty & Cacioppo, 1986, p. 8). While the ELM is quite broad theoretically, this breadth comes at the expense of a lack of specificity. As we argued earlier, the ELM lacks precision in identifying the cognitive processes that underlie the effects of messages on attitudes.

Shortcomings aside, these two models have made significant contributions to understanding speaker, message, and receiver factors that affect attitude change. Specific tests of these models have produced an overwhelming volume of persuasion research during the past three decades (Chaiken & Lederwood, 2012; Petty & Briñol, 2012). Though far from complete, these research programs reflect the dramatic shift from the source-centered approaches to persuasion that were prevalent into the 1970s to the receiver-centered focus that is apparent in much of today's theorizing about persuasive communication.

THE UNIMODEL

Although the ELM and HSM have been the leading persuasion theories for three decades, a new model was introduced during the late 1990s to challenge the underlying tenets of these models. The key concept embodied in the *Unimodel*, which was introduced by Kruglanski and colleagues (Kruglanski, Erbs, Pierro, Mannetti, & Chun, 2006; Kruglanski & Thompson, 1999; Thompson, Kruglanski, & Spiegel, 2000), is the notion that there is no need for two routes or modes of message processing, because central and peripheral (or systematic and heuristic) processing are both examples of the same underlying process.

When applied to the study of persuasion, this general model of information processing posits that persuasion "is a process during which beliefs are formed on the basis of appropriate evidence." In turn, *evidence* is "information relevant to a conclusion" (Kruglanski & Thompson, 1999,

p. 89). Given these definitions, both message arguments and persuasive (or heuristic) cues represent forms of evidence that are more similar than they are different. According to the Unimodel, the distinction between heuristic (or peripheral) cues and message arguments is a difference in *evidence content* relevant to a conclusion rather than any qualitative difference in how that content is processed (Kruglanski & Thompson, 1999, p. 90). In this regard, the Unimodel assumes that message arguments and heuristic/peripheral cues are processed in the same way. What looks like two persuasion processes occurs because source information is presented, and is typically processed, *before* message arguments.

Although it has been more than a decade since the Unimodel was introduced, it has received mixed reviews (Chaiken, Duckworth, & Darke, 1999; Crano, 2006; Lavine, 1999; N. Miller & Pederson, 1999; Petty & Briñol, 2006; Petty, Wheeler, & Bizer, 1999; Strack, 1999; Strahan & Zanna, 1999; Stroebe, 1999; Wegener & Claypool, 1999; Wyer, 2006). One concern is that the persuasive outcomes predicted by the Unimodel can also be derived from the HPM and ELM (for a detailed discussion, see D. J. O'Keefe, 2013). At this point, there appears to be no theoretical advantage or empirical foundation for preferring the Unimodel over the dual process models that have become the staple of persuasion research in communication and social psychology. Nevertheless, the advantage of theoretical formulations like the Unimodel is that they cause scholars to reexamine the underlying assumptions and predictive utility of our models of persuasion.

SUMMARY

This chapter examined three cognitive models of persuasion. After reviewing research by Tesser and his colleagues (Sadler & Tesser, 1973; Tesser, 1978; Tesser & Conlee, 1975; Tesser, Martin, & Mendolia, 1995) that documented the effects of "mere thought" on the polarization of people's attitudes, the ELM was introduced as one model of persuasion that posits an important role for message receivers' cognitive responses. The ELM specified conditions that cause people to carefully consider the substance of persuasive messages and argued that when such conditions were met message characteristics such as argument quality and supporting evidence would influence attitudes. According to the model, when people are unwilling or unable to carefully scrutinize message content, they base their message evaluation on persuasion cues that are peripheral to the message itself. Several concerns were raised about the theoretical structure of, and empirical support for, the ELM that call the model's validity into question. The HSM was introduced as one alternative that is free of several of these limitations. Although they have many similarities, the HSM and the

ELM represent distinct conceptualizations about the persuasion process. For example, the HSM reflects a single theoretical approach rather than the ELM's concept of integrating many different theoretical perspectives. In addition, the HSM explicitly accommodates the ability of message receivers to simultaneously conduct systematic and heuristic processing. Finally, the Unimodel was presented as an alternative to both the ELM and the HSM. Although the "jury is still out" on the utility of the Unimodel for scholars of persuasion, it has focused renewed interest on the underlying assumptions about the ways that people process persuasive information, including traditional conceptions of persuasive cues and message arguments.

In summary, these models reflect a movement among persuasion scholars to pay more attention to the contributions of message receivers in the persuasion process. Theorizing about this issue has stimulated scholarly inquiry and debate and promises to provide a more comprehensive understanding of persuasive communication.

NOTES

1. Although early tests of the ELM uniformly associated the persuasive effects of argument quality with central processing and the persuasive effects of source expertise with peripheral processing, Petty and Cacioppo (1986) later specified that these variables could play multiple roles. As is revealed later in the chapter, this conceptual flexibility raises serious concerns about whether the model can be falsified.

2. Petty and Cacioppo (1990) disparaged the conceptual and methodological decisions by Johnson and Eagly (1989). However, the quality of Johnson and Eagly's (1990) rebuttal of this critique reaffirms the serious challenge their findings pose for proponents of the ELM.

3. Working from functional approaches to attitudes (see Chapter 1), Chaiken, Lieberman, and Eagly (1989) asserted that two other motives might also operate in social influence situations. Specifically, they argue that those with a *defensive* motivation are chiefly seeking to maintain their particular set of beliefs, attitudes, or values, while those with an *impression* motivation want to express their beliefs or attitudes because they consider them socially appropriate (Chaiken et al., 1989).

PART II

COMPONENTS OF PERSUASIVE TRANSACTIONS

This part of the book explores the most essential characteristics of persuasive transactions. In many regards, David Berlo's (1960) Source–Message–Channel–Receiver Model of communication remains an effective organizing tool for discussing research on persuasive communication more than a half-century after its introduction. Chapter 6 reviews key research on the characteristics of persuasive *sources*. The next two chapters summarize the research on persuasive message characteristics, with the first focusing on *rational* messages and the second on *emotional* messages. Chapter 9 identifies the features of message *receivers* that most affect the effectiveness of a persuasive appeal. Finally, closing this part, Chapter 10 describes the characteristics of persuasive situations that influence the persuasion process.

CHAPTER 6

Source Characteristics in Persuasive Communication

LOOKING AHEAD . . . This chapter examines the characteristics of message sources that enhance the effectiveness of persuasive messages. We begin by identifying two key dimensions of source credibility, namely, expertise and trustworthiness. We then examine how people form judgments about these factors and how these judgments affect their attitudes and behavior. The chapter concludes with a discussion of two related source characteristics, perceived similarity and physical attractiveness, and the effects of these factors on persuasion.

Are the characteristics of message sources important factors in persuasive communication? Are they important in *all* persuasive contexts? Is the credibility or attractiveness of a message source more persuasive than the content of the message itself? Although there are no simple answers to these questions, source characteristics are often critical to the success or failure of a persuasive transaction. Indeed, sometimes they are the most important persuasive features. Public hearings, courtroom testimony, and political campaigns are situations in which effective communication skills, personal background, and personal demeanor are essential for persuasive communication.

The Senate confirmation hearings of then Supreme Court nominee Clarence Thomas in October 1991 underscored the persuasive effects of source credibility. During the hearings, the national television audience's attention was riveted on Professor Anita Hill's allegations that Thomas sexually harassed her several years earlier when they both worked for the Equal Employment Opportunity Commission (which he headed at the time). Her allegations and his responses generated conflicting accounts of Thomas's personal and professional behavior. Moreover, there was little or no physical evidence to directly substantiate either person's account. Ultimately, judgments about the validity of Anita Hill's claims of sexual harassment and the suitability of Clarence Thomas as a Supreme Court justice were based on viewers' assessments of the credibility of the two people most involved.

More recently, during the early stages of the Republican primary season in 2015, Donald Trump's presidential aspirations were buoyed by a series of derisive comments he made about women and Mexican immigrants. While these comments were doubtless offensive to a large number of potential voters, Trump's in-your-face bluster nonetheless resonated with a significant number of Republicans, who despised both government and politicians in general. While initially 16 other Republican candidates struggled to gain traction, Trump's histrionics immediately catapulted him to the Republican nomination. While these high-profile examples provide compelling evidence for the importance of source credibility in persuasion, such source factors are equally significant in common ordinary persuasive transactions. Consumers prefer honest and likable salespeople, television viewers prefer news media personalities who share their values, and many sports fans pay to watch athletes based not solely on their on-field performance but also on their beliefs and how they interact with their fans.

This chapter examines the influence of specific source characteristics in persuasive communication. Because much of the research investigating source characteristics has focused on source credibility, most of the chapter will be devoted to this issue. Following this discussion, the persuasive influence of additional source characteristics, such as likability and perceived similarity, will be examined. It bears mentioning that there is a growing literature on media credibility and the credibility of specific websites. Given this book's primary focus on persuasive communication in personal and group settings, however, we defer to scholars of mass communication on any discussion of mass media credibility.

SOURCE CREDIBILITY

Source credibility as a construct can be traced back to the fourth-century B.C.E. Greek philosopher Aristotle. In his seminal work *The Rhetoric*, Aristotle claims that *ethos* (i.e., the character of the speaker) "is the most potent of all the means to persuasion" (1932/1960, p. 10). During the early 1950s, Hovland and colleagues (1953) conducted the first modern social science research on the components and effects of source credibility.[1] Not surprisingly, they found that source credibility (how believable the source is) is likely to be a significant determinant of persuasion irrespective of culture.

However, the specific characteristics underlying the concept of credibility do differ across cultures. For example, Whittaker and Meade (1967) found that a given source's gender was a component of credibility (i.e., with male sources assumed to be more credible than female sources) in Brazil, Hong Kong, and India, but not in Jordan or Rhodesia.

Over the past half-century, research in the United States has helped identify areas of agreement and disagreement among scholars as to the nature of source credibility (Pornpitakpan, 2004; Rieh & Danielson, 2007). First, while scholars generally agree that source credibility is multi-dimensional (i.e., is composed of more than one dimension or component), considerable disagreement exists as to the number and nature of these dimensions. Second, there is general agreement that source credibility is a *perceptual* variable. Specifically, source credibility is the audience's *perception* of the source rather than a commodity that the source brings to a particular persuasive context. Third, perceptions of source credibility and message quality influence one another and affect attitudes (Hahn, Harris, & Corner, 2009; Reimer, Mata, & Stoecklin, 2004). The dimensionality and perceptual nature of source credibility are issues that we will turn to next. The mutual influence that credibility and message quality have on each other and on attitudes is examined in more detail in our discussion of rational appeals in Chapter 7.

Dimensions of Credibility

One of the early empirical debates in the scientific study of persuasive communication focused on the definition and measurement of source credibility. Hovland and colleagues (1953) initially defined source credibility as a combination of two factors: *source expertise* and *source trustworthiness*. They defined expertise as "the extent to which a communicator is perceived to be a source of valid assertions" (p. 21). In short, expertise is the extent to which an audience member perceives the source as being well informed on the topic at hand. Source trustworthiness, on the other hand, is an audience member's "degree of confidence in the communicator's intent to communicate the assertions he considers most valid" (p. 21). In short, trustworthiness represents an audience member's perceptions that the source will tell the truth as he or she knows it.

Later, Berlo, Lemert, and Mertz (1969) conducted two studies that examined the dimensions people used to make judgments about a source's credibility. Using factor-analytic procedures,[2] they found three dimensions—safety, qualification, and dynamism—that explained most of the variance in people's ratings of a source's credibility. The qualification dimension found by Berlo and colleagues was similar to the expertise dimension identified by Hovland and colleagues (1953). However, the safety dimension identified by Berlo et al. was much broader in scope than the Hovland group's trustworthiness. In addition to truthfulness (the key component in Hovland and colleagues' definition), safety in the Berlo et al. (1969) study included such descriptors as "calm, safe, patient, friendly, kind, congenial, gentle, hospitable, and warm" (p. 574). The third dimension identified by Berlo, dynamism (i.e., how animated and outgoing the source was seen as being), was previously not identified in the literature.

The Berlo and colleagues paper circulated for nearly a decade before it was published, in 1969 (Cronkhite & Liska, 1980). During that period, McCroskey (1966) examined the dimensions of source credibility in a series of factor-analytic investigations. Though he intended to measure the dynamism dimension, he consistently found only two dimensions of source credibility—authoritativeness and character—that corresponded to the dimensions reported by Hovland et al. McCroskey's authoritativeness dimension (see Table 6.1) was consistent with Hovland and colleagues' (1953) expertise dimension and accounted for a large amount of the variation (47%) in people's responses. The character dimension (see Table 6.2) was consistent with Hovland and colleagues' trustworthiness dimension

TABLE 6.1. McCroskey's (1966) Authoritativeness Scale

1. I respect this person's opinion on the topic.
2. The speaker is *not* of very high intelligence.
3. This speaker is a reliable source of information on the topic.
4. I have confidence in this speaker.
5. This speaker lacks information on the subject.
6. This speaker has high status in our society.
7. I would consider this speaker to be an expert on the topic.
8. This speaker's opinion on the topic is of little value.
9. I believe that the speaker is quite intelligent.
10. The speaker is an unreliable source of information on the topic.
11. I have little confidence in this speaker.
12. The speaker is well informed on this subject.
13. The speaker has low status in our society.
14. I would *not* consider this speaker to be an expert on this topic.
15. This speaker is an authority on the topic.
16. This speaker has very little experience with this subject.
17. This speaker has considerable knowledge of the factors involved with this subject.
18. Few speakers are as qualified to speak on this topic as the speaker.
19. This speaker is *not* an authority on the topic.
20. This speaker has very little knowledge of the factors involved with the subject.
21. The speaker has had substantial experience with this subject.
22. Many people are much more qualified to speak on this topic than this speaker.

Note. Recommended response options are Strongly Agree, Agree, Undecided, Disagree, and Strongly Disagree. From "Scales for the measurement of ethos" by J. C. McCroskey, 1966, *Speech Monographs, 33,* 65–72. Copyright 1966 by the National Communication Association. Reprinted by permission.

TABLE 6.2. McCroskey's (1966) Character Scale

1. I deplore this speaker's background.
2. This speaker is basically honest.
3. I would consider it desirable to be like this speaker.
4. This speaker is *not* an honorable person.
5. This speaker is a reputable person.
6. This speaker is *not* concerned with my well-being.
7. I trust this speaker to tell the truth about the topic.
8. This speaker is a scoundrel.
9. I would prefer to have nothing at all to do with this speaker.
10. Under most circumstances I would be likely to believe what this speaker says about the topic.
11. I admire the speaker's background.
12. This speaker is basically honest.
13. The reputation of this speaker is low.
14. I believe that this speaker is concerned with my well-being.
15. The speaker is an honorable person.
16. I would *not* prefer to be like this person.
17. I do *not* trust the speaker to tell the truth on this topic.
18. Under most circumstances I would *not* be likely to believe what this speaker says about the topic.
19. I would like to have this speaker as a personal friend.
20. The character of the speaker is good.

Note. Recommended response options are Strongly Agree, Agree, Undecided, Disagree, and Strongly Disagree. From "Scales for the measurement of ethos" by J. C. McCroskey, 1966, *Speech Monographs, 33*, 65–72. Copyright 1966 by the National Communication Association. Reprinted by permission.

and accounted for a smaller (though still significant) amount of the variation (29%) in responses to the credibility measure.

In summary, these three reports (and others; see Pornpitakpan, 2004, for a review) suggest that two factors, trustworthiness and expertise, adequately represent people's judgments about a source's credibility. Although these studies' factor-analytic procedures have been criticized and other dimensions of credibility have been suggested (Cronkhite & Liska, 1976, 1980), most persuasion scholars now describe credibility as a combination of a source's perceived expertise and trustworthiness.[3]

Defining Credibility as a Receiver Perception

Perhaps the greatest point of consensus in the research on this construct is that credibility is a perception held by message recipients. Eschewing a source-oriented approach to credibility, Hovland and his colleagues (1953) defined credibility as a perceptual state, not a characteristic of message sources. Cronkhite and Liska (1980) also reflected that perspective when they wrote that "it is not merely the needs/goals of sources which must be assessed" (p. 105). In their view, evaluations of source credibility must focus on judgments made by message receivers. This receiver-oriented emphasis led persuasion scholars to define credibility in terms of the perceptions that message recipients have about a given source's expertise and trustworthiness. In this construct, credibility is not an objective characteristic that message sources possess but, rather, the perception of trustworthiness and expertise that sources are able to engender in a target audience.

McCroskey's measures of expertise (i.e., what he calls authoritativeness; see Table 6.1) and trustworthiness (i.e., what he calls character; see Table 6.2) were intended to quantify audience members' perceptions of a source's credibility. These scales can differentiate people with divergent views on the same source. For example, a person who has a favorable impression of U.S. Senator John McCain as an authority on foreign policy would likely agree or strongly agree with statement 1 on the expertise scale, while a person with a negative view of his ability would disagree or strongly disagree with that statement.

McCroskey used many items to measure expertise and trustworthiness (22 and 20, respectively) to improve both reliability and validity of his scales. In general, the greater number of items or statements used to measure a concept, the more reliable the measure will be. Moreover, because the credibility dimensions are conceptually broad, multiple items were needed to best capture the expertise and trustworthiness dimensions.

Another point of general agreement is that perceived trustworthiness and expertise are considered separate (though related) constructs. Although these perceptions are often strongly related, it is possible for a message source to be perceived as expert without being seen as trustworthy (or vice versa). For example, President Richard Nixon was generally believed to possess considerable expertise in foreign policy. However, in the aftermath of Watergate most Americans no longer thought him to be trustworthy. Conversely, message sources can be seen as trustworthy but not expert. At the end of his presidency, Jimmy Carter was regarded as highly trustworthy, but many voters felt he lacked the political or professional expertise to run the country. As a result, "credibility" as a general factor or concept lacks the precision needed in productive persuasion research. Thus, instead of describing a source's credibility, persuasion scholars have preferred to rely on the more precise constructs of expertise and trustworthiness.

Variations in Perceived Expertise and Trustworthiness

Because trustworthiness and expertise are perceptions held by individual message recipients, these judgments are likely to differ among audiences as well as members of the same audience and to change over time. First, it is likely that perceptions of credibility will vary considerably from one target audience to another. As a result, a high school physics teacher may be perceived as highly expert when talking to students in his or her classroom but may simultaneously be seen as less of an authority when presenting a paper before an audience of esteemed scholars at an international conference on nuclear physics. Similarly, an inmate at a federal penitentiary might be considered relatively trustworthy by other inmates but not by citizens living outside of the prison's walls.

Second, perceptions of a single source's credibility will likely vary among members of any broad-based audience. For example, it is likely that Bono will be perceived as a more credible source among middle-age people than younger people.

In addition, perceptions of a source's expertise and trustworthiness can change over time. For example, an untrustworthy coworker may gain credibility over time by exhibiting reliability and commitment to the workgroup. Moreover, a recent college graduate may be perceived as "green" and lacking the experience necessary to manage an important business account. Over time, that same college graduate may gain expertise and become indispensable to the organization.

Along similar lines, perceived expertise likely varies from topic to topic; however, perceptions of trustworthiness are likely to be relatively stable across topics. A renowned economist will likely be perceived by many people to have expertise when talking about government deficit-reduction options. However, the same person may lack the perceived expertise to speak persuasively about child development.

BOX 6.1. Credibility (Like Stock Market Investments) Can Be Here Today and Gone Tomorrow

For nearly three decades, Bernie Madoff was perceived as a financial wizard by Wall Street. Reports of fantastic investment returns and his extravagant personal style led charitable foundations, hedge fund managers, and the super-rich to entrust him with management of their investments. By all accounts, people were lining up to give him money to invest for them. All the while, Mr. Madoff was perpetrating the largest Ponzi scheme in history, eventually defrauding investors out of nearly $20 billion. When the scheme finally unraveled beginning in December 2008, sophisticated investors were left wondering how they could have been deceived for so long. The answer to that question was Mr. Madoff's carefully cultivated trustworthiness (as well as the investors' good old-fashioned greed). Over the course of a couple of weeks, Bernie Madoff went from being a highly respected financial genius to being regarded as a common criminal, vilified by everyone who knew him (as well as many who did not).

SOURCE CREDIBILITY AND ATTITUDE CHANGE

There are ample data to suggest that source credibility influences attitude change, at least some of the time (see Pornpitakpan, 2004, for a thorough-going review). In one of the early investigations, Hovland and Weiss (1951) measured college students' attitudes toward a wide variety of subjects. Five days later, under the guise of a guest lecture, students in a college history class were exposed to messages on four of the subjects measured earlier (i.e., over-the-counter sale of antihistamines, the feasibility of building nuclear-powered submarines, a steel shortage, and the future of movie theaters). Each message was attributed to either a high-credibility source or a low-credibility source. For example, the message on the future of movie theaters was attributed to either *Fortune* magazine (a high-credibility source) or a movie gossip columnist (low-credibility source). After reading each message, participants indicated their opinion and responded to a number of other measures.

For three of the four topics (and for the overall results combined across topics), Hovland and Weiss (1951) reported that messages attributed to the high-credibility source created much more attitude change toward message recommendations when compared to the low-credibility source. In addition, the highly credible source was judged to have presented the facts more fairly and to have provided more justifiable conclusions when compared to the low-credibility source (Hovland & Weiss, 1951). This final result is interesting because the messages were *exactly* the same across the credibility conditions.

Source credibility is one of those constructs that we, as scholars, would like to think will always influence attitude change (e.g., McCroskey & Teven, 1999). The accumulated research, however, indicates that this is not always the case (Pornpitakpan, 2004). In his meta-analysis, Jim (Stiff, 1986) reported that the influence of source credibility on attitude change varied dramatically across studies. Many studies found that highly credible sources were more persuasive than less credible ones. Other studies found that credibility has no effect on attitudes. Still other studies have found that low-credibility sources can be more persuasive than highly credible sources, particularly when presenting messages that receivers initially disagree with (Bochner & Insko, 1966). For this reason, during the 1960s and 1970s scholars had a difficult time summarizing the credibility literature. In the ensuing decades, though, our understanding of the role of credibility has improved dramatically. Indeed, three moderator variables—issue involvement, existing attitudes and knowledge, and the timing of source identification—have been shown to affect the persuasiveness of source credibility.

Issue Involvement

The cognitive response models (i.e., the Elaboration Likelihood Model of persuasion [ELM; Petty & Cacioppo, 1981, 1986] and the Heuristic Model of persuasion [HSM; Chaiken, 1980]) that we discussed in Chapter 5 have helped to improve our understanding of the persuasive impact of source credibility. In those models, variables can act as message arguments, persuasive cues, or influence the amount of cognitive effort receivers exert when processing a persuasive message. Source credibility (in most instances) plays the role of a persuasive cue. Credibility judgments can typically be made simply and quickly from brief descriptions of the source. When a recipient doesn't want to pay a lot of attention to the message but wants to hold the correct attitude on the issue, credibility judgments are a simple way of drawing a conclusion about the message recommendation. Specifically, relying on the recommendation of a highly credible source increases the probability of holding the correct attitude.

The ELM and HSM posit that source credibility will have a greater influence on attitudes when people are paying attention to the source but *not* engaged in effortful evaluation of the message arguments. According to the ELM, the influence of a credible source is evidence of peripheral processing, while the HSM suggests that source credibility is a heuristic (simple decision rule) that can be used to make decisions about message recommendations without having to scrutinize message content. Information about a source's expertise and the decision rule that "experts are generally correct" can substitute for careful message evaluation.

These predictions are consistent with Jim's (Stiff, 1986) meta-analytic data on the persuasive effect of source credibility. Specifically, Jim found that source credibility had a stronger influence on attitudes when issue involvement was moderate (as compared to either low or high). At very low levels of issue involvement (e.g., if a message about tariffs between Thailand and Kenya is presented to American college students), receivers are so unmotivated that they are unlikely to attend to either the message content or the source cues. As involvement increases to a moderate level, however, the influence of source credibility increases. When receivers are highly involved with the message topic, receivers focus much of their cognitive effort and attention on message arguments and evidence, thereby diminishing the effect of source credibility on attitudes.

Existing Attitudes and Knowledge

A recent meta-analysis by Kumkale, Albarracín, & Seignourel (2010) limits the effects of issue involvement and source credibility on attitudes even further. Specifically, these researchers argue that source credibility cues are persuasive only when message recipients have no preexisting attitudes and very little information about the topic. If a message receiver has an existing attitude or has been exposed to information on the topic previously, he or she likely already has a sufficiently strong opinion base from which to form a judgment. Under these conditions, message receivers tend to rely on information and evaluations they have in memory, instead of the credibility of the message source, when deciding whether or not to change their attitudes (Kumkale et al., 2010). It is only when those receivers have no preexisting attitude or very little information that they rely on the source information to form their attitude. In terms of Miller's (1980) definition of persuasion (set forth in Chapter 1), the existing knowledge and source credibility interaction affects the attitude-shaping processes but not the attitude-changing processes. Indeed, this type of empirical finding is precisely what G. R. Miller (1980) had in mind when he argued that it was important to distinguish among response *shaping, changing, and reinforcing* processes in persuasion.

Timing of Source Identification

Another factor that influences the effect of source credibility on attitudes is whether the message source is identified before or after the persuasive appeal. Studies examining this issue manipulate the timing of the source identification to occur either before or after the message is presented (Pornpitakpan, 2004). D. J. O'Keefe (1987) performed a meta-analysis of research that examined how the timing of source identification affected the persuasiveness of source credibility. This review found that high credibility sources are most persuasive when introduced before rather than after the message presentation. Low credibility sources, on the other hand, are most persuasive when introduced after rather than before the message presentation.

Moreover, the *difference* in persuasiveness between high- and low-credibility sources is greatest when the sources are introduced before the message. On the other hand, when sources are introduced after the message, there is much less difference between the persuasiveness of high- and low-credibility sources (D. J. O'Keefe, 1987, p. 68).

When sources were identified following the message presentation, the persuasive impact of source credibility declined dramatically because message receivers are persuaded by the message content before it is attributed to a source. The low-credibility source benefits from this arrangement, however, because the effect of message content is stronger (largely because it comes first) than the inhibiting effect of the negative source identification. The timing of the identification of the source has become quite an important issue in recent persuasion research that we will consider further when we discuss the "sleeper effect."

Tormala and colleagues (Tormala, Briñol, & Petty, 2007) examined how the timing of source credibility information affects the confidence that people have in their attitudes. These scholars found that when the source's credibility is introduced after the message content it enhances people's confidence in the attitudes that were formed about the message content. However, when source cues are introduced before the message, these cues have their greatest effect on the valence of receivers' issue-relevant thinking (as noted in Chapter 5).

In conclusion, if source credibility has its greatest impact when message receivers are moderately involved (Stiff, 1986), have no existing attitude and relatively little information already on the topic (Kumkale et al., 2010), and the source is identified before the message is presented and perceived as credible (D. J. O'Keefe, 1987). When presented after the message, source cues improve the confidence with which an attitude is held, and when presented prior to the message, they affect the direction of issue-relevant thinking about it (Tormala et al., 2007). The emphasis on receiver perceptions and thoughts—paramount to the definition of source expertise and trustworthiness—highlights the importance of factors that affect the judgments people make about message sources. The next section examines this perceptual process in greater detail.

ATTRIBUTIONS ABOUT MESSAGE SOURCES

After reaching agreement on the definition and measurement of credibility, researchers turned their attention to understanding how people make initial judgments about a source's expertise and trustworthiness. One approach suggests that the expectations recipients have about the source and the positions he or she might advocate are important in understanding their perceptions of the source's likely expertise and trustworthiness. Consider three examples. Following the *Deepwater Horizon* oil spill in 2010, BP employed a number of scientists to report on the environmental effects of the oil spill on wildlife along the Gulf Coast. Second, following presidential debates, candidates from both parties have a number of "surrogates" who assemble in the media room to offer their impressions (and "spin" their candidate's talking points). Third, every time Apple launches a new product, the company holds a media event during which the CEO or other high-level executive introduces the product and describes its attributes and features. In each of these persuasive situations, the target audience has expectations about the motives, experience, and knowledge of the speaker(s) and those expectations affect perceptions of perceived source credibility and the persuasiveness of the message.

In a series of studies, Eagly and her colleagues investigated the influence of receiver expectancies on perceptions of source expertise and trustworthiness (Eagly & Chaiken, 1976; Eagly, Chaiken, & Wood, 1981; Eagly, Wood, & Chaiken, 1978). These investigations employed Kelley's (1967) Attribution Theory to explain how message recipients make causal inferences about message sources. Kelley argued that people behave like naive psychologists as they attempt to develop explanations for many things, including other people's behaviors. More specifically, Attribution Theory is concerned with understanding how people identify the causes of other people's behavior.

In Attribution Theory, two major categories of causal inferences exist: *dispositional* (or personal) characteristics or *environmental* (or situational) characteristics. In dispositional attributions, the behavior is attributed to some intrinsic characteristic of the person, him- or herself. Imagine that you are waiting to go to a concert with a friend who is 45 minutes late in picking you up. If your friend is *always* late (e.g., for class, parties, and work), you might conclude that some characteristic of the person (i.e., his or her disposition) causes the consistent tardiness. On the other hand, when we make a situational attribution, we conclude that something about the context caused the behavior. If your friend is always punctual, but is late picking you up for the concert, you are much more likely to infer that some extenuating circumstance led to the tardiness.

Attributions, Expectancies, and Credibility Assessments

Eagly and colleagues (1981) argued that message recipients initiate a similar causal analysis when evaluating a message source's credibility. When we don't know a source very well, we use existing information about the source and situation to generate expectations (i.e., predictions of) the position the speaker will advocate. Referring back to our prior example of the *Deepwater Horizon* oil spill, receivers might expect BP's scientists to minimize the damage caused by the oil. Similarly, one might well assume that surrogates for a presidential candidate will have only positive impressions of their candidate's debate performance. Likewise, no one expects an Apple executive to provide critical commentary about an iPhone or iPad.

Receivers use the positions they predict a speaker will advocate to look for evidence of bias. In this model, there are two types of bias: knowledge bias and reporting bias. *Knowledge bias* refers to the judgment, based on available information, that the source does not possess accurate information about the message topic. This bias presumes that there is something about the source (e.g., his or her background or position/occupation) that leads him or her to have only a partial or even slanted mindset about a particular topic. For example, you might perceive that a salesperson in an

Apple store might know everything there is to know about Apple products but still have limited (and/or slanted) information about a competitor's products. This represents a *knowledge bias* because receivers think that the salesperson's background and position prevent him or her from being credible or objective when comparing Apple products with the competition's. In this case, the presumption is that the salesperson is telling the truth as he or she knows it but lacks complete information about a competitor's product to give an unbiased opinion. In short, the source might be seen as trustworthy but still lacking relevant knowledge (or expertise).

Reporting bias, on the other hand, reflects the belief that a source is unwilling to report accurate or full information about the message topic (Eagly et al., 1978). For example, you might assume that the BP scientist in our example will underreport the extent of environmental damage created by the oil spill. The BP scientist, in this example, might have accurate information but is unwilling to tell the whole truth, as he or she knows it. "A reporting-biased communicator, then, willfully misleads his or her audience" (Eagly & Chaiken, 1993, p. 357). That is, the scientist is perceived as an expert but is nonetheless lacking in trustworthiness.

BOX 6.2. Expectancy Confirmation and Familiar Speakers

Expectancy violations relating to source credibility occur most commonly when audience members are unfamiliar with the speaker addressing them. In situations where the speaker is well known to them, confirmation of the audience's expectations may have less impact on the persuasiveness of the message. For example, those who were gathered on the National Mall in Washington, DC, on August 28, 1963, had come to listen to (foremost among others) Dr. Martin Luther King, Jr., talk about racial equality. The audience members (mostly, civil rights advocates and their followers) likely had well-ingrained attitudes about the issue at hand and equally well-settled expectations about the positions that Dr. King (the universally acknowledged civil rights leader of the time) would advocate. In what came to be known as his "I Have a Dream" speech, Dr. King confirmed his listeners' best expectations and did nothing to undermine his credibility with them or others.

Is this set of observations about a key historical moment inconsistent with Alice Eagly's model relating to the effects of expectancy violations? Not if one considers that the model works best in estimating *initial* judgments about source credibility (Dr. King's credibility was long-established and deeply felt in the minds of the audience members on that day). This occasion was the backdrop for one of the greatest orations in U.S. history.

Expectancy Violations and Attitude Change

Message receivers' prior expectations are based solely on available information about the source's personal preferences or background (e.g., his or her job or employer) and situational pressures (e.g., the nature of the context or audience). These message expectations take the form of a *mini-theory* (or commonsense theory, as we called it in Chapter 2) concerning what position the source will advocate. These mini-theories are either confirmed or disconfirmed by the position the communicator *actually takes* in presenting the message (Eagly et al., 1981). When premessage expectations (or mini-theories) are actually tested, receivers may attribute the views expressed by the speaker to what the speaker really believes, his or her background, or the pressures impinging on the situation. These causal attributions lead to the perception that the speaker is (or is not) biased. These judgments are important because if a source is perceived as being biased, his or her message is unlikely to be persuasive because message receivers will not believe that it accurately reflects the true state of affairs for the issue being discussed (Eagly et al., 1978, 1981).

When a source *disconfirms* premessage expectations that he or she is biased, message recipients generate a different mini-theory to explain *why* the speaker advocated that surprising position. Generally, this different mini-theory suggests that especially compelling evidence must have made the communicator overcome the expected bias that was thought to influence message content. When expectations of bias are disconfirmed, receivers are likely to think that the source must really believe what he or she is saying. Such explanations lead to perceptions that the source is *unbiased* and enhance the persuasive effect of the message because of the source's unexpected honesty and sincerity.

Several investigations by Eagly and her colleagues (Eagly & Chaiken, 1976; Eagly et al., 1978; W. Wood & Eagly, 1981) examined the persuasive effects of expectancy disconfirmations. In one study (Eagly et al., 1978), participants read a pro-environment message that was attributed to a mayoral candidate who had either a pro-business or a pro-environment background. The background attributed to the source created an expectation of *knowledge bias*, that is, the perception that the source would possess (and express) either pro-business or pro-environment information. Participants who heard a message advocating a pro-environment position that was attributed to the candidate with an environmental background had their knowledge bias expectancies confirmed (i.e., the source was indeed biased). Those exposed to the pro-environment message attributed to the candidate with a business background experienced a disconfirmation of their knowledge bias expectancies (i.e., the source wasn't biased, after all).

In order to create *reporting bias* expectancies, participants were told that a pro-environment message was presented to either a pro-environment audience or to a pro-business audience (Eagly et al., 1978). When presented to the pro-environment audience, the message confirmed the reporting bias expectancy. However, when the audience was pro-business, the pro-environment message disconfirmed the reporting bias expectancy.

When an audience's expectancies of bias were disconfirmed by the position advocated in the message, the message source was judged to be less biased and more persuasive. Apparently, following expectancy disconfirmation, audience members concluded that the factual evidence must have been so overwhelming as to cause the message source to sincerely advocate the unexpected position (i.e., the source really believed what he or she said). When premessage expectancies of bias were confirmed, message recipients attributed the position advocated to the source's background characteristics or to situational constraints (i.e., the source had biased information or wasn't telling the truth) that limited the message's persuasive effect (Eagly et al., 1978). This process is depicted in the model shown in Figure 6.1.

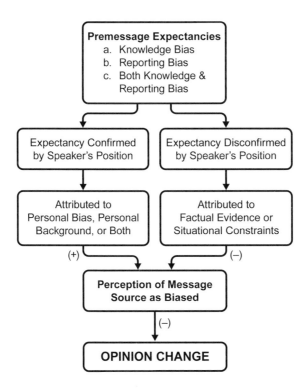

FIGURE 6.1. An expectancy model of opinion change.

PERSISTENCE OF CREDIBILITY EFFECTS

Although most scholars agree that the expertise and trustworthiness dimensions of source credibility are persuasive under certain circumstances, the *persistence* of credibility effects is less certain. The long-term persuasive effect of source credibility was initially studied by Hovland and colleagues (1949), who subsequently "showed that some opinion changes in the direction of the communicator's position are larger after a lapse of time than immediately after the communication" (Hovland & Weiss, 1951, p. 636). They referred to this curious phenomenon as the *sleeper effect.* Although they were not certain of the cause of the delayed change, they hypothesized that immediate attitude change might be reduced because receivers initially questioned the message source's motives but that, over time, they forgot who the source was and began to accept what was said. At that point, receivers "may then be more inclined to agree with the position which had been presented by the communicator" (ibid.).

Hovland and Weiss (1951) tested this sleeper effect hypothesis and found that, immediately following message exposure, messages attributed to a highly credible source were more persuasive than messages attributed to a less credible source. When they measured attitudes 4 weeks later, however, they discovered something interesting: attitude change declined over time for the message attributed to the high-credibility sources. In contrast, messages attributed to the low-credibility sources produced more favorable attitudes (for three of the four topics and for the overall results) after 4 weeks, as compared to immediately following the message.

Over the past 60 years, a number of researchers have attempted to replicate these early findings but have met with only limited success (Gruder et al., 1978; Pratkanis, Greenwald, Leippe, & Baumgardner, 1988). Several alternative definitions and explanations of the sleeper effect have emerged to account for the inconsistent findings in this body of research. Moreover, two meta-analyses (Allen & Stiff, 1989; Kumkale & Albarracín, 2004) statistically reviewed this research thread, identified differences among four explanations of the sleeper effect, and evaluated the evidence supporting each explanation. Although these meta-analytic reviews have provided some clarity, the sleeper effect literature remains a hodgepodge of explanations, experimental manipulations, and statistical effects that is difficult to summarize. If you have a long afternoon available (or a bout of insomnia), we encourage you to read the meta-analytic reviews because they describe all of the theoretical models and their empirical support in great detail. For now, we will simply present the highlights.

First, at least four different theoretical mechanisms have been proposed to explain the sleeper effect: *the Traditional Model, the Forgetting Model, the Disassociation Model,* and *the Differential Decay Model.*

These models posit the same general pattern: (1) persuasive messages attributed to high-credibility sources are initially more persuasive than if the same message is attributed to a low-credibility source; (2) over time, persuasion induced by the high-credibility source decays, presumably because the credibility of the source becomes separated in memory from the content of the message; and (3) over time, resistance induced by the low-credibility source also decays, causing attitude change to increase as the inhibiting effect of the low-credibility source gradually becomes disassociated from the content of the message.

Second, models designed to explain the sleeper effect have been investigated only sporadically. Although the sleeper effect had been studied for over a half-century, Kumkale and Albarracín (2004) found only 24 studies that met the criteria for inclusion in their meta-analysis.

Third, the models explaining the sleeper effect have been offered as *post-hoc* explanations of unanticipated research findings. For example, the Traditional Model stemmed from Hovland and colleagues' (1949) speculation that participants (army recruits) were suspicious of the source. That model, however, provided no theoretical reason why a low-credibility source would produce *more* attitude change over time. The Forgetting Model posits that message receivers forget the message source but retain the message content, but it also provides no explanation for why memory should operate in this manner. While the phrase "I don't remember where I heard this, but someone said . . . " is anecdotal evidence of the Forgetting Model at work, one can easily conjure up counterexamples. For example, jurors often report posttrial that they do not recall the specific details of testimony from an expert witness but that they do recall being impressed by the witness's credibility. Finally, the Disassociation Model and Differential Decay Model emerged because evidence suggested that receivers actually eventually remember the message source over time. According to the Disassociation Model, the message source is remembered but comes to be "disassociated" from the content of the message. However, one is left wondering whether there is any practical distinction between *disassociating* the source from the message and *forgetting* the source entirely. The point is that these models were developed as *post hoc* explanations for unexpected research findings and therefore lack a solid theoretical foundation.

Fourth, evidence suggests that the sleeper effect is likely to occur only under certain circumstances. Specifically, for the sleeper effect to occur the source must be identified *after* the message is presented (Kumkale & Albarracín, 2004); if the source is identified prior to the message, the sleeper effect is unlikely to occur. Second, the sleeper effect requires that message receivers engage in central (or systematic) message processing. Kumkale and Albarracín (2004) reported that the sleeper effect is much more likely to occur when recipients are able and motivated to process message content. Third, for the sleeper effect to occur, the message content must be persuasive and yet the negative impact of the low-credibility source (the discounting cue) should be strong enough to offset the positive impact of the message content. The researchers found that the sleeper effect is strongest when there is no initial attitude change from messages attributed to low-credibility sources. Thus, while messages from high-credibility sources are immediately more persuasive than messages from low-credibility sources, the persuasive impact of a message attributed to a low-credibility source can increase over time. Presumably, under these conditions, the low-credibility source *initially* inhibits (or offsets) the persuasive effects of the message content. Over time, however, the inhibiting effects of the low-credibility source fade more rapidly than the persuasive effects of the message content. Once the effects of the low-credibility source fade, the persuasive effects of the message content become more apparent, generating increased attitude change over time (Kumkale & Albarracín, 2004).

Implications of the Sleeper Effect

The meta-analytic reviews of this literature suggest that the sleeper effect is real and moderate in size but that it only occurs in limited persuasive situations. Although the theoretical explanations for this effect are not totally clear, a number of practical implications have emerged from the sleeper effect literature. First, the persuasive effects of source expertise and trustworthiness are relatively short-lived. These investigations have demonstrated that the initial persuasive effects of source expertise and trustworthiness decay relatively quickly.

Second, these findings suggest that the long-term effects of a single message presentation are more a function of message content than source characteristics. Once the effects of source credibility diminish, the more lasting effects of the message content are all that remain. And yet, the persuasive effects of the message are not permanent, either; they will also eventually decay. However, the decay of the message effect appears to be slower than that of the source effect. So, for short-term persuasive effects, both message and source cues are important. For longer-term attitude change, however, source cues are less important, because their effects will decay first.

Of course, one caveat bears mentioning: Investigations of the sleeper effect focus on long-term attitude change, but they employ only a single-message presentation. Advertising, health promotion, and political campaigns generally rely heavily on source credibility factors but also involve the use of repeated message presentations. Though the influence of source characteristics may be temporary, repeated exposure to these factors during a persuasive campaign may facilitate the reinforcement of an attitude.

Unfortunately, research on the sleeper effect (and persuasion more generally) has not investigated the long-term effects of repeated exposure to messages and sources.

RELATED SOURCE CHARACTERISTICS

Although researchers have mainly focused their efforts on understanding the persuasive effects of source expertise and trustworthiness, additional source characteristics have also received some attention. While these other research literatures are not as extensive, a sufficient number of investigations have examined the effects of source similarity and attractiveness to permit discussion about the influence of these factors in persuasive transactions.

Perceived Similarity

Practitioners have long believed that effective persuasion begins by establishing a personal connection between the message source and the target audience. Salespeople often spend a few minutes trying to establish or maintain a good rapport with clients by claiming some degree of similarity in interests or background before focusing on the sale itself. Before the Iowa Straw Poll, presidential candidates often arrange for photo opportunities in which they are shown hanging out at the state fair. In Ohio and Michigan, there are obligatory visits to auto manufacturing plants. When the primaries move to southern states, the candidates begin talking about the grits they ate for breakfast. The underlying goal of all these activities is to create impressions of mutual respect and familiarity between the candidate and local voters.

A number of psychological theories inform us that people should be more susceptible to the persuasive appeals of similar—as opposed to dissimilar—others. Early investigations of similarity effects (Berscheid, 1966; Brock, 1965) led textbook authors to conclude that perceived similarity may be an important characteristic of persuasive message sources (Bettinghaus & Cody, 1987; Petty & Cacioppo, 1981). In a thorough review of the literature, however, Simons, Berkowitz, and Moyer (1970) concluded that the persuasive effects of perceived similarity are less clear.

Simons and his colleagues identified two dimensions of source similarity: *membership similarity* and *attitudinal similarity*. Membership similarity focuses on demographic and social characteristics, personal experiences, and affiliations with groups and organizations that are shared with the target audience. Politicians often refer to their association with whatever city, state, or region they might be in to create a sense of geniality with the audience. Though perhaps less calculated, college students often establish a bond of peership during their initial interactions with one another. Beyond even that, for example, sorority and fraternity members will often describe themselves in terms of their mutual membership in a particular organization and wear clothing bearing Greek letters to advertise that membership.

Correspondingly, attitudinal similarity is established when speakers proudly proclaim opinions and values that are shared by members of their target audience. TV evangelists, for example, attempt to reinforce their perceived trustworthiness by continually expressing values and opinions that are deeply held by their target audience. The credibility enjoyed by those in the electronic ministry is constantly tested whenever appeals for financial contributions are made. In Texas, the owner of Jim's lawn service company described himself as a "good Christian man" when discussing the services he could provide. He assumed that Jim might share his religious beliefs and hoped that that prospective bond might lead Jim to evaluate him and his company more favorably.

Not all similarities (either membership or attitudinal), however, are equally relevant to the persuasive context (Simons et al., 1970). Irrelevant similarities, researchers argued, are offered simply to build rapport and lack persuasive influence. Relevant similarities, on the other hand, may lead to greater perceptions of source trustworthiness or expertise and thus indirectly influence attitudes. After reviewing research on the persuasive effects of similarity, Simons and colleagues concluded that perceived similarity is not always a persuasive cue (i.e., a cue that is considered peripherally, in ELM parlance).

In fact, Goethals and Nelson (1973) have argued convincingly that agreement from dissimilar others can sometimes be more compelling evidence for a point of view than agreement from similar others. They found that when considering a statement of fact (i.e., a verifiable claim) agreement from *dissimilar* others increased the confidence with which people held their beliefs. Apparently, agreement from similar others leads people to question whether their assessment of the issue is correct or whether, instead, it reflects personal biases and predispositions held in common. When agreement comes from a dissimilar other (i.e., a person who does not share the same biases and predispositions), however, people are more confident about the position they hold because the agreement is not likely attributable to similar opinions or personal biases. Although Goethals and Nelson focused on judgmental confidence, as opposed to attitudes, their finding is consistent with the following proposition about the persuasive influence of source similarity: "Attitude change toward the position advocated by the source depends on the extent to which interpersonal similarities or dissimilarities are perceived as having instrumental [or useful] value for the receiver" (Simons et al., 1970, p. 12).

BOX 6.3. Guilt by Association

There are times when membership similarity and attitude similarity overlap or intertwine. Politicians often emphasize their membership in particular national organizations in order to build a sense of rapport and trust with their target audience. Just as often, political candidates focus on an opponent's membership in an organization or other affiliations as a way of negatively characterizing that person's beliefs and values. For example, during the 1988 presidential campaign GOP candidate Vice-President George Bush "accused" Democratic nominee Michael Dukakis of being a member of the American Civil Liberties Union (ACLU). Aware of the negative attitude that many Republicans held toward the ACLU, Bush strategically associated Dukakis with the liberal values of the ACLU while at the same time aligning himself with conservatives who oppose the organization. Similarly, during the 2004 presidential campaign, President George W. Bush criticized John Kerry for his participation in early 1970s antiwar demonstrations following his return from Vietnam. Recalling Senator Kerry's association with antiwar demonstrators helped foster the perception he was antimilitary at a time (2004) when the United States was involved in wars in Iraq and Afghanistan. During the 2008 presidential campaign, U.S. Senator Barack Obama was criticized for his friendship with the Reverend Jeremiah Wright, a United Church of Christ pastor in Chicago who had made a number of inflammatory racial comments in his sermons. This controversy stoked racial fears at a time when voters were considering electing a black president. These are all instances of attempted guilt by association.

Applied to the Goethals and Nelson (1973) findings, this proposition suggests that agreement from similar others about a statement of fact had little informational value for people. However, agreement from a dissimilar other was more informative, because the other was not influenced by the same biases and predispositions. In much the same fashion, Simons and colleagues (1970) concluded that source similarity was not informative when it lacked relevance to the issue under consideration.

Presently, it is safe to advance three conclusions about source similarity's role in persuasive communication. First, source similarity does not always serve as a persuasive cue; in many situations, it is unrelated to the persuasion process. Second, when similarity influences attitudes or behaviors, it likely does so as a persuasive cue (i.e., is processed peripherally or heuristically). Third, when similarity serves as a persuasive cue, it has a direct effect on source trustworthiness and a smaller, indirect, effect on attitudes.

Physical Attractiveness

Laboratory and field investigations of the persuasive effects of physical attractiveness have produced a variety of conflicting findings. In a review of this literature, Chaiken (1986) concluded that, like perceived similarity, source attractiveness does not always generate attitude change and that, when physical attractiveness does influence response change it seems to have its greatest influence in persuasive situations that are relatively unimportant for message receivers. However, more recent research by Trampe et al. (2010) found that source attractiveness can also be very persuasive in situations where receivers are highly involved in the topic and the attractiveness of the source is relevant to the message recommendation.

Like the research findings on source similarity, the persuasive effects of physical attractiveness are not as straightforward as we once believed. Over the years, three different explanations have been advanced to account for the influence of source attractiveness (Chaiken, 1979, 1986). These explanations focus on social reinforcement, cognitive processes, and social skills.

Social Reinforcement Explanation

The *social reinforcement* explanation argues that the persuasive effects of physical attractiveness stem from the social rewards attractive people provide. It is well established that we find attractive people to be socially rewarding, and when given a choice we select attractive acquaintances over unattractive ones (Berscheid & Walster, 1974). Kelman (1961) argued that *identification* increases susceptibility to influence from attractive sources. Thus, the social reinforcement explanation suggests that our desire to associate with attractive people leads us to accept influence from them. This is similar to the instrumental function of attitudes (as discussed in Chapter 1). Using this functional perspective, we agree more with attractive sources because we seek the social rewards that affiliation with them (as compared with unattractive sources) may provide.

However, this *social reinforcement* effect does not appear to work equally for all people. Specifically, the reinforcing nature of attractive sources is likely moderated by the desire of message receivers to identify with, or liken themselves to, socially and physically attractive people. DeBono (2000) used a functional perspective to identify *self-monitoring* as influencing the persuasive impact of a source's physical attractiveness. According to Snyder (1986), high self-monitors are individuals who are concerned with the image that they project in social situations. Essentially, high self-monitors want to act appropriately in social situations and have the ability to modify their behavior to do just that. High self-monitors, then, typically apply an instrumental (what DeBono calls *social-adjustive*) function to the determination of their attitudes. Thus, adjusting their behavior enables them to receive social rewards in a wide variety of contexts. Low self-monitors, on the other hand, are concerned with acting in a way that is consistent with their personal interpretation of the social situation. Low self-monitors want their own behavior to be a reflection of their own beliefs, moods, attitudes, and values. DeBono claims, then, that low self-monitors primarily embrace a value-expressive function for their attitudes because their behaviors reflect important values and attitudes that they hold.

DeBono, Ruggeri, and Foster (1997, cited in DeBono, 2000) investigated this relationship between self-monitoring and attitude functions in a study relating to evaluations of a consumer product. They claimed that high self-monitors (i.e., those favoring an instrumental function) will respond to the image presented in an advertisement to a greater extent than the actual characteristics of the product. Low self-monitors (i.e., those embracing a value-expressive function) will respond to the characteristics of the product itself more than to the image projected in an advertisement. In this case, self-monitoring is a classic example of a moderator variable (see Chapter 2) because it changes the nature of the relationship between source attractiveness (as the independent variable) and persuasion (as the dependent variable). In their study, DeBono and colleagues had high and low self-monitors look at one of two forms of a print advertisement for a new brand of chocolate. The two versions differed only in the physical attractiveness of the person depicted in the ad. Participants were then asked to sample one of two chocolate candies (one of which tasted much better than the other).

Consistent with the researchers' predictions, high self-monitors evaluated the chocolate associated with the attractive source more positively than that associated with the less attractive source. This was true regardless of the actual quality of the chocolate they sampled. Evaluations made by low self-monitors, on the other hand, were influenced by the nature of the chocolate sampled. The attractiveness of the person depicted in the advertisement did not influence the low-self monitors' ratings of the chocolate.

In summary, results of the DeBono and colleagues (1997, cited in DeBono, 2000) study indicates that the physical attractiveness of the source would be influential for some—but not for all—people. Individuals working from primarily instrumental attitude functions (high self-monitors in their study) will be influenced to a greater extent by physically attractive sources. Conversely, individuals working from a value-expressive function will be uninfluenced by an attractive source, because they are careful to make their behavior consistent with their own values and beliefs.

Cognitive-Processing Explanation

A *cognitive-processing* explanation has also been advanced to account for the persuasive effects of source attractiveness (Chaiken, 1980, 1987). In Chapter 5, we discussed Chaiken's HSM, which posits that people often rely on heuristics to make judgments about message recommendations. Research has shown that heuristics are most prominent when the issue is relatively unimportant. Under those circumstances, simple decision rules substitute for careful thinking about the persuasive message in determining receiver responses. For example, one heuristic, the "likability–agreement heuristic" suggests that we tend to agree with people we like. Because physical attractiveness has been associated with likability (Chaiken, 1986), the likability-agreement heuristic may be the basis for agreement with attractive sources.

Consistent with the HSM of persuasion (and the ELM), Chaiken (1980, 1987) argued that when the persuasive situation is relatively unimportant to message receivers, source attractiveness acts as a cue that can be persuasive during heuristic processing. In other words, when the issue is of little personal consequence, people do not spend the cognitive effort necessary to engage in careful scrutiny of the message content and instead source attractiveness becomes a persuasive cue.

However, recent research by Trampe and colleagues (2010) has demonstrated that attractive sources can also be persuasive when the situation *is* important to message receivers. However, this only occurs when the attractiveness of the source is relevant to the persuasive appeal and there is little verbal argument provided. For example, when attractive models introduce vehicles at the Detroit Auto Show, their physical attractiveness is unrelated to the product being advertised. However, when a supermodel promotes cosmetics or hair-styling products, the attractiveness of the model *is* relevant to the product being advertised. This analysis is consistent with the discussion in Chapter 5 (see also Petty & Briñol, 2012; Petty & Wegener, 1999) that the same variables can be processed in multiple ways. Sometimes source attractiveness is processed heuristically (or peripherally), and sometimes it is effectively considered a message argument.

Trampe and colleagues (2010) found that when the persuasive message was unimportant to message receivers, ads including attractive sources were more persuasive than ads including less attractive sources. Moreover, this was true regardless of whether or not the attractiveness of the source was relevant to the message presentation (i.e., for a diet product *or* a deodorant). This finding is consistent with the large body of research stemming from the HSM and the ELM discussed in Chapter 5. However, Trampe and colleagues (2010) found that, when the message topic was important for message receivers, the relevance of source attractiveness to the message appeal determined the persuasiveness of that cue. When the message was important and when source attractiveness was relevant to the persuasive appeal (the diet plan), the attractive source was more persuasive than the less attractive source. However, if attractiveness was not relevant to the persuasive appeal (the deodorant), then the source's level of attractiveness was unrelated to persuasion. In this regard, the *relevance* of physical attractiveness to the persuasive appeal and the *importance of the message* are both moderator variables because they combine to change the nature of the relationship between the physical attractiveness (independent variable) and persuasion (dependent variable).

Another cognitive-processing explanation of the persuasive advantage of physically attractive people is called the "halo effect" (sometimes called the "what is beautiful is good stereotype"; Dion, Berscheid, & Walster, 1972). Physically attractive individuals are generally considered to have a number of other, positively evaluated, characteristics. Attractive individuals are generally evaluated as being more likely to be successful, more sociable, more popular, and more competent (Dion et al., 1972; Hatfield & Sprecher, 1986; see Eagly, Ashmore, Makhijani, & Longo, 1991, for a meta-analytic review). This stereotype acts as a heuristic in which attractive individuals are often evaluated as being more expert and trustworthy as compared to their less attractive counterparts. These increased perceptions of credibility might be yet another way that attractive individuals are more persuasive.

Social Skills Explanation

Finally, the *social skills* explanation suggests that physically attractive people are more persuasive because they have better social skills than less attractive people. In one of the early studies on the relationship between attractiveness and persuasion, Chaiken (1979) found that attractive sources were significantly more persuasive (i.e., they generated greater attitude change and petition signing) than less attractive sources. What is more, attractive sources were more fluent, spoke slightly faster, and reported higher SAT scores. Attractive sources also reported more favorable self-impressions and were more confident of their persuasive skills than less attractive communicators. Although Chaiken did not specifically test the relationship between communication skills and attitude change, these factors likely contributed to the persuasive successes of attractive sources. The social skills explanation is basically that attractive sources are more persuasive because they are generally more confident and skilled communicators than unattractive sources.

Thus, Chaiken's (1979) research suggests that, in situations where message recipients consider source characteristics (i.e., during peripheral or heuristic processing), attractive sources enjoy a persuasive advantage over their less attractive counterparts. It bears mentioning that the three explanations for this effect are not mutually exclusive. More likely, some combination of the three explanations accounts for the persuasive effects of source attractiveness.

The finding that attractive people have a clear persuasive advantage over unattractive people has significant predictive utility for persuasion practitioners. However, it is critically important to recognize that these effects are not simple and they are rarely straightforward. Instead, there are different processes, message situations, and receiver characteristics that interact to determine the effectiveness that an attractive source is likely to have in any persuasive situation.

SUMMARY

This chapter examined several characteristics of message sources that affect the persuasion process. We began by discussing two dimensions of source credibility, source expertise and source trustworthiness, and argued that, although often related, they are two separate dimensions that people typically employ to evaluate a source. Next, we discussed the expectations people have about message sources and the positions the sources are likely to advocate. We argued that when these expectations are confirmed, people perceive the source to be biased and hence less convincing. However, when these expectations are disconfirmed, the source is perceived as less biased and more persuasive. We concluded the discussion of source credibility effects by reviewing research on the sleeper effect. Here, we argued that source credibility has its greatest persuasive influence in the short term and that, over time, people separate the source of a message from the message content. Thus, in the long run, message content features are often more persuasive than source characteristics.

Source similarity and physical attractiveness are two other factors that may affect the persuasion process. When characteristics of a message source that are relevant to the persuasive message are similar to characteristics of the audience, the trustworthiness of the source may be enhanced. In addition, research has shown that source attractiveness is only persuasive in certain situations. Several possible explanations for these effects were discussed.

NOTES

1. Since Hovland and colleagues' research (1953; Hovland, Lumsdaine, & Sheffield, 1949) broke ground in several areas of persuasion, we will return to their seminal work several times in this book.

2. Factor analysis is a statistical technique that groups questions together based on how people respond to them. Groupings of questions (factors) reflect various dimensions of the concept being measured.

3. McCroskey and Teven (1999) reported a new measure of source credibility that also includes a *goodwill* dimension (i.e., the extent to which the source has the receiver's best interest in mind). Much of the research on goodwill appears to focus on either instructor credibility or physician credibility, a dimension that appears to be relevant to situations where message receivers have repeated interactions with a particular source.

CHAPTER 7

Persuasive Message Characteristics

RATIONAL APPEALS

LOOKING AHEAD . . . The next two chapters examine the features of messages that are most influential in the persuasion process. In this chapter, we begin by discussing rational appeals—specifically, how message receivers process evidence and when it is likely to be most effective. Then we examine the effectiveness of one- and two-sided messages. Later on, in the next chapter, we take up the subject of emotional appeals—in particular, the broad area of research on fear appeals and the relatively new research on guilt-arousing appeals.

In discussing the means by which one is persuaded, Aristotle (1932/1960) posited three primary means of persuasion: *ethos*, *logos*, and *pathos*. We discussed *ethos* (i.e., the character of the speaker) in the preceding chapter when we took up the subject of source credibility. Aristotle's other means of persuasion have to do with the message. Specifically, *logos* refers to the use of logic or rational appeals in a persuasive message. This chapter examines the findings from message effects research that relate to rational appeals. Aristotle's third means of persuasion, *pathos*, concerns messages that attempt to persuade by tapping audience members' emotions. The next chapter focuses on emotional appeals. The topics chosen for these chapters were selected because they made significant contributions to the understanding of persuasive communication and because they continue to motivate persuasion research even a half-century after the message effects research paradigm was born.

   This chapter begins with a review of the research on the persuasive effects of evidence. Following this discussion, we examine several models of rational argumentation and then conclude with some observations on the effectiveness of one- and two-sided message presentations.

A NOTE ABOUT RATIONAL AND EMOTIONAL APPEALS

Before beginning though, we feel compelled to admit the somewhat arbitrary nature of our organizational scheme in these two chapters. While textbooks continue to draw a distinction between rational and emotional appeals that is reflective of the Western tradition of divorcing reason from emotion, several persuasion scholars have rightly noted that separating rational from emotional appeals may create a false dichotomy (S. L. Becker, 1963; Gass & Seiter, 1999). Few messages are either entirely rational or entirely emotional. Instead, most messages generate some degree of both rational and emotional processes.

For example, some messages designed to be rational appeals can create any number of emotional reactions in recipients. An otherwise rational message on critical food shortages in third-world countries might foster fear, pity, guilt, and probably other emotions in receivers. Moreover, as we will discuss in the next chapter, while explanations for the persuasive effectiveness of fear appeals (e.g., Rogers, 1975; Witte, 1992) once drew a clear distinction between cognitive and emotional processes, more recent research considers them to be clearly related processes (Mongeau, 2013). As a consequence, while the distinction between rational and emotional appeals might be a useful organizational tool in a textbook, drawing a clear conceptual distinction between the two in practice is a much more difficult task.

RATIONAL PERSUASIVE APPEALS

Persuasive messages that contain rational arguments are based on the assumptions that people have an implicit understanding of formal rules of logic and that they apply these rules when they make judgments about a source's recommendations. Rational arguments derive their influence from sound reasoning and the quality of evidence that is offered in support of the conclusion. Though there are many types of rational appeals, the most basic form of an argument contains three components: a claim, data to support that claim, and a warrant that provides a logical connection between the data and the claim (Toulmin, 1964).

In Toulmin's terms, a *claim* is the conclusion of the argument, the position supported by reasoning and information. Typically, the claim is the position a source is advocating in a message. *Data* are evidence that provide support for the claim. McCroskey (1969) defined evidence as "factual statements originating from a source other than the speaker, objects not created by the speaker, and opinions of persons other than the speaker that are offered in support of the speaker's claims" (p. 170). Finally, a *warrant* is a propositional statement that connects the data to the claim. Its specific form may vary, but a warrant always provides the logical connection between the data and the claim. It is the justification for the claim, given the data provided.

For example, consider the following argument: "Recent tuition increases at most state universities make it increasingly difficult for people from lower- and middle-income families to obtain a college degree. Thus, we should cap tuition increases in order to make public education accessible to students from all economic backgrounds." In this argument, the claim is that we should cap tuition increases. Support for this claim comes from the first sentence, which states that tuition increases make it difficult for students in lower socioeconomic groups to attend college. However, this evidence is not relevant to the claim unless we also consider our long-standing national commitment to make public education accessible to everyone. Hence, the warrant that connects the data to the claim is the statement that we must maintain our commitment to make public education accessible to everyone.

In our example above, the warrant was included as part of the argument (i.e., the warrant was explicit). This is not true of all arguments. Some messages include an implicit warrant. Consider a version of the tuition cap argument we presented above: "We should cap tuition increases at most state universities because they make it difficult for people from lower- and middle-income families to obtain a college degree." In this case, the claim and the data are the same as in the previous example; however, the warrant (i.e., that it is important to keep a college education available to everyone) is missing.

Toulmin's model of argument specifies an important role for evidence in the persuasion process and suggests two important questions for persuasion scholars (Shen & Bigsby, 2013). First, under what conditions is evidence persuasive? Second, how do rational appeals work to influence message receivers' attitudes and beliefs? In the next sections of this chapter we examine each of these questions. We begin with a discussion of the persuasive effects of evidence and then review studies that have modeled the effectiveness of rational appeals.

PERSUASIVE EFFECTS OF EVIDENCE

There are few notions in persuasive communication that are more intuitive than the hypothesis that the presence of high-quality evidence will increase the persuasiveness of a message. For example, while their terminologies may vary, public speaking textbooks all strongly suggest that persuasive speeches contain data, evidence, or supporting materials (e.g., German, Gronbeck, Ehninger, & Monroe, 2013).[1] However, as noted in the preceding chapter regarding the influence of source credibility, early reviews of evidence research painted a far murkier picture than our intuition would suggest. Lacking an overarching theoretical perspective, researchers conducted studies whose results were seemingly very inconsistent, and early reviewers had difficulty summarizing this literature (e.g., Kellermann, 1980; McCroskey, 1967b, 1969).

Not until the 1980s did some clarity emerge concerning the persuasive impact of evidence (see Reinard, 1988; Reynolds & M. Burgoon, 1983; Shen & Bigsby, 2013). Reinard (1988) argued that past inconsistencies in research on the persuasive impact of evidence were caused by different ways of manipulating (or controlling) evidence as well as by differences in the terminology used to describe these manipulations (see also Kellermann, 1980; Reynolds & M. Burgoon, 1983; Shen & Bigsby, 2013). For example, while several studies compared the persuasive effects of messages containing "evidence" and "no evidence," they differed strongly on what those two terms meant. One study might define evidence as statistical information while another defined it as statements made by individuals other than the message source. To make matters even worse, what might count as "no evidence" differed across studies as well (Hample, 1978).

When John Reinard (1988) grouped studies according to conceptual (and operational) definitions of evidence, a much clearer picture emerged. He concluded that various characteristics of evidence have different effects on attitudes and behaviors. Specifically, he postulated that five internal characteristics were consistently related to attitude and behavior change: the credibility of the evidence source, its probative force, the quality of the evidence, the amount of it available, and the novelty or recency of the evidence. Reinard (1988) concluded that, once one compares studies based on these characteristics, "Evidence appears to produce general persuasive effects that appear surprisingly stable" (p. 46; see also Reynolds & M. Burgoon, 1983; Reynolds & Reynolds, 2002; Shen & Bigsby, 2013).

Research on the persuasive effects of various types of evidence continues apace. Specifically, numerous studies have examined the comparative effectiveness of *statistical* and *narrative* evidence. Statistical evidence describes information from (typically) a large number of people that is combined and presented using a quantifiable metric like a rate, average, or probability. In contrast, narrative evidence is anecdotal and most often describes the experiences of a single person.

Two early reviews of this literature comparing the persuasive impact of statistical and narrative evidence found no large differences (Allen & Preiss, 1997; Reinard, 1988). More recent research, however, has suggested that statistical evidence and narrative evidence are both persuasive but produce different outcomes and do so in different ways. For example, Kopfman, Smith, Yun, and Hodges (1998) reported that statistical evidence enhances cognitive responses (i.e., thinking) while narrative evidence facilitates affective (or emotional) responses. These processing differences may explain why Greene and Brinn (2003) reported that statistical evidence had a stronger effect on beliefs, while narrative evidence had a stronger influence on intentions.

Remember, however, that the early literature reviews (e.g., the Allen & Preiss [1997] meta-analysis and Reinard, 1988) failed to highlight the differences between narrative and statistical evidence. Zebregs, van den Putte, Neijens, and de Graaf (2015) noted that the Allen and Preiss (1997) meta-analysis failed to conduct separate analyses for various persuasive outcomes (e.g., attitudes and intentions) and that they may have missed important differences in the effects of narrative and statistical evidence. Working from the theory of planned behavior (Ajzen, 1985), Zebregs and colleagues (2015) hypothesized that statistical evidence, being based on large numbers of individuals, likely activates cognitive processes and would have the greatest influence on beliefs and attitudes. In contrast, narrative evidence was hypothesized to encourage affective processing, perhaps because messages include information about an actor's emotions (e.g., Kopfman et al., 1998). Such information is typically absent in messages featuring statistical evidence. Affective processes (e.g., anticipated regret) have been shown to predict behavioral intentions above and beyond those explained by other cognitive factors (Sandberg & Conner, 2008). Therefore, Zebregs et al. (2015) predicted that narrative evidence would have its greatest impact on behavioral intentions.

To test their hypotheses, the Zebregs team (2015) performed a meta-analysis that considered the separate influences of statistical versus narrative evidence on attitudes, behaviors, and intentions. Consistent with their hypotheses, they found that statistical evidence had stronger effects on beliefs and attitudes than did narrative evidence, while narrative evidence had a stronger impact on behavioral intentions than did statistical evidence.

Although the literature on the persuasive effects of evidence is clearer now than it was once thought to be, we need to be careful not to oversimplify it. Indeed, the influence of persuasive evidence appears to depend on a variety of intervening and moderating variables. For example, Reinard (1988) noted that (among other variables) source credibility and message receivers' prior attitude and knowledge about the message topic influence the persuasiveness of evidence. Moreover, the cognitive models of persuasion discussed in Chapter 5 suggest that a message receiver's motivation to process the message may also affect the persuasiveness of the evidence. We will consider each of these variables in the next sections.

BOX 7.1. Politicians' Use of Statistical and Narrative Evidence

Politicians routinely use both statistical and narrative evidence to argue a point. For example, a politician promoting the benefits of "Obamacare" may use statistical evidence to talk about the number of people who have signed up for health insurance, the decline in the rate of uninsured people, the change in the cost of health insurance premiums, and newfound efficiencies in the system. Although the statistical data may be persuasive, politicians also understand that stories or narratives that personalize this information may also motivate voters to act. Thus, the same politician may also describe the experience of a family caring for a child with a life-threatening illness that is able to access insurance that was previously unaffordable; or a family with three children who are able to remain on their parents' health insurance plan until they reach the age of 26. Combining narrative with statistical evidence has become a staple of modern political discourse, because narrative accounts help to add extra meaning and emotional punch to statistical data.

Source Credibility and the Persuasive Effects of Evidence

Early research on source credibility by McCroskey and colleagues found support for the proposition that, while low-credibility sources are more persuasive when they use evidence, the effects for highly credible sources are more complicated. Specifically, early research found that highly credible sources do not derive any *immediate* persuasive advantage from the use of evidence (Luchok & McCroskey, 1978; McCroskey, 1967a, 1967b, 1969; McCroskey & Dunham, 1966). Speakers who lack credibility can benefit from supporting information originating from third parties (who presumably are more credible). However, highly credible speakers are less dependent on information from third parties to buttress their arguments.

In contrast, research that measured *delayed* attitude change several weeks after the message presentation found that highly credible sources do gain a persuasive advantage from the use of evidence. M. Burgoon and J. K. Burgoon (1975) concluded that, when attitude change is measured over time, evidence enhances the persuasive effects of messages from both highly and less credible sources.

Thus, quality evidence appears to enhance the persuasiveness of low-credibility sources in both the short term and long term as well as the persuasiveness of highly credible sources—but only in the long term. This finding appears consistent with the differential decay explanation of the sleeper effect (covered in Chapter 6). Over time, the effects of source credibility decay faster than the persuasive effects of message content (i.e., evidence). When persisting attitude change is the goal, evidence is an important component of message appeals because the influence of source credibility is short-lived.

McCroskey (1970) argued that, while evidence may not enhance the persuasiveness of highly credible sources in the short term, message receivers who have come to expect evidence in support of a conclusion may punish speakers who do not provide such evidence. In such cases, the absence of evidence may diminish the credibility of the source. In this regard, Reinard (1988) concluded that "evidence may influence and be influenced by source credibility" (p. 42).

Indeed, there appears to be a symbiotic relationship between source credibility and argument quality. For example, in one of the early tests of the ELM, Petty, Cacioppo, and colleagues (1981) reported that the argument quality manipulation had a stronger effect of perceptions of credibility than did the source credibility manipulation, a finding consistent with the hypothesis that judgments about argument quality are used to draw inferences about the expertise of the message source (Reimer et al., 2004). Moreover, evidence from the source credibility literature suggests that source credibility affects perceptions of the quality of message arguments (Hahn et al., 2009; Hovland & Weiss, 1951).

Receivers' Motivation and the Persuasive Effects of Evidence

We know from our discussion of the HSM (Chaiken, 1980) and the ELM (Petty & Cacioppo, 1981, 1986) in Chapter 5 that message receivers' ability and motivation to process a persuasive message have significant impacts on the persuasiveness of message content. Specifically, issue involvement affects people's motivation to scrutinize persuasive message content. When message receivers are highly involved with the message topic, such characteristics as the strength of supporting evidence should influence attitude change. Conversely, when message receivers are relatively uninvolved with the message topic, they will be less motivated to consider message content and the persuasive effects of evidence will be minimal. In other words, the greater the message receiver's involvement with the message topic, the more strongly evidence should influence attitude change.

A meta-analytic review of the evidence literature provided support for this general hypothesis (Stiff, 1986). When the findings of 30 investigations were cumulated, Stiff (1986) found an overall positive correlation between the use of evidence and attitude change (average $r = .18$). However, consistent with the cognitive models of persuasion, there was an interaction between message recipient involvement and the persuasiveness of message evidence. Specifically, when the message topic was relatively uninvolving for recipients, evidence was least persuasive (i.e., the correlation between evidence quality and attitude change was weak; average $r = .12$). For moderately involving topics, the correlation between the amount or quality of evidence and attitude change was somewhat stronger (average $r = .18$). Finally, the correlation was strongest when the topic was highly involving for message receivers (average $r = .30$). Although relatively small in size, the differences among these effect sizes were statistically significant. Thus, the meta-analysis of the effects of supporting information on attitudes was consistent with the effects derived from the ELM.

The investigations included in Jim's meta-analytic review (Stiff, 1986) contained several ways of manipulating evidence. Some studies manipulated the *amount* of evidence contained in the message, other studies compared the *presence or absence* of evidence in a message, and still others manipulated evidence by varying the *quality* of arguments contained in a message. Petty and his colleagues (Petty et al., 1987) criticized the decision to collapse these different types of evidence manipulations into a single category. They argued that the different types of evidence manipulations would produce different persuasive effects. However, subsequent reanalysis of these studies produced the same pattern of effects for each type of evidence manipulation (Stiff & Boster, 1987).

Thus, the pattern of findings that emerged from Jim's (Stiff, 1986; Stiff & Boster, 1987) meta-analysis appears quite robust. Across many studies and several operational definitions, the persuasive effects of evidence appear to depend on recipients' motivation to scrutinize message content. As we discussed in Chapter 5, in addition to involvement in the message topic, a person's *need for cognition* affects the extent to which he or she is motivated to engage in effortful processing of persuasive messages (Petty & Cacioppo, 1986; Petty et al., 2009). When motivated to consider message content, receivers are likely to be influenced by the quality of the message's supporting evidence.

Prior Attitudes and the Persuasive Effects of Evidence

Just because evidence is cognitively processed, that does not imply that it will be processed *logically*. It is well established that when people have an established attitude on an issue they are prone to making errors in logical reasoning when considering persuasive messages about that issue.

In an early study, Janis and Frick (1943) hypothesized that people are likely to let their agreement with an argument's conclusion affect their judgments concerning the logical validity of that argument. The two researchers found that when students agreed with an argument they tended to judge an invalid argument as valid. Moreover, if they disagreed with a conclusion, they evaluated a valid argument as invalid. This finding provided early evidence for the proposition that established opinions affect the ways in which people process message evidence.

Bettinghaus and his colleagues (Bettinghaus, Miller, & Steinfatt, 1970) extended this analysis and found that, because of their rigid cognitive style, highly dogmatic people tend to let their preference for an argument's conclusion guide their evaluation of the argument's validity to a greater extent than do less dogmatic people.

Together, these studies suggest that people tend to make systematic errors when they judge the validity of arguments. Though the accuracy rates in these studies were quite high because they involved college students who likely had some training in formal logic and reasoning, it is important to realize that people can and do make errors in their reasoning when processing persuasive messages and that these errors are often influenced by their existing attitudes on the subject of the message.

BOX 7.2. "Birthers" Need No Evidence

Although research into the persuasive effects of evidence has focused primarily on the attitude formation process, there is reason to believe that evidence has only limited persuasive appeal in situations where people have entrenched attitudes. Perhaps there is no better example of the limits of evidence than the "birther" movement within the Republican party.

Following Barack Obama's election as president in 2008, members of the Republican party were strongly opposed to his presidency and even questioned its legitimacy. Conservative talk radio hosts started a campaign to convince listeners that Obama was not born in the United States and therefore was not constitutionally eligible to serve as its president. Soon, many Republican politicians took up the cause and began to sow seeds of doubt about President Obama's place of birth.

By April 2011, 45% of all Republicans believed that President Obama was not born in the United States, and another 22% indicated "don't know" in response to the question (Condon, 2011). In May 2012, Ken Bennett, Arizona's secretary of state and cochair of Mitt Romney's Arizona campaign for president, considered blocking President Obama's name from being placed on the Arizona ballot for the 2012 presidential election.

Despite clear evidence that Obama was born in Honolulu, Hawaii, in 1961, only one-third of the Republicans were willing to acknowledge that he was legitimately a U.S. citizen. We know from this and many other examples that people who maintain firmly held convictions are unwilling to consider evidence that is contrary to their belief system. In this regard, evidence may be more persuasive in *attitude-shaping* and *attitude-reinforcing* processes than it is in *attitude-changing* processes.

While it is fair to conclude that evidence is generally persuasive (Reinard, 1988; Stiff, 1986), these findings further limit the conditions under which evidence will influence response change. In many instances, people with established attitudes will make errors in reasoning, while those who lack the motivation to scrutinize the content of persuasive messages will not be persuaded by the evidence contained in them.

MODELING THE EFFECTS OF RATIONAL APPEALS

The preceding discussion of the limitations of rational appeals was not intended to create the impression that logical arguments and supporting information are ineffective in creating, changing, or reinforcing attitudes and behavior. Rather, it was intended to provide readers with a better understanding of the situations in which the influence of rational appeals is likely to be limited. Given that rational appeals are effective under certain circumstances, it is also important to understand *how* they persuade targets.

Mathematical models of belief formation and change provide some insight into how rational persuasive appeals operate (Hample, 1977, 1978, 1979; McGuire, 1960; Wyer, 1970; Wyer & Goldberg, 1970). These models are derived from logic and assume that humans are rational beings.

McGuire's Probabilistic Model

Belief in an argument's claim (or conclusion) is not always an all-or-nothing proposition. That is, typically people believe claims with a wide latitude of probability. Sometimes they hold the beliefs with a high degree of certainty—in fact, those who are absolutely convinced that their belief in a statement is 100% correct might characterize the belief statement as "absolutely true." Beliefs about abortion rights or the right to life, for example, tend to be held with a high degree of certainty or conviction by their proponents (i.e., with a probability at or near 1.00). That is, abortion rights advocates and their anti-abortion adversaries often express all-or-nothing beliefs about abortion. The battle lines have been clearly drawn, and for many people on opposite sides of this continuing debate there is no gray area, no common ground.

On the other hand, our beliefs about most issues are held with less certainty. For example, we may believe that government regulation and close oversight of the banking industry help to protect consumers, or that grade school students would benefit from a longer academic school year, but we may be less certain of these beliefs than we are about our beliefs surrounding the abortion issue. That is, we may hold these beliefs with a probability of much less than 1.00.

To explain the variation in the extent to which people accept an argument's claim (or conclusion), McGuire (1960) developed a probabilistic model of beliefs. The foundation of this model is a form of argument known as the logical syllogism. Logical syllogisms have three components: a major premise, a minor premise, and a conclusion. If an argument is valid, its conclusion can be deduced from the major and the minor premises, provided they are true. Consider the following example:

Major premise: If I attend every class session and study 3 hours a week, I will receive an "A" in my persuasion course.

Minor premise: I will attend every class and study 3 hours a week.

Conclusion: I will receive an "A" in my persuasion course.

In this example, if both the major premise and minor premise are true, then the conclusion is true by definition. Thus, if attending every class and studying 3 hours a week is sufficient to receive an "A" in your persuasion course, then you should expect an "A" if you attend class and study 3 hours a week. However, McGuire (1960) argued that you may be less than entirely certain about the major or the minor premise and yet still believe the conclusion. For example, you may believe with a high probability—say, 80%—that the major premise is true, and believe with a somewhat lower probability—say, 70%—that the minor premise is true. According to McGuire's model, if either the major or minor premise (or both) is held with less-than-certain probability, then the conclusion will also be held with less-than-certain probability.

McGuire's model is actually quite simple, and can be easily represented in the following equation:

$$p(B) = p(B/A)\, p(A) \tag{7.1}$$

where $p(B)$ (read: the probability of B) is the probability that the conclusion is true; $p(B/A)$ (read: the probability of B, given A) is the probability that the major premise is true; and $p(A)$ (read: the probability of A) is the probability that the minor premise is true.

Thus, to estimate your belief in the conclusion of an argument, you simply multiply the probability that you believe the major premise is true by the probability that you believe the minor premise is true. Applying this model to the earlier syllogism about receiving an "A" in your persuasion course highlights the effects of probabilistic beliefs. Assume that you believe the probability of the major premise (i.e., that if you attend every class and study 3 hours a week, you will get an "A") to be .80 and the probability of the minor premise (that you will actually attend every class and study 3 hours a week) to be .70. Then, the probability that you believe the conclusion, that is, that you will receive an "A" in the course, should be .56 (i.e., .80 multiplied by .70). Conversely, the probability that you will receive something other than an "A" is .44 (or 1.00 − .56).

It bears mentioning that, like any other model or theory of persuasion, McGuire's model is hypothetical, one that describes how the components of logical syllogisms determine people's beliefs about an argument's conclusion. Tests of this hypothesis were relatively straightforward. People were asked to indicate the probability that a number of belief statements were true. Embedded in this list of belief statements were minor premises, major premises, and conclusions from syllogisms. By multiplying a person's belief probability for the major premise of an argument by that person's belief probability of the minor premise, researchers could obtain a predicted value for the person's belief in the conclusion. To specifically test McGuire's model, the person's reported belief in the conclusion is compared with the predicted belief in the conclusion. A strong positive correlation between the predicted and reported probabilities of belief in the conclusion indicates the extent to which the model describes how people form beliefs about an argument's conclusion. McGuire's model produced the anticipated significant correlations between predicted and observed belief probabilities, thus providing support for this model (McGuire, 1960).

McGuire's (1960) probabilistic model presumes that people are being entirely logical when judging the validity of an argument's conclusion. This represents what he called the "logical consistency" of beliefs and attitudes. McGuire recognized, however, that people are not always logically consistent. He suggested that "hedonic consistency" (or wishful thinking) also influences people's judgments about an argument's validity. Thus, in addition to exhibiting logical consistency, McGuire (1960) reported that people had a tendency to consider conclusions that depicted favorable outcomes as valid (even if they were entirely illogical). As a consequence, while the probabilistic model is useful in understanding how audience members cognitively construct arguments, there will always be more to the story than logic.

Wyer's Extension of McGuire's Model

Although studies supported McGuire's model, correlations between predicted and observed belief probabilities were far from perfect. In an effort to improve its predictive value, Wyer (1970) and Wyer and Goldberg (1970) proposed an extension of McGuire's original model. They hypothesized that factors other than those included in an argument influenced the probability in which people believe the argument's conclusion. In fact, Wyer hypothesized that people could believe the conclusion of a syllogism even if they did not believe the major and minor premises. For example, you may believe you will receive an "A" in your persuasion class even if you don't go to class every day and study regularly. Instead, you may believe that you will receive an "A" because you are brilliant, cheat well, or believe the class is remarkably easy. Wyer's extension can be represented in the following equation:

$$p(B) = p(B/A) \, p(A) + p(B/\overline{A}) \, p(\overline{A}) \qquad (7.2)$$

where the first part of the equation (before "+") is identical to McGuire's model. Specifically, the $p(B)$, $p(B/A)$, and $p(A)$ terms are identical to Equation 7.1. Wyer's extension appears after the addition sign. In this part of the model, $p(B/\overline{A})$ (read: the probability of B, given *not-A*) is the probability that the conclusion is true even if the minor premise is false; and $p(\overline{A})$ (read: the probability of *not-A*) is the probability that the minor premise is false. By definition, the value of $p(\overline{A})$ is $1 - p(A)$.

Thus, Wyer's (1970) model suggests that a person's belief in the conclusion is determined by his or her belief in the major and minor premises *plus* the effects of factors not included in the syllogism. Extending our example about the grade you believe you will receive, recall that your belief in the major premise is .80, your belief in the minor premise is .70, and the product of these two belief probabilities is .56. So far, Wyer's equation works the same as McGuire's.

Wyer's model (1970) requires that you also consider your belief that you will receive an "A" even if you do not attend every class and study 3 hours a week, $p(B/\overline{A})$. In Wyer's extension, the value of $p(B/\overline{A})$, or the probability that you will receive an "A" even if you do not attend every class and study 3 hours a week, is multiplied by $p(\overline{A})$, or the probability that you will not attend every class and study 3 hours a week.

Assume that you believe the probability that you will receive an "A" even if you do not attend every class and study 3 hours a week is .40. Because $p(\overline{A})$ equals $1 - p(A)$, you believe the probability that you will not attend class and study 3 hours a week is .30. Multiplying these latter two values produces a belief in the conclusion (i.e., that you will receive an "A" even if you don't attend class and study 3 hours a week) of .12 (i.e., .40 multiplied by .30) because of factors other than those contained in the original argument. Combined with the probability that the conclusion is true because the major and minor premises are true (.56), the overall belief probability in the conclusion is .68 (i.e., .56 + .12).

Thus, in this example, Wyer's (1970) model predicts that you believe there is a .68 probability of getting an "A" in your persuasion class, compared to the .56 probability predicted by the McGuire model. As does the previous model, Wyer's probabilistic model represents a hypothesis about the structure of people's beliefs. Tests of this hypothesis, however, produced disappointing results. In comparative tests of the two models, Hample (1979) found that the McGuire model predicted beliefs much better than the Wyer model.

Hample's Refinement of Wyer's Model

Hample (1979) argued that, when added together, the two components in the Wyer model tended to offset each other. Because the $p(A)$ is inversely related to $p(\overline{A})$—recall that $p(\overline{A}) = 1 - p(A)$—the values for the first multiplicative term (i.e., before the "+") in Wyer's equation were negatively correlated with the values of the second multiplicative term (i.e., following the "+") in the equation. The result was a model with less predictive validity than the original model offered by McGuire.

To alleviate this problem, Hample suggested applying a weight to each of the multiplicative components in the Wyer model. We discussed the concept of weights in Chapter 3 when we covered the Theory of Reasoned Action. Weights in this case represent the relative importance of the two parts of Wyer's model. By applying weights, these two components can vary independently of each other rather than being negatively related.

Using regression analysis, Hample (1979) demonstrated that applying weights to both parts of the Wyer model allowed each to work independently to predict people's belief in the conclusion of an argument. That is, the weights allow both components in Wyer's model to contribute without canceling each other out. In short, Hample applied a statistical solution to the problems associated with Wyer's model. He further demonstrated that his weighted version of Wyer's model produced uniformly strong correlations between people's predicted and reported beliefs in the conclusions of various arguments. Hample's revision of the Wyer model provided a better approximation of people's beliefs in the conclusion than either the Wyer (1970) or the McGuire (1960) models.

Why These Models Are Important

Students often question the value of these mathematical models for persuasion practitioners. We frequently field inquiries about the relevance of probabilistic models for everyday interaction or even for the development of persuasive campaigns. Although their value may not be intuitively obvious, these models provide considerable insight into the role that evidence plays in persuasion.

Recall our earlier discussion of Toulmin's (1964) model of argument. A valid argument contains a claim, data to support that claim, and a warrant that connects the data to the claim. Hample (1978) argued that, whatever verbal form an argument may ultimately take, its warrant must serve the logical function of asserting "if D then C, where D represents the data and C represents the claim" (p. 220). In a logical syllogism, the argument's warrant is consistent with the major premise. The data are expressed in the minor premise, and the argument's claim is represented in the conclusion. Thus, the probabilistic models describe the effect of an argument's evidence and warrant on adherence to its claim. Hample's (1979) revision of Wyer's (1970) model accurately predicted people's acceptance of an argument's conclusion and thus provides insights into the operation of evidence in the persuasion process.

Hample's (1979) model underscores the importance of evidence in the success of a logical appeal. Furthermore, the model implies that belief in the argument's warrant is as important as the acceptance of the supporting evidence. Given the importance of the warrant to the overall acceptance of the argument, sources may gain a persuasive advantage by explicitly stating the connection between the data and the claim and avoiding the use of implicit warrants. Because they are unstated, implicit warrants enable message targets to provide their own connections between the data and the claims or to leave the evidence logically unconnected. Indeed, M. Burgoon (1989) cautioned against the use of implicit conclusions for the same reason. He argued that "persuaders must be cautious in assuming that the audience will draw the *correct* conclusion from the data" (p. 144). Arguments with explicit warrants also require less cognitive participation from message targets who may be content to adopt the logic, and hence the conclusions, of a source's arguments.

ONE- AND TWO-SIDED RATIONAL APPEALS

One characteristic of rational persuasion is that two or more opposing positions can be advocated for any persuasion topic. Because there are at least two sides to every story, persuaders must decide how much attention they should direct toward opposing viewpoints. The extent to which messages recognize and attempt to refute those opposing viewpoints is called *message sidedness*. Messages can be crafted to focus exclusively on arguments in favor of a source's position, or they can be expanded to acknowledge the existence of (and, perhaps, refute) opposing arguments. Messages that contain only supporting arguments are labeled *one-sided messages*; those that also address opposing viewpoints are labeled *two-sided messages*.

BOX 7.3. Contrast Advertisements in Political Campaigns

One familiar type of two-sided message is the contrast ad in a political campaign. In a typical negative advertisement, the records of the two competing candidates are contrasted. Such a message might compare two candidates' voting records on issues such as tax increases or immigration policy. Two positions are compared, and one (i.e., the one held by the candidate sponsoring the ad, of course) is asserted to be superior. In contrast, a one-sided political advertisement might simply extol an incumbent's experience in office and role as a community leader without mentioning the challenger's name or record.

As is true with several research areas in persuasive communication, Hovland and colleagues (1949) were the first to investigate the relative persuasiveness of one- and two-sided messages. Like most variable analytic researchers of their day, Hovland's group was motivated by a practical (rather than a theoretical) concern: they wanted to determine which message structure would enjoy the greatest persuasive success.

Initial investigations of this issue found that premessage agreement with the position advocated in the message and the educational level of the message recipients influence the relative persuasiveness of one- and two-sided messages. Participants who already agreed with the position advocated in a message were persuaded more by one-sided messages, whereas two-sided messages were more effective with targets who initially disagreed with the source's position (Lumsdaine & Janis, 1953). Moreover, two-sided messages proved more successful for targets with some high school education, whereas one-sided messages were more successful for less educated targets (Hovland et al., 1949).

These early research efforts sparked considerable interest in the structure of persuasive messages. One additional question that emerged from Hovland and colleagues' research was the extent to which one- and two-sided messages influenced credibility assessments of the speaker. Presumably, well-informed audiences and audiences that disagree with the speaker's position are cognizant of opposing viewpoints and expect the source to address both sides of the issue. One-sided message presentations to these types of audiences were hypothesized to produce lower judgments of source expertise and trustworthiness and to limit the effectiveness of the message.

Unfortunately, subsequent investigations of message sidedness produced an array of conflicting findings. Some studies found two-sided messages to be more persuasive, others found one-sided messages more persuasive, and yet others revealed no effects for message sidedness. More-over, the pattern of findings in these investigations did not support the anticipated effects of audience characteristics.

Three related meta-analytic reviews have been conducted on this lit-erature. The first review was an unpublished paper by Jackson and Allen (1987) that laid the conceptual groundwork for two published meta-analyses (Allen, 1991, 1998) and original research that was conducted by Allen and colleagues (Allen et al., 1990). One important aspect of the early meta-analytic reviews is that they noted widespread differences in the ways that message sidedness was manipulated in prior research. Although the construction of one-sided messages was relatively consis-tent across studies, the nature of two-sided messages varied in important ways. For example, some investigations constructed two-sided messages that acknowledged, but did not refute, opposing arguments. Allen and colleagues (1990) labeled these as "two-sided nonrefutational messages." Other researchers developed two-sided messages that not only recognized opposing viewpoints but also refuted them. These were labeled as "two-sided refutational messages."

In the meta-analytic reviews, Allen and colleagues (Allen, 1991; Jack-son & Allen, 1987) produced the hypothesis that message sources who recognize the existence of opposing viewpoints but do not refute them are likely to be perceived as less credible and less persuasive than sources who recognize *and* refute opposing viewpoints. In fact, they expected that two-sided nonrefutational messages would be less credible and less persuasive than one-sided messages, which in turn would be less credible and persua-sive than two-sided refutational messages (Allen, 1991; Jackson & Allen, 1987).

Consistent with his predictions, the results of the Allen (1991) meta-analysis indicated that the two-sided refutational messages were signifi-cantly more persuasive than one-sided messages. One-sided messages, in turn, were more persuasive than two-sided nonrefutational messages. Moreover, although not particularly large, the effect sizes Allen reported indicated that two-sided refutational messages were about *20% more effec-tive* than one-sided messages, whereas two-sided nonrefutational messages were about *20% less effective* than one-sided messages. It also bears men-tioning that early predictions of the relative effectiveness of one-sided mes-sages for favorable and less-educated audiences and two-sided messages for unfavorable and more educated audiences were not confirmed in Allen's review. He found that audience favorability toward the topic was unrelated to message effectiveness.[2]

The Jackson and Allen (1987) and Allen (1991) meta-analyses pro-vided evidence for the relative persuasiveness of these three different mes-sage types (i.e., refutational two-sided messages are more persuasive than one-sided messages, which are more persuasive than nonrefutational two-sided messages). No single study in the meta-analyses, however, had utilized all three message types, as each one compared one-sided to either a two-sided refutational or nonrefutational message (but not both).

To directly test the differential effectiveness of all three message types, Allen and colleagues (1990) conducted three studies involving 17 topics, 51 messages, and over 1,000 research participants. For each of the 17 topics, they developed three persuasive messages: a one-sided message, a two-sided refutational message, and a two-sided nonrefutational message. These messages were presented to research participants, and their attitudes and perceptions of source credibility were measured following the message. A consistent pattern of findings emerged from their analyses. Two-sided refutational messages were more persuasive than one-sided messages, and one-sided messages were more persuasive than two-sided nonrefutational messages. The pattern for source credibility assessments was consistent with the attitude data. People who read the two-sided refutational messages provided the most favorable assessments of source credibility, followed by those who read the one-sided messages and the two-sided nonrefutational messages, respectively (Allen et al., 1990).

Hale, Mongeau, and Thomas (1991) employed cognitive response measures (i.e., indicators of what message receivers were thinking about during the message's reception) to explain the enhanced persuasiveness of two-sided refutational messages. The cognitive response approaches suggest that message receivers' thoughts are important in determining the effectiveness of a message. Hale and colleagues found that two-sided refutational messages produced more favorable thoughts about the message recommendation, which led to a more favorable evaluation of the message and greater attitude change, than did one-sided messages. In turn, one-sided messages produced more positive thoughts and were more persuasive than two-sided nonrefutational messages. In combination, the findings of Allen's (1991) meta-analysis and Hale and colleagues' (1991) study suggest that two-sided refutational messages are more persuasive, because they produce more favorable thoughts about the message recommendation and more favorable evaluations of the source's credibility.

FILLING IN THE BLANKS

There are several findings in the preceding sections that suggest that making message arguments explicit will increase attitude change. First, we argued that an important implication of Hample's Attitude Change Model is that both an argument's data and its warrant should be explicitly stated. Second, two-sided refutational messages may be superior to two-sided nonrefutational messages because they clearly show why one position is superior to another. In both these cases, message sources gain a persuasive advantage by making their arguments as complete as is possible, so receivers are not left to *fill in the blanks* left by an incomplete message.

Two meta-analyses speak to the issue of filling in the blanks in persuasive messages. First, D. J. O'Keefe (1997) conducted a meta-analysis of the relative impact of implicit versus explicit message conclusions. The issue he studied was the extent to which messages are more persuasive when they contain an explicit statement of the message's conclusion (as compared to messages that simply allow message receivers to fill in that information). O'Keefe found that messages that explicitly described the message's conclusions (i.e., "filled in the blanks," in our parlance) were more persuasive than those that left such information only implicit.

D. J. O'Keefe (1998) argued that leaving it to recipients to fill in the blanks by using implicit warrants or conclusions might make them work harder to draw their own conclusions about the message. There is also a tendency for audience members to consider their own thoughts to be stronger or more enlightened than message arguments (what Perloff and Brock [1980] call the "ownness bias"). When audience members' thoughts influence their attitudes, however, they may not fill in the blanks the way the source intends them to. If message or argument elements are implicit, the audience might take what information is available to them and come to a conclusion that is consistent with their initial attitudes rather than the conclusion intended by the source (Bettinghaus et al., 1970; Janis & Frick, 1943).

SUMMARY

This chapter examined the use of rational appeals in persuasive messages. We began by examining the structure of rational appeals and how they functioned to influence attitudes and behavior. We concluded that when people are motivated and able to process the content of a persuasive message, rational appeals are an effective persuasive technique. Moreover, the quality of supporting information in these appeals determines the persuasiveness of the message. Although we are often accurate judges of the logical validity of a rational appeal, when we do make errors, they tend to be systematic and reflect our personal agreement or disagreement with the argument's conclusion. We also considered the relative merits of one- and two-sided rational appeals and concluded that two-sided refutational messages were more effective than both one-sided messages and two-sided nonrefutational messages. Finally, the research suggests that speakers who use implicit warrants and conclusions and invite message receivers to "fill in the blanks" run the risk that the receivers may draw their own conclusions about the message topic rather than accept the conclusions desired by the source.

1. As we begin this discussion, it is important to distinguish the concept of *evidence* as we discuss it here from Petty and Cacioppo's (1986) concept of *argument quality*. Recall from Chapter 5 that, in the ELM, the argument quality manipulation is designed to influence the valence (i.e., positive or negative nature) of recipients' cognitions *if they actively process the message*. The ELM's definition of argument quality says nothing about the quality or strength of an argument (Petty & Cacioppo, 1986; Petty & Wegener, 1999). In contrast, when we discuss *evidence* in this chapter we are referring to data, facts, and third-party statements that are offered in support of a proposition. The concept of evidence is distinct from the concept of *argument quality* because the former focuses on the specific nature and validity of the arguments in the message.

2. D. J. O'Keefe (1993) questioned Allen's meta-analytic conclusions, based on the latter's classification of studies as using two-sided refutational or two-sided non-refutational messages. After changing six studies from two-sided refutational to two-sided nonrefutational, O'Keefe concluded that two-sided refutational messages were more persuasive than either one-sided or two-sided nonrefutational messages (which did not differ from each other). In Allen's (1993) response, he stands by his original conclusion (though not totally satisfactorily) that two-sided refutational messages are more persuasive than one-sided messages, which are in turn more persuasive than two-sided nonrefutational messages. Other results consistent with Allen's conclusions (Allen et al., 1990; Hale et al., 1991) bolster our confidence in these findings, even in the face of O'Keefe's concerns.

CHAPTER 8

Persuasive Message Characteristics
EMOTIONAL APPEALS

LOOKING AHEAD . . . In this chapter we continue our consideration of the characteristics of persuasive messages. In the preceding chapter, we covered several key topics relevant to rational appeals. Here we review the major theory and research relating to two types of emotional message appeals, namely, fear appeals and guilt appeals. We review the long history of studying fear appeals and the explanations that have been developed to explain their effectiveness. We also discuss the research associated with changing a message target's attitudes and behaviors through the creation of guilt. While guilt appeals have not generated nearly the amount of research or theorizing that fear appeals have, creating attitude and behavior change through guilt appears to be an interesting and complex phenomenon.

Emotions have been the focus of scholars representing a variety of disciplines, ranging from philosophy to biology. Even within the study of communication, scholars look at emotions in a number of ways and in a number of different contexts (e.g., Andersen & Guerrero, 1998). As a consequence, "Defining emotion is a tricky proposition" (Guerrero, Andersen, & Trost, 1998, p. 5). Spearheading the resurgence in the study of emotion within communication scholarship, Dillard (1998) argued that human beings, as a species, "have evolved to meet adaptive challenges posed by the environment and . . . emotions represent the reactions that occur in response to these environmental changes" (p. xvii). As environments change, people have to decide whether these changes are good or bad for them. The cognitive activity that takes place during this evaluative process determines what emotions a person experiences.

Consider an example. While hiking in the Rocky Mountain wilderness outside Missoula, Montana, you suddenly encounter a large bear. This represents a drastic change in your environment, from appreciating awesome natural beauty to confronting a wild animal that may be bent on making you his lunch. Given such an environmental change, many people would report experiencing an emotion that they would describe as fear.

However, emotions like "fear" include several components (Guerrero et al., 1998). First, emotions have a cognitive component representing a person's interpretation of the environmental changes. You might interpret the large hungry-looking bear as a threat to your health and well-being. Dillard and Seo (2013) make an important distinction when they point out that the bear, per se, does not create the fear. Rather, the interpretation of the bear as a large, likely hungry, carnivore is what causes the emotion. More relevant to the present context, it isn't the fear appeal that is persuasive, but rather the audience's *interpretation* of the appeal.

Second, emotions have a positive or a negative feeling component (generally called *affect*; see Dillard & Seo, 2013; Guerrero et al., 1998). Most people's affective reactions to a bear are likely to be negative. Unexpectedly encountering a rare and endangered bird in the wilderness, however, would likely create a *positive* affective response in a birdwatcher. Generally speaking, if an environmental change is evaluated as being positive for us, our affective reaction will be positive, whereas if the change is evaluated as being bad for us, our affective reaction will be negative.

Third, emotions involve a physiological component. Encountering a large bear in the wilderness (thereby unleashing certain cognitive and affective reactions) is likely to generate considerable physiological arousal, which might well include increases in one's heart rate, respiration, and blood pressure; pupil dilation; and the release of adrenaline into the bloodstream.

Most relevant to the study of persuasive communication, the final component of emotions is behavioral. "The primary function of emotion is to guide behavior" (Dillard & Meijnders, 2002, p. 318). The cognitive (i.e., this is a dangerous animal), affective (i.e., this is bad for me), and physiological (i.e., arousal) reactions to the bear all function to create a behavioral response: run![1]

It is the behavioral component of emotions that makes them particularly well suited to persuasive communication in a variety of settings. If particular emotions generate a characteristic behavioral response, then persuasive messages may be able to exploit this effect (Dillard & Seo, 2013).

Recent research and theorizing indicates that there are a relatively small number of discrete emotions (though scholars disagree about their nature and exact number; see Guerrero et al., 1998; Nabi, 2002, 2010). For example, Fehr and Russell (1984) reported that people's listing of emotions most consistently included joy, hate, fear, love, sadness, anger, and happiness. Moreover, recent theorizing suggests that some emotions are discrete, including "anger, fear, sadness, guilt, happiness, and contentment" (Dillard & Seo, 2013, p. 17; see also Nabi, 2010). By *discrete,* we mean that emotions are considered distinct in terms of the four components described above. Thus, a particular emotion, like fear, is the result of an environmental change (i.e., a threat) that creates a unique pattern of cognitive, affective, physiological, and behavioral reactions. The pattern of reactions for fear will be different from the pattern for other discrete emotions, like anger, sadness, and guilt.

Just as there are a number of emotions, there are many types of emotional appeals (ranging from humor to sympathy) that may be persuasive. Fear appeals, however, have received the most attention from persuasion scholars and practitioners. As a consequence, we will spend most of this chapter reviewing fear appeals research and the various explanations that account for such appeals' success. We then devote the remainder of the chapter to discussing the effectiveness of guilt appeals as an approach to persuasion.

FEAR APPEALS

Fear appeals are frequently employed in prevention and safety campaigns directed at adolescents. For example, "Don't text and drive" campaigns routinely use fear-arousing messages to get teenagers' attention and motivate them to refrain from texting while driving. Despite fear appeals' popularity, however, many scholars have questioned their efficacy, with some even pointing out that they can occasionally "backfire" (Witte & Allen, 2000, p. 591; see also Geller, 1989). Thus, the primary question to consider in reviewing this literature is: Are fear appeals persuasive? The answer to this question is a qualified "Yes." Fear appeals can be persuasive, but only with certain types of messages and audiences. In this section of the chapter, we examine the fear appeal literature. We begin by defining a fear appeal and identifying models that describe how fear appeals work. Then, we summarize some of the important findings from previous studies of this category of persuasive messages.

Defining Fear Appeals

Over the years, a number of definitions have been used to separate fear appeals from other types of persuasive messages. For the most part, these definitions focus on either message content or audience reactions to a message (D. J. O'Keefe, 1990). For example, early definitions tended to describe fear appeals as messages containing gruesome content (Leventhal, 1970).

The gory films depicting car crash victims that continue to be used in high school driver education classes reflect this *message content definition* of fear appeals, as do more recent fear appeals that typically describe a threat and then the behaviors that receivers may adopt to avoid it.

A second approach defines a fear appeal as simply a message that provokes considerable fear in recipients. Studies adopting this *message response definition* create messages that are designed to arouse fear and then measure the amount of fear people report after their exposure to the messages. In Chapter 2, we referred to such measures as manipulation checks because they assess the effectiveness of the message manipulation. Messages that produce significant levels of self-reported fear in message recipients are defined as fear-arousing (or high-fear) messages.

BOX 8.1. Fear Appeals in Driver Training Classes

Short films like *Mechanized Death* (check it out on YouTube) were once a staple of driver education classes during the 1960s and 1970s, when Paul and Jim learned to drive. Videos produced by highway patrol officers and departments of public safety graphically depicted carnage on the highways caused by reckless driving. The shocking images of horribly disfigured corpses were intended to scare young drivers into obeying traffic laws and thereafter driving sensibly.

This past fall, Paul took his son to a driving school class, where similar films continue to be shown. While these efforts do not rise the standard of grossness typified by *Mechanized Death,* these films contained obvious fear appeals that were presented to both students and parents. One included footage from a camera at an intersection where a red-light infraction caused an accident, with two cars running over (and presumably killing) two pedestrians. There was also a shot of a driver in a fatal accident that was taken by a dashboard camera. It was a rollover accident, and the driver was violently thrown into the backseat and killed. There was also a professionally produced PSA that was highly graphic (though not *Mechanized Death*-gory).

While these fear-appeals videos continue to be shown to young drivers, there is no evidence that they have produced any meaningful positive results in traffic death reductions (for a review, see Lewis, Watson, Tay, & White, 2007). The U.S. Census Bureau reported in 2009 that teenagers were 2.5 times more likely to be involved in an accident than drivers over the age of 20, and 65% more likely to be involved in a fatal accident. By most accounts, more training appears to be the solution. A 2007 Massachusetts law increased the required number of parent-supervised driving hours to 40 and doubled the amount of time spent driving with an instructor, to 12 hours. Since this law's implementation, the number of teenage accidents on Massachusetts roads has dropped by half.

Although some studies adopt only one of these two approaches, many investigations incorporate features of both. That is, many studies define a fear appeal in terms of message content but also employ manipulation checks to assess audience perceptions of fear. For our purposes, *a fear appeal can be defined as a persuasive message that arouses fear by depicting a personally relevant and significant threat, followed by a description of feasible recommendations for deterring the threat* (see Witte, 1992).

Embedded in this definition are three concepts that have guided our thinking about fear appeals for over 60 years: *fear, perceived threat,* and *perceived efficacy.* "Fear" is a negative emotion that is accompanied by a high level of arousal (Witte, 1992, p. 331). "Perceived threat" is a message receiver's sense that he or she is susceptible to some negative situation or outcome. For example, a message that links texting to auto accidents is likely to be perceived as threatening by many who text while driving because it pairs their behavior with a negative outcome. Finally, "perceived efficacy" is similar to the concept of perceived behavioral control that we discussed in Chapter 3. As applied in the fear appeal literature, perceived efficacy is a person's belief that message recommendations can be implemented and will effectively reduce the threat represented in the message (Mongeau, 2013; Rogers, 1975; Witte, 1992; Witte & Allen, 2000).

Although these concepts are not new, they are consistent with the modern theory of discrete emotions and more recent fear appeal explanations (Dillard & Seo, 2013; Mongeau, 2013; Nabi, 2002). Fear appeals make vivid a potential environmental change that presents a threat to audience members' health and well-being. The depicted threat serves to launch an appraisal process that generates closer analysis of the perceived threat and, eventually, perceived efficacy. Threats perceived as significant and likely to occur generate physiological arousal and the emotion of fear. In turn, fear motivates individuals to avoid the threat (though specifically *how* differs radically, as we discuss later in this chapter; e.g., Leventhal, 1970; Witte, 1992).

Three families of explanations have dominated fear appeal research: *drive theories, parallel response models,* and *subjective expected utility models* (Dillard, 1994; Mongeau, 2013; Witte, 1992; Witte & Allen, 2000). Each of these models is described below.

Modeling the Effects of Fear Appeals

Humble Beginnings

As we have for several other literatures, our review of research on the persuasive effects of fear appeals is decidedly historical in nature. We believe that the best way to understand current conceptualizations is to recognize the historical foundation upon which they are built. The rich history of fear appeal research provides insight into the scientific study of persuasion and explains the development of current models of the role of fear in persuasive communication.

One of the first investigations of fear-arousing persuasive messages (Janis & Feshbach, 1953) speculated about the possibility of a curvilinear (inverted-U) relationship between the amount of fear-arousing content and the relative acceptance of message recommendations. Janis and Feshbach hypothesized that "when emotional tension is aroused, the audience will become more highly motivated to accept the reassuring beliefs or recommendations advocated by the communicator" (p. 78). However, they cautioned that the arousal of extreme emotional tension could activate defensive mechanisms that might thwart the message's persuasive effectiveness. Under conditions of high fear, for example, persuasive targets might stop paying attention to the message in hopes of alleviating their extreme anxiety. In the researchers' view, a *moderate* level of fear would produce the greatest amount of attitude change.

To test their hypothesis, Janis and Feshbach (1953) exposed 200 high school students to messages advocating better dental hygiene. The strong-fear message contained several references to the painful consequences of tooth decay, gum disease, and worrisome trips to the dentist that would result from poor dental hygiene. The moderate-fear message contained the same information but was less graphic in its depiction of the effects of poor dental hygiene. Finally, the minimal-fear message contained the same hygiene information but rarely described the negative effects of poor hygiene. Each message was accompanied by a series of slides that corresponded to the amount of fear imparted in the verbal message. Both 1 week before and 1 week after exposure to the persuasive messages, participants in the study completed a questionnaire describing their dental hygiene practices.

Janis and Feshbach's (1953) findings disconfirmed their expectations: they found no support for the curvilinear relationship they had hypothesized. Instead, they found that the minimal-fear message induced the *most* compliance with message recommendations and the strong-fear message produced the *least* amount of compliance. In other words, their findings confirmed a negative linear relationship instead of a curvilinear one.

Although their study found no evidence for the effectiveness of fear-arousing messages, the counterintuitive nature of Janis and Feshbach's (1953) results ignited considerable research and theorizing about the persuasive effects of fear appeals.[2] Specifically, this early research laid the conceptual groundwork for the family of fear-appeal models known as Drive Models.

Drive Models

The first theoretical explanation for the effects of fear-arousing messages conceptualized fear as an acquired drive (Hovland et al., 1953; Janis & Feshbach, 1953; McGuire, 1968; G. R. Miller, 1963). *Drive* is a psychological term for an unpleasant state that people strive to reduce or eliminate (e.g., fear, hunger, or thirst). These bodily states initiate activity and are frequently experienced as feelings of tension or restlessness (Newcomb, Turner, & Converse, 1965, p. 23).

Applied to fear appeals, fear is a drive state that can be initiated through graphic descriptions of negative consequences likely to occur if receivers do not adopt a message's recommendations. According to this explanation, TV commercials depicting the consequences of texting while driving are designed to create fear as a drive state. The Drive Model also predicts that whatever reduces the drive is reinforcement, because it is rewarding to message receivers. "When a response reduces fear, it is reinforced and becomes part of one's permanent response repertory" (Leventhal, 1970, p. 123).

Thus, the Drive Model suggests a sequence in which an appeal arouses fear in message receivers, and that fear in turn acts as a drive. Acceptance of message recommendations reduces this fear and the corresponding drive state, and that attitude or behavior change is thereby reinforced. However, message receivers might also reduce their fear by denying that the negative consequences (say, of texting while driving) are likely to occur. This denial, if it reduces the drive, is also rewarding, but it is unlikely to produce attitude and behavior change in recipients. Denial of the threat is particularly relevant for adolescents, who sometimes feel invulnerable. The mechanism that reduces this fear, whether adaptive (e.g., behavioral change) or maladaptive (e.g., denial), is reinforced and becomes the preferred response to the threat (Janis, 1967; Hovland et al., 1953). This process is depicted in Figure 8.1 and implies that "a fear appeal should have two components: a part of the message that instills fear and another that assuages it" (Dillard, 1994).

Consistent with the rationale proposed by Janis and Feshbach (1953), Drive Models posit a curvilinear relationship between the level of fear aroused by a message and message acceptance (Hovland et al., 1953; Janis, 1967; McGuire, 1968). According to the Drive Models, messages that arouse moderate levels of fear will be more effective than those that arouse very low or very high levels of fear (see Figure 8.2).

Even though the Drive Model dominated the fear appeal literature during the 1950s and 1960s, little evidence was garnered to support it. Multiple subsequent meta-analytic reviews of this literature produced no evidence of a curvilinear relationship between the fearsomeness of messages and the target's responses (Boster & Mongeau, 1984; Sutton, 1982; Witte & Allen, 2000). Indeed, by the 1970s the lack of empirical support

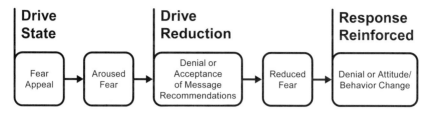

FIGURE 8.1. A Drive Model of fear appeals.

and growing concerns about the specification of variables that moderate the relationship between fear and message acceptance led Leventhal (1970) to propose an alternative model, the Parallel Response Model, to explain the persuasive effects of fear appeals.

Parallel Response Model

Findings from early research on the effectiveness of fear appeals were inconsistent. A few studies found low-fear messages to be most persuasive (e.g., Janis & Feshbach, 1953). In many other studies, however, high-fear messages were found to be more persuasive than low-fear messages (e.g., Hewgill & Miller, 1965). Still other studies found that the level of fear had no effect on attitude or behavior change (e.g., Wheatley & Oshikawa, 1970; see Mongeau, 2013, for a recent review).

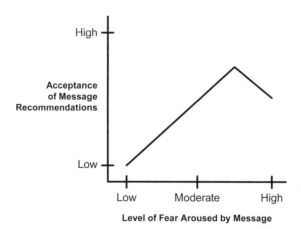

FIGURE 8.2. The relationship between aroused fear and message acceptance predicted by the Drive Model.

In the wake of these inconsistent findings, Leventhal (1970) proposed that fear-arousing messages can create two separate, but parallel, responses—fear control and danger control. *Fear control* is basically an emotional response, whereas *danger control* is primarily a cognitive process. When people engage in fear control, they look inward for cues enabling them to reduce their fear. Outcomes of the fear control process include avoidance of the message and denial of the threat contained in the message. In contrast, when people engage in *danger control* processes, they look for external cues that enable them to reduce the threat. Outcomes of the danger control process are much more likely to include attitude and behavior change (see Figure 8.3). Thus, adaptive behavior results from the danger control process, while maladaptive behavior is attributed to the fear control process (Mongeau, 2013).

Leventhal's (1970) distinction between fear control and danger control was a significant shift in theorizing about fear appeals. As Sutton (1982) observed, "The importance of the parallel response model lies largely in its movement away from the notion of fear as the central explanatory concept" (p. 324). Dillard (1994) assessed the contribution of Leventhal's Parallel Response Model to theory as follows: "During the heyday of drive theories, fear was at the center of the theoretical stage. With the coming of the Parallel Response Model, it was forced to share the limelight with the cognitive machinations of the danger control process" (p. 301).

Although the Parallel Response Model was the first one to balance the emotional and cognitive components of fear appeals, a major shortcoming was that it lacked precision. The model failed to specify when recipients would engage in fear or danger control (Beck & Frankel, 1981; Rogers, 1975; Sutton, 1982). This failure made it impossible to test. Although it lacked empirical support, the Parallel Response Model provided the conceptual framework for a third family of fear appeal models, the Subjective Expected Utility Models.

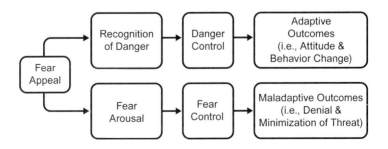

FIGURE 8.3. The Parallel Response Model of fear appeals.

Subjective Expected Utility Models

Subjective Expected Utility (SEU) Models have been developed to explain a variety of human behaviors. For example, in Chapter 3 we discussed Reasoned Action Theories. Another SEU model, the Health Belief Model (M. H. Becker, 1974), includes fear appeal elements and has been applied in many public health settings. This family of models, which adopts a rational view of humans, posits that people choose behaviors that maximize rewards and minimize punishments (Edwards, 1961; Lewin, 1935). According to these models, a person faced with two or more alternative courses of action will choose the one with the greatest SEU. The SEU for a course of action is a function of the subjective value (or utility) of the outcome associated with a particular course of action and the subjective probability (expectation) that that action will produce the specified outcome (Sutton, 1982, p. 325). Thus, the basic structure of these models is a simple equation in which the dependent variable is a multiplicative function (the product) of two or more independent variables (Dillard, 1994).

Protection Motivation Theory (Rogers, 1975, 1983) is an application of an SEU model to the study of fear appeals. Rogers argued that the effectiveness of a fear appeal depended on its ability to create three perceptions in message receivers: the perceived severity or noxiousness of the threat contained in the message, the perception of personal susceptibility to the threat, and the perception that the recommended response will effectively reduce or eliminate the threat.

The original formulation of this model (Rogers, 1975) proposed that all three components were necessary ingredients in an effective fear appeal. That is, the model proposed that protection motivation (i.e., a person's intention to adopt a recommended behavior) was a multiplicative function of *perceived noxiousness, perceived susceptibility,* and *perceived efficacy of the response* (see Figure 8.4).

By the 1980s, several studies had failed to find evidence of the multiplicative relationship (i.e., the predicted three-way interaction) among these three variables and raised doubts about the validity of Rogers's model. In response, alternative SEU models were introduced (Sutton & Eiser, 1984), and modifications to the original model were suggested. For example, Beck and Frankel (1981) distinguished between *response efficacy* (i.e., the perception that a recommended response will effectively reduce the threat) and *self-efficacy* (i.e., the perception that one can personally execute the response), and they suggested that *both* dimensions of efficacy were important features of fear appeals. By 1983, Rogers (1983) revised his Protection Motivation Theory by incorporating the concept of self-efficacy, altering the predictions concerning the separate and combined effects of the four predictor variables, and extending the model to areas beyond the scope of

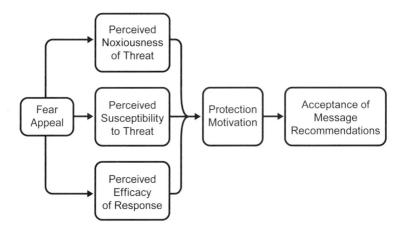

FIGURE 8.4. The Protection Motivation Model of fear appeals.

fear appeals (for more complete discussions of these models, see Dillard, 1994, and Mongeau, 2013).

Tests of these models produced mixed findings regarding the respective outcomes associated with perceived noxiousness of the threat, perceived susceptibility to the threat, and the efficacy of the recommended responses on one's intentions to adopt the recommended action. Nevertheless, two important implications emerged from investigations of these models. First, these perceptual variables were judged to be "important sources of information for individuals attempting to determine what response to make to a potential threat" (Dillard, 1994). Second, the emergence of this family of models virtually excluded the concept of fear as an emotion from the study of fear appeals (Dillard, 1994; Mongeau, 2013; Witte, 1994). Instead of describing emotional reactions to a fear-arousing message, the SEU models emphasized cognitive, or rational, reactions to these messages. Indeed, over a 30-year period, beginning with Janis and Feshbach's (1953) seminal study, theorizing about fear appeals had evolved to the point where fear was no longer an essential construct.

Extended Parallel Processing Model

Another attempt at explaining the persuasive successes and failures of fear appeals is the Extended Parallel Processing Model (EPPM; Witte, 1992, 1994; Witte & Allen, 2000). Kim Witte attempted to combine the other fear appeal models mentioned above into one comprehensive and testable package. The EPPM borrows the concepts of fear control and danger control from Leventhal's (1970) Parallel Response Model and the threat and

---

BOX 8.2. Response Efficacy, Self-Efficacy, and Lung Cancer

Each year millions of people die from smoking-induced lung cancer. Recently, Jim's mom succumbed to the disease that resulted from nearly 60 years of smoking cigarettes. She continued to smoke through several decades of constant exposure to antismoking messages. Despite his best efforts as a *so-called expert* in persuasion, Jim was unable to convince his mother to stop smoking. His mother was convinced that she could not stop smoking, because the addiction to nicotine and the social nature of smoking were simply too strong. In this regard, antismoking messages based on *self-efficacy* failed to convince her because she simply believed that she could not break the addiction.

In addition, after smoking for six decades, she also concluded that it was futile to stop. By the time she developed emphysema several years ago, Jim's mom was convinced that she had been smoking so long that the die had been cast. Given these beliefs, persuasive appeals lacked *response efficacy* because Jim's mom believed that there was nothing she could do to improve her lung capacity or reduce the probability of developing cancer. Despite messages from doctors, the media, and family, she never believed that adopting the recommended behavior would achieve the desired outcome of a longer and healthier life.

---

efficacy components of fear-arousing messages from Rogers's (1983) Protection Motivation Theory.

Witte (1992, 1994) argued that the threat component of a message motivates recipients to respond, while the efficacy component of the message determines the nature of that response. The EPPM predicts that if a message depicts a minor threat, recipients will be unmotivated to respond and no attitude and behavior change should occur. No threat, no sweat, message recipients conclude. When the message depicts both a significant threat and an effective coping response, the model predicts that recipients will engage in danger control and significant attitude and behavior change should result. If the message depicts a significant threat but the recommended response is ineffective, recipients are predicted to engage in fear control (i.e., denial, defensive avoidance, and/or reactance; Witte & Allen, 2000). If recipients engage in fear control, no attitude or behavior change is expected.

A meta-analysis of the fear appeal literature (Witte & Allen, 2000) provided mixed support for the EPPM. The EPPM's central prediction is that the severity and susceptibility of the threat (conjoined into what Witte and Allen called *threat*) combine with self-efficacy and response efficacy (conjoined into what they called *efficacy*) to produce attitude change. Thus, while threat and efficacy are predicted to combine multiplicatively to influence attitudes and behaviors, only the high-threat–high-efficacy condition should produce strong levels of attitude and behavioral change. The other combinations of threat and efficacy should each produce no change (though for different reasons). Meta-analytic results, however, are not consistent with these predictions. Witte and Allen's (2000) meta-analytic results are most consistent with an additive model where threat and efficacy contribute separately to the production of attitude and behavior change (Mongeau, 2013).

While the results are not entirely consistent with either model, both Rogers's Protection Motivation Theory and Witte's EPPM highlight the importance of efficacy in the fear appeal process. Results of the Witte and Allen (2000) meta-analysis clearly indicate that messages that create high levels of perceived threat and efficacy are maximally effective. This finding suggests that effective fear appeals must include information that poses a threat to message receivers and then prescribes effective action for alleviating the threat. Fear appeals that fail to accomplish *both* objectives are unlikely to be very persuasive.

Summarizing the Research Findings

While none of the theories can fully explain the findings from fear appeal research, the strength of fear appeals appears to be positively correlated with attitudes, behavioral intentions, and behaviors. Specifically, Witte and Allen (2000) assert that "the stronger the fear aroused by a fear appeal, the more persuasive it is" (p. 601). Indeed, there is a small positive relationship between the strength of a fear appeal and subsequent attitudes and behaviors. Across meta-analyses, the average fear–attitude correlations have ranged from .14 to .21, while the average fear–behavior correlations have ranged from .10 to .17 (for reviews, see Boster & Mongeau, 1984; Dillard, 1994; Sutton, 1982; Witte & Allen, 2000; also see Mongeau, 2013). Moreover, there is little evidence that strong fear messages will backfire, and there is no evidence in any of the reviews for the curvilinear (inverted-U-shaped) pattern predicted by the Drive Model.

As we suggested in Chapter 2, one reason for these weak relationships is that the manipulations of fear appeals have not been terribly effective. In fact, the average fear–perceived fear correlations across meta-analyses have ranged from only .30 to .36. While manipulations appear to be getting stronger over time (Witte & Allen, 2000), differences in recipients' levels of experienced fear across the low- and high-fear appeals are not terribly large. If fear manipulations are not strong, then the correlation between the strength of a fear appeal and attitudes or behaviors will not be strong either (Boster & Mongeau, 1984).

Fear Appeals and the Creation of Other Emotions

One of the complexities involved in studying emotional appeals is that, while some emotions are separate and distinct, other emotions are more complicated and intertwined with one another. Consequently, a single message can produce several related emotions. For example, a fear appeal might also generate anger, sadness, or surprise. Dillard and colleagues (1996) noted that "fear appeals do more than scare people" (p. 44). This complicates the persuasive process because each aroused emotion involves a unique combination of cognitive, affective, physiological, and behavioral components. Some of these emotions might facilitate attitude and behavior change, while others might inhibit it.

Dillard and colleagues (1996) investigated the extent to which fear appeals created emotional reactions beyond fear and how these multiple reactions influenced the persuasiveness of messages. In their study, they used 31 PSAs concerning AIDS/HIV that had previously been identified as fear appeals. College students viewed a number of these messages and indicated their emotional reactions (i.e., fear, anger, puzzlement, happiness, sadness, and surprise) as well as their ratings of the persuasiveness of the messages.

The results of the Dillard et al. (1996) investigation indicated that all but one of the 31 PSAs produced statistically significant changes in two or more emotions (and over half of the messages generated changes in three or more emotions). So, it is clear that fear appeals do more than simply create fear. Equally important, the Dillard team reported that these emotions varied considerably in how they related to judgments of the messages' persuasiveness. Fear, surprise, and sadness were positively related to persuasiveness judgments, while puzzlement and anger were negatively related to the same judgments. Only happiness was unrelated to judgments of message persuasiveness.

The Dillard and colleagues (1996) findings are important because they reinforce the meta-analytic data that indicates that fear appeals are persuasive. Strong fear appeals generate the emotion of fear in audience members and are positively related to the message's level of persuasiveness. However, the finding that fear appeals create different patterns of emotional and affective reactions might explain why correlations between fear appeals and attitude and behavior vary so much from study to study.

Directions for Future Research

There appears to be a rekindled interest in the study of fear appeals (for recent examples, see de Hoog, Stroebe, & de Wit, 2005, 2007). This interest may be caused in part by the continued evolution of fear appeal explanations and in part to the continued application of fear appeals in everyday persuasion campaigns. Conceptual developments have revived an interest in studying the "fear" component of fear-arousing messages. In a thoughtful review of the fear appeal literature, Dillard (1994) chronicled the decreasing emphasis on fear in fear appeal models. He also suggested that the reestablishment of the fear construct, and a renewed interest in emotional reactions to fear appeals, might be essential to our better understanding their effects (see also Mongeau, 2013). Witte (1992), reflecting a similar concern, introduced the EPPM to explain the effects of fear appeals. At this point, it is clear that we know more about the cognitive evaluations inherent in danger control than we do about the far messier, emotionally driven, fear-control processes (Mongeau, 2013). Further investigation into fear appeals is needed in order to fully understand the interconnected nature of these processes.

Compared to the amount of research and theorizing on fear appeals, relatively little research has been devoted to other types of emotional appeals. However, scholars have become interested in the persuasive effects of inducing guilt in message recipients (D. J. O'Keefe, 2000, 2002). The following section discusses research on the relationship between guilt and persuasion.

GUILT AND PERSUASION

Scholars have proffered a number of different definitions for the concept of guilt (Baumeister, Stillwell, & Heatherton, 1994; Cotte, Coulter, & Moore, 2005; Mongeau, Hale, & Alles, 1994; D. J. O'Keefe, 2000, 2002). However, most agree that guilt arises when people act in ways that are inconsistent with their personal standards (e.g., D. J. O'Keefe, 2002). (The related question of the difference between guilt and cognitive dissonance is treated in Aronson's [1992] Later Dissonance Theory.) Three types of guilt particularly relevant to persuasive communication have been identified: reactive guilt, anticipatory guilt, and existential guilt (Cotte et al., 2005; Izard, 1977; Rawlings, 1970).

Reactive guilt occurs after you have behaved in a manner that is inconsistent with your values and morals. In this case, the action has already occurred, and you feel badly as a result. Consider the example of a middle school student who observes a friend being bullied because he is gay by a group of more popular students. If this student fails to stand up for his friend, he might later feel guilty because he failed to support him in a time of need.

Anticipatory guilt represents the negative emotional state people experience when they are *about to* behave in a way that is inconsistent with their own values and morals. For example, if you are in a committed romantic relationship but contemplating an amorous fling with an attractive class-mate in your physics lab, you might experience anticipatory guilt as a result of simply thinking about cheating on your romantic partner.

Existential guilt occurs when people feel a sense of remorse or regret after comparing their own circumstances with those of less fortunate others. Soldiers returning from war or those who have lived through devastating auto accidents often experience "survivor's guilt" when they contemplate why they are still alive when other friends or family members in the same circumstances were unable to escape the carnage. International relief organizations often attempt to arouse existential guilt in TV viewers by producing commercials that depict the plight of impoverished children immediately before soliciting contributions.

Guilt is a negative emotion. That is, people don't *want* to feel guilty if they don't have to. As a result, if people *do* feel guilt they are immediately motivated to get rid of it. What is more, like all other emotions, guilt has a behavioral component. In this case, the typical behavioral response to feeling guilty is to atone for one's transgressions or omissions (whether real or anticipated; Nabi, 2002). As with effective fear appeals, guilt appeals should be most persuasive when they both arouse guilt in message receivers and recommend actions that effectively relieve it. However, it is important to keep in mind that, like any persuasive message, the cognitive, emotional, and behavioral responses generated by the same guilt appeal will vary across receivers.

The current literature indicates that the persuasive influence of guilt appeals is as complicated as the results across studies are inconsistent. Part of the discrepancy stems from the particular *type* of guilt that is aroused. First, we will consider research focusing on reactive guilt appeals. After that, we consider several issues identified in recent research on the impact of guilt appeals on charitable donations. These studies focus on a combination of anticipatory and existential guilt arousal.

Several studies have investigated the role of reactive guilt in persuasion (see D. J. O'Keefe, 2000, 2002, for reviews of this literature). For example, Coulter and Pinto (1995) exposed working mothers to advertisements about one of two products, either bread or dental floss. For each product, the researchers created messages reflecting three levels of guilt (low, moderate, and high). After exposure to the message, the participants reported their levels of guilt, anger, and happiness, their attitudes toward the advertisement and the brand depicted, and their intentions to purchase the product.

Participants in Coulter and Pinto's study (1995) reported the greatest perceived guilt *and* the most positive attitudes toward the brand advertised in the moderate-guilt message condition. Participants in the high-guilt message condition felt angry, evaluated the message as manipulative, and viewed the company as simply out to make money. Participants in this condition likely evaluated the message as attacking their behavior and ability as a mother. Specifically, levels of anger increased across the low-, moderate-, and high-guilt message conditions. Moreover, reports of guilt were strongly correlated with reports of anger. Thus, as was true with fear appeals (i.e., Dillard and colleagues, 1996), Coulter and Pinto (1995) reported that guilt appeals generate multiple emotions (some of which were intended and some were not; see also Cotte et al., 2005).

In terms of persuasion outcomes, Coulter and Pinto reported that strong guilt appeals simply do not work. As guilt appeals moved from moderate to high, attitudes toward the advertisement and the specific brand became more negative and intentions to purchase the product declined. This pattern of results is, for the most part, consistent with a meta-analysis of the guilt appeal literature. D. J. O'Keefe (2000) reports that, although increasing the strength of a guilt appeal increases the amount of guilt that message recipients experience, the strength of a guilt appeal is negatively related to persuasiveness.[3] In short, guilt appeals appear to be effective in producing guilt but ineffective in producing attitude and behavior change in the direction of the message's recommendations.

Why Don't Guilt Appeals Work?

The accumulated research findings reported in D. J. O'Keefe's (2000) meta-analysis clearly indicate that persuasive messages emphasizing guilt appeals induce reactive guilt but are ineffective in producing attitude and behavior change. However, O'Keefe (2000, 2002) reports that inducing guilt may influence attitudes and behaviors in two specific contexts: the hypocrisy paradigm and the transgression–compliance paradigm.

In Chapter 4, we discussed a modern application of cognitive dissonance theory known as the "hypocrisy" phenomenon. Specifically, we discussed Stone and colleagues' (1994) study in which participants in the hypocrisy condition were asked to record a message for high school students advocating safe-sex practices and then to recall privately instances when they themselves failed to engage in the safe behaviors. As compared to those participants who either wrote a message but did not present it or those who did not recall past risky behavior, participants in the hypocrisy condition were more likely to purchase condoms (and purchased more condoms) with the money they received for participating in the study.

Stone et al. (1994) concluded that purchasing condoms was motivated by (and was an effort to reduce) cognitive dissonance. D. J. O'Keefe (2000, 2002), on the other hand, argued that results from the hypocrisy paradigm could be explained just as well in terms of guilt. Specifically, engaging in unsafe sex practices represents a behavior that violates personal standards that are made particularly salient while recording the message. As a consequence, the hypocrisy condition could have created guilt instead of (or perhaps in addition to) dissonance. Purchasing condoms, then, could be interpreted as guilt reduction (trying to avoid making the same mistake in the future). To date, there are insufficient data to choose between the guilt or dissonance explanation of the hypocrisy effect (see, e.g., Fointiat, Morisot, & Pakuszewski, 2008), or whether there is a substantive difference between these two constructs.

A second area of research on guilt involves investigations of the "transgression–compliance" paradigm (D. J. O'Keefe, 2000, 2002). In transgression–compliance studies, participants engage in some transgression (e.g., knocking over a stack of papers, spilling a drink, or breaking someone else's equipment) and are later asked to do someone a favor. D. J. O'Keefe's (2000) meta-analytic investigation of research on this

---

BOX 8.3. Has Cognitive Dissonance Morphed into Reactive Guilt?

D. J. O'Keefe's (2000, 2002) reinterpretation of the hypocrisy paradigm highlights the question of how reactive guilt and cognitive dissonance differ. Early conceptualizations depicted cognitive dissonance as a state of arousal created when two cognitive elements are inconsistent (see Chapter 4). Given this broad view, all instances of reactive guilt (i.e., when one's behavior violates a personal standard), by definition, are examples of cognitive dissonance. However, not all cases of cognitive dissonance, as it was initially defined, produce reactive guilt (because not all cognitions are related to personal standards). Thus, early definitions of cognitive dissonance are broader than the concept of reactive guilt.

Aronson's (1992) more recent view (frequently called Later Dissonance Theory) adopted a much narrower view of cognitive dissonance. Specifically, he argued that dissonance did not stem from inconsistent cognitions but, rather, from the belief that one is sensible and yet admittedly behaved in an unsensible manner. As we noted in Chapter 4, Aronson (1992) argued that "dissonance is greatest and clearest when it involves not just any two cognitions but, rather, a cognition about the self and a piece of our behavior that violates that self-concept" (p. 305). This later and narrower conceptualization of cognitive dissonance appears to overlap considerably, if not entirely, with reactive guilt. Has the narrowing and clarification of cognitive dissonance proposed by Aronson allowed the concept to morph into reactive guilt? At a minimum, there is a great deal of conceptual overlap between the two concepts, as both posit that negative arousal occurs when behavior violates a person's beliefs about personal standards.

phenomenon provides clear findings. Participants who engaged in some transgression were much more likely to comply with a subsequent request than those who did not. This result is generally interpreted as an indication of guilt, because participants have done something wrong and wish to make up for it (D. J. O'Keefe, 2000, 2002).

Given that guilt appears to work as an effective persuasive tool in both the hypocrisy (apparently) and the transgression–compliance paradigms, why don't guilt appeals work to influence attitude and behavior change? One explanation might be that appeals that attempt to arouse strong levels of guilt also arouse other negative emotions that interfere with the persuasion process. As we noted above, Coulter and Pinto (1995) found that self-reports of guilt were strongly correlated with feelings of anger and irritation. Anger-irritation in the Coulter and Pinto study was more strongly and negatively related to both attitudes and behaviors than was guilt. Jimenez and Yang (2008) observed similar findings when they studied the influence of guilt appeals on reactions to green advertising. They found that the more negative self-conscious emotions or angry or irritating emotions a guilt appeal produced, the more negative receivers' attitudes toward the product turned out to be.

Our speculation is that negative reactions to guilt appeals are related to the source of the message. We get angry at people who try to make us feel guilty (particularly someone we don't know). In both the hypocrisy and the transgression–compliance paradigms, there is no one trying to *make* participants feel guilty. Instead, in both cases, an internal consideration of personal behavior as it relates to personal standards creates the guilt. In this regard, no one may be quite as good at arousing guilt in a target person as the target him- or herself.

This is not to say that other people cannot make us feel guilty. Parents, close friends, and romantic partners may be best at inducing us to feel guilty. Two studies (Baumeister et al., 1994; Vangelisti, Daly, & Rudnick, 1991) found that "one of the central issues in the elicitation of guilt was the transgressor's violation of relationship obligations or norms" (Vangelisti & Sprague, 1998, p. 138). This suggests that eliciting strong levels of reactive guilt from a target will be difficult for those who are not in close relationships with that target.

Given this view of guilt, mass advertising may be at a disadvantage when trying to persuade consumers with guilt appeals. Because audience members do not have an existing relationship with the message source (e.g., a corporation, a faceless voice, or a celebrity spokesperson), there are likely to be no relational obligations or norms that can be violated. The very notion that a stranger might attempt to create guilt may create the anger and irritation that participants reported in the Coulter and Pinto (1995) and Jimenez and Yang (2008) studies.

Guilt and Charitable Donations

How effective guilt is as a persuasion tool and the process through which it operates, however, might depend upon the type of guilt aroused. Not all guilt appeals focus on reactive guilt (as the studies in the preceding section did). For example, consider the use of a common guilt appeal that depicts emaciated and abused animals and then solicits contributions to an animal rescue organization. These ads appear to be trying to arouse a combination of existential guilt (these animals are much worse off than you are) and anticipatory guilt (i.e., if you don't help these poor animals, you will be violating a personal standard to help those in need). These appeals differ markedly from those used in the Coulter and Pinto (1995) study. In the animal rescue messages, you haven't done anything wrong—yet.

The particular emotional reactions to the animal rescue appeals likely vary across people. For some viewers, the commercial may arouse existential and anticipatory guilt. Other viewers might experience anger, particularly if they consider the advertisement as attempting to manipulate their feelings. To be effective, guilt appeals must be associated with particular kinds of cognitive responses. For example, Cotte and colleagues (2005) found that when message receivers consider a message to be manipulative, it becomes so closely associated with negative impressions of the sponsor that its effectiveness is radically reduced.

To be effective, the ad requesting contributions for the animal rescue organization should generate a sense of personal responsibility in message receivers. People are unlikely to feel responsible for the abuse, but instead they might feel some responsibility to help those in need. Such responses will likely occur in some people and increase the probability of charitable donations. Basil, Ridgway, and Basil (2006) demonstrated that a feeling of responsibility is an important mediating variable in the process. In their study, guilt appeals that promoted a sense of personal responsibility were more likely to produce a desired response than those that failed to engender it.

Additionally, considering the significant role of self-efficacy in the fear appeal literature (Rogers, 1983; Witte, 1992), one could argue that the perceived efficacy of the desired response might prove determinative in a guilt appeal's capacity to produce a desired action. Extending the animal rescue example, if people accept the suggestion that every donation helps, they may be motivated to donate money. However, if message receivers conclude that their donation will not make a difference—either because the problem is overwhelming or because they believe that the animal rescue organization is (or charities in general are) a bloated bureaucracy that spends most of its money on overhead and advertising and not enough money rescuing animals—then they will be less inclined to make a contribution.

In summary, the amount of guilt aroused by a reactive, anticipatory, or existential guilt appeal is generally positively related to attitude and behavior change. Getting people to feel guilty, however, is quite tricky. Making people feel a sense of responsibility to help those in need is an important component of guilt arousal and is persuasive (Basil et al., 2006). On the other hand, if people feel as though they are being manipulated by those appeals, reactance likely occurs (Brehm, 1966) and attitude change is unlikely (Cotte et al., 2005). Moreover, it is likely that the amount of guilt a message receiver feels will depend on the audience member's level of empathy for the subject of the message and the perceived efficacy of one's personal response.

THE CHOICE BETWEEN RATIONAL AND EMOTIONAL APPEALS

Prior research has documented the effectiveness of both rational and emotional persuasive appeals. Although we seem to understand the process of rational argument more clearly than we do emotional appeals, research supports the persuasive value of both types of appeals. Given this finding, one might speculate about the merits of integrating rational and emotional appeals within a single persuasive message.

Though no research bears directly on this issue, investigations of the influence of heightened arousal on cognitive processing suggest that rational appeals may lose their effectiveness when combined with fear-arousing content. For example, investigations of short-term memory (Bacon, 1974; Mandler, 1984) suggest that heightened arousal may interfere with information processing. In fact, these investigations indicate that a variety of stressors can contribute to memory impairment. However, an investigation of college women found that arousal was unrelated to their learning and recall of contraceptive information (Goldfarb, Gerrard, Gibbons, & Plante, 1988). Thus, the relationship between arousal and cognitive processing appears unclear. In addition, there may be some conceptual slippage between the arousal of fear and the physiological arousal induced in these studies. Specifically, we know much more about cognitive responses to fear appeals than the corresponding physiological responses (and how the two work together; Mongeau, 2013). Nevertheless, these investigations provide little reason to expect that the arousal of fear or anxiety will facilitate the persuasive influence of rational appeals.

Because emotional and rational appeals appear to be incompatible persuasive companions, persuaders often rely on one or the other. One particular investigation provided information that may assist persuaders in choosing between the two alternatives. M. G. Millar and K. U. Millar (1990) hypothesized that cognitively based attitudes are more susceptible to affective appeals and affectively based attitudes are more susceptible to rational appeals. They argued that when attitudes and the arguments against them are based on the same type of information (whether rational/cognitive or emotional/affective), the argument threatens the way in which the person has thought about the object (p. 217). Because receivers often react defensively to threatening messages, such arguments may be ineffective. In the three investigations that provided support for their general hypothesis, when attitudes were formed through cognitive processes, affective appeals were more persuasive. Conversely, when attitudes were affectively based, rational appeals were more persuasive (Millar & Millar, 1990). Although the affective appeals in these studies were not fear appeals, these findings provide some recommendations for the use of rational and emotional persuasive appeals. Knowledge about the affective or cognitive basis of a target's attitude may be instructive in determining whether to construct a rational or an emotional appeal to alter that attitude.[4]

SUMMARY

Our review of emotional appeals focused primarily on the fear appeal literature. The development of this literature, from the Drive Models to parallel response and SEU models, coincided with the reduced emphasis on the role of fear in these appeals. We concluded that all three families of models are instructive but that none provides a satisfying description of the effects of fear appeals. Nevertheless, summaries of this literature provide a number of empirical conclusions that can be confidently drawn about the effects of fear appeals. Recent theoretical developments provide important recommendations for future research. The chapter concluded with a discussion of the effectiveness of emotional and rational appeals for changing affectively based and cognitively based attitudes.

We also briefly reviewed the guilt-appeal literature. Several studies show that guilt appeals are ineffective as a mass persuasion strategy. However, guilt appears to be a powerful persuasive force in interpersonal situations. Further conceptual and theoretical work is necessary to explain when and how guilt is most effective in producing attitude and behavior change.

NOTES

1. While scholars from many disciplines recognize that emotions encompass these four components, they differ on the importance assigned to each. For example, psycho-physiologists tend to emphasize physiological responses, paying much less attention to the other components. Cognitive scholars tend to emphasize

interpretive and behavioral components. However, fully understanding emotional appeals requires that we give all four components—cognitive, affective, physiological, and behavioral—their due.

2. In the realm of persuasion research, early counterintuitive findings sparking considerable subsequent theorizing are not unique to the study of fear appeals. As discussed in Chapter 3, LaPiere's (1934) finding that no correspondence existed between people's stated intentions and actual behaviors sparked considerable research and theorizing about the attitude–behavior relationship. Moreover, in Chapter 6, the sleeper effect literature emerged from counterintuitive findings by Hovland and his colleagues (1953). In point of fact, counterintuitive findings often generate more persuasion theory research than findings consistent with scholars' expectations.

3. Few if any researchers other than Coulter and Pinto (1995) have created three levels of guilt. Much more typically the comparison is between low-guilt and high-guilt appeals.

4. Edwards (1990) on the other hand, argued that affect-based attitudes are most susceptible to affective appeals and that cognition-based attitudes are most susceptible to rational appeals. Three studies provide support for these predictions and appear to contradict the Millar and Millar (1990) findings. However, important differences exist between these investigations. For example, the manipulations employed in the Edwards studies appear to create a positive or negative mood state in participants. The stimuli used to create these mood states are unrelated to the attitude objects investigated in these studies. By comparison, the latter's studies assess the affective and cognitive dimensions of *existing* attitudes. Moreover, these dimensions were directly related to the attitude objects investigated in Millar and Millar's studies. Although the Edwards studies have important implications for the role of affect in persuasion, the Millar and Millar investigations are more relevant to the notion of affective-based and cognitive-based attitudes.

CHAPTER 9

Receiver Characteristics

LOOKING AHEAD . . . A receiver-oriented approach to persuasion focuses attention on those characteristics of message receivers that affect the persuasion process. In this chapter we review the research on these characteristics and discuss how they influence persuasion. We begin with a discussion of gender and answer the question "Are women more easily persuaded than men?" Then we look at the message discrepancy literature and describe how the difference between a receiver's opinion and the position advocated in the message affects the persuasiveness of the message. We then discuss the influence of personal involvement on the processing and effectiveness of persuasive appeals. Researchers have traditionally employed a variety of conceptual definitions for the term *involvement*; as a result, investigations of the effects of involvement have produced apparently contradictory findings. Each of these definitional approaches, along with their related research findings, is examined in this chapter. Finally, we look at the influence of function matching, or the extent to which persuasive messages match the underlying functions of receivers' attitudes.

In the preceding three chapters we focused on the characteristics of persuasive messages and persuasive message sources. Although carefully crafted messages from highly trustworthy sources can promote response formation, reinforcement, and change processes, persuasion scholars have long recognized the importance of message receivers in the persuasion process. The persuasive effects of target characteristics were initially investigated by Hovland and his colleagues (1953) and gained prominence in the development of cognitive response theories during the late 1960s and 1970s (Greenwald, Brock, & Ostrom, 1968; Petty, Ostrom, & Brock, 1981).

This chapter examines the role of receiver characteristics in the persuasion process. Historically, persuasion scholars have paid considerable attention to four characteristics of persuasive targets: gender, message discrepancy, involvement, and function matching. In fact, these four characteristics continue to motivate contemporary programs of research on persuasive communication.

SEX/GENDER DIFFERENCES IN PERSUADABILITY

For years, a colloquial truism about persuasive communication held that women were more easily persuaded than men. Indeed, until relatively recently social scientists argued that clear and convincing evidence existed to support such a proposition. However, close scrutiny of the research on this subject reveals that there is insufficient proof to sustain this belief. This heightened focus on the differences between men and women in social influence studies indicates that the small differences that exist are more a function of the research design than any inherent differences between the sexes.

While their research is some three decades old now, Eagly and her colleagues were chiefly responsible for accurately condensing the gender-difference research down to a cohesive set of conclusions (Eagly, 1978; Eagly & Carli, 1981; see also B. J. Becker, 1986). Thus, the following discussion draws heavily on their review findings. Before beginning, however, three brief comments are in order.

First, while questions about the relative persuadability of men and women have largely been set to rest, reviewing this literature is beneficial because it highlights the importance of social science research over commonsense observations and also illustrates how conceptual thinking about research methods, narrative reviews, and meta-analytic procedures combined to reverse the course of thinking about a fundamental issue in the field.

Second, it is important to distinguish between the variables of sex and gender. Specifically, *sex* refers to the biological differences between males and females. An individual's sex is indicated by anatomical and biological characteristics such as genitalia, chromosomes, and hormones. *Gender* (i.e., how masculine or feminine an individual is), on the other hand, is a psychological characteristic. Cultures determine which behaviors are considered *masculine* (i.e., expected of males) and which are considered *feminine* (i.e., expected of females) (J. T. Wood, 2011). In North America, for example, characteristics or traits typically considered masculine include being "strong, ambitious, successful, rational, and emotionally controlled" (p. 21), while those considered feminine include being "physically attractive, deferential, emotionally expressive, nurturing, and concerned with people and relationships" (p. 22). A person (either a man or a woman) who exhibits the former behavior set is considered masculine, while a person (again, either a man or a woman) who exhibits the latter set of behaviors is considered feminine.

Although the female versus male distinction is frequently cited in persuasion research, the field's researchers are rarely as interested in the biological differences between men and women as they are in the socialization and cultural differences between individuals. Although cultural and social (i.e., gender) differences are invoked to *explain* persuasion differences between men and women, they are rarely measured in persuasion research. The biological definition of sex frequently used in persuasion research is an imprecise way of measuring the social and cultural differences that exist among people, because a biological definition of sex inevitably miscategorizes people who have not experienced traditional sex-role socialization and do not identify with the social characteristics of their biological group. Nevertheless, owing to its widespread use in prior research, our review of gender effects will perforce employ this imperfect categorization of differences between men and women as message recipients.[1]

Our third comment relates to the nature of the differences between men and women. Historically, it has been popular to cast men and women as representative of different cultures (or even planets!) (Gray, 1992). But there are precious few data that support such an extreme view (e.g., Canary & Dindia, 1998). Instead, most scholars believe that men and women are basically more similar than different (Canary & Hause, 1993). As applied to social influence, this perspective implies relatively little qualitative differences between the sexes.

Eagly's Narrative Review

Eagly (1978) conducted a narrative review of research on gender differences in social influence. She noted that several prior reviews of the persuasion and conformity literature had found strong gender effects in prior research. She then divided the studies into two categories: traditional persuasion studies in which the message receivers were individually exposed to a persuasive message and conformity studies in which the participants formed a small group and attempted to achieve consensus on an issue. Three types of findings were recorded for these studies: either women were more easily persuaded or conformed more than men; men were more easily persuaded or conformed more than women; or there were no differences in persuadability or conformity between the two. Of the 62 persuasion studies included in her review, Eagly found that 51 (82%) revealed no gender difference in persuadability. Ten studies (16%) concluded that women were more easily persuaded than men, while only one (2%) found that men were more easily persuaded than women. The conformity studies yielded larger differences. Of the 61 group conformity studies, 38 (62%) found no gender differences, 21 (34%) concluded that women conformed more than men, and 2 studies (3%) found that men conformed more than women. These findings seriously undermined the claims of strong gender effects that had been advanced in prior literature reviews.

Eagly (1978) speculated that the studies in her review that found significant gender differences might be partially explained by cultural and experimental factors. She noted that many of the studies that found significant gender differences had been conducted prior to 1970 and the real heyday of the feminist movement in the United States. In addition, she argued that many of these studies employed sex-biased persuasion topics. That is, the studies concluding that women conformed more readily or were more easily persuaded than men tended to use male-oriented topics (e.g., auto mechanics and football rather than nutrition and child development). Eagly argued that the use of sex-biased topics prior to the women's liberation movement may have made women appear more susceptible to influence in certain studies. In fact, prior research has found that both men and women

---

BOX 9.1. Knowledge and Persuadability in Juries

The fact that message recipient knowledge plays an important role in persuadability is well known among jury consultants. During the past 25 years, Jim has conducted more than 550 focus group and mock trial projects for clients across the country on a wide variety of civil lawsuits. Although the specific research findings are proprietary, one remarkably consistent finding occurs time and again: when jurors assert that they have some special knowledge of, training in, or experience with the subject matter, they are able to exert a disproportionate amount of influence over the other jurors. For example, jurors who claim some experience in applying for patents will normally have more influence during deliberations on a patent infringement case. Those who claim to have experience in negotiating or managing contracts, similarly, will have more influence over other jurors in a commercial contract case.

It is a natural tendency for jurors lacking specialized knowledge to defer to those who have more knowledge on a particular subject. As a result, these self-proclaimed *local experts* often exert a disproportionate influence on verdict decisions. For this reason, trial lawyers usually use *voir dire* (or question) jurors to identify people who have special knowledge and consciously focus on those jurors for peremptory challenges (or strikes) that excuse them from jury service.

are more susceptible to influence when they lack knowledge of (McGuire & Papageorgis, 1961) or are uninterested in the persuasion topic (N. Miller, 1965). If these factors combined to influence susceptibility to persuasion in the earliest studies, then it is even less likely that gender is a key characteristic involved in more modern-day persuasive exchanges.

Eagly and Carli's Meta-Analytic Review

Eagly's (1978) narrative review was limited by the use of a "counting procedure" for summarizing the findings of prior research. Because this review predated the development of more sophisticated meta-analytic procedures (see Chapter 2), a subsequent meta-analytic review of this literature was conducted to assess the impact of cultural and experimental factors in studies reporting gender effects (Eagly & Carli, 1981).

The primary advantage of the meta-analytic review is a precise estimate of the *size* of any gender difference in each study. Averaging these effect sizes across studies provides a much more precise estimate of gender differences in persuasion than is possible in a narrative literature review. Although the meta-analysis found that, for both persuasion and group conformity studies, women were statistically significantly more susceptible to influence than men, the size of this effect was quite small. Consistent with Eagly's (1978) narrative review, the effect sizes in group conformity studies were significantly stronger than those in the persuasion studies. Even with these larger effects in conformity studies, less than 1% of the variance in susceptibility to influence was attributed to subject gender. Eagly and Carli (1981) concluded that "a sex difference as small as this may have few implications for social interaction" (p. 11).[2]

In addition, Eagly and Carli (1981) failed to find evidence of gender bias in the topics employed in prior research as they had previously speculated. To examine this issue, they presented students with a list of topics from these studies and asked them to rate their interest and knowledge about the topics. Some topics were found to be biased in favor of men (e.g., football, soccer, the military, automobiles), some were found to be biased in favor of women (e.g., cancer checkups and social work), and others were found to be gender-neutral. Although many of the topics were gender-biased, there was no support for the position that male-oriented topics were overrepresented in prior studies. That is, the average gender difference on the interest and knowledge ratings for topics used in these studies was not significantly different from zero (Eagly & Carli, 1981). It should be emphasized that the students who made these interest and knowledge ratings as part of the meta-analysis were not the original participants in the studies that are reviewed. Given that the majority of the studies included in this review were conducted prior to 1970, it is possible that participants in many of these original studies may have had different knowledge and interest levels than the students who made the ratings for this review in 1981. Thus, the findings concerning the bias in message topics should be interpreted cautiously (Eagly & Carli, 1981).

Summary of Gender Effects Research

Together, these reviews provide little evidence to suggest that the sex of persuasion targets is an important feature of persuasive transactions. Although this belief was once widespread among both scholars and lay community, the findings of these two reviews have nearly laid this issue to rest (for a dissenting view, however, see M. Burgoon & Klingle, 1998). No doubt, there are some persuasion situations in which women (or men) find themselves more susceptible to influence than members of the opposite sex (e.g., M. Burgoon & Klingle, 1998; Carli, 2001), but these situations are not sufficiently frequent to uphold the belief that important gender differences exist in persuadability.

MESSAGE DISCREPANCY AND PERSUASION

The goal of many persuasive transactions is to change a target person's or an audience's attitudes in a particular direction. When persuaders attempt to alter attitudes or behaviors, the position advocated in the persuasive message may differ from the position held by message recipients. This difference is generally referred to as *message discrepancy,* that is, the extent to which a persuader's message recommendation differs from the position held by the target person or audience.

In Chapter 1 we defined *attitude* as, in part, a positive, negative, or neutral evaluation of a target. Thus, a continuum may be conceived as representing the differing positions people hold for most attitude objects. At the risk of conflating legal, financial, and moral issues as well as appearing overly simplistic, let's consider the variety of positions people hold on abortion rights (or, alternatively, "the right to choose"). Some people oppose abortion under any circumstances, their position being represented at the extreme right end of the continuum shown in Figure 9.1. Moving progressively leftward on the continuum, others might generally oppose abortion but regard it as acceptable when the life of the mother is at stake—and yet others might support a woman's right to choose to terminate her pregnancy when her life is at risk *or* in cases of rape or incest. At the extreme other (left) end of the continuum are those who support the right of every woman to choose an abortion, *whatever* her financial circumstances.

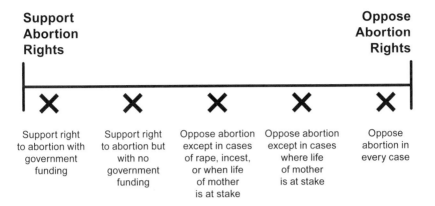

FIGURE 9.1. Hypothetical attitude continuum.

The diversity of viewpoints on the abortion issue is apparent in this example. As with many potential subjects of persuasion, people may hold similar general views about abortion and yet differ when more precise scenarios or alternatives are outlined. As a result, persuaders who blindly assume that an audience's views on a topic are homogeneous may overlook subtle but important nuances in the positions held. In other words, it is important to recognize that even when people generally agree on an issue, they are likely to differ somewhat in the specific attitudes they hold. Indeed, this may be one reason why politicians become "fuzzy" on some issues when speaking to diverse audiences. In their attempt to appeal to a wide spectrum of voters, politicians often attempt to minimize the perceived discrepancy between their own viewpoint and the positions held by their constituents.

Most persuasive messages advocate acceptance of a particular position, while the attitudes held by audience members will vary from person to person. It follows, then, that message discrepancy is likely to differ among message recipients. Extending the abortion rights example further, we can conclude that a persuasive message advocating a ban on all abortions will be mildly objectionable to some people (e.g., those who favor abortion only under extenuating circumstances) and highly objectionable to others (e.g., those who believe that every woman should have the right to an abortion regardless of the circumstances). If message discrepancy (i.e., the difference between the position advocated by a speaker and the position held by the receivers) affects attitude or behavior change, then some recipients will experience more attitude change than will others.

The concept of message discrepancy raises two questions for persuaders. First, and most important, is message discrepancy an important factor in persuasive communication? If so, then effective persuaders should be interested in a second question: How does message discrepancy influence the attitudes and behaviors of message recipients? Two theories, Social Judgment Theory and Information Processing Theory, agree that message discrepancy is an important factor in the persuasion process; however, the two theories disagree on almost everything else. Each theory and its supporting evidence will be discussed next.

Social Judgment Theory

One of the first theories to address the issue of message discrepancy was Social Judgment Theory (M. Sherif & Hovland, 1961; C. W. Sherif et al., 1965). C. W. Sherif, M. Sherif, and their colleagues classified attitudes along a continuum that ranged from acceptance to rejection.[3] The *latitude of acceptance* represents the positions on the attitude continuum that a person finds acceptable. By definition, a person's ideal or preferred position is included within this latitude. Positions that are unacceptable to a message recipient constitute the *latitude of rejection*. People holding a moderate position on an issue may have a latitude of rejection on both sides of their latitude of acceptance (see Figure 9.2). However, when a person's attitude is extreme, then a single latitude of acceptance will be located on one end of the latitude continuum, and a latitude of rejection will be located on the other end (see Figure 9.3). In both Figures 9.2 and 9.3, the ideal or preferred position is marked with an X.

Predicting Attitude Change

According to the Social Judgment Theory, attitude change can be reliably predicted from knowledge about the latitudes of acceptance and rejection: "Attitude change increases with [message] discrepancy as long as the message falls within the latitude of acceptance, but then it decreases if the

FIGURE 9.2. Latitudes of acceptance and rejection for a moderate attitude.

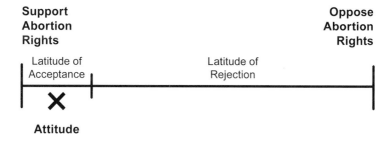

FIGURE 9.3. Latitudes of acceptance and rejection for an extreme attitude.

discrepancy is so large that the message falls in the latitude of rejection" (Hunter, Danes, & S. H. Cohen, 1984, p. 57).

Underpinning the attitude change process is a series of perceptual judgments people make about message content and message sources. When people perceive that a message recommendation falls within their latitude of acceptance, *assimilation* is hypothesized to occur. That is, receivers judge the message recommendation as being closer to their own position than it actually is. For example, voters who are opposed to abortion under any circumstances might perceive their views to be aligned with those of a "pro-life" political candidate who favors abortion *only* when the life of the mother is at risk. However, when a message recommendation is perceived to fall within the latitude of rejection, *contrast effects* are hypothesized. A contrast effect causes receivers to judge the message as more discrepant from their own position than it actually is. Extending the example, a person who opposes abortion under any circumstances might reject the views of a candidate who supports abortion rights in the case of rape or incest, fearing that such a position would enable any woman who wanted an abortion to claim that she had been raped. In short, reflecting the features underlying the latitudes of acceptance and rejection, as well as assimilation and contrast effects, Social Judgment Theory predicts a curvilinear (i.e., inverted-U-shaped) relationship between message discrepancy and attitude change (see Figure 9.4).

Predicting Changes in Source Credibility

Social Judgment Theory did not predict the impact of message and attitude discrepancy on perceived source credibility. However, descriptions of the theory provide a clear set of expectations regarding this relationship. "When messages fall within the latitude of acceptance, the source is viewed as more truthful, factual, and less biased" (C. W. Sherif et al., 1965, p. 227). However, they identified source derogation as one outcome

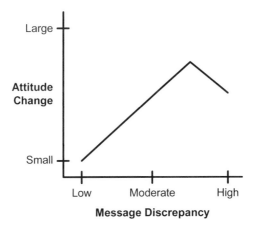

FIGURE 9.4. Curvilinear relationship between message discrepancy and attitude change as predicted by the Social Judgment Theory.

of extreme message discrepancies. Editorial cartoon caricatures depicting President Obama as Adolph Hitler during the health care debate in 2010 and occasional left-wing references to Tea Party activists as "wingnuts and lunatics" are classic examples of source derogation that may result from extreme message discrepancy.

Interest in the role of source derogation led Hunter and colleagues (1984) to argue that *if* predictions regarding message discrepancy and source credibility had been posited by social judgment theorists, the hypothesized relationship would mirror the message discrepancy–attitude change prediction. That is, when a message falls within the latitude of acceptance, message discrepancy is positively related to changes in source credibility. When a message falls within the latitude of rejection, source derogation occurs, producing a negative relationship between message discrepancy and changes in source credibility (see Figure 9.5). In short, Social Judgment Theory would predict a curvilinear (inverted-U-shaped) relationship between message discrepancy and source credibility change (Hunter et al., 1984).

Evidence Supporting Social Judgment Theory

A considerable number of studies have found evidence of the curvilinear relationship between message discrepancy and attitude change (Aronson, Turner, & Carlsmith, 1963; Bochner & Insko, 1966; C. W. Sherif et al., 1965; Whittaker, 1967). These studies provided evidence of a "discrepancy curve" reflecting a positive relationship between message discrepancy and

BOX 9.2. Source Derogation and Message Discrepancy

Perhaps the most extreme example of source derogation stemming from message discrepancy occurred during the late 1790s and early 1800s as Aaron Burr and Alexander Hamilton argued in newspapers and public forums about the proper role of the federal government. The sharp political differences between these two men escalated to personal disparagement as well, and the ensuing public spectacle grew so intense that the two men ultimately agreed privately to a duel of honor intended to settle their differences. On the morning of July 11, 1804, the two men rowed across the Hudson River from Manhattan to the cliffs of Weehawken, NJ (where pistol duels had not yet been outlawed). Because the firearms they used were notoriously inaccurate at the time, the duel could have been settled honorably by each man firing and intentionally missing the other. However, Vice President Aaron Burr shot former Treasury Secretary Alexander Hamilton, who died 31 hours later. The duel marked the culmination of years of public animosity and disparagement that grew and ultimately festered from the two former friends' markedly different political views.

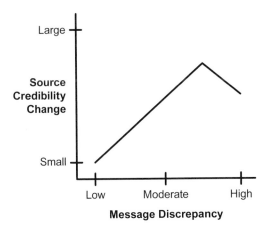

FIGURE 9.5. Curvilinear relationship between message discrepancy and changes in perceived source credibility as predicted by the Social Judgment Theory.

attitude change up to a point, beyond which further increases in discrepancy decreased the amount of observed attitude change. These findings are consistent with the pattern of attitude change predicted by Social Judgment Theory (for a contrasting view, see Fink & Cai, 2013).

Unfortunately, evidence for the predicted change in source credibility is less apparent. In an extensive investigation of message discrepancy effects, Hunter and colleagues (1984) failed to find evidence of a curvilinear relationship between message discrepancy and source credibility change. Instead, they found that message discrepancy was positively correlated with changes in source credibility. These findings were consistent with prior message discrepancy studies that showed a positive linear relationship between message discrepancy and measured changes in source credibility (Bochner & Insko, 1966; Rhine & Severance, 1970; Tannenbaum, 1953).

In summary, the attitude change data suggest that discrepancy is positively related to attitude change until the message becomes so divergent from the recipients' beliefs that it falls within his latitude of rejection. In this regard, there is support for Social Judgment Theory. However, predictions concerning source credibility pose problems for the theory. Although C. W. Sherif, M. Sherif, and their colleagues did not specifically offer source credibility predictions, the curvilinear relationship hypothesized by Hunter et al. (see Figure 9.5) is consistent with the theory. Studies measuring source credibility effects, however, failed to find evidence of this curvilinear relationship.

Therefore, Social Judgment Theory fails to provide a completely satisfying explanation for the impact of message discrepancy on attitude change and source credibility. A second perspective, Information Processing Theory, provides an alternative way of understanding the effects of viewpoint discrepancy on attitudes toward the message and its source.

Information Processing Theory

Information Processing Theory is a generic label for a family of persuasion models that maintain a common set of assumptions about the cognitive evaluation of persuasive messages (Anderson, 1959, 1971; Hovland & Pritzker, 1957; McGuire, 1968; Wyer, 1970). The fundamental assumption of Information Processing Theory is that messages have affective value. The value of a message can be represented along the same continuum that we developed to represent a person's attitude on a topic. The position of a message along the continuum is determined by the value of the attitude reflected in the message recommendation (Hunter et al., 1984). For example, the value of a message advocating a total ban on abortions would be represented on the right end of the continuum shown in Figure

9.1. Conversely, the value of a pro-choice message could be represented on the left end of this continuum.

According to the theory, message processing involves an internal comparison of one's own position to the position advocated in the message. The difference between these two positions is defined as message discrepancy, which stimulates attitude change. Several theorists propose a "distance-proportional" model in which attitude change is proportional to message discrepancy and is always in the direction advocated by the message (Anderson, 1959; Anderson & Hovland, 1957; Hunter et al., 1984, p. 36).

Linear Discrepancy Model

Hunter and colleagues (1984) demonstrate that the attitude change predictions of Information Processing Theory are formally equivalent to a simple Linear Discrepancy Model in which the amount of attitude change produced by a persuasive message will be a linear function of message discrepancy:

$$\Delta a = \alpha(m - a) \qquad (9.1)$$

where Δa represents attitude change, m is the value of the attitude reflected in the message, a is the receiver's premessage attitude, and α is the coefficient that represents the strength of the relationship between message discrepancy $(m - a)$ and attitude change (see Fink & Cai, 2013, for a more detailed discussion of such models).

There are two important differences between the predictions of Information Processing Theory and Social Judgment Theory. First, Social Judgment Theory predicts a curvilinear (inverted-U-shaped) relationship between message discrepancy and attitude change, whereas Information Processing Theory predicts a positive linear relationship between message discrepancy and attitude change (see Figure 9.6). Second, Social Judgment Theory suggests that source derogation will occur when message discrepancy is large, producing a curvilinear relationship between message discrepancy and changes in perceived source credibility. Information Processing Theory, on the other hand, predicts that changes in perceived source credibility are a linear function of message discrepancy (see Figure 9.7).

Evidence Supporting Information Processing Theory

Several experiments provide support for the predictions of Information Processing Theory. First, there is considerable evidence of a linear relationship between message discrepancy and attitude change. Tests of Anderson's

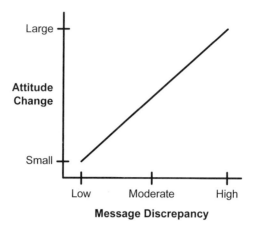

FIGURE 9.6. Linear relationship between message discrepancy and attitude change as predicted by the Information Processing Theory.

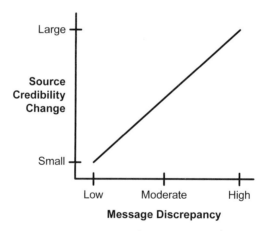

FIGURE 9.7. Linear relationship between message discrepancy and changes in perceived source credibility as predicted by the Information Processing Theory.

Information Integration Model (Anderson, 1971, 1981) and the Linear Discrepancy Model (Hunter et al., 1984) provide evidence of a positive linear relationship between message discrepancy and attitude change. That is, greater persuasive effects are associated with increased, not decreased, message discrepancy.

Perhaps the most compelling evidence for the information processing explanation of discrepancy effects stems from the source credibility data presented by Hunter and colleagues (1984). Consistent with the predictions of Information Processing Theory, the studies they reviewed and conducted all found a linear relationship between message discrepancy and changes in perceived source credibility.

Explaining the "Discrepancy Effects"

In summary, two different theories make contrasting predictions concerning the persuasive impact of message discrepancy. Social Judgment Theory predicts a curvilinear relationship between message discrepancy and attitude change, while Information Processing Theory predicts a positive linear relationship. There are studies, moreover, that are consistent with both of these predictions, however, on the whole, there is more support for Information Processing Theory than Social Judgment Theory.

How do we make sense of these competing explanations and results? It is possible that both theories offer correct explanations of message discrepancy, because each theory has a different theoretical domain and different boundary conditions. In discussing Social Judgment Theory, C. W. Sherif et al. (1965) argue that, in order to produce the curvilinear relationships between message discrepancy and attitude change, audience members must be ego-involved in the topic. Social Judgment theorists used the term *ego-involvement* to reflect a set of core values or beliefs that constitute a person's self-concept. Thus, ego-involving attitudes define a person's system of values. For example, for many people, attitudes about immigration reform and gay marriage reflect their core political and cultural values.

Studies finding a curvilinear relationship have tended to include highly ego-involved participants who already have a strong commitment to an issue. Highly ego-involved persons have a narrow latitude of acceptance and a wide latitude of rejection. Messages falling in the latitude of rejection must be rejected if the person is to maintain his or her preexisting values.

Information Processing Theory studies, on the other hand, tend to use topics that are not closely linked to participants' values and self-concepts. Participants in these studies are unlikely to be ego-involved in the topic and therefore have a wider latitude of acceptance. Participants can drastically change their attitudes without having to restructure their self-concepts.

In summary, curvilinear relationships between message discrepancy and attitude change are likely to occur under a specific set of circumstances, most specifically, when one's ego involvement in the message is high. When the message topic is not related to the receiver's core values, however, Information Processing Theory predicts a positive relationship between message discrepancy and attitude change.

While Social Judgment Theory and Information Processing Theory provide compelling explanations of message discrepancy effects, a third explanation stems from investigations that have examined the effects of *positional* and *psychological* discrepancy (Fink & Cai, 2013; Fink, Kaplowitz, & Bauer, 1983). *Positional discrepancy* refers to the absolute difference between a receiver's attitude and the position advocated in the message, while *psychological discrepancy* relates to the difference a receiver perceives between his or her attitude and the position advocated in the message.

For example, consider the issue of capital punishment. Assume that a voter who opposes the death penalty in *all* circumstances attended a candidate panel discussion on the issue. Candidate A spoke first and advocated use of the death penalty only in certain types of cases (e.g., for repeat violent offenders or the murder of a law enforcement officer), the position advocated by this candidate would be discrepant from the voter's position on the issue. The objective difference between their respective positions is referred to as "positional discrepancy." If, then, Candidate B spoke next and advocated *widespread use* of the death penalty, his or her position would be even more discrepant from the voter's attitude than Candidate A's. If both candidates were speaking sequentially as part of the same panel, the voter would likely perceive Candidate A's position as *psychologically* less discrepant from his or her own attitude than Candidate B's position.

In a test of the importance of positional and psychological discrepancy, Fink and colleagues (1983, 2013) found that positional discrepancy was associated with greater attitude change; however, they found that greater psychological discrepancy inhibited attitude change. Moreover, they found that surrounding messages influenced the psychological discrepancy of a message.

Applied to Information Processing Theory, these findings suggest that messages with extreme positional discrepancy may also serve to heighten psychological discrepancy in message recipients. If these two types of discrepancy are confounded, one would expect the nonlinear relationship between discrepancy and attitudes that was observed in prior tests of Social Judgment Theory.

Regardless of the correct theoretical interpretation of these effects, the practical implications of message discrepancy research are clear. In many situations, highly discrepant messages will produce greater attitude change than less discrepant messages. However, when the message topic is linked to receivers' core values, highly discrepant messages (those falling within a receiver's latitude of rejection) may cause receivers to discount the message, counterargue against it, and/or perceive it to be more psychologically discrepant than it objectively is. Any of these outcomes could limit the persuasiveness of the message.

RECEIVER INVOLVEMENT AND PERSUASION

A third characteristic of message receivers that has captured the attention of persuasion researchers is *involvement*. Over the years, receiver involvement has assumed a variety of theoretical roles in the development of several persuasion theories. Beginning with the Social Judgment theorists in the early 1960s, *involvement* referred to the activation of ego-defensive mechanisms in message receivers that motivated them to reject discrepant persuasive appeals (C. W. Sherif et al., 1965). By the late 1960s social-cognitive theories of persuasion began to investigate these issues, and by the 1980s they dominated persuasion research (Greenwald et al., 1968; Petty, Ostrom, et al., 1981). This theoretical shift led to the development of several social-cognitive theories in which involvement was hypothesized to stimulate thinking in message receivers (Chaiken, 1987; Petty & Cacioppo, 1981, 1986). In yet a third conceptual approach, Cialdini and his colleagues (Cialdini, Levy, Herman, & Evenbeck, 1973; Cialdini, Levy, Herman, Kozlowski, & Petty, 1976) argued that receiver involvement can stimulate impression management behaviors and influence the persuadability of message receivers.

Across at least six decades, the term *involvement* has been used in widely different ways that have produced a body of persuasion studies that appear to be contradictory. In their review of the literature, Johnson and Eagly (1989) attempted to explain these contradictions by identifying three distinct conceptual meanings of involvement and clarified the various roles that involvement plays in the persuasion process.

Johnson and Eagly (1989) defined *involvement* as "the motivational state induced by an association between an activated attitude and some aspect of the self-concept" (p. 293). Working from this general definition, they described three research traditions as germane to involvement—*value-relevant, outcome-relevant,* and *impression-relevant*—each of which reflects different functions that the concept plays in the persuasion process. Although Johnson and Eagly did not endorse a functional perspective for defining involvement, such a framework provides an excellent conceptual backdrop for understanding the essential characteristics of these research traditions. The four psychological functions of attitudes—*ego-defensive, instrumental, value-expressive,* and *social-expressive* (D. Katz, 1960;

Smith et al., 1956)—that we discussed in Chapter 1 highlight the differences among the three traditions of research on involvement. These traditions and their psychological functions are reviewed in the remainder of this chapter.

Value-Relevant Involvement

This tradition of research on the persuasive effects of involvement evolved from investigations of Social Judgment Theory (C. W. Sherif et al., 1965; M. Sherif & Hovland, 1961; M. Sherif & Sherif, 1967). Earlier in this chapter we discussed the predicted effectiveness of messages falling within the latitudes of acceptance and rejection as well as how ego-involvement determines the width of these latitudes. Social Judgment Theory posits that when message receivers are highly ego-involved in a message topic, their latitudes of rejection become wider, increasing the number of positions along the attitude evaluation continuum that are unacceptable. Conversely, when receivers are uninvolved, their latitudes of rejection become narrower, increasing the number of positions that receive an acceptable evaluation.

Johnson and Eagly (1989) labeled this type of involvement *value-relevant involvement* because it reflects a concern about the core values that define a person's self-concept. For example, a privacy rights advocate would consider a message advocating the more expansive use of cell phone monitoring by federal law enforcement agencies to be inconsistent with his or her core values. Such an appeal would have high value relevance for the privacy rights advocate. Regardless of the label, Levin, Nichols, and Johnson (2000) maintain that this type of involvement serves either an ego-defensive or a value-expressive function, as defined by Katz (1960). People become highly concerned about particular topics because these issues allow receivers to express important values or defend their self-concepts from attack (Levin et al., 2000).

Given this function, the predicted relationship between value-relevant involvement and attitude change should be obvious. Value-relevant involvement should increase the number of unacceptable positions along the attitude–evaluation continuum and inhibit attitude change. Johnson and Eagly's (1989) meta-analytic review found a moderately strong negative correlation between value-relevant involvement and attitude change. In short, this type of involvement appears to inhibit attitude change.

Outcome-Relevant Involvement

Johnson and Eagly (1989) labeled a second category of involvement *outcome-relevant involvement*. This tradition of involvement research began with the social cognitive approaches to persuasion. As we noted in Chapter 5, during the 1980s, both the Heuristic–Systematic Model of persuasion (Chaiken, 1987) and the Elaboration Likelihood Model (Petty & Cacioppo, 1986) posited that outcome-relevant involvement is one factor that motivates receivers to carefully scrutinize the content of persuasive messages.

In this research tradition, involvement serves an *instrumental function* similar to the one described by Katz (1960). This type of involvement reflects a concern about achieving particular positively evaluated outcomes (Levin et al., 2000). A typical ELM investigation, for example, might manipulate outcome-relevant involvement by presenting college students with messages that warn of comprehensive exams for undergraduates or higher tuition rates. Both topics, while central to students' educational goals (thus making them high in outcome-relevant involvement), would nonetheless be unlikely to tap students' values or self-concept.

Outcome-relevant involvement is likely to rise as people work toward achieving an issue-related goal and decline once the goal has been achieved. This variability distinguishes outcome-relevant involvement from value-relevant involvement. Value-relevant involvement is likely to be much more stable because of its connection to a person's core values (C. W. Sherif et al., 1965).

Again, as we noted in Chapter 5, social cognitive models of persuasion posit that highly involved message recipients will scrutinize the content of persuasive messages more than less involved recipients will. Thus, the persuasive effects of this type of involvement depend upon the quality of the arguments and supporting material in the message. Consistent with this general prediction, Johnson and Eagly (1989) found that involvement enhanced the persuasive effects of strong persuasive messages and inhibited the effectiveness of weak persuasive messages.[4] Thus, when outcome-relevant involvement of message receivers is high, the quality of arguments and evidence in the persuasive message will determine the extent of attitude change.

Impression-Relevant Involvement

The third tradition of involvement research emphasizes *impression-relevant involvement*. Investigations by Cialdini and his colleagues (Cialdini et al., 1973, 1976; Cialdini & Petty, 1981) evolved from Zimbardo's (1960) concept of response involvement. Impression-relevant involvement occurs when individuals are concerned about the social consequences of expressing an attitude. Research on this type of involvement has consistently found that when people are concerned about the impressions they make on others, they are reluctant to endorse positions that are incompatible with those of message sources. Cialdini's research found that when people are under public scrutiny they tend to advocate more flexible and moderate attitudes as compared to when their position is unlikely to be publicly evaluated.

Because concerns about impression management influence the attitudes people endorse, Johnson and Eagly (1989) prefer the label "impression-relevant involvement" to Zimbardo's "response involvement." Individuals high in impression-relevant involvement "employ their attitudes as a means of advancing interpersonally oriented goals" (Levin et al., 2000, p. 166). In this regard, Levin and colleagues (2000) argue that impression-relevant involvement serves what Smith and colleagues (1956) called a "social-adjustive function." In the social-adjustive function of attitudes, the expression of a particular attitude serves to "promote or preserve relationships with important others, or to break from those relationships no longer considered valuable to the attitude holder" (Hullett & Boster, 2001, p. 135). For example, this concern is evident in the behavior of many job applicants who are cautious not to endorse extreme attitudes unless they are certain their potential employer endorses the same attitudes.

Given its social function, it should come as no surprise that impression-relevant involvement inhibits attitude change (Johnson & Eagly, 1989). Although the size of this effect was small, highly involved receivers were less likely to change their attitude or to endorse an extreme position when compared to receivers who were less concerned with impression management.

Summarizing the Effects of Involvement

Johnson and Eagly (1989) offer convincing evidence of the theoretical and empirical distinctions among these three research traditions of involvement research.[5] Although the pattern of effects for value-relevant and impression-relevant involvement is similar, their theoretical foundations are clearly distinct. Whereas value-relevant involvement reflects concern about a set of core values, impression-relevant involvement stems from more superficial concerns about self-presentation.

For scholars of persuasion, differences among the research traditions highlighted by Johnson and Eagly may help resolve many of the apparent inconsistencies among prior investigations of the persuasive effects of involvement. For persuasion practitioners, this analysis calls for considerable caution in developing and presenting persuasive appeals. Because the specific type of receiver involvement is likely to influence the effectiveness of persuasive messages, persuaders are cautioned to carefully consider the values and goals that message receivers bring to each persuasion transaction.

FUNCTION MATCHING

Persuasion scholars have in recent times reexamined the nature of attitudes and the functions they serve for people (see, e.g., Carpenter et al., 2013; Hullett & Boster, 2001; Petty, Wheeler, & Bizer, 2000). One prediction made by the earliest proponents of the functional approach to attitudes (D. Katz, 1960; Smith et al., 1956) was that persuasive messages are likely to be particularly successful when the arguments they contain match the functions that underlie audience members' attitudes. For example, an individual whose attitudes are based on the instrumental function (i.e., to gain rewards and avoid punishments) will likely positively evaluate—and be persuaded by—a message promising rewards or one that describes ways of avoiding punishments. That same individual will be unpersuaded by an appeal to values.

Much research on the functional approach has been hindered by a lack of clear methods for identifying various attitude functions (Carpenter et al., 2013; Hullett & Boster, 2001). During the past two decades, research on functional approaches (and function matching) has been facilitated by the development of either direct measures of attitude functions (Clary & Snyder, 1992; Herek, 1988) or personality measures that serve as indirect indicators of attitude functions. For example, several studies used the self-monitoring scale to identify value-expressive and social-adjustive functions (e.g., Snyder & DeBono, 1985; see also Carpenter et al., 2013).

Hullett and Boster (2001) investigated the extent to which functional matching influenced attitude change following exposure to a persuasive message on tuition increases. They developed measures to determine the extent to which participants valued conformity (i.e., a social-adjustive function) or self-direction and independence (i.e., a specific value-expressive function). Hullett and Boster measured conformity and self-direction values and then exposed participants to one of two versions of a message advocating a tuition increase. The "conformity" message indicated that the typical student in favor of tuition increases valued "politeness, self-restraint, and getting along with others" (p. 142), while the "self-direction" message associated agreement with tuition increases with students exhibiting "self-sufficiency, self-reliance, ability to choose one's own goals, and independence" (ibid.).

Hullett and Boster's (2001) results were, for the most part, consistent with the functional matching hypothesis. Specifically, they found that the values students espoused were related to their evaluations of the persuasive messages. Students who strongly endorsed the conformity value found the conformity message to be of higher quality than students who did not espouse that value. In addition, students who strongly endorse the self-direction value found the self-reliance message to be of higher quality than students who did not espouse that value. In all cases, evaluation of message quality was positively related to agreement with the message's conclusions (i.e., to increase tuition).

SUMMARY

This chapter examined four characteristics of persuasive targets that have received considerable attention from persuasion scholars. We concluded that, although some weak effects were found in prior research, the gender of message receivers is not an important predictor of the effectiveness of persuasive messages. That is, there is scant evidence to suggest that women are more easily persuaded than men.

The discussion of message discrepancy effects was considerably more complicated. Social Judgment Theory and Information Processing Theory offered competing predictions about the persuasive effects of message discrepancy. Although some evidence supported both interpretations in different conditions, Information Processing Theory can more fully explain the findings of prior investigations. Regardless of the underlying theoretical mechanism, however, we concluded that message discrepancy appears to enhance attitude change unless the discrepancy is so large as to appear ridiculous or when audience members' values are involved in the message topic (Bochner & Insko, 1966; Fink & Cai, 2013).

Involvement is an important message receiver characteristic. We described three types of receiver involvement along with the functions they serve. The ego-defensive function served by value-relevant involvement has a moderately strong inhibiting effect on attitude change. Outcome-relevant involvement interacts with message quality to influence the effectiveness of message appeals. Lastly, impression-relevant involvement appears to have an inhibiting effect on attitude change, but this effect is much weaker than the one found for value-relevant involvement.

Finally, function matching appears to be another receiver factor that influences persuasion. Several studies have found that successful persuasive messages contain messages that match the functions underlying receivers' attitudes.

NOTES

1. This discussion leads us to one of the very few substantive issues upon which we (i.e., Jim and Paul) disagreed. Specifically, what do we *call* the differences between men and women? Jim argued that if differences between men and women in persuadability do exist, they are almost certainly the result of

differential socialization and, as a consequence, should be called "gender differences." Paul, on the other hand, argued that, while Jim is almost certainly correct, the data being reviewed focus on biological sex and as a consequence should be called "sex differences." Jim is first author, so we will call them "gender differences."

2. Eagly and Carli's (1981) research effectively ended the academic conversation on sex differences in persuadability. In a rare reconsideration of this issue, M. Burgoon and Klingle (1998) pointed out that Eagly and Carli's (1981) data showed that between "20% and 25% of women tend to be more persuadable than the population of men. This is clearly neither a small nor trivial difference" (p. 273). Moreover, they suggested that, contrary to the common misconception, the observed gender difference was less attributable to women being easily influenced than it was to a certain percentage of men refusing to change their attitudes and beliefs *under any circumstances*. Moreover, Carli (2001) noted that men were particularly unlikely to change their attitudes when the message source was female (see, e.g., Ridgeway, 1981).

3. Some variations of the theory also include the latitude of noncommitment, which represents a range of positions that are neither acceptable nor unacceptable. Unfortunately, few testable hypotheses were ever offered about attitudes falling within this latitude.

4. As we discussed in some detail in Chapter 5, Johnson and Eagly (1989) reported that Petty, Cacioppo, and their colleagues consistently found this effect, but other scholars were unable to replicate them.

5. It bears mentioning that not everyone endorsed the conceptual distinctions drawn by Johnson and Eagly (1989). Petty and Cacioppo (1990) criticized the distinction between value-relevant and outcome-relevant involvement, opting instead for a broader concept they labeled "personal involvement." They also criticized the merits of the meta-analytic review that supported Johnson and Eagly's distinction. Interested readers are encouraged to carefully examine the comprehensive response to Petty and Cacioppo's critique that was provided by Johnson and Eagly (1990).

CHAPTER 10

Characteristics of Persuasive Settings

LOOKING AHEAD . . . This chapter examines three situational characteristics that influence the persuasion process. We begin with a discussion of the relative effectiveness of various communication modes used in presenting persuasive appeals, including an examination of the large and growing literature on persuasive communication in online settings. After this, we explore the influence of distracting stimuli on the persuasiveness of a message. The chapter concludes with a discussion of group influences in the persuasion process.

In the preceding four chapters, we used Berlo's (1960) Source–Message–Channel–Receiver (i.e., SMCR) Model to parse the influence of source, message, and receiver characteristics on persuasive transactions. To explicate Berlo's model completely, this chapter might focus singlemindedly on the effects of persuasion channels. Although we examine various persuasion channels (including the recent literature on persuasive communication in online settings), our scope is broader and includes *all* the settings in which persuasive messages are communicated.

We begin with a discussion of traditional modality research and review the relative effectiveness of video, audio, and written modes of presenting persuasive messages. Next, we focus on the burgeoning literature that examines *online persuasion* through a variety of social media outlets. Then, we review the distraction literature, which encompasses the influence of distracting stimuli on the comprehension and effectiveness of persuasive messages. The chapter concludes with a discussion of the persuasion process within small groups. Though few persuasion textbooks consider the persuasive effects of small groups, a considerable portion of persuasive activity occurs in group settings. We review two avenues of research that reflect important social and informational influences of groups on individuals' attitudes and behaviors. Our review of these context effects is necessarily less integrated than the research literature reviews in previous chapters, but we believe that each distinct literature warrants consideration. Persuasion in interpersonal settings is then treated in Chapters 11 and 12.

TRADITIONAL MODALITY RESEARCH

Perhaps the most fundamental decision facing would-be persuaders is how best to present their persuasive appeals. With a wider variety of technological alternatives available to persuaders, this choice has become somewhat more complicated in recent years. Advertisers, politicians, business organizations, and relational partners routinely choose among several methods of message presentation. Sometimes these choices are based on research, but more often they reflect personal preferences based on prior persuasive success. Since the mid-1970s, for example, television has been the media staple of politicians seeking to present their positions and cultivate their images. This trend was marked by the election of Ronald Reagan in 1980—Reagan was a former actor with a strong television persona. Recent campaigns have seen an increase in the use of the Internet by candidates (e.g., Atkin & Rice, 2013; Benoit, 2007; Kaid & Bystrom, 1999). Advertisers and relational partners have also expanded to social media as an important conduit for communication.

Although these choices often become routine, one might question their effectiveness. Is television the most effective method for outlining the political positions of a candidate? When are various forms of media effective for achieving the particular goals of advertisers? Are face-to-face interactions the most effective method for making persuasive appeals to relational partners? Most likely, these questions require complex answers that depend on a variety of source, receiver, and message characteristics. Nevertheless, a growing body of research provides some preliminary insights into the persuasive merits of various modes of message presentation.

Research on the effects of message modality has found no simple effects for any mode of message presentation. That is, no overall persuasive advantage exists for live, video, audio, print, or computer-mediated messages. Instead, message modality serves to influence other factors, including the salience of the source and message comprehension, which in turn determine the effectiveness of a persuasive message.

Message Modality and Source Salience

Early on, two studies (Andreoli & Worchel, 1978; Worchel, Andreoli, & Eason, 1975) found that live and video messages were more effective in focusing receivers' attention on the characteristics of the message source than were written messages. When the source was perceived as trustworthy, this attention enhanced the persuasiveness of the message presentation. However, when the source was perceived as untrustworthy, this heightened attention decreased the persuasiveness of the message.

Chaiken and Eagly (1983) also investigated this issue and found similar effects. They argued that video presentations would make communicator-based cues more salient to message receivers than audio or written messages. Consistent with this hypothesis, they found that a video presentation presented by a likable source was more effective than the same message presented in audio or written format. Conversely, for unlikable sources, audio and written message presentations were more persuasive than video message presentations. Moreover, Braverman (2008) found that informational messages were most effective when they were delivered through a written rather than audio mode, because the written presentation provided greater opportunity for message elaboration. However, testimonials were more effective when they were delivered through an audio mode because the latter contained vocal information like emotion that could not be conveyed in a written format.

Taken together, these investigations provide a consistent pattern of effects. Live and video presentations focus more attention on the source of the message than audio and written presentations do. If the source's attributes are evaluated positively, this attention should enhance the effectiveness of the message. However, if the source lacks trustworthiness or is for some reason unlikable, then the use of a live or video presentation may inhibit the persuasiveness of the message. Although the findings from some individual studies are more complicated (e.g., Booth-Butterfield & Gutowski, 1993), research on modality effects provides a straightforward set of recommendations for persuaders: live or video presentations should be most effective for favorable message sources, whereas sources who are viewed less favorably should be more persuasive when using written and audio presentations. Moreover, written messages permit cognitive elaboration for those interested in more systematic processing of the content.

Modality and Message Comprehension

Message modality has also been related to message comprehension. Once again, however, the persuasive effects of this relationship are not straightforward. Chaiken and Eagly (1976) argued that the relative persuasiveness of video, audio, and written messages depends on the difficulty of the message content. In one study they manipulated message complexity by creating one message that contained sophisticated language but was equivalent in all other respects to a more easily understood second message. After presenting these difficult and simple messages in alternative video, audio, and written formats, they found that *comprehension* of the simple message did not vary across the three presentation modes. However, the difficult message was best comprehended when it was presented in a written format, as compared to the audio or video format. This finding should come as no surprise when one considers that messages presented in written format afford receivers the opportunity to reread portions of the message that are not initially understood. Similarly, Braverman (2008) found that informational messages were more convincing when delivered in writing, because written messages provide an opportunity to more carefully review and consider the message.

Given the positive relationship between message comprehension and message acceptance, these findings are easy to interpret: the difficult message was more persuasive when presented in a written format because message comprehension was highest in that format. The finding that the video presentation was most effective for the simple message may reflect an increased salience of favorable source characteristics or increased attentiveness to the message when it was presented in a video format.

Consistent with this information processing explanation of media effects, Grabe, Kamhawi, and Yegiyan (2009) found that a message receiver's level of education interacts with presentation medium to affect one's recall of the information. Specifically, less educated recipients (i.e., those with no more than a high school education) demonstrated greater recall of news presented on TV than in newspapers or on the Internet. In contrast, highly educated recipients (i.e., those with an advanced degree such as a PhD or JD) had greater recall of news information when it was presented in written formats (whether in newspapers or on the Internet) than on television (Grabe et al., 2009).

Summary of Modality Effects

In combination, research on source salience and message comprehension provides a clear description of the persuasive effects of message modality. When a source's attributes are favorable and likely to engender attitude change, video and live message presentations are the effective ways to emphasize these characteristics. If a source's characteristics are unfavorable and likely to inhibit persuasion, written and audio message formats appear most effective, because they do not accentuate these qualities.

A similar interaction effect was found for message comprehension. Written messages afford receivers the opportunity of reviewing and elaborating the content, making that format generally more effective for difficult content. However, the receiver's level of education also determines the effectiveness of the medium of presentation. Less educated message receivers have better recall of television messages than written messages, while highly educated receivers recall written content better than video content.

ONLINE PERSUASION

Over the past two decades, the Internet has emerged as an important tool of persuasion for communication professionals and ordinary people alike. Technological advances have created an ever widening array of options for sending messages designed to shape, reinforce, and change target audiences' responses. While Facebook and Twitter may have originally been intended primarily as social media, they have become a powerful organizational tool for tech-savvy political activists. For example, during the 2008 Obama presidential campaign, supporters were actively recruited to use the campaign's social media site to create their own web pages, post their own content, and disseminate information to their social media "friends" (Dutta & Fraser, 2008). The Occupy Wall Street protests against income inequality that occurred during the fall of 2011 were another set of events that demonstrated the power of social media as a source of persuasive communication. The movement began in New York City on September 17, 2011, and aided greatly by people's prolific use of Twitter, Facebook, and YouTube—quickly spread to many cities in the United States and elsewhere around the world (Schwartz, 2011).

In the preceding edition of this textbook, we made two predictions about online persuasion: first, that research in this area would increase dramatically; and, second, that summarizing it would prove difficult. We were correct on both accounts. The research literature on online persuasion is large, varied, and confusing (Atkin & Rice, 2013). Because it addresses a variety of questions stemming from a variety of theoretical frames (see, e.g., Portnoy, Scott-Sheldon, Johnson, & Carey, 2008; Webb, Joseph, Yardley, & Michie, 2010), it is naturally next-to-impossible to summarize coherently. Even cataloging the wide array of *modalities* falling under the rubric of "online communication" is a daunting task. Websites (both static and interactive), Facebook (and other social media such as Twitter, Tinder, Tumblr, etc.), YouTube, chat rooms, text messaging, and email are just some of the computer-mediated communication channels available to people creating social influence messages. The traditional modality research reviewed above provides some insights into the potential perils of online persuasion. Specifically, countless online analogues to traditional print (e.g., Twitter), audio (e.g., podcasts), and video (e.g., YouTube) media sources are routine in the modality research. A key issue in online persuasion research is the extent to which online media differentially focus more attention on the source rather than the message itself. Text-based blogs, for example, are unlikely to focus readers' attention on the source, while You-Tube videos typically emphasize the source characteristics over message content. Of course, the nature of the information contained on a website (as well as the nature of the website itself) is likely to affect message processing. For example, perusing a medical website for information on cancer prevention is likely to generate a different set of cognitive, emotional, and persuasive outcomes than reading a cancer survivor's blog or participating in an online cancer-survivor support group.

Platforms such as YouTube, however, also enable users to *respond* to persuasive messages (e.g., political speeches and advertisements) by posting their own video messages for others to view and critique. Thus, a higher level of *perceived interactivity* between the message source and receivers is another important feature of online communication. McMillen and Downes (2000) suggest that perceptions of interactivity are a function of two factors: the directionality of the communication between the message source and receiver (i.e., one-way vs. two-way) and the actual amount of control that the message receiver has over the communication process.

BOX 10.1. Social Media and the Arab Spring

The Arab Spring revolutions that began, first in Tunisia and then Egypt, in December 2010 quickly spread to Libya and ultimately Yemen. Both Twitter and Facebook served as important catalysts for these uprisings, as they provided real-time electronic forums for exchanging political views, organizing protests, and disseminating information to thousands and even millions of people instantaneously (Wolman, 2013). These uprisings were decentralized in that there was no formalized opposition party or preappointed leader who could be held accountable by the government authorities. Instead, the most popular social media platforms became powerful tools for organizing and persuading people en masse to join the insurrections. More recently, ISIS has exploited media sources such as YouTube to promote its cause and parade its acts of brutality against its perceived enemies, seeking thereby to recruit new members. Social media sites are very effective tools of persuasion and have become, in effect, "the great equalizer" in that they are readily accessible to all and provide for the unfettered exchange of information and opinions.

Interactivity is important to how today's social media have revolutionized online persuasion. Thanks to social media, audience members are no longer passive receivers of messages but, rather, active participants in creating, transforming, and passing along persuasive messages. The term *Web 2.0* was coined to emphasize the role of user-generated content in this transformation. For example, consumers routinely use company websites (in addition to independent ones like Yelp) to rate products, services, restaurants, and hotel accommodations. On the other hand, such practices limit a company's control over persuasive appeals and content on its website.

Additionally, such platforms as Facebook enable message receivers to endorse ("like") and disseminate ("share") messages created by message sources through a simple mouse click. Personalized testimonials or accounts, such as consumer reviews, can be quite compelling and value-added. Such researchers as Berthon and colleagues (Berthon, Pitt, Plangger, & Shapiro, 2012; Pitt, Berthon, Watson, & Zinkhan, 2002) have reported that consumers typically value other consumers' input more highly than the promotional information posted on commercial websites. Campbell and colleagues (Campbell, Pitt, Parent, & Berthon, 2011) have developed a typology of these consumer-generated messages, arguing that they can be arrayed along two dimensions, cognitive versus affective and collaborative versus oppositional. In this typology, cognitive responses are primarily concerned with questions about how the ad was created or came to exist, while emotional responses reflect affective (positive or negative) responses to the consumer-generated comment. The collaborative versus oppositional distinction reflects the extent to which the consumer either agrees with or is antagonistic toward the original ad's creator (Campbell, Pitt, Parent, & Berthon, 2011).

While technology has radically transformed the modern face of social influence, investigations of persuasion via these social media have nonetheless relied primarily on traditional theories of persuasion. For example, Chang and colleagues used the Elaboration Likelihood Model (ELM; see Chapter 5) to investigate the effects of online post popularity, source attractiveness, and argument quality on the usefulness of information and intention to share the information with other users (Chang, Yu, & Lu, 2015). Steyn and colleagues (Steyn, Ewing, Ven Heerden, Pitt, & Windisch, 2015) also relied on the ELM to make predictions about the credibility of both consumer-generated ads and those created by an advertising agency. Meanwhile, Social Cognitive Theory (Bandura, 2001) has also been used to study selective exposure to online appeals (Knobloch-Westerwick & Sarge, 2015).

Research about online persuasion remains in its infancy and to this point has focused primarily on product advertising and health communication messages. For example, Campbell and colleagues (2011) examined the messages that consumers generate in response to online product advertisements, while Knobloch-Westerwick and Sarge (2015) investigated selective exposure to online weight-loss messages. To date, traditional theories of persuasion appear capable of handling most of the questions about effective online messages, including the roles of interactivity and consumer-generated messages, the perceived credibility of source attribution, and strategies for processing affective and emotional content. What remains to be seen is whether traditional models of persuasion will be helpful in understanding the loss of control that a source concedes when allowing message recipients to play an active role in creating, commenting on, and disseminating persuasive appeals. It is too early to determine whether current models of persuasion will prove sufficient—or, alternatively, whether models focused specifically on questions related to online persuasion will become necessary to fully understand the dynamic nature of persuasion via social media (for a discussion of theoretical challenges, see Okazaki & Taylor, 2015).

Another feature of some persuasive situations is the presence of distracting stimuli. The next section describes two types of distracting stimuli and examines their influence on persuasive outcomes.

PERSUASIVE EFFECTS OF DISTRACTING STIMULI

When he was a college student in the 1970s, Jim went shopping for a waterbed and experienced firsthand the use of distraction as a persuasive strategy. He entered a waterbed store and was immediately approached by a slick salesperson who was eager to describe the line of waterbeds the store had to offer. After listening to his sales pitch for several minutes, Jim had some questions about the reliability of the mattress and heating element. Just as the salesperson stopped to ask if Jim had any questions about the beds, another salesperson came over and told them a joke that was in poor taste. After the second salesperson left, the first one asked, "Well, are there any more questions I can answer before you make a decision?" When Jim reminded him that his partner's rude interruption had prevented him from asking any questions at all, the salesperson looked somewhat disappointed. Luckily, Jim was able to recall the questions he had intended to ask before the interruption. Afterward, Jim was wondering to himself whether the interruption had been a planned distraction. After talking with several friends who were former salespeople, however, he became convinced that the sudden interruption was indeed a deliberate ploy. Most of these former salespeople indicated that planned interruptions were part and parcel of their sales pitches, and most of them believed that these distractions actually benefited their sales performance.

Fortunately, a large body of scientific research provides some insights about the practical application of distraction techniques. Since a seminal investigation by Festinger and Maccoby (1964), many persuasion scholars have examined the effects of a variety of distracting stimuli on the attitudes and behaviors of persuasive targets.

A cursory review of these investigations reveals that researchers have created a wide variety of stimuli that act as distractions in their studies. These various manipulations can be simplified by placing them into two relatively distinct categories of distraction research, namely, *external distractors* and *communicator-relevant distractors*. External distractors are stimuli that are outside the message presentation itself, such as using flashing lights (Osterhouse & Brock, 1970), playing audio feedback (Zimbardo & Ebbesen, 1970), or having receivers eat while they read a persuasive message (Janis, Kaye, & Kirschner, 1965). These distractors are thought to divert attention away from the message presentation and toward the source of the distraction.

In contrast, communicator-relevant distractors are behaviors intentionally manipulated by the speaker that cause receivers to shift attention away from the content of the message and toward characteristics of the speaker (Buller, 1986). Manipulations of this type include varying the synchrony of a source's nonverbal behaviors (Woodall & J. K. Burgoon, 1981), violating interpersonal distancing expectations (J. K. Burgoon, Stacks, & Burch, 1982), and using intense language (M. Burgoon et al., 1978).

Studies employing external or communicator-based distractors reflect researchers' fundamentally distinct questions about persuasive communication. Studies of external distractors are primarily concerned with the effect of divided attention on message processing and subsequent attitude change. Conversely, studies of communicator-relevant distractors are primarily concerned with the effect of unusual or off-putting communicative behavior on perceptions of source credibility and subsequent attitude change.

Examining the Effects of External Distraction

Researchers have developed a number of explanations for the persuasive effects of external distractions. However, two types, the *Cognitive Response* and the *Information Processing* theories of persuasion, have received the most attention. Cognitive response explanations were initially invoked to explain the findings of Festinger and Maccoby's (1964) seminal investigation. In that study, college students in an "ordinary film" condition watched a movie of a professor presenting a message denouncing college fraternities. In the "distraction" condition, students *heard* the professor give the same speech, but an "amusing and absorbing short film" (*Day of the Painter*) was shown instead of video of the professor. Festinger and Maccoby hypothesized, and found, that students listening to the speech while watching the amusing but topically irrelevant video would be distracted from generating thoughts to counter the position advocated by the speaker (and thus be more susceptible to persuasion). Shortly thereafter, McGuire (1966, 1969) applied information processing theories as an alternative explanation of distraction effects.

Consistent with these competing explanations, a number of investigations provide support for the prediction that distraction hinders the creation of counterarguments and message comprehension. For example, Osterhouse and Brock (1970) found that, in the case of counterattitudinal messages (i.e., those that receivers disagree with), external distractors reduced the number of counterarguments generated by receivers and increased attitude change. More recently, Jeong and Hwang (2012) found that multitasking (for example, surfing the Internet while watching television or performing a household task while watching television) reduces both message comprehension and counterarguing.

Kupor and Tormala (2015) conducted five studies that examined the effects of *interruptions* on curiosity, thought favorability, and behavioral intentions. Using a variety of interruptions (e.g., a confederate interrupting a presentation to ask for directions, a pause in a video presentation that simulated the loading of content in an online presentation), these authors found that interruptions were positively related to thought favorability, which was positively related to behavioral intentions. Moreover, the interruption also had a direct positive effect on behavioral intentions. While Kupor and Tormala argued that the external distractions produced curiosity and hedonic reactions that resulted in favorable thoughts about the message, their findings are also consistent with the hypothesis that the interruptions interfered with counterarguments, resulting in more favorable evaluations of the message.

In the next two sections, we consider the evidence supporting cognitive response versus information processing explanations for the effects of external distractors. Both explanations focus on how distractors have evolved in our thinking and how distractors can interfere with the processing and integration of information in persuasive messages.

Cognitive Response Explanations

As we discussed in Chapter 5, cognitive response approaches to persuasion assume that the thoughts that receivers generate during message processing contribute significantly to the effectiveness of the persuasive appeal. If receivers actively process a message, they generate their own favorable or unfavorable impressions about the message that combine with the information presented in the message itself to influence their postmessage attitudes.

According to a cognitive response explanation, distracting stimuli interfere with cognitive processing that would otherwise be expected to occur. For instance, when the message recommendation is counterattitudinal, the predominant cognitive response in the message recipient, under normal conditions, would be to generate counterarguments. Since distracting stimuli inhibit the formulation of counterarguments (Festinger & Maccoby, 1964; see also Osterhouse & Brock, 1970, and Zimbardo & Ebbesen, 1970), distracted recipients should therefore experience more attitude change than they might otherwise (Festinger & Maccoby, 1964).

On the other hand, when the message recommendation is consistent with the recipient's preexisting attitudes, distractors are hypothesized to limit the generation of favorable thoughts (Harkins & Petty, 1981; Insko, Turnbull, & Yandell, 1974; Petty, Wells, & Brock, 1976). Because they cannot formulate as many positive cognitive responses as they could have without the distraction, recipients will exhibit less attitude change in reaction to an appealing message than recipients who are not distracted.

Thus, the number of positive thoughts and counterarguments generated by message recipients are important variables that mediate the relationship between distraction and attitude change. While both positive cognitions and counterarguments are important components of cognitive response explanations, most distraction studies measure only counterarguments, if they measure cognitive responses at all.

Information Processing Explanations

A second category of explanations stems from Information Processing Theory. Information processing explanations suggest that in order for messages to be persuasive, the supporting arguments and evidence must be received and understood by recipients. The failure to appreciate the arguments underlying a recommendation should reduce the effectiveness of the persuasive appeal (McGuire, 1969).

According to information processing explanations, external distractors interfere with message comprehension and hence reduce the persuasiveness of the message. Because distractors divert attention away from the message, receivers have greater difficulty understanding the supporting arguments and evidence and committing them to memory (Haaland & Venkatesen, 1968; Vohs & Garrett, 1968). Message comprehension, rather than self-generated thoughts about the message, is the important intervening variable in information processing explanations of the persuasive effects of distraction. Specifically, both message recall and attitude change should be negatively correlated with distraction.

Specific Predictions and Supporting Evidence

In short, both the cognitive response and information processing explanations posit that distractors divert one's attention from message processing, but the specific hypothesized effects of this distraction differ, depending upon the explanation. Cognitive response theorists argue that distractions aimed at counterattitudinal messages inhibit counterarguments, thereby enhancing acceptance of the message's recommendations. However, distractions interfering with congruent messages diminish receivers' favorable impressions, thus inhibiting the persuasive effects of the messages.

Evidence for the proposition that messages consistent with a recipient's preexisting attitudes will be less persuasive when a distraction is present, however, has been limited. Petty and colleagues (1976) did find that distractions enhanced attitude change when the message presentation was counterattitudinal and inhibited message acceptance when the message was pro-attitudinal. However, this investigation found no positive relationship between distractions and the production of favorable thoughts and counterarguments, thus diminishing confidence in the cognitive response explanation.

While the research provided mixed support for the cognitive response explanation, certain studies of distraction effects produced findings that are consistent with Information Processing Theory. Studies supporting this explanation found that distractions reduced message recall (an indication of learning) and led to less acceptance of message recommendations (Haaland & Venkatesen, 1968; Vohs & Garrett, 1968).

Although the findings from these studies are contradictory, a meta-analytic review of this literature revealed some support for both explanations. However, support for the information processing hypothesis was somewhat stronger than for the cognitive response hypothesis (Buller, 1986). Across studies employing various manipulations of external distractions, Buller (1986) consistently found that both the number of counterarguments and the degree of message comprehension were negatively correlated with attitude change. However, Buller also reported a consistently stronger negative relationship between distractions and message comprehension than between distractions and the generation of counterarguments. This finding provides stronger support for the information processing explanation than for the cognitive response explanation. Although the strength of the relationship varied depending upon the type of external distraction used, in general Buller's analysis also found that distractions were negatively related to attitude change, providing additional support for the information processing explanation.

Thus, although some individual studies provide evidence for each of these explanations, a cumulative summary of these studies suggests that the persuasive effects of an external distraction are mediated primarily by the distraction's negative effect on message comprehension. However, several researchers have noted (see Buller, 1986) that a significant distraction is needed to create the reduction in message comprehension necessary to reduce message effectiveness. That is, rather small distractors are unlikely to produce the significant reduction in comprehension necessary to reduce one's acceptance of message recommendations.

Examining the Effects of Communicator-Relevant Distractions

A second category of distraction studies has produced much more consistent findings. Investigations of communicator-relevant distractions hypothesize that the distractions divert attention away from the content of the messages and toward the characteristics of the communicator. Information processing and cognitive responses are not central to this phenomenon. Instead, the persuasive effects of communicator-relevant distractions are more dependent on the specific features of the source that created the distraction in the first place.

Buller's (1986) review found that communicator-relevant distractions enhanced attitude change when the source was highly credible and decreased attitude change when the message source lacked credibility. For example, over the years Jim has observed many witnesses whose persuasiveness was affected by such distractors. In one case, the male jurors in a mock trial focused attention on the attractiveness of a former beauty queen who testified about her marketing activities for a cosmetics company. In another case, a computer engineer tended to blink excessively, and the jurors ended up by focusing more on that distraction than his testimony about the technology he had developed—and, consequently, his testimony was rendered ineffective.

Buller (1986) found the correlation estimates for these effects were directionally consistent across studies, though small in size. Specifically, the difference between the persuasive effect of communicator-relevant distraction among high-credibility (average $r = .15$) and low-credibility ($r = -.10$) sources provides compelling support for the importance of this explanation. In addition, Buller found that communicator-relevant distraction was unrelated to counterarguing (average $r = .00$) and message recall ($r = -.02$), providing further evidence of the distinction between source-based and external distractors.

More recent research on the effects of speaker disfluency (Carpenter, 2012) is consistent with the findings of this meta-analysis. Carpenter found that disfluencies by a speaker produced cognitions related to the source of the message. These source-related cognitions (labeled "attitude defensive cognitions") undermined judgments about the speaker's competence and the persuasiveness of the message. Speaker disfluencies affected message processing when the message was presented by high-reward sources but not when presented by low-reward sources.

Summary of Distraction Effects

Differences in the persuasive effects of external and communicator-based distractions underscore the importance of the differences in manipulations created by researchers across studies. More importantly, they provide a fuller understanding of the situational features underlying the persuasion process. Both internal and external distractors can divert attention away from the message. If the distraction is external, it limits processing of the message, and as a result attitude change is reduced. If the distraction is source-related, the receiver's focus shifts from the message content to the source. If the source's characteristics are favorable, the distraction enhances persuasion, but if they are negative, then message acceptance is diminished.

PERSUASIVE INFLUENCES OF COLLECTIVES

Another important situational factor that influences persuasion is the presence of others. Every day, we spend a considerable amount of time working and socializing with others. Whether we communicate in large organizations or small groups, we are rarely immune from the social influences of collectives (i.e., groups). Although communication scholars and social psychologists have sought to understand the persuasive effects of social and work collectives, these social effects are routinely neglected in persuasion textbooks. While a complete discussion of these effects is beyond the scope of this book (see Andrews, Boster, & Carpenter, 2013, and Forsyth, 2010, for recent reviews), the remainder of this chapter examines two types of influence that various group dynamics exert on individual members. This section begins with a discussion of conformity effects and concludes with an examination of the persuasive effects of group discussion.

Conformity Effects

Most of the communicative messages that are exchanged in small groups and organizations are expressions of the values, beliefs, and goals of the people in those entities. Over time, these individual expressions are codified into a collective set of values, beliefs, and goals that establish the norms of acceptable behavior for individual group (or organization) members. Once these norms have been established, social pressure is exerted on individual members to adopt and maintain them. Pressures toward attitudinal and behavioral uniformity in collectives have been well documented (for a review, see Forsyth, 2010). *Conformity,* a general label for this type of social influence process, is commonly defined as "a change in attitude, belief, or behavior as a function of real or perceived group pressure" (Aronson, 1999, p. 17). People often conform because they perceive that the collective (or its individual members) is exerting pressure on them to behave in a particular manner. However, overt pressure is not necessary to produce conforming behavior: all that is required is the *perception* of group pressure.

The Asch line experiments provide a compelling example of the influence that groups can have on their members. Solomon Asch (1955, 1956) was interested in the effect of apparent group consensus on individuals' judgments. His experiment involved several confederates who played the role of research participants and one actual research participant who did not know the real purpose of the study. Asch presented the confederates and research participant with a series of 18 card pairs. For each pair, one card contained three lines, each of a different length. On the other card was a single line that was the same length as one of the lines on the first card. The task was to determine which line on the first card was the same length as the line on the second card.

When participants completed this task alone, they made correct judgments over 99% of the time. However, when they were placed in a group setting, their decisions were influenced by the confederates' choices. Asch (1956) secretly (in concert with the confederates) identified 12 of the 18 trials as critical trials. For critical trials, all confederates were instructed to choose the same *wrong* response; however, on noncritical trials they were to choose the correct response. The experimenter asked each confederate for their judgment before asking the only true research participant (because he was seated at the end of the row).

On each trial, the confederates' judgments established a group norm. For critical trials, this norm was obviously incorrect. Those participants who made these judgments alone were correct over 99% of the time, indicating that the correct response was obvious. Asch (1956) was interested in knowing how often research participants would choose the incorrect response in order to conform with the group norm. The findings were remarkable. He found that more that 75% of the participants conformed to the group norm on at least one of the 12 critical trials. In fact, over 35% of the total judgments made on critical trials were wrong! While only a very small percentage of people conformed to the group norm on all 12 critical trials, once the real participant conformed on one critical trial, it was much more likely that he or she continued to conform on all subsequent trials.

It is worth noting that the confederates and each true participant in this study did not form a "group" in the everyday sense of the term. That is, there was no group history, no group leader, and no anticipation of future group interaction. It also bears mentioning that the confederates exerted no overt pressure on the one true research participant; they simply established a norm by unanimously choosing the wrong response. As a consequence, conformity rates in the Asch (1956) studies likely underestimate conformity in actual functioning groups. While the true participants had little commitment to the group and were subject to no overt pressure to conform, nonetheless the pressures of an established group norm influenced them. Subsequent research has demonstrated that group norms can be quickly established, and once that happens members tend to maintain the norms even when members are no longer present (M. Sherif & C. W. Sherif, 1956). These studies demonstrate the pervasive effects of conformity influences on individual behavior.

Conformity occurs in a variety of ways—when an employee agrees to work late at the boss's request, for example, or when teenagers wear a particular style of clothing or college students engage in binge drinking just to be like their peers. Kelman (1958) provided a conceptual framework for categorizing conformity behavior by identifying *compliance, identification,* and *internalization* as three distinct types of conformity processes.

Compliance

When compliance occurs, people accept influence from a group or organization in hopes of attaining some future reward or avoiding some punishment. Festinger (1953) defined this type of influence as public conformity without private acceptance. That is, compliance does not require an actual change in attitude, but rather only a change in observable behavior. People routinely engage in conforming behavior without necessarily changing their underlying attitudes or beliefs. For example, many car drivers routinely exceed the posted speed limits so long as they are unconcerned about being stopped for speeding. Sighting a highway patrol vehicle, however, triggers an immediate reflex action in most people's driving behavior. The sudden appearance of a compliance agent increases the likelihood of sanctions for noncompliance, causing drivers to stay within the speed limit or exceed it only by an acceptable margin. The fact that so many drivers routinely disobey posted speed limits suggests that they privately believe that the limits are unreasonable. In this case, only surveillance and the threat of a fine or other penalties can assure compliance with the law.

Compliance, however, can be motivated less by a desire to avoid punishment than to gain or reap rewards. A young professional may work overtime in hopes of impressing his or her supervisor and gaining the inside track on an upcoming promotion. Hospital volunteers follow the rules and procedures of their assigned hospital in order to enjoy emotionally rewarding work with patients. College students may agree to participate in a persuasion experiment in order to gain extra academic credits. Although behaviors like these are motivated by the rewards they offer and not by the threat of reprisal, they are still considered a form of compliance because the behavior being performed is considered the means to a specified end.

Regardless of the motivation, however, the fundamental characteristic of compliance processes is that they are motivated by one's desire to *avoid punishment* or *gain a reward*. As a result, compliance is only effective so long as the controlling agent is likely to apply sanctions for noncompliance or offer rewards for compliance. Although we have focused chiefly on the ways that groups or collectives enforce this type of conformity, compliance processes are also prominent in interpersonal interactions (which is the key focus of Chapter 11).

Identification

A second type of conformity identified by Kelman (1958) is identification, which occurs when people accept influence from a controlling agent in order to "develop and maintain a favorable self-defining relationship with the controlling agent" (p. 35). These self-defining relationships allow people to construct favorable self-images. Identification processes are sufficiently subtle that they often go unrecognized by sources and targets of influence. For example, college fraternity and sorority members often cultivate similar hair styles or wear similar clothing that effectively reinforces their membership in the organization. Although the decision to purchase and wear clothing bearing certain labels is clearly an identification process, few people would argue that this form of influence is a conscious effort to promote conformity among a given organization's members. Nevertheless, these identification processes do represent a type of conformity that facilitates the adoption of collective norms and values.

Though frequently subtle, identification processes can also be quite explicit. More than a dozen years after he ended his NBA career, for example, Michael Jordan continued to advertise men's underwear in national ads. Though often less explicit than Jordan's, most ad campaigns that involve a prominent sports figure's endorsement derive their effectiveness from identification processes.

Kelman (1958) observed that the success of identification appeals depends to a significant extent on maintaining a favorable social relationship between the source of the influence and the target audience. As people get older over time, their relative attraction to various reference groups changes, thus altering the effectiveness of persuasion agents that rely on identification processes. Because the social attractiveness of an individual, group, or organization can be subject to sudden and dramatic change, influence stemming from identification processes may not persist for extended periods of time.

Internalization

Kelman's (1958) third type of conformity was labeled internalization. Internalization processes are similar to traditional conceptions of attitude change. When people internalize a particular behavior, they do so after careful consideration of the reasons offered to adopt it for themselves. This type of conformity may be likened to Festinger's (1953) concept of public conformity with private acceptance. That is to say, internalization involves concurrent changes in both behaviors *and* attitudes. In this regard, internalization reflects the use of rational message appeals (treated in Chapter 7) that are the cornerstone of Information Processing Theory (discussed in detail in Chapter 9).

Internalization is the most stable form of Kelman's three types of conformity in that internalized behaviors stem from a person's own beliefs and values and thus are likely to persist in the absence of a controlling agent. Whereas behavior change created by compliance is dependent upon the continuing presence of a controlling agent, behavior change created by internalization will endure so long as one's attitudes, beliefs, and/or values remain intact.

Summary of Conformity Effects

Regardless of their specific characteristics, conformity processes are a prominent form of social influence in groups or collectives. Normative expectations emerge from interactions with other people, and, once formed, they exert pressure on people to conform with them. Although compliance, identification, and internalization are qualitatively distinct forms of conformity, they all stem from the desire of individuals in collectives to behave in a uniform or predictable fashion. The pressure exerted toward uniformity is most apparent in group discussions that require a single decision. In the next section, we extend the discussion of group influence by examining the effects of group discussion on the attitudes of individual members.

POLARIZATION IN GROUP DECISIONS

Investigations of group decision-making processes shed further light on the influence of group interactions on the attitudes and behaviors of individual members. Beginning in the 1960s, social psychologists examined what was initially labeled the "risky shift phenomenon," the tendency for groups to make riskier decisions than individuals. The discovery of the risky shift was surprising, because it was generally believed that groups are cautious and less willing than individuals to make bold and risky decisions.

Investigations of the risky shift relied primarily on the methodology of choice dilemma items (Kogan & Wallach, 1967). This methodology presents research participants with a problem and two potential solutions. One solution is almost certain to resolve the dilemma and has a moderately rewarding outcome. The probability of success for the second alternative is less likely, but if successful it will provide a much more rewarding outcome. Perhaps the adage "A bird in the hand is worth two in the bush" represents the dilemma created by items like these. Respondents must choose between a certain but less rewarding alternative and an uncertain but potentially more rewarding alternative. For example, financial planning often involves choosing between a safe investment that almost certainly will produce moderate profits and a risky investment that if successful will produce much greater returns but if unsuccessful will lose money.

Researchers investigating this phenomenon typically ask research participants to read a choice dilemma scenario and make an individual choice prior to participating in a group discussion of the dilemma. A risky shift is said to occur when the group decision, or average postdiscussion choices of individual group members, is riskier than the average prediscussion decision choices of the individual members.

Using this methodology, several early investigations found that small-group discussions produced riskier decisions than those made by individuals (Dion, Baron, & N. Miller, 1970; Kogan & Wallach, 1967). Subsequent research, however, found evidence that groups may also make more cautious decisions than individuals (Baron et al., 1974; Stoner, 1968), leading researchers to relabel the risky shift phenomenon as the "polarity shift phenomenon." That is, groups tend to make more extreme (or polar) decisions—more risky or cautious ones—than individuals. When the group is somewhat cautious to begin with, group discussion will generally produce cautious shifts, but when the group is somewhat risky initially, discussion generally produces a risky shift.

Since these initial investigations, several studies have provided evidence of a polarity shift phenomenon in group discussions (for reviews, see Andrews et al., 2013; Boster, 1990; Lamm & Myers, 1978). How can these opinion shifts be explained? The most likely explanation stems from the influence of group interactions on the attitudes and judgments of individual group members. Although a wide variety of explanations have been offered, two theoretical explanations that emphasize group communication have received the most attention from researchers. Consistent with Deutsch and Gerard's (1955) distinction between normative and informational social influence, researchers have examined the merits of the *social comparison* and *persuasive arguments* explanations of the polarity shift phenomenon.

Social Comparison Explanations

Social normative explanations of the polarity shift phenomenon evolved from both Festinger's (1954) description of Social Comparison Theory and Deutsch and Gerard's (1955) concept of normative social influence. Social Comparison Theory posits that people are concerned about the correctness or appropriateness of positions they hold, and this concern motivates them to validate their positions through interaction with others. In highly ambiguous situations, people are less certain about the validity of their positions, and so in these situations social comparison processes become more important.

Social comparison processes occur in daily interactions. For example, college students often engage in social comparison processes after an exam when they gather just outside the classroom to discuss their impressions about the test's difficulty, fairness, and the like. The reason students engage in this comparison process is to reduce their uncertainty about the exam. Social pressure to conform to a normative position about the perceived difficulty of the exam may be limited, but a normative position is likely to emerge during discussions like these. That is, students participating in these discussions may collectively conclude that the exam as a whole was too difficult or that a particular question was unfair.

In much the same fashion, group discussions are social comparison processes that produce normative positions about the issue under consideration. As group members begin discussing an issue, they quickly assess the preferences and opinions of one another, a group norm emerges, and social pressure develops to conform to the norm.

The fundamental assumption of Social Comparison Theory is that people view themselves individually as better than the average group member in terms of the abilities, traits, and attitudes valued by the group (Lamm & Myers, 1978, p. 176). Lamm and Myers (1978) provide considerable evidence to support this assumption, including findings that most business people view themselves as more ethical than the average business person (Baumhart, 1968) as well as research indicating that most people believe they are less prejudiced than the average person (Lenihan, 1965). But, as Lamm and Myers (1978) point out, people's perceptions that they are superior to the average person are distorted (not to mention self-serving), because "the average person is not better than the average person" (p. 176).

Applied to the polarity shift phenomenon, a social comparison (or normative influence) explanation posits that initially (i.e., before the discussion) group members will report a position that they assume is more favorable (i.e., extreme in the right direction) than the group norm. Group discussions, according to this explanation, disconfirm this assumption. If discussion reveals that the group is more cautious than was originally expected, then members striving to maintain the perception that they are more favorable than the average group member will advocate a position that is more cautious than the group norm. On the other hand, if group discussion reveals a riskier norm than was expected, members will endorse a position that is more risky than the group norm. The result of social comparison processes is to cause individuals to endorse a more extreme position than the group norm (whether more risky or cautious). The result of these individual position shifts is a postdiscussion position that is more extreme than the prediscussion position of the group.

Persuasive Arguments Explanations

A more straightforward explanation of the polarity shift phenomenon has also been proposed. The persuasive arguments explanation posits that group discussions expose members to novel arguments that are persuasive. Consistent with Information Processing Theory (discussed in Chapter 9), this explanation holds that if the group norm represents a cautious position, then the distribution of these novel arguments is likely to be skewed in the cautious direction. That is, a greater proportion of novel arguments will favor a cautious position than a risky one. On the other hand, if group members favor a risky position, then a greater proportion of novel arguments are likely to favor risk more than caution.

The informational influence of these novel arguments is hypothesized to produce opinion shifts in group discussions. Group discussions produce more reasons for advocating the normative group position than individual members could develop on their own. Armed with these additional new arguments, individual members become more confident in their judgments and advocate a more extreme position following group discussion. Thus, when the group norm favors caution, group discussion should produce a more cautious decision than the average prediscussion decision of individual group members. However, if the normative position is risky, group discussion should produce a decision that is riskier than the average prediscussion position of individual group members.

Testing Competing Explanations

Examining the validity of these two explanations is a difficult task. Social comparison explanations posit that all that is required to produce a group shift is knowledge of the positions held by group members. Persuasive arguments explanations assert that it is novel informational content, not the normative positions of individual members, that is responsible for the polarity shift phenomenon.

Unfortunately, these two explanations are difficult to differentiate because the two forms of information contained in them (i.e., group members' attitudes versus the arguments supporting those attitudes) are confounded in naturally occurring group discussions. As Boster (1990) aptly noted, any argument offered during the group's discussion includes both types of information: it provides knowledge of which members advocate which positions on the issue as well as their individual reasons for advocating those positions. Thus, if a given argument is persuasive, social comparison theorists might conclude that it more likely reflected the source of the opinions and arguments and not the quality of the arguments. However, persuasive arguments theorists would contend that the arguments themselves were persuasive. If a person offered an opinion statement with no explicit argument to support it, social comparison theorists would argue that any persuasive effects were caused by the normative information in the opinion statement. However, persuasive arguments theorists might conclude that opinion statements include implicit arguments and that these arguments, rather than group pressure, are responsible for the persuasive effects of the message (Boster, 1990).

To examine each of these explanations, researchers have employed a variety of experimental procedures that systematically control group composition and the number of risky and cautious arguments that emerge during the group discussion. For example, one study created groups with either a risky or cautious majority by selecting members on the basis of their prediscussion responses to a choice dilemma item. These groups then discussed an issue that tended to produce either a risky or a cautious shift (Boster, Fryrear, Mongeau, & Hunter, 1982). These researchers argued that a group's composition and the specific type of choice dilemma item they discussed would together influence the number of risky and cautious arguments that emerged during group discussion. Boster and Mayer (1984) employed a more direct manipulation of persuasive arguments and normative influences by having research participants observe videotaped discussions that varied both the number of arguments favoring a risky and a cautious position *and* the proportion of group members with risky and cautious positions. Although this procedure did not involve research subjects in a group discussion, it more precisely controlled the social normative information and persuasive arguments to which they were exposed.

Investigations like these have examined the relative merits of the social comparison and persuasive arguments explanations (for reviews, see Lamm & Myers, 1978; Mayer, 1986). Support for the social comparison explanation has been found in studies where participants altered their positions after being exposed solely to the positions of others. Evidence of this *mere exposure effect* was found in a meta-analysis of group polarization experiments. Isenberg (1986) reported that the average effect of social comparison processes in these studies was substantial (average r = .44).

Considerable support has also been found for the persuasive arguments explanation. In fact, Isenberg's (1986) review found the average effect of persuasive arguments processes was extremely strong (average r = .75). Indeed, further support for the persuasive arguments explanation has emerged from studies employing the Linear Discrepancy Model (see Chapter 9) to explain group polarization effects (Boster et al., 1982; Boster, Mayer, Hunter, & Hale, 1980).

Evidence supporting both explanations might cause one to question whether social comparison or persuasive argument influences are responsible for group polarization effects. Most likely, both social normative and informational influences affect polarity shifts in group discussions (Boster, 1990). One study that was designed to examine the relative importance of both processes found evidence supporting both explanations, although the persuasive arguments explanation accounted for more variance in polarity shifts than did the social comparison explanation (Mayer, 1986). This finding is consistent with Isenberg's (1986) meta-analytic review, which found a much stronger persuasive arguments effect, though the influence of social comparison processes was also large. Furthermore, a strong correlation between the persuasive arguments and social comparison effects led Isenberg to conclude that "at this point in time there is very good evidence that there are two conceptually independent processes even though outside of the laboratory they almost always co-occur" (p. 1149). Regardless of the relative contributions of these theoretical processes, investigations of the polarity shift phenomenon provide compelling evidence for the influence groups have on their individual members.

What Do Persuasive Arguments Look Like?

While there is substantial research consistent with the persuasive arguments explanation of polarization (Isenberg, 1986), relatively little of this research helps us to identify what aspects of group discussions are most persuasive. Renée Meyers and her associates (e.g., Meyers, 1989; Meyers, Brashers, & Hanner, 2000; Meyers & Seibold, 1990) spent a considerable amount of time trying to understand the interactive processes that create persuasive argument effects in group discussions. In the Meyers et al. (2000) study, 15 groups were asked to discuss and reach consensus on three issues. The researchers categorized group members as holding a view that was accepted by the majority (labeled "attitudinal majority") or holding a minority viewpoint (labeled "attitudinal minority"), based on their prediscussion opinions. They also identified the winning and losing factions by identifying the subgroup that held the attitude that was consistent with the group's final decision. Adapting the Conversational Argument Coding Scheme (Canary, Brossmann, & Seibold, 1987), Meyers and colleagues investigated the arguments made by the winning and the losing factions on each issue.

Consistent with prior research, the researchers found that the initial attitudinal majority "won" the discussion (i.e., the eventual group decision was consistent with their initial positions) nearly 80% of the time. They also found some important differences between the arguments made by the attitudinal majority and minority subgroups. Majority factions used more statements indicating agreement with other group members (i.e., bolstering: "That's a good point, Jim, I agree with you") and fewer statements of disagreement as compared to minority faction members. Statements of agreement reinforced the perception of majority faction unanimity (what they referred to as "tag team arguing") because, while just one person might present an argument, other faction members could validate it with bolstering comments. Tag team arguing can also occur when one member extends the argument begun by another faction member. This bolstering and tag-team arguing is, in itself, persuasive, because it reflects both social comparison and persuasive arguments processes.

Members of the minority factions, on the other hand, were less likely to use agreements and spent more time disagreeing with the majority faction. If you are the lone dissenting voice in a group, you have no one to agree with, and your only choice may be to disagree with the larger majority. This suggests that attitudinal minority factions will be more persuasive when they have at least two members. Minority factions with multiple members can use the same bolstering and tag-team arguing that is typical of majorities' behavior.

Meyers and colleagues (2000) also found differences in the arguments made by winning and losing factions. Their findings regarding winning minorities were particularly interesting. It has long been suggested that, in order to be persuasive, attitudinal minorities have to be consistent in the way that they present their arguments (e.g., Moscovici, Lage, & Naffrechoux, 1969). Confirming this belief, Meyers and colleagues reported that the attitudinal minorities that ended up convincing the initial majority were those who argued most consistently. In order to win the argument, however, a consistent minority had to be pitted against a less consistent majority. Moreover, the more consistent the arguments presented by a particular faction, the less likely those faction members were to change their attitudes during the discussion. This was particularly true for losing, as opposed to winning, subgroups.

BOX 10.2. Group Majorities in Jury Deliberations

In the classic 1957 movie *12 Angry Men* Henry Fonda immortalized the role of a single juror faced with the prospect of having to convince 11 other jurors to change their minds and find a defendant not guilty of murder. In the 2003 movie *Runaway Jury,* John Cusack played the role of a juror who cunningly sways the opinions of his fellow jurors to deliver the verdict he wants. Although these actors defied the odds in their respective movies, that outcome is extremely rare in real life (Davis, Kerr, Atkin, Holt, & Meek, 1975). While it is true that a single juror can force a hung jury verdict in cases where a unanimous one is required, a single juror is rarely able to persuade the majority to change their minds. The key to a successful process is for the initial minority member to gradually enlist *lieutenants* who in turn change their position to agree with the minority member.

The far more common outcome is for the one or two minority members to ultimately concede their position because they simply do not have the staying power to sustain repeated arguments from the majority. Indeed, after conducting more than 550 mock jury research projects, Jim has consistently observed that the size of the majority at the outset of deliberations (i.e., 10–2 vs. 7–5) is often much more important than the quality of the arguments advanced during the deliberations. Once one or two members of a minority coalition waiver in their opposition, the momentum created by the concession makes it extremely difficult for the remaining minority group members to maintain their position (for a recent review, see Laughlin, 2011).

SUMMARY

This chapter examined the characteristics of persuasive situations that influence the attitudes and behaviors of persuasive targets. The persuasive effects of any given mode of message presentation are moderated by the characteristics of both the message and the message source. Live and video presentations focus attention on message sources and enhance the persuasiveness of highly attractive and credible sources, while written presentations are more effective for complex messages that require more effort on the part of the audience to comprehend.

Distracting stimuli are situational factors that also affect the persuasiveness of messages. Distractions external to the message source effectively interfere with message learning, restricting the persuasiveness of the message. However, the effect of communicator-based distractions is to direct attention toward the message source, either enhancing the persuasiveness of highly credible sources or limiting the effectiveness of less credible ones.

Finally, investigations of conformity effects and the polarization of individual attitudes provided clear evidence of the influence that groups or collectives have on their individual members. Conformity research suggests that social norms are developed in the presence of others. Once these norms are established, groups and organizations exert influence on their members to adopt them. Investigations of the polarity shift phenomenon reflect a different type of influence that groups have on individual members. These investigations found that group discussion causes individuals to advocate more extreme positions (either risky *or* cautious) than they did prior to group discussion. Social comparison effects and the influence of novel persuasive arguments are two prominent explanations that help to account for these outcomes.

PART III

PERSUASION MODELS

This last part of the book describes persuasion models that incorporate the essential features of persuasive transactions discussed in Part II. This part is divided into three chapters. Chapter 11 examines the major strategies and techniques employed to gain the target's compliance in interpersonal situations. Chapter 12 focuses on the production of compliance messages as well as the research on compliance resistance strategies. Chapter 13 examines persuasive communication campaigns, particularly the stages of persuasion and the role of tailored persuasive appeals in campaigns. Chapter 13 also explores the use of Social Cognitive Theory and Inoculation Theory in these campaigns.

Models of Interpersonal Compliance

LOOKING AHEAD ... The next two chapters review the major research on interpersonal influence. Chapter 11 focuses on the selection and efficacy of compliance-gaining strategies and techniques, while Chapter 12 reviews research describing how people produce and resist influence messages in interpersonal contexts. This chapter examines both the *compliance-gaining* and *sequential-request* traditions of interpersonal persuasion research. We examine the theoretical foundations of each tradition and the empirical findings brought to light by major studies within each. Along the way, we identify the shortcomings of each approach and attempt to integrate the findings into these research traditions.

The past several chapters have examined how various components of persuasive communication (i.e., the source, message, receiver, and setting) influence the nature of persuasive communication. Now we shift our attention to examining the characteristics of messages in interpersonal persuasive transactions. For the most part, the research examined in this chapter focuses on persuasion in one-on-one situations (such as college student organizations soliciting new members or donations during orientation week); however, one could certainly envision the strategies described in this chapter as applying also to larger groups of people. Moreover, much of this research is focused on face-to-face interactions, though the explosion of social media has broadened the application of interpersonal persuasion to mediated channels as well. This chapter focuses on two avenues of research that encompass the evaluation, use, and effectiveness of messages designed to gain receivers' compliance in a broad array of interpersonal settings (Wilson, 2010).

The first avenue is known as *compliance-gaining message selection* research. Though advanced primarily by communication scholars, this research path originated in the field of sociology. In 1967 sociologists Gerald Marwell and David Schmitt identified a typology of persuasive strategies that individuals might use to gain compliance from one another. This typology was subsequently adopted by communication scholars who focused on the situational factors affecting the evaluation of these strategies (G. R. Miller, Boster, Roloff, & Seibold, 1977). Together, these early investigations provided a research paradigm for examining compliance-gaining messages (for a review, see Seibold, Cantrill, & Meyers, 1985). Though these investigations were typically labeled as compliance-gaining *message selection* or *message use* studies, relatively few of them examined actual communicative behavior. Instead, researchers were content to rely on research participants' reports of the *likelihood* that they would use various strategies to gain compliance in a particular situation. This failure to investigate actual communicative behavior raised serious questions about the predictive utility of these evaluations and the generalizability of this research paradigm (Dillard, 1988; Seibold et al., 1985).

Concurrent with the efforts of communication scholars, a second avenue of research was instigated by social psychologists who studied the effectiveness of several sequential-request strategies. Unlike compliance-gaining research in communication, many of these investigations observed actual communicative behavior and focused attention on persuasive outcomes rather than on the generation of interpersonal persuasive messages (for reviews, see Cialdini, 2009; Cialdini & Goldstein, 2004).

COMPLIANCE-GAINING MESSAGE SELECTION

One avenue for investigating interpersonal persuasion has been labeled "message selection research." Compliance gaining involves situations in which one person wants to convince a second person to do something for him or her. Given this definition, the term *compliance gaining* is a misnomer; a better term would be *compliance seeking* (Wilson, 2002). However, we will use the established terminology. One consistent question in this area of inquiry has focused on identifying the strategies that people use when they attempt to gain receivers' compliance.

Before reviewing this body of research it is important to mention that, given the rapid emergence of social media and their role in persuasive communication (see Chapter 10), the traditionally sharp distinction between interpersonal and mediated communication is less meaningful today than it was when research on compliance-gaining messages began in the 1970s. Thus, while most of this research envisioned communication in face-to-face circumstances, there is nothing that inherently limits its application to face-to-face interactions. While there are likely some elements of these message strategies that are specific to face-to-face interactions, they may be just as effective (if not more so) in social media settings or other forms of mediated communication.

Relying primarily on French and Raven's (1960) survey of power and influence, Marwell and Schmitt (1967) developed a list of 16 compliance-gaining strategies. To examine how people would evaluate each of these strategies, Marwell and Schmitt created hypothetical scenarios that described a source attempting to gain compliance from a target. For example, a mother might attempt to persuade her son, Mike, to improve his study habits. For each scenario, Marwell and Schmitt developed a message that reflected each of the 16 compliance-gaining strategies. Research participants then read each scenario and indicated how likely they would be to use each of the 16 messages to gain compliance from the son in the hypothetical situation.

G. R. Miller and his colleagues (1977) brought this research paradigm to the field of communication and examined situational characteristics that affected the selection of these message strategies. Soon thereafter, a burgeoning body of research on compliance-gaining message selection developed as communication scholars set out to create their own representative lists (or typologies) of compliance-gaining strategies (Boster, Stiff, & Reynolds, 1985; Clark, 1979; Delia & O'Keefe, 1979; Wiseman and Schenck-Hamlin, 1981; for a review, see Kellermann & Cole, 1994).

In addition to developing these typologies, researchers focused on the situational and personality factors that most influenced the selection of compliance-gaining strategies. Sillars (1980) applied a Subjective Expected Utility Model to this question and posited that the acceptability of a message strategy is a function of the perceived importance of the situation and the relational costs and rewards associated with the use of the strategy. For example, the use of threats or guilt to gain compliance may have a greater relational cost than the use of promises. Meanwhile, Boster and Hunter (1978) developed a model that focused on a person's *ethical threshold* and suggested that some messages were sufficiently negative that they might be deemed unethical for use in certain situations.

These models suggest that aspects of the compliance-gaining situation and a person's personality characteristics influence the types of strategies people are likely to use. Armed with lists of compliance-gaining messages and hypothetical situations, researchers examined various situational characteristics (e.g., relational intimacy, the perceived benefits of compliance) and personality characteristics (e.g., Machiavellianism, dogmatism) that might affect the selection of specific compliance-gaining strategies (for reviews, see Boster & Stiff, 1984; Cody & McLaughlin, 1985).

During the decade following the publication of G. R. Miller and col-leagues' (1977) article, over 100 journal articles, book chapters, and con-vention papers employed hypothetical scenarios to investigate compliance-gaining message selection. However, after nearly a decade of research, it became increasingly apparent that the strategies selected by undergraduate students in response to hypothetical compliance-gaining scenarios bore little resemblance to the messages that people actually use in persuasive interactions. For example, Boster and Stiff (1984), in a study that sought to have college students actually gain compliance from another person, failed to find evidence of the complex message strategies identified by Marwell and Schmitt (1967) and Clark (1979). Dillard (1988) found very little cor-respondence between the strategies selected in response to the hypothetical compliance scenarios and those used in role-play situations. In 1987, G. R. Miller and colleagues (Miller, Boster, Roloff, & Seibold, 1987) had con-cluded that "most previous research on the selection of compliance-gaining strategies has used procedures that do not capture the interactive nature of compliance gaining" (p. 103).

As an alternative to the "message selection" paradigm, in a few stud-ies college students were asked to generate messages that they would use to gain compliance in a hypothetical situation (Clark, 1979; Clark & Delia, 1979). There is evidence that this message generation procedure is more representative of actual compliance behavior than the message selection procedure. For example, Applegate (1982) found that the number of per-suasive strategies people generated in response to a hypothetical situation was positively correlated with the number of strategies they employed in face-to-face persuasive situations ($r = .31$).

Over time, communication researchers realized that studies of hypo-thetical compliance-gaining situations lacked the ecological and predic-tive validity necessary to gain much understanding of persuasion in natu-rally occurring interpersonal situations. Although many studies employed hypothetical compliance-gaining scenarios following G. R. Miller and colleagues' (1977) investigation, at this point researchers have abandoned the message selection and message generation paradigm for studying compliance-gaining behavior.

SEQUENTIAL REQUEST STRATEGIES

About the same time that Marwell and Schmitt (1967) published their seminal investigation of compliance-gaining message selection, Jonathan Freedman and Scott Fraser (1966) initiated a program of research on more complex compliance-gaining strategies. Unlike studies that employed hypo-thetical scenarios to generate evaluations of compliance-gaining messages, this line of research examined the effectiveness of specific compliance strategies and studied actual compliance behavior.

Such studies have investigated techniques that employ either single or multiple messages that are commonly applied in everyday persuasive encounters. Examples of single-request strategies include the *every-penny-can-help* technique (Cialdini & Schroeder, 1976) and the *that's-not-all* technique (Burger, 1986). For the remainder of this chapter, however, we focus on sequential-request strategies. Three *sequential-request* techniques—the foot-in-the-door, the door-in-the-face, and the lowball techniques—are representative of this body of literature. Although there are differences among these techniques, *sequential-request strategies* generally have two attributes. First, they involve multiple (rather than just one) requests. Second, the nature and timing of the two requests are intentionally structured to increase compliance. In these strategies, agents are really interested in compliance with the *second* request, which is the goal of the interaction.

The Foot-in-the-Door Technique

In 1966, Freedman and Fraser published their seminal investigation of an influence strategy known as the *foot-in-the-door* (FITD) technique. This technique requires a persuader to send two sequential messages in order to gain compliance. The first message, which we will refer to as the *FITD request,* is relatively innocuous and sufficiently small that most targets will agree to it. The second request (or the *target request*) asks for a much larger response than the FITD request. What is more, the target request might come several days after the initial request and can be even made by another person. Compliance with the initial FITD request is a means to an end, as persuaders are really interested in gaining compliance with the second, larger, request. The thinking underlying the strategy is that persons who agree to the FITD request will eventually be more willing to comply with the larger target request.

The FITD gets its name from a strategy employed by door-to-door salespeople who ask for a glass of water or to come in from the sun or rain (literally getting their "foot in the door") before attempting to sell their product. Salespeople in these situations may perceive that getting their persuasive target to do them a small favor may increase the likelihood that the target will comply with a subsequent, and much larger, request like purchasing a product. Freedman and Fraser (1966) conducted two studies to assess the effect of compliance with a small initial request on compliance with a larger second request. In Study 1, they canvassed a residential neighborhood in Palo Alto, California, and asked housewives if they would answer a brief survey about household products they use. Three days later, these same housewives (i.e., the experimental group), along with others who were not initially contacted (i.e., the control group), were asked if they would allow a team of researchers to spend 2 hours in their home cataloging the types of household products they used. The pattern of compliance was remarkable. Over half (55%) of participants who participated in the brief survey 3 days earlier agreed to the larger request to allow researchers in their home. Conversely, only 22% of the people who had not received the initial request agreed to the larger request.

In Study 2, Freedman and Fraser (1966) asked some residents to sign a petition or place a small sign in the front window of their homes (experimental group). The topic of the petition and sign was either safe driving or a "Keep California Beautiful" campaign. Once again, this initial FITD request was sufficiently small that most people agreed to it. Other residences were bypassed during the initial phase of this study (control group). Different researchers canvassed the neighborhood 2 weeks later and asked everyone—both those who had received the small initial request and those who had been bypassed—if they would be willing to place a large sign promoting safe driving in their front yard. Targets were shown a photograph of the crudely lettered sign in front of a house that was so large it obscured the doorway. The target was told that "our men will come out and install it and later come and remove it. It makes just a small hole in your lawn, but if this is unacceptable to you we have a special mount which will make no hole" (Freedman & Fraser, 1966, p. 200).

Once again, Freedman and Fraser found that those who had complied with the initial FITD request were more likely to comply with the larger target request (54%) than control group participants who did not receive the initial small request (16%). Thus, in both studies, large compliance effects were obtained when participants were first asked to comply with a small initial request.

BOX 11.1. FITD and Political Campaign Contributions

Politicians and political action committees (PACs) have mastered the use of FITD techniques in fundraising appeals. Using extensive email lists of supporters or like-minded people, the FITD strategy begins with an email request asking the message recipient to sign an online petition on a particular issue or cause. As soon as the recipient's electronic signature is completed, a second window opens and asks for a small contribution to support the candidate or cause. Although the organizations are interested in obtaining signatures to the petition, the request they are most interested in is embodied in the fundraising appeal. Message receivers who have supported the candidate or cause by signing the petition are more likely to contribute money to the campaign than those who do not sign.

Evidence for the FITD

Scores of published articles have examined the FITD since Freedman and Fraser's (1966) seminal investigation. Several meta-analytic reviews have synthesized the findings of these studies (Beaman, Cole, Preston, Klentz, & Steblay, 1983; Burger, 1999; Dillard, 1991; Dillard, Hunter, & M. Burgoon, 1984; Fern, Monroe, & Avila, 1986). Findings from these reviews paint a consistent picture of the effectiveness of this technique, though each review highlights the influence of different moderator variables.

The overall effect of the FITD on compliance in prior studies was small; ranging from average $r = .09$ to .17 in the five meta-analyses (Burger, 1999). However, subgroup analyses indicated that the FITD is more effective than one might conclude from these overall analyses.

PURE TESTS

Two reviews considered *pure tests* of the FITD. Because the FITD requires an initial request that is sufficiently small that most people will comply with it, researchers defined *pure tests* as those studies in which at least 80% of participants complied with the initial request (Beaman et al., 1983; Fern et al., 1986). Among studies that met this 80% criterion, the FITD was somewhat more effective. The average effect was average $r = .14$ in the Beaman and colleagues (1983) study and average $r = .21$ in the Fern and colleagues (1986) study.

PERFORMANCE OF INITIAL REQUEST

Whether or not people actually perform the initial request also affects agreement with the larger target request. Four studies tested this issue directly by creating three conditions—a control group with no initial request (only the larger target request), a nonperformance group where people were asked but not given the opportunity to perform the first request before being asked the second request, and a performance group where people were given the opportunity to perform the first request before they were asked to comply with the target request.

Burger's (1999) meta-analysis of the four studies that tested this performance question directly found that the FITD effect only works when people are given the opportunity to actually perform the small initial request. When people were not required to perform the initial request, their compliance with the larger target request (24%) was not significantly greater than compliance by people in the control condition (20%). However, when people performed the initial request, compliance with the larger target request averaged 32%. The performance group produced significantly more compliance than the control group ($r = .12$).

PRO-SOCIAL REQUESTS

In addition, Dillard et al. (1984) found that the FITD was effective only when the compliance request was pro-social and when targets were *not* offered incentives to comply with the FITD request (average r = .16). A pro-social request is one that does not directly benefit the person making the request (e.g., a charitable donation where the money goes to the organization rather than to the requestor). In studies where the request was self-oriented (i.e., directly benefiting the requestor) or targets were offered incentives for compliance, the FITD effect was trivial.

INVOLVEMENT WITH THE INITIAL REQUEST

Burger (1999) also examined the role of involvement to test whether self-perception theory explains the success of the FITD effect. Self-Perception Theory suggests that targets of FITD requests recall their performance of the initial smaller request when deciding whether to comply with the second larger request. According to self-perception theory, people who see themselves as having been helpful in the past are more likely to accept the larger request. Thus, if the initial request is inconsequential or uninvolving, it is less likely to affect the target's self-perception when the second request is made. For example, compliance with such small requests such as signing a petition or giving directions may be insufficient to alter the way people think about themselves. However, compliance with a memorable or consequential request should affect the target's self-perception about how helpful he or she is (Burger, 1999, p. 307).

To test this hypothesis, Burger examined eight FITD studies where targets were asked (and given the opportunity) to comply with either a low-involvement (inconsequential) or high-involvement (consequential) initial request before being presented with a second, larger, request. As predicted from Self-Perception theory, Burger's meta-analysis revealed that the low-involvement requests produced a small FITD effect (average r = .08). However, when a high-involvement initial request was provided, the FITD effect was stronger (average r = .17). Averaged across all eight studies, people in the control condition (where only the target request was made, no initial request) complied with the target request 28% of the time. By comparison, people in the low-involvement conditions complied 36% of the time, while those in the high-involvement conditions complied 44% of the time. Thus, the more consequential or memorable the initial request, the greater the compliance with the target request.

These subgroup analyses suggest that when certain conditions are met the FITD is an effective technique for gaining compliance. In summary, when the initial request is small enough to produce compliance from most targets, when people are given the opportunity to perform the initial request, when the compliance requests are pro-social (vs. self-oriented), when no incentives are provided for compliance, and when the initial request is involving (or consequential), the FITD should increase compliance rates by about 20%.

Theoretical Basis of the FITD

The most frequently cited theoretical explanation of the FITD effect is Self-Perception Theory (Bem, 1967, 1972). Recall from our discussion in Chapter 4 that Bem's theory hypothesized that people look to their own behaviors for evidence of their underlying attitudes and beliefs. Applied to FITD studies, Self-Perception Theory predicts that when people comply with the FITD request they conclude that their attitude toward the issue or the source of the compliance request must be favorable. After inferring that their attitudes are favorable toward the issue, the requestor, or both, people are then more likely to comply with a second target request.

Although the general pattern of compliance behavior in prior FITD studies is consistent with this interpretation, most of these investigations failed to directly test the self-perception explanation. A study by Dillard (1990b) is a rare exception. He argued that evidence of a self-perception explanation would be reflected in attitude change following compliance with the first request. He measured general attitudes toward the topic of the request and toward several specific reasons for complying with the request. Analysis of the attitude data revealed that compliance with an FITD request to support an environmental organization indicated more favorable attitudes toward the environment as a general issue but *less* favorable attitudes toward several specific reasons for compliance (i.e., the source, emotional benefit, as well as appearances and obligations) (Dillard, 1990b).

Dillard concluded that, although a self-inference explanation was a viable account of his findings, the specific predictions of Self-Perception Theory were not supported in his study. Specifically, neither the size of the initial request nor actual compliance with the initial request (vs. simply agreeing to comply) predicted compliance with the larger second request (Dillard, 1990b). Gorassini and Olson (1995) also found that agreeing to a small request affected people's perceptions of their own helpfulness but that those perceptions did not predict agreement with the second request.

Burger's (1999) meta-analysis, however, found "a great deal of evidence to support a self-perception explanation" (p. 323). Recall that Burger found that both compliance with the initial request and involvement with the initial request increased the effectiveness of the FITD technique. If the initial request is not complied with or if it is inconsequential, then acceptance of the initial request is unlikely to affect people's perceptions about themselves. However, if the initial request is both performed *and* consequential, then it will likely affect self-perceptions and lead to greater compliance with the target request.

Thus, while self-perception processes explain some of the FITD research findings, direct tests of the Self-Perception Theory explanation for the FITD produced mixed results. We concur with Burger's (1999) conclusion that "self-perception processes contribute to the effectiveness of the FITD procedure" (p. 323), but additional theorizing about these self-inference processes may be necessary to fully explain the FITD phenomenon.

The Door-in-the-Face Technique

The FITD technique's reverse counterpart is the door-in-the-face (DITF) technique. The DITF begins with an initial compliance request (referred to as the DITF request) that is so large that it is rejected by most targets. After rejection of the initial request, the source proceeds with a second, smaller, request (i.e., the target request). The DITF technique is similar to the FITD technique in that both techniques are designed to increase compliance with the *second* of two sequential requests. Presumably, people who refuse an initial large request are more likely to comply with the more moderate second request than people who only receive the moderate request.

A variety of organizations attempt to use the DITF to generate sales or donations. For example, Paul is a regular donor to his alma maters (Arizona State and Michigan State) and is contacted annually by both institutions. Several years ago Paul received a call from one of the schools asking for alumni donations. On this particular occasion, however, the student making the call suggested a $1,000 donation that would qualify him to join an elite group of donors. This was a large request, because Paul had never given more than $100 in any prior donation. When Paul refused the request to donate $1,000, the student asked if he would donate the same amount he gave the year before. Paul agreed and even gave a little more than the preceding year.

Cialdini and his colleagues (1975) were the first to investigate the effectiveness of the DITF technique. In the first of three studies, the DITF request asked college students if they would be willing to work as counselors to juvenile delinquents for at least 2 years. None of the students agreed to this initial request. Following their refusal, the moderate target request was made: the students were asked to act as chaperones for a group of juvenile delinquents on a 2-hour trip to the local zoo. Of the students who refused the large initial request, 50% agreed to the smaller second request. By contrast, less than 17% of the people in a control condition—who only received the target request, agreed to act as chaperones on the trip to the zoo (Cialdini et al., 1975). In this study, the DITF produced compliance rates with the target request that were three times greater than those obtained in the control condition (where the target request was not preceded by the DITF). Cialdini and his colleagues also reported the findings from two additional studies that revealed the same patterns of compliance. They argued that, following the rejection of the initial request, anyone seeking greater compliance must concede to lowering the goal, reflected in the much smaller second request. Such a concession on the requester's part establishes an implicit obligation among the targets who refused the initial request to make a concession of their own—specifically, to comply with the second, more moderate, request. Respondents in the control group received a single moderate request, there being no concession involved, and therefore they felt much less obligation to comply with it.

A second process likely facilitated the effectiveness of the DITF technique (Cialdini, 2009). Specifically, Cialdini argued that *perceptual contrast* is the difference between two things that are presented one after another, and this contrast likely influences how targets perceive and evaluate the second request. Applied to the DITF, the second, smaller, request is likely to seem even smaller because it comes immediately following the larger first request. To go back to our earlier example about giving money to one's alma mater, $100 did not seem like such a large donation to Paul because of its time proximity to the initial $1,000 request.

Evidence for the DITF

Since the seminal investigations by Cialdini and his colleagues, scores of published articles have reported investigations of the DITF. Several meta-analytic reviews have synthesized the findings of these studies (Dillard et al., 1984; Feeley, Anker, & Aloe, 2012; Fern et al., 1986; D. J. O'Keefe & Hale, 1998, 2001). The findings from these reviews paint a consistent picture of the effectiveness of this technique, though once again each review highlights separate moderator variables. For example, Fern and colleagues (1986) found that the overall correlation between the use of DITF and compliance was small (average $r = .07$), but a subsequent analysis revealed that the timing of the second request had a significant impact on compliance rates. When there was no delay between refusal of the initial request and the second request, the DITF techniques had a positive effect on compliance (average $r = .09$). However, when there was a delay between the first and second requests, the DITF technique had a negative effect on compliance (average $r = -.08$). Although neither correlation is very large, the absolute difference between these effect sizes (.17) is noteworthy. Subsequent meta-analytic reviews have confirmed this pattern—the DITF technique is only effective in situations where refusal of the initial request is followed during the *same* interaction by a second, smaller, request (Feeley et al., 2012).

The Dillard and colleagues (1984) review found that two factors maximized the effectiveness of this technique. They too found that the DITF was most effective when there was no delay between the two requests, but they also found that the effect was most prominent when the request was prosocial (average $r = .15$). When these conditions are met, the DITF technique increases compliance rates by about 17%.[1] In contrast, as had been previously found, the DITF approach appears to be ineffective when a source's request is self-oriented or when there is a delay between a target's refusal of the first request and the subsequent smaller request (Feeley et al., 2012).

D. J. O'Keefe and Hale's (1998, 2001) meta-analyses differed in method, but generated similar results: compliance with the second request increased when the same person made both requests and when both requests benefited the same person or group. While O'Keefe and Hale (1998, 2001) found that the DITF technique was more effective face to face than over the telephone, Feeley and colleagues (2012) concluded that it was equally effective in mediated contexts (including telephone, online, and written appeals) as in face-to-face contacts.

Perhaps most important, Feeley and colleagues (2012) distinguished between verbal compliance and behavioral compliance (performance) with the target request. Consistent with the prior meta-analytic reviews, and recognizing that the overall correlations are relatively small, the DITF appears to be a reliable technique for significantly increasing verbal compliance with a target request (i.e., getting people to *agree* to do something). However, the DITF technique "does not outperform control conditions in securing behavioral compliance" (Feeley et al., 2012, p. 334). In this regard, while the technique appears to be effective in increasing verbal compliance with an immediate request, it is not effective in securing actual behavior at a later point in time.

Theoretical Basis of the DITF

Three conceptual explanations have been advanced for understanding the DITF phenomenon. The first stems from Gouldner's (1960) concept of the norm of reciprocity, which suggests that "you should give benefits to those who give you benefits" (p. 170). Cialdini and colleagues (1975) extended this discussion by identifying the concept of reciprocal concessions as, basically, "You should make concessions to those who make concessions to you" (p. 206).

Applied to the DITF phenomenon, Dillard et al. (1984) argue that this norm suggests that "two conditions are necessary to activate the normative force that increases the likelihood of compliance to the second request.... (1) The original appeal must be rejected and ... (2) the target must perceive a concession on the part of the requestor" (p. 464). Consistent with this notion, Cialdini and colleagues (1975, Studies 2 and 3) found in two studies that the success of the DITF technique required that targets view the smaller second request as an admitted concession from the source's original position. This is consistent with the meta-analytic reviews that concluded that the DITF approach was effective only when the second request immediately followed the first one. Indeed, as previously noted, if there is a long delay between the two requests, if the two requests come from different people, or if the target's compliance benefits unfamiliar parties, then there is a more tenuous connection between the two requests (and thus the target will be less likely to perceive his or her response to the second request as a deliberate concession).

Not all of the accumulated data, however, are totally consistent with the reciprocal concessions explanation. For example, some research has demonstrated that the size of the concession is unrelated to the degree of compliance with the target request (D. J. O'Keefe & Hale, 1998, 2001). Similarly, Feeley and colleagues (2012) have hypothesized that if the *reciprocal concessions* explanation is correct, greater compliance rates should appear where the concession from the DITF and target requests is large and lower where the difference between the DITF and target requests is small. However, the data do not support that hypothesis (Tusing & Dillard, 2000; Feeley et al., 2012).

A second explanation for DITF effects centers on the creation and reduction of *guilt* (D. J. O'Keefe, 2000, 2002; D. J. O'Keefe & Figgé, 1997). As noted in Chapter 8, *reactive guilt* appears when we recognize that we have behaved in a way that is inconsistent with our own values and morals. Because helping others in need is a widely accepted norm, rejecting a request for help can generate guilt because it violates that personal norm.

Guilt can be a powerful influence tool. Rejecting a pro-social DITF request creates guilt if it violates a personal standard (e.g., to help those in need). Agreeing to the second request, then, gives the target an opportunity to reduce his or her guilt (D. J. O'Keefe & Hale, 1998, 2001). The guilt-based explanation is consistent with the two moderating variables identified in the various meta-analyses. Recall that the meta-analyses suggested that the DITF approach works best when the request is pro-social and when there is no delay between the two requests. Guilt wanes over time, and so compliance with a second request should be greatest when the second request immediately follows the initial request. If rejecting the first request produces guilt, then immediately agreeing to a smaller second request might be the easiest way to reduce it.[2]

Although guilt is a compelling explanation for the DITF phenomenon, studies of this explanation have also produced mixed results (Feeley et al., 2012). For example, in the first of three studies, D. J. O'Keefe and Figgé (1997) found that respondents reported higher levels of guilt after rejecting a pro-social request to volunteer for a health study than did those who rejected a profit-driven request to volunteer for a market research company. However, their researchers' two other studies provided no evidence that acceptance of the target request reduced feelings of guilt. For example, those who rejected the DITF request but then accepted the target request did *not* report lower feelings of guilt than people who rejected both requests. Moreover, while Millar (2002) found experimental support for the guilt explanation, Turner, Tamborini, Limon, & Zuckerman-Hyman (2007) found no evidence that guilt explained the DITF effect. Thus, despite the guilt explanation's conceptual appeal, further investigation is needed since the empirical evidence to date has proven inconclusive (Feeley et al., 2012).

A third explanation for the DITF phenomenon is *social responsibility* (Tusing & Dillard, 2000; Turner et al., 2007). The social responsibility explanation is a hybrid of the norm of reciprocity and the guilt explanations, discussed previously. Tusing and Dillard (2000) posited that rejecting a pro-social request violates a social or personal norm to help others. That is, violating that social norm may result in a range of negative feelings, including guilt, self-deprecation, or loss of self-esteem. Following refusal of the DITF request, "one feels an obligation to comply with the target request in order to avoid self-criticism or so as to refrain from appearing in violation of the norm to help the requester" (Feeley et al., 2012, p. 337).

Because this latter explanation emerged only after the first few meta-analytic reviews were published, Feeley and colleagues (2012) provide the only meta-analytic commentary on the social responsibility explanation. They concluded that "the social responsibility explanation for how the DITF technique operates appears to be the most viable explanation for the pattern of findings" (p. 337). The initial DITF request forces people to violate the norm to help others. The DITF effect is greatest when the initial request is "implausible or is seen as beyond one's capacity to help" (p. 337). The larger the initial request, the stronger the obligation not to violate the personal norm a second time, and the higher the level of compliance with the second request.

Conceptual Integration of Sequential-Request Techniques

Given the obvious similarities between the FITD and the DITF techniques, scholars have sought to develop a single theoretical explanation of both phenomena. The separate explanations of the FITD and DITF phenomena that we described above are incompatible with each other. For example, Self-Perception Theory, frequently invoked to explain the FITD, cannot account for the DITF approach's effects. According to Self-Perception Theory, turning down the initial request should cause DITF targets to infer that their attitudes toward the issue or source of the request are unfavorable, decreasing the likelihood of their complying with a second request (whatever the amount or sacrifice in question). Similarly, neither the norm of reciprocal concessions nor either guilt-based and/or social responsibility explanations invoked to explain the DITF phenomenon can account for the effects of the FITD. Because no concession is made in the FITD, the norm of reciprocal concessions cannot explain its effectiveness. Similarly, agreeing to a *smaller* request should produce no guilt, per se, so the guilt-based explanation cannot readily explain the FITD's effects either.

Several researchers have attempted to identify a single theoretical process that allows for conceptual integration of the FITD and DITF techniques. One such explanation is the *availability hypothesis,* which posits that favorable information available in a person's cognitive framework tends to guide one toward compliance with requests (Tybout, Sternthal, & Calder, 1983). As applied to the FITD's effect, the availability hypothesis would suggest that one's initial compliance with a small request increases the favorable information one relies on in memory to guide his or her response to the second, larger, request. On the other hand, as applied to the DITF's effects, the availability hypothesis suggests that one's perception of a concession in the source's second (smaller) request is favorable information whose availability inclines one to comply with the second (less demanding) request.

In assessing the viability of this explanation, Dillard (1991) concluded:

> Though conceptually elegant and empirically promising in its first tests (Tybout et al., 1983), the availability model does not comport well with the meta-analytic data. Fern et al. (1986) derive several hypotheses that are closely modeled on the reasoning of Tybout et al. (1983). . . . But, by my count only three of those seven hypotheses received support. . . . In short, despite its hopeful beginning, the information availability perspective does not appear adequate to the task of providing a unified theoretical account of sequential-request phenomena. (p. 286)

Thus far, scholars have been unsuccessful in discovering a unifying theoretical process to explain the FITD and the DITF. It may be time to conclude that the DITF and FITD techniques are separate phenomena guided by fundamentally different processes. This suggestion is bolstered by several studies indicating that source factors such as power and legitimacy work differently in FITD and DITF contexts. For example, Stahelski and Patch (1993) reported that people see a greater power differential between requester and target in typical DITF situations as compared to typical FITD situations. Williams and Williams (1989) reported that the requester's relative power amplified the DITF situation but had little or no effect in the FITD process. Finally, Patch (1988) observed that when requests are made by sources low in legitimacy, FITD strategies are effective but DITF strategies are not.

That such source variables as power and legitimacy should so differentially influence DITF and FITD processes suggests that these structurally similar techniques are rooted in fundamentally different persuasive processes. While a recent meta-analysis of studies directly comparing the effectiveness of the FITD and DITF techniques found that both are successful in gaining compliance (Pascual & Gueguen, 2005), the search still continues for a unifying process that might explain their mutual efficacy. Most likely, two theoretically distinct processes drive these two sequential-request strategies.

While DITF and FITD are the two examples of sequential-request strategies for gaining compliance that have received the most interest from persuasion scholars, let us not end this section without examining the third one, namely, lowball procedures (Cialdini, Cacioppo, Bassett, & Miller, 1978).

The Lowball Technique

The *lowball technique* is a sequential-message technique that involves initially securing compliance from a target and then changing the request such that the cost of performing the behavior is increased. The lowball technique is a staple of salespeople, and it is especially prevalent among new-car dealers (Cialdini et al., 1978). This technique can take a number of forms. For example, new-car dealers often negotiate the price of a new car in combination with an offer to purchase a customer's used car. In these situations, the sales price of the new car may not be very attractive, but a generous trade-in offer makes the total cost of purchasing the new car quite appealing. After the customer agrees to the new car's sales price and the trade-in value, the salesperson leaves the negotiation to seek a supervisor's approval of the deal. Upon returning, the lowball tactic is confirmed whenever the salesperson indicates that he or she has mistakenly offered too much for the trade-in and that the supervisor has rejected the deal. The salesperson pleads that the company "would lose money" on the original deal and then attempts to renegotiate (i.e., reduce) the value of the customer's trade-in. Customers typically feel sufficiently committed to their initial decision to purchase the new car that they end up accepting a lesser amount for their trade-in. Although the agreed-upon retail price of the new car has not changed, the total cost of the sale to the customer may be significantly greater than he or she had agreed to originally.

BOX 11.2. The Prius Lowball

A number of years ago when the Toyota Prius was first introduced, Paul was feeling particularly "green" (i.e., environmentally responsible) and therefore decided that he wanted one. Because early demand for the Prius was much greater than the supply, some dealers were selling the cars at a hefty premium (i.e., a price well above the sticker price) and most all dealerships had long waiting lists for the car. Paul went to a local Toyota dealership and was told that they had a 6- to 9-month waiting list, so he put his name down on a list of about 20 people and went home.

A few days later, Paul received a phone call from a salesperson who said that—because he was a "special" customer (probably meaning that he walked into the dealership)—they had moved his name up to number 2 on the waiting list. The salesperson then told Paul that a new Prius would be delivered to the dealership in the next few days and that if the person in front of him on the list did not want the car, then Paul would be able to purchase it. A few days later, Paul received another phone call informing him that the person ahead of him on the waiting list was unable to obtain financing for the vehicle and that Paul could purchase the Prius if he still wanted it. Every time he spoke with someone at the dealership, Paul was asked, "You do still want the car, don't you?" These repeated questions sought a verbal commitment from Paul in order to solidify his intention to purchase the car.

After several more phone calls, Paul was finally back at the dealership. He looked at the car (color, "tideland pearl"). He had the keys in hand. But when it came time to sign the contract, the dealer listed a price that was several thousand dollars higher than the previously agreed-upon price. When Paul asked the salesperson where the higher price came from, he indicated for the first time that there was a $3,500 premium above the sticker price. Apparently the dealer figured that—because Paul had waited and repeatedly expressed interest in purchasing the car over a period of several days—surely he would not back out of the deal that far into the process. This classic example of a lowball technique did not work well with Paul, however, who immediately tore up the contract and walked out of the dealership. However, it is quite likely that someone a little further down on the "waiting list" soon succumbed to the pressure and agreed to pay a premium for the vehicle. For his part, Paul waited 8 months until supply caught up with demand and then became the proud owner of a Prius (color, "millennium silver metallic"), purchased without paying a premium.

Of course, there are any number of ways that the lowball technique can play out in real life. Several years ago, Jim decided to buy a convertible sports car with a hardtop option. When the car was delivered several weeks later, he was told that the hardtop option had gone up in price. Although he had a signed contract, the salesman wanted Jim to pay an additional $700 for the car! Indeed, the salesman attempted to use a lowball technique to increase his profit. Just as happened with Paul and the Prius, the salesman anticipated that, after waiting several weeks for the car, Jim would be so eager to take delivery that he would cave in on the price increase, or at least agree to a portion of it. While the salesman's ploys ultimately proved unsuccessful, this is but one example of the countless ways that the lowball technique comes into play daily (especially on new-car lots).

Evidence of the Lowball Technique

Cialdini and his colleagues (1978) conducted three experiments that provided evidence of the effectiveness of the lowball technique. In one study, undergraduate students were contacted by phone and asked if they were willing to participate in an experimental study in order to fulfill a psychology class requirement. Students in the control condition were told that the experiment was to take place at 7:00 A.M. *prior* to being asked if they were willing to participate. Students in the lowball condition were asked to participate, and if they said "Yes," only then were they told that the experiment would be conducted at 7:00 A.M.; they were then asked again if they were willing to participate.

Participants in the lowball condition agreed to participate significantly more often (56%) than participants in the control condition (31%). More importantly, behavioral commitment was similar across the two conditions: 95% of the participants in the lowball condition and 79% in the control condition who agreed to participate actually showed up at 7:00 A.M. Cialdini et al. (1978) reported the findings of two additional studies providing further evidence of the effectiveness of the lowball technique (see Cialdini & Goldstein, 2004, for a review).

Theoretical Basis of the Lowball Technique

In an attempt to explain the effectiveness of the lowball technique, Cialdini and his colleagues (1978) tested the efficacy of dissonance, self-perception, and commitment explanations. In an experiment designed to separate these effects, the researchers found that the notion of psychological commitment was the most viable explanation for this effect. According to Kiesler (1971), committing (even if only tentatively) to a particular decision makes it more difficult to change one's mind. Applied to the lowball technique, this formulation posits that, once people agree to a request, they feel psychologically committed to their decision and are less likely to change it—even if the nature of the request changes. This explanation suggests that, once people have committed to purchasing a car, they generally (albeit not Paul!) are unlikely to change their minds even if the ultimate cost of the car is more than they originally agreed to pay. Of course, however, J. M. Berger and Cornelius (2003) demonstrated that without a "public" commitment (i.e., a verbal response witnessed by someone) to accept the initial offer, the lowball technique will not generally be effective.

We only applied the lowball technique to new-car sales situations, but this technique has proven to be quite effective across a variety of compliance settings. There are similarities between the FITD and the lowball technique, but Cialdini et al. (1978) drew important conceptual and empirical distinctions between these two sequential-request strategies. Although the technical aspects and theoretical foundations of the FITD, the DITF, and the lowball procedures differ, these techniques all reflect the influence that sequential-compliance requests can have on the behavior of persuasion targets.

SUMMARY

This chapter reviewed two distinct traditions of research on interpersonal influence. The research on compliance-gaining message selection encompassed situational and personality factors that affect the ways in which people evaluate strategies for gaining compliance. Though relatively few studies in this tradition examined communicative behavior, they nonetheless provided a framework for understanding how people approach persuasion situations. A second tradition of research on interpersonal influence paralleled the growth of the message selection tradition. Studies of compliance-gaining behavior focused on the relative effectiveness of sequential-request strategies for gaining compliance. Specifically, we discussed three strategies (i.e., FITD, DITF, and lowball) that attempt to gain compliance by sending multiple messages in a sequence. While similar in structure, the FITD, DITF, and lowball strategies are distinct and appear to operate in fundamentally different ways.

NOTES

1. While the average correlations may not seem terribly different, a 17% increase in compliance is significant. Consider a sales situation where hundreds (or perhaps thousands) of sales calls are being made every day. Using the DITF strategy

to increase compliance would generate a much larger number of people agreeing to the second request (and generate substantial amounts of money) than if the second (target) request was made without a preliminary one.

2. Part of what makes D. J. O'Keefe's (2002) guilt-based explanation so interesting is that he has extended it beyond the DITF context. For example, in Chapter 4 we noted that D. J. O'Keefe argues that some dissonance study conclusions can be explained equally well through guilt processes (e.g., the Stone et al. [1994] study's findings on increasing condom use by spotlighting hypocrisy); and in Chapter 8 we challenged whether the conceptual distinction between guilt and cognitive dissonance was truly clear-cut.

CHAPTER 12

Producing and Resisting Influence Messages

LOOKING AHEAD . . . In this chapter, we take a more detailed look at BOTH the process of producing and resisting influence messages. First, we investigate how one's own goals and plans affect the production of influence messages. We focus specifically on the nature of influence goals and the role of plan complexity in message production. We also consider how influence agents deal with multiple simultaneous influence goals and the role of message design logics in interpersonal influence. Finally, we discuss how and why people resist influence attempts. After examining resistance in general, we examine these issues in the context of resisting drug and alcohol influence attempts.

The body of research on compliance-gaining message selection discussed in the preceding chapter provided useful insights into the selection and effectiveness of strategies for gaining compliance in interpersonal situations. That research tradition, however, offered little guidance about the factors most affecting the *production* and actual use of compliance messages, which we treat in the first part of this chapter. During the past couple of decades, many communication scholars have focused on developing a better understanding of how compliance-gaining messages are created, and this chapter begins with a review of their research. Following this review, we examine recent research on the use of compliance *resistance* strategies, which for us represents a marked shift in focus. Instead of examining how sources produce messages, compliance resistance research explores how the message receivers actually defend themselves *against* persuasive appeals. In much the same way that we examined the role of counterargument in resisting persuasive messages in several earlier chapters, understanding how people resist persuasive appeals is essential to understanding the nature of compliance-gaining transactions.

Numerous studies of message production have examined how people form persuasive goals (Dillard, Segrin, & Hardin, 1989; B. J. O'Keefe & Shepherd, 1987; Wilson, 1990, 1997), how these goals are translated into action, the effects of these persuasive goals (Dillard et al., 1989; Sabee & Wilson, 2005; Wilson, Aleman, & Leatham, 1998), and how they function in interpersonal influence interactions (B. J. O'Keefe, 1988, 1990; B. J. O'Keefe & McCornack, 1987). We examine each of these lines of research below.

GOALS, PLANS, AND ACTION IN INTERPERSONAL INFLUENCE

Cognitive theoretical frameworks have guided much of the recent research on message production (see Roskos-Ewoldsen & Monahan, 2007, for an overview of these perspectives). Many of these theoretical perspectives, in one way or another, focus on the concept of goals (Wilson, 1997). A number of scholars have used the goal concept (though they sometimes label it differently) to help explain interpersonal influence (e.g., Caughlin, 2010; Dillard, 1990a; Hample & Dallinger, 1987; Samp & Solomon, 1998; Wilson & Feng, 2007). The approach that we will use as a guide to describe this research derives from a combination of James Dillard's Goals, Plans, Action (GPA) Model of interpersonal influence and Charles Berger's Theory of Planning. These frameworks posit that people in interpersonal influence situations develop interaction goals that lead them to plan and select particular message strategies. Once developed, these plans are implemented as persuasive message appeals (Dillard, 1989, 1990b). Because message production processes appear to be guided by the persuader's goals, understanding the nature of influence goals and how they are transferred into action is essential to our understanding of the message production process.

The Nature of Influence Goals

Dillard (1990a) defines goals as "future states of affairs which an individual is committed to achieving or maintaining" (p. 43). There are a number of different persuasive goals that people can bring to influence interactions (for descriptions, see Cody, Canary, & Smith, 1994; Dillard, 1989; Rule, Bisanz, & Kohn, 1985; Wilson & Feng, 2007). Some goals represent the particular outcome desired by the persuader. Dillard and colleagues (1989) refer to these as *primary goals*: "In interpersonal influence attempts, the desire to bring about behavioral change in a target person is the primary goal" (p. 20). For example, an influence situation may involve giving advice, asking for a date, or obtaining information.

Primary goals are important because they define the nature of the influence situation, direct behavior, and represent yardsticks for measuring the effectiveness of an influence attempt (Dillard, 1990a). Primary goals also help message sources identify and evaluate behavior that occurs in influence interactions. For example, if your primary influence goal is to get your roommate to quit smoking, then the success or failure of your influence attempt should be based upon whether or not he or she actually quits (or cuts down on) smoking.

Several studies (Cody et al., 1994; Dillard et al., 1989; Rule et al., 1985) provide compelling evidence that there are a relatively small number of primary influence goals. Despite using different research methods, these studies generated similar lists of goals. Primary influence goals include changing a relationship (whether by initiation, escalation, or decline), asking for a favor, giving advice, sharing activities, and a broader range of attitude and behavior modifications (Schrader & Dillard, 1998; for a summary, see Kellermann, 2004).

However, other goals, such as relational maintenance and impression management, also operate in interpersonal influence situations. Dillard (1989, 1990a) refers to these outcomes as *secondary goals*: "Rather than driving the influence episode, as does the primary goal, secondary goals act as a counterforce to it and as a set of dynamics that help to shape planning and message output" (1990a, p. 46). Perhaps the best evidence for these secondary goals is the fact that people often avoid using coercive influence strategies (as we discussed in the preceding chapter), especially when they judge more socially desirable strategies to be equally effective. If these secondary goals did not exist, then people would routinely use the most forceful compliance strategy available to them regardless of its impact on the target or its reflection on the source. For example, you might really want your roommate to stop smoking in the room you share, but you do not want to criticize his or her behavior too harshly for fear of damaging your relationship with him or her.

Just as is true for primary goals, there are multiple secondary goals that may operate in any particular influence situation. In one study, Dillard and colleagues (1989) asked students to imagine themselves in hypothetical compliance-gaining situations. For each situation, students were then given Wiseman and Schenck-Hamlin's (1981) list of compliance-gaining strategies and asked to indicate whether or not they would use each strategy and provide a written justification for each decision. These written justifications were content-analyzed and provided the basis for establishing the secondary goals that help determine strategy use.

This analysis revealed that five secondary goals—*identity, interaction, resource, arousal,* and *influence*—were represented in people's reasons for rejecting a message strategy (see Table 12.1) (Dillard et al., 1989). *Identity* goals reflect concerns about a person's internal moral standards (e.g., be honest) and appeared in 34% of the justifications offered by respondents. *Interaction* goals reflect concerns about social appropriateness and impression management. These goals were present in 9% of the justifications. For example, an aggressive strategy might be rejected because it may be socially inappropriate for a particular situation and may project an image that the persuader does not wish to send. *Resource* goals are revealed through concerns about relational and personal costs and rewards associated with the compliance attempt. For example, threatening strategies may be avoided because they may damage the relationship and are incompatible with the resource goal of relational maintenance. These goals were apparent in 5% of the justifications. *Arousal,* the fourth secondary goal, is focused on managing the anxiety or emotional turmoil that might be present in some influence situations. Arousal was least frequently cited (only 1%) as a reason for not selecting particular compliance-gaining strategies. The fifth category,

TABLE 12.1. Justifications for Rejecting Message Strategies

Goal category	Frequency	Proportion	Exemplar statements
Influence	865	44%	It won't work. It's irrelevant.
Identity	672	34%	It's immoral. Not my style.
Interaction	180	9%	That would make me look bad. This is inappropriate for the situation.
Resource	98	5%	This would cost me our friendship.
Arousal	8	1%	This would make me apprehensive. Makes me too nervous.
Uncodable	136	7%	This is stupid. You must be kidding.
Total	1,959	100%	

Note. From "Primary and secondary goals in the production of interpersonal influence messages" by J. P. Dillard, C. Segrin, & J. M. Hardin, 1989, *Communication Monographs, 56,* 19–38. Copyright 1989 by the National Communication Association. Reprinted by permission.

influence, was cited 44% of the time, indicating that people frequently eliminated a strategy because they did not think that it would be effective. This category reflects the view that people prefer to choose strategies that are most likely to succeed. In a second study, Dillard and his colleagues (1989) developed and validated self-report measures for each of these secondary goals.

Goal Formation

A Cognitive Rules Model has been introduced that describes the formation of interaction goals (Wilson, 1990). This model proposes that people possess cognitive rules for developing goals. These rules are stored in long-term memory and are activated when there is a "match between the perceived features of the situation and the situational conditions represented in the rule" (Wilson, 1990, p. 82). The accessibility of a cognitive rule and its fit with the persuasion situation affect the creation of persuasive goals. For example, Wilson (1990) found that "people were more willing to form supporting goals if a situational feature associated with those goals recently had been activated, making the relevant cognitive rules accessible" (p. 97). The activation process described in the Cognitive Rules Model depicts people as parallel information processors. This suggests that rules for forming primary and secondary goals can be simultaneously activated. How people create these multiple goals represents an important theoretical issue.

Goals and Plans

Dillard's (1990a) discussion of primary and secondary goals suggests that persuaders will enter most influence situations with multiple goals (i.e., one or more primary goals linked with one or more secondary goals). For example, a person might attempt to achieve a primary goal of convincing his or her roommate not to smoke in their room while at the same time attempting to achieve the secondary goals of not looking foolish, not making the roommate look foolish (i.e., interaction goals), and not violating personal standards (i.e., identity goal). The fact that most influence situations involve multiple goals suggests that the production of influence messages is unlikely to be a simple process. Instead, the complexity of goal structures highlights the importance of the second stage of Dillard's GPA Model, planning.

In both Dillard's (1990a) GPA Model and C. R. Berger's (1997) Theory of Planning, the intermediate process between an influence goal and the production of an influence message is *planning*. Planning represents the cognitive work that goes into realizing primary and secondary goals. The end result of the planning process is the development of one or more plans.

Plans are "hierarchical cognitive representations of goal-directed action sequences" (Berger, 1997, p. 25). There are several aspects of this definition that require further consideration. First, this definition highlights the fact that plans are developed in an effort to reach goals. Second, plans are not behaviors, but rather the thoughts that are related to those behaviors. Third, plans are hierarchical because they can and do occur at varying levels of abstractness. If your goal is to get your roommate to stop smoking in your shared room, you might develop an abstract plan to "reward him or her." After considering different types of rewards, a specific plan can be developed that fulfills the general one (e.g., promise to take him or her to dinner at a favorite restaurant if he or she doesn't smoke in the room for a week).

Berger (1997) assumes that people have a number of "canned plans" stored in long-term memory. "Canned plans" are those that individuals have used before in goal-related influence situations and—because they were successful in the past—might want to use again. Because people have limited information processing capacity and cannot generate an entirely new set of plans every time they enter an influence situation, they prefer to use these canned plans rather than ones they might have to develop from scratch. If the goal and situation closely match what is required for the plan to work, Berger assumes that the canned plan will be used. This is similar to the argument that S. R. Wilson (1990) made in discussing the production of goals.

According to Berger (1997), plans differ in how simple or complex they are. They can be complex in either (or both) of two ways. First, their complexity depends upon their level of detail. To continue the smoking example, a complex plan might involve developing and mentally rehearsing everything that you will say (down to the specific gestures you will use and when) to your roommate. If, on the other hand, you enter the interaction with only a vague sense of how to convince your roommate, then your plan is quite simple.

Second, plan complexity may reflect the number of contingencies that must be considered. A *contingency* represents an attempt to deal with events that might interfere with the plan's successful implementation (Berger, 1997). For example, you might plan a primary means of attempting to get your roommate to stop smoking in the room. You expect, though, that your roommate may well object to your primary plan by claiming that it is his or her room too and that he or she has the right to smoke there. A plan contingency would involve developing a "subplan" of how you might respond to that particular objection. In short, the greater number of contingencies in a plan, the more complex it is. For example, if you wanted to achieve a primary goal of relational initiation by asking someone out on a first date, developing a complex plan might include thinking through who you would ask, when you would ask, what specifically you would say, what sort of response you would expect, and how you might react to that response. The complexity of this plan is apparent when it is contrasted with a plan to ask a committed relational partner out on a date. In the latter case, one might not be concerned about the specific language used or anticipating how to react to a variety of possible responses. With a committed partner, much of the uncertainty—and hence, plan complexity—is reduced.

While developing a plan featuring numerous contingencies might be useful in making a message source feel better prepared, it might also make presenting the messages more difficult. A complex plan replete with many contingencies likely requires message sources to closely monitor the recipient's responses and decide the extent to which the influence attempt is going "according to plan." A complex plan might give the message source a lot of things to think about—and all this while presenting the influence message. It would seem, then, that complex plans might be more difficult to present smoothly.

C. R. Berger, Karol, and Jordan (1989) were interested in the role complexity might play in terms of verbal fluency when producing influence messages. They had college students in two experimental conditions write out a plan designed to convince a fellow student that alcohol consumption should be banned in dormitories (an important campus issue at the time). In one condition (i.e., plan-question), the experimenter looked at the plan and asked the participant what he or she would do if four specific aspects of his or her plan were to fail. In the other condition (i.e., plan-only), participants were not questioned about their plans.

After the participants developed their respective plans (in the plan-only condition), or after the experimenter asked participants to reconsider their plan (i.e., the plan-question condition), each participant was taken to a different room and asked to convince another student of his or her position. Unbeknownst to the participants, the other student was a confederate. A *confederate* is someone who acts as if he or she is a genuine participant in the study but in reality is actually working for the experimenter and has been instructed to act in a particular way. In this particular study, the confederate was instructed to act in a neutral fashion initially but to become more skeptical of the source's position as the influence attempt went on.

Berger and colleagues (1989) presumed that facing the experimenter's questions about the plan would cause participants to become more aware of alternative plans and to increase the number of contingencies in their existing plans. Thus, participants in the plan-question condition should have had more complex plans than participants in the plan-only condition. Given that participants had relatively little time to rehearse the (revised) influence attempt, increased plan complexity was expected to reduce message fluency, particularly when the recipient asked questions.

BOX 12.1. Plan Complexity and Witness Testimony

Jim routinely encounters the issue of plan complexity whenever he helps attorneys prepare their witnesses for trial testimony. Often the witnesses are quick to provide answers on direct examination, particularly if the questions and answers are rehearsed prior to the trial. They generally require less planning when answering questions from their own attorney or friendly counsel. However, as soon as cross-examination begins, the demeanor of witnesses often changes, and the amount of time they pause before answering a question typically increases. Witnesses often require more time to respond to cross-examination questions, because they do not trust the examiner, worry more about the implications of their responses, and attempt to anticipate potential follow-up questions that their answers will provoke. Although Jim forewarns witnesses not to engage in a "chess match" with opposing counsel, the fact is that cross-examination is a significantly more complex process that requires significantly more planning. Unfortunately, the time required for planning responses to complex cross-examination questions increases the time it takes to respond to questions, and jurors usually interpret longer response times or periods of silence negatively. Witnesses who take *too* long to answer a question are often perceived as reluctant, afraid, or unwilling to tell the truth. In that regard, excessive plan complexity can have a significant impact on the credibility of witnesses.

The results of the study were consistent with the researchers' predictions. Participants in the plan-question condition (i.e., those who were asked to reconsider their plan before its presentation) were judged as being less fluent than participants in the plan-only condition. Berger and colleagues concluded that, once the initial message was questioned, the more complex plans that resulted made it more difficult for participants to change their persuasive approach and/or the strategy of their message. In summary, while greater plan complexity might make a person feel better prepared to make an influence attempt, it might also make it more difficult for that person to change the plan to meet unexpected circumstances.

Goals, Planning, and Message Production

In an effort to link primary and secondary goals with the production of plans and persuasive messages, Dillard and his colleagues (1989) asked research participants to recall and describe a recent interaction in which they attempted to influence someone with whom they were well acquainted. The participants were also asked to indicate how much planning and effort was involved in their influence attempt (Study 3). Trained coders evaluated these influence descriptions to determine the level of directness, positivity, and logic reflected in them. The participants also responded to measures of primary and secondary goals in influence situations (Study 2). These scales assessed the influence, identity, interaction, relational resource, and arousal goals that people bring to interpersonal influence situations.

The goals that people reported in these influence situations were related to the characteristics of the messages they produced. Respondents' concerns with the primary goal of influence were positively related to their level of planning of, and effort exerted in producing, persuasive messages, as well as to the level of logic and reasoning reflected in them. In addition, secondary goals were associated with planning and the characteristics of persuasive messages. Identity goals were positively associated with both the level of planning and logic, and negatively related to the directness of the message. Interaction goals were positively related to planning and the level of positivity in the message. Relational resource goals were positively associated with message positivity. Finally, concerns about arousal management were negatively related to the directness, positivity, and logic of message appeals.

The overall pattern of effects in these findings suggests an important relationship between goals, planning, and message production. The strongest relationships were observed between the primary goal of influence and message production. Moreover, greater degrees of planning went into messages that reflected primary influence goals and the secondary goals of identity and interaction concerns. What is more, significant relationships were also observed between secondary goals and characteristics of the persuasive messages. Some of these relationships were negative, whereas others were positive—a finding that underscores the problem of goal management and the complexity of interpersonal influence attempts. For example, identity and interaction goals were positively associated with message positivity, but arousal management goals were negatively related to message positivity. Also, the primary goal of influence was positively associated with the logic of message appeals, but arousal management was negatively associated with message logic. These results are consistent with the notion that "the primary goal serves to initiate and maintain the social action, while the secondary goals act as a set of boundaries which delimit the verbal choices available to sources" (Dillard et al., 1989, p. 32).

When the secondary goal of impression management (i.e., presenting a positive image) has consequences for an influence attempt, politeness is likely to be a very important concern. Influence messages that are perceived as impolite may be ineffective because they present the message source as being rude. A message that is too polite, however, may be ineffective, because it may be so indirect as to be easily avoided or interpreted in different ways. As a consequence, Dillard, Wilson, Tusing, and Kinney (1997) attempted to identify those characteristics of influence messages that are related to judgments of politeness. According to Brown and Gilman (1989), "Politeness means putting things in such a way as to take account of the feelings of the hearer" (p. 161). Achieving persuasive goals may depend on finding the right balance between presenting the most effective message while at the same time being polite. For example, Wilson et al. (1998) examined the importance of face-saving goals and their constraints on message production. Extending research from Brown and Levinson (1987), Wilson and colleagues argued that the primary goals of asking favors or enforcing an obligation create different face-saving goals for the message sources. Message sources identify potential threats to their self-image as well as the target's as they evaluate the politeness and appropriateness of message strategies.

Dillard and colleagues (1997) were interested in the extent to which three message characteristics—directness, dominance, and logic—influenced judgments about politeness. They developed videotapes of 320 influence messages that were based on college students' actual influence experiences. Different groups of students rated the messages on dominance, argument, explicitness, and politeness. When they compared these various judgments, the research team found that dominance (i.e., the extent to which the source uses power to influence) was by far the factor most strongly related to politeness judgments. Messages containing high levels of dominance were judged as very impolite. Moreover, they reported that the dominance communicated in the verbal message (i.e., linguistic dominance) and the dominance communicated nonverbally combined to have the strongest effect on perceptions of impoliteness.

As Dillard et al. (1997) expected, messages judged to be high in logic (i.e., that provided at least one reason for the influence attempt) were judged as being more polite than messages that contained no reasons. Finally, they were surprised to find that directness was positively related to politeness (rather than negatively related, as they expected), which may be attributable to the generally close relationships participants recalled. In a close relationship, coming right out and directly asking for something might be considered more polite than "beating around the bush."

Multiple Goal Management

The preceding discussion clearly indicates that the development of influence goals and plans as well as the presentation of an influence message are complex matters. One source of complexity in the goals–plans–action sequence occurs when primary and secondary goals are incompatible with one another. In many influence situations, the management of these competing goals requires the use of complex tactics that enable sources to gain compliance without harming their own image or their relationships.

B. J. O'Keefe and Shepherd (O'Keefe, 1988; O'Keefe & Shepherd, 1987) describe three strategies people use to manage the conflict created by incompatible primary and secondary goals. Their first goal management strategy, *selection*, allows people to resolve this conflict by choosing between the conflicting goals. Applying the Dillard and colleagues (1989) distinction between primary and secondary goals, the selection strategy requires people to assign priority to either the primary goal of influence or to subsidiary goals such as relational maintenance and identity management. For example, if you wish to collect an overdue $50 loan from your roommate, your primary goal may be to reclaim the unpaid money. However, the secondary goals of relational maintenance (you have to live with this person) and identity management (you don't want to appear cheap or petty) may affect the nature of your compliance request. In order to adopt the selection strategy to manage the apparent conflict between these primary and secondary goals, you give priority to *either* the primary or the secondary goal. If priority is given to the primary goal, you might produce a compliance message that reflects little concern about your own image or your relationship with your roommate—for example, "You still haven't repaid the $50 loan I gave you, and I want the money today." However, maintaining a favorable relationship with your roommate may be a higher priority than reclaiming the money you are owed. If priority is assigned to the secondary goals of relational maintenance and identity management, you might construct a more tactful message even if it is less likely to prompt your roommate to repay the loan—for example, "Gee, I could really use some money to buy books for my persuasion class."

The second strategy for managing conflicting goals is *separation*. O'Keefe and Shepherd (1987) argue that a separation strategy involves placing priority on the primary goal and then addressing the secondary goals by elaborating the request with phrases that are designed to account for, minimize, or repair the negative characteristics of the primary message (p. 401). Applied to the hypothetical loan situation, a separation strategy might involve a direct and forceful request to achieve the primary goal of loan repayment along with another statement or phrase that explains why the money is important to you. For example: "You haven't repaid the $50 I loaned you weeks ago, and I really need the money today. I'm sorry about being so direct, but I don't get paid until next week, and I have to buy books for my persuasion class."

Integration is a third strategy for managing competing goals. Integration strategies resolve the competing demands of primary and secondary goals by redefining the persuasive situation (O'Keefe & Shepherd, 1987). Returning again to the hypothetical loan scenario, an integrative strategy might cause you to generate a message that redefines the loan obligation as a willingness between roommates to help each other. Such a message might permit you to request payment of the loan from your roommate without threatening the relationship—for example, "I am happy that we have the type of friendship that allows us to ask each other for help when we need it. And right now, I really need to ask for the $50 I loaned you a couple weeks ago. You see, I need to buy books for my persuasion class and don't get paid until next week."

In a study examining the influence of these goal management strategies, O'Keefe and Shepherd (1987) had college students engage in a discussion on a controversial campus topic with a person they disagreed with. When considering what the partners said, they found that none of the strategies used to deal with competing goals was unrelated to persuasion outcomes. However, greater use of integration strategies, and less use of the separation strategies, was associated with interpersonal success ratings. The more people used an integration management strategy and the less they used the separation strategy, the more they were liked and perceived as competent by their interaction partners (p. 415). These findings and others like them (Bingham & Burleson, 1989; B. J. O'Keefe & McCornack, 1987) suggest that, although the three goal management strategies may be equally effective for achieving the primary persuasive goal, use of an integration goal management strategy appears most effective for simultaneously achieving both primary and secondary goals such as identity management and relational maintenance.

MESSAGE DESIGN LOGICS AND MESSAGE PRODUCTION

In the cognitive rules and planning approach to message production reviewed above, goals and obstacles to achieving desired outcomes represent the framework for understanding message production. On the other hand, B. J. O'Keefe (1988) argued that message producers have "a theory of communication" (p. 83) that specifies how verbal messages can be used to achieve practical goals. What is more, by understanding these implicit theories of communication, we can understand how people move from goals to the messages they produce (O'Keefe, 1988).

To better explain people's implicit theories of communication, O'Keefe (1988) introduced the concept of *message design logics*, which encompasses three fundamentally different belief systems about communication that people use in creating their messages. Understanding these implicit theories or belief systems is important, according to O'Keefe, because knowledge about the situation constraints is insufficient to fully understand how people move from their goals to producing actual messages. Thus, it behooves us to understand the message design logic of each message producer.

The most simple design logic one can possess is based on the premise that "language is a medium for expressing thoughts and feelings" (O'Keefe, 1988, p. 84). People using *expressive design logics* experience difficulty in separating their thoughts and feelings from the messages they produce. Described as "dumpers," they openly express their thoughts and feelings and assume that others interact in the same fashion (O'Keefe, 1990). Caughlin and colleagues (2008) asked research participants how they would respond to a sibling's disclosure that he or she was HIV-positive. These responses were then coded as indicative of one of the three message design logics identified by O'Keefe (1988). One example of a message reflecting an expressive design logic was: "Oh my God! Are you serious? I cannot believe this. How did this happen? Are you sure? You've been to the doctor and everything?!" (Caughlin et al., 2008, p. 666).

In contrast, people embracing *conventional design logics* view "communication as a game that is to be played cooperatively, according to socially conventional rules and procedures" (O'Keefe, 1988, p. 86). They regard the characteristics of communicative situations as static elements that define the rules of appropriate interaction.

Individuals using conventional design logics, unlike expressives, are likely to pay close attention to the context and the audience in fashioning their messages. For example, Caughlin and colleagues (2008) reported this response to a disclosure about HIV as indicative of a conventional design logic, "I would ask my brother questions to better understand his condition and to help comfort if he is upset. I would first ask, 'Have you told Ann?' I would then ask, 'In what ways can I help you most in this time?' and 'How are you doing emotionally with the news?'" (p. 667).

Finally, people employing *rhetorical design logics* view communication as the "creation and negotiation of social selves and situations" (O'Keefe, 1988, p. 87). For this kind of person, the primary function of messages is to negotiate or arrive at, a consensus about the social reality people find themselves in. Rather than merely reacting expressively, or viewing the situation as a fixed set of elements, rhetoricals attempt to define the situation in a manner that is beneficial to the achievement of their goals. Caughlin and colleagues (2008) set forth this example (in the circumstances already noted) of a comforting message that reflects a rhetorical design logic:

> "My initial response would be to say, 'I am so sorry' and just hug my sister. We are not a very physical family, so this act of physical support would be important. Then I would say, 'Well, this is really a shock, but life will go on. Focus as much as you can about making the best of this

situation. You've been such a positive person all your life. I have confidence that you will make this a positive situation as well. Just have faith that God will help you and guide you.' Past that, I would definitely ask a lot of questions and figure out medically and emotionally how she is doing." (p. 668)

B. J. O'Keefe and Shepherd (1987) argue that expressive, conventional, and rhetorical design logics can be ordered on a developmental continuum in which the expressive design logic is viewed as the least cognitively developed while the rhetorical design logic is viewed as the most cognitively developed. Using this developmental ranking, B. J. O'Keefe and McCornack (1987) assessed the perceptions people have of messages that reflect these design logics. Their research participants rated messages with a rhetorical message design logic as more favorable and potentially more persuasive than messages reflecting either conventional or expressive design logics. Interestingly, in their study of comforting messages in response to a sibling's HIV disclosure, Caughlin and colleagues (2008) found that messages exhibiting greater sophistication in the management of relevant goals were rated as higher quality than those reflecting less sophistication. In another study, Bingham and Burleson (1989), however, reported that, although messages suggestive of rhetorical design logics were perceived as more communicatively competent, they were not perceived as more effective than messages reflecting conventional and expressive design logics.

Together, these findings provide some support for the preferential status generally accorded to rhetorical design logics. Presumably, people who employ these logics are likely to be judged as more competent communicators than those drawn to more conventional and expressive design logics. These findings also suggest that persuaders who employ rhetorical design logics *may* be more influential in certain persuasion situations.

While these empirical findings appear to reinforce the legitimacy of the concept of message design logics, one should note that the participants in all of these investigations were undergraduate students enrolled in communication courses. It should come as little surprise that students enrolled in courses where one goal is to improve communication skills would perceive polished messages (i.e., those reflecting a rhetorical design logic) to be more competent, satisfying, and successful than the less developed messages that reflect an expressive design logic. Members of various social, cultural, and economic communities, however, may place a *higher* value on messages that are more direct expressions of their feelings and values. For example, B. J. O'Keefe, Lambert, and Lambert (1997) suggested that people who value direct, open expression of their thoughts and emotions may not react favorably to messages that attempt to reframe or negotiate social relationships through rhetorical methods.

All interpersonal influence situations involve at least two people, an influence agent (i.e., the person trying to persuade) and the target (i.e., the person being persuaded). Our discussion to this point and in the preceding chapter has focused almost exclusively on the influence agent. Comparatively speaking, relatively little research that we have discussed has dealt with the *target* of these influence attempts. When research *does* focus on the targets of persuasion efforts, it is generally to study how these individuals resist the attempts to influence them. We now turn our attention to that discussion.

RESISTING INFLUENCE ATTEMPTS

Research indicates that compliance-gaining strategies generally meet with success (Cody et al., 1994; Dillard, Anderson, & Knobloch, 2002). There are times, however, when the targets of influence messages simply do not *want* to comply with the influence agent's request. Put simply, there are going to be times when targets of influence messages actively wish to resist the would-be persuaders' efforts.

Most of the compliance-gaining research that we have covered has focused on the messages that participants send without necessarily considering the targets' responses. Compliance-*resistance* messages, on the other hand, are clearly part of the ongoing interaction between the two parties. The study of compliance-resistance messages presumes that there was a prior influence attempt to which the persuasive target is now responding. Moreover, the structure and content of the resistance message is likely to have an important impact on subsequent influence message attempts (if any) that the agent generates.

Consider the following example. Imagine that you are back in high school "hanging out" at a friend's house with a group of several friends and acquaintances. Some of these people are good friends of yours, while others are "friends of friends"—people that you don't know very well. You are having a good time when someone you don't know very well reaches into his or her backpack and pulls out a joint. The joint is lit, passed around, and handed to you. Assuming that you do not want to smoke pot, what do you do?

In situations where influence targets do not want to comply with a request, Ifert (2000) argued that there is a natural tension between the desire to comply and the desire to resist complying. The desire to comply likely stems, in part at least, from relational concerns and obligations. Ifert pointed out that compliance research (on both compliance resisting and compliance gaining) "assumes that, for the most part, a fairly intimate relationship exists between requester and request target" (p. 127). In our smoking pot example, the forces pushing for one's compliance might include the desire to maintain a positive relationship with your friends and to be viewed favorably by everyone present. The relational forces pushing targets toward compliance are particularly significant for influence messages related to drugs—in part, because most drug offers (including offers of alcohol) come from friends and thus are much more difficult for targets to refuse (Alberts, Miller-Rassulo, & Hecht, 1991).

On the other hand, the forces pushing influence targets toward resistance have generally been conceptualized in terms of obstacles to compliance (Ifert, 2000). Such obstacles could include not wanting to comply, not being able to comply, or not liking the person seeking compliance. In our smoking pot example, the primary obstacle to compliance might well be (as indicated above) that you are proud of your ability to resist using alcohol and other drugs up to this point in your life and you do not want to begin now.[1] We will have more to say about obstacles to compliance later, but for now they can be considered the key reasons why a person might not want to comply.

Our subject in this section is compliance-resistance research, beginning with a focus on compliance-resistance strategies. We then consider the major obstacles to compliance and their relation to politeness. Finally, we explore the research examining influence and resistance as it relates to adolescent drug use.

Compliance-Resisting Strategies

Following the lead of compliance-gaining researchers, scholars interested in compliance resistance initially developed several lists of verbal strategies that individuals could use to resist compliance (e.g., Alberts et al., 1991; McLaughlin, Cody, & Robey, 1980; see Ifert, 2000, for a detailed review of these typologies). As an example, consider the compliance-resistance strategy typology developed by McLaughlin and colleagues (1980). Based on previous research on conflict, they described five compliance-resistance strategies. *Nonnegotiation* refers to strategies where the target clearly and unequivocally refuses the influence attempt (e.g., "Just say 'No'"). *Identity management* strategies involve manipulating the identity of either the target or the requester (e.g., by flattering the influencing agent or by acting incompetent). *Justifying* strategies involve attempting to explain the reason for noncompliance by focusing on the positive or negative outcomes that compliance would generate for oneself (i.e., the target) or for others. *Negotiating* strategies involve the target's suggesting an alternative activity to the one specified by the requestor. Finally, *emotional appeals* are those strategies that directly involve affect (e.g., pleading or playing with the requestor's affection) (McLaughlin et al., 1980).

While the various lists of compliance-resisting strategies differ in several important respects (Ifert, 2000), they also contain numerous overlapping strategies. For example, the strategies of deception, withdrawal, justification, negotiation, and nonnegotiation are included in multiple typologies (Ifert, 2000). These typologies are helpful in identifying some of the common ways that people resist compliance. However, they are subject to several of the same problems associated with compliance-gaining typologies (e.g., Marwell & Schmitt, 1967; Wiseman & Schenck-Hamlin, 1981). Concerns over compliance-resistance typologies include (among other things) how representative and truly generalizable they are. Ifert (2000) argued that it may be impossible to create a category scheme that really includes all of the possible resistance strategies available to potential resistors in every situation (e.g., Kellermann & Cole, 1994).

Given that an "ideal" list of compliance-resisting strategies will likely never be agreed upon and that arguing about the merits of one typology over another rarely generates useful knowledge, several researchers have turned their attention from *how* people resist compliance toward the question of *why* people resist. As we noted above, many scholars consider this phenomenon under the label of "obstacles to compliance."

Obstacles Inhibiting Compliance

In order for one to comply with a message or request, the influence target must be both motivated and able to comply (Francik & Clark, 1985). In broad terms, then, people resist compliance because they lack either the motivation (i.e., the desire) or ability (i.e., means) to comply.

When influence attempts are rebuffed, the person refusing is generally expected to explain *why* he or she is not complying. Rather than creating lists of obstacles, research has attempted to identify the dimensions along which the obstacles differ (Ifert, 2000). For example, Wilson, Cruz, Marshall, and Rao (1993) argued that obstacles vary along three dimensions: stability, locus, and controllability. *Stability* refers to how permanent or temporary an obstacle is. *Locus* refers to the extent to which the obstacle is internal (to the target) or external. Finally, *controllability* refers to the extent to which the obstacle is under the target's control. For example, refusing a date because you find the other person unattractive is likely to be a stable, internal, and uncontrollable obstacle. Refusing a date because you are busy on the particular night that the person asked about, on the other hand, is unstable (temporary), external, and uncontrollable.

Even though obstacles inhibiting compliance can and do vary independently along these three dimensions, the obstacles that are actually expressed (i.e., the reasons or excuses given) tend not to use the full range of the continua. For example, in a study of date refusals, Folkes (1982) found that the reasons stated for refusing a date differed significantly from the real reasons for the rejection. Folkes reported that stated obstacles tended to be unstable ("I'm sorry, but I'm busy that night"), while unstated obstacles tended to be internal and stable ("I don't find you physically attractive"). Along a similar line, Ifert and Roloff (1994) found that students reported inability obstacles to a greater extent than they reported unwillingness obstacles.

In resisting influence attempts, people are more likely to provide some obstacles as stated reasons (or excuses) for refusals than they are to provide certain other reasons or excuses. Why might this be? One likely explanation for this finding is that some ways of refusing are seen as more polite than others. We argued above that, in making requests, there is generally a preference for developing influence messages that are polite. The same is true of resistance messages. Being polite while refusing a request is one way of managing the tension between the forces pushing toward compliance and those inclined toward refusal (Ifert, 2000). For example, Besson, Roloff, and Paulson (1998) reported that, even when a request for a date is directly refused, stated refusals contained apologies, statements of concern for the requester's feelings, and statements of appreciation. Thus, even though the date (i.e., influence attempt) is refused, the stated obstacles allow both parties to maintain face (i.e., positive identities).

While polite refusals may be easy to give (and to receive), they are somewhat problematic because they may be so indirect and take the requester's feelings into account to such an extent that they may be too ambiguous to be effective (Ifert, 2000). For example, Metts, Cupach, and Imahori (1992) found that one highly polite sexual rejection message indicated that the target was not ready to engage in sexual activity. This strategy was seen as being polite because it was comfortable to give and took the target's feelings into account. This same strategy, however, was ineffective because it suggested that the obstacle was unstable ("I'm not ready *right now*") and left the requester with the mistaken impression that sexual activity with the target might be possible in the future (Metts et al., 1992).

Resisting Drug Influence Messages

One important context where resisting influence messages is crucial is that of adolescent drug and alcohol use. Consider the smoking pot example we described earlier in this chapter. As we noted, this example represents a difficult situation because the target of the influence is likely caught between competing demands. As explained earlier, on the one hand, the obstacles to compliance are that the target may be proud of his or her ability to resist using alcohol and other drugs to this point in his or her life and does not want to start using them now. At the same time, the target doesn't want to alienate him- or herself from a group of friends and doesn't want to be evaluated negatively by them or others present. What does the target person do? How do individuals resist the peer pressure to take drugs while at the same time maintaining positive relationships with those around them?

Research has found that in many cases adolescents initially say "No" to a drug[2] offer (either to themselves or to the person offering) and then use the drug anyway (Miller, Alberts, Hecht, Trost, & Krizek, 2000; Trost, Langan, & Kellar-Guenther, 1999). Refusing a drug offer is particularly difficult for middle school and high school students who may not have developed the cognitive complexity necessary to develop and use effective resistance strategies. There are similarities between producing compliance messages and resisting them. First, both are communication phenomena (McLaughlin et al., 1980). In the drug scenario, it would be impossible to effectively refuse the drug offer without sending some message (even if it is to "just say 'No' "). Second, as suggested above, resisting influence messages can be described while invoking the same primary and secondary goals used in describing message production (Dillard, 1990a; McLaughlin et al., 1980; M. A. Miller et al., 2000). Applying Dillard's (1990a) terminology to the smoking pot example, the primary goal might be to resist the influence attempt (i.e., not to smoke pot). The secondary resistance goals in this case might be to still manage to maintain a positive relationship with others in the situation (particularly your good friends), still be seen as "cool," and yet maintain a drug-free identity. Dillard would refer to these secondary goals as resource and identity goals, respectively.

Reaching both the primary goal of resistance *and* the secondary goals of maintaining one's identity and relationships requires a delicate balancing act (Harrington, 1995; McLaughlin et al., 1980). According to M. A. Miller and colleagues (2000), "Competently maintaining relationships and sustaining a nonuse identity, while meeting one's instrumental goal of refusal, is a difficult task to assume" (p. 43). Strategies that are the most direct and effective ones in resisting the influence attempt might harm the relationship, while indirect and "relationship-friendly" strategies may prove ineffective in maintaining resistance.

Maintaining relationships is likely to be an important secondary resistance goal because most drug and alcohol use among adolescents consists in social activities—that is, something done with friends and romantic partners (M. A. Miller et al., 2000). Moreover, counter to certain stereotypes, relatively few drug offers actually come from total strangers (Alberts et al., 1991; Hecht, Trost, Bator, & MacKinnon, 1997; Trost et al., 1999). Same-sex friends are more likely to offer drugs than any other group (e.g., relatives, acquaintances, family members, or strangers). Drug offers from friends also are more likely to involve greater social pressure, as they likely occur in a social setting (e.g., at a party or other informal gathering) with several friends and acquaintances (Alberts et al., 1991; Hecht et al., 1997). Finally, a majority of respondents who indicated that they took drugs even though they did not want to indicated that they did so because of peer pressure or the acceptance of those who were around at the time (M. A. Miller et al., 2000).

The Nature of Drug Offers

Successful compliance resistance must begin by considering how the compliance was sought in the first place. Thus, to better understand the nature of drug resistance strategies, we need to consider how drug offers are made.

Most drug offers are initially simple; they generally involve either a simple request (e.g., "Want some [beer, pot, tobacco, etc.]?") or a nonverbal pass (e.g., being handed a joint without an attendant verbal offer). These simple initial requests tend to contain very little overt social pressure. Even though they apply at best very little social pressure, "a direct request challenges the target to construct a message that not only effectively resists the influence attempt, but pacifies the interaction partner as well" (M. A. Miller et al., 2000, p. 54).

Refusing an initial simple offer, however, rarely ends the episode (except in samples from junior high schools, where more complex offers are relatively rare; see Alberts et al., 1991). Following the initial refusal, the person offering is likely to respond with multiple repeated offers or even more elaborate counteroffers. Trost and colleagues (1999) observed that drug offer interactions contain numerous *types* of offers. More directly overt social pressure to take the drugs generally descends on one only *after* the first offer is refused. Once the first attempt is refused, the person offering is likely to come back with a more complex offer that contains more overt social pressure (particularly in high school and college-age samples; Alberts, Hecht, Miller-Rassulo, & Krizek, 1992).[3] The escalating nature of multiple drug offers clearly indicates that the advice once given to adolescents to "just say 'No' " may well prove ineffective, because it leaves them unprepared to resist the more complex, and potentially more persuasive, subsequent counteroffers.

Drug Resistance Messages

The escalating nature of drug offers indicates that an effective resistance strategy must include an explanation that appeases the person making the offer. Some strategies are likely to be ineffective because they do not directly focus on the secondary goals of relationship maintenance or one's nonuser identity. For example, if the person refusing explains that he simply does not "like" drugs, he may generate a negative reaction in the person offering, who is implicitly being painted in a negative light. By just indicating that he doesn't want to take the drug, the person's resistance efforts "may simply be seen as a weak response and an invitation for encouragement" (M. A. Miller et al., 2000, p. 59).

So, what is an effective drug resistance strategy? It is overly optimistic and simplistic to claim that a single message (or strategy type) will be effective in all resistance situations. Instead, what will be an effective resistance message almost certainly depends on the nature of the person refusing, the nature of the person offering, and their relationship. Moreover, the context within which the refusal is given (including what drug is being offered and how many other friends are around) also are likely to influence the effectiveness of a given resistance strategy.

There are individuals who can effectively refuse drug offers while at the same time maintaining their friendship with the person offering (Alberts et al., 1991). Given participants' own stories of successful refusals, M. A. Miller and colleagues (2000) developed the REAL system of refusing drug offers. The REAL system presents a series of escalating resistance messages that will likely match the escalating drug offers being made. The four steps in the REAL system are *R*efuse (a simple "No"), *E*xplain (repeat one's "No" but with an explanation), *A*void (avoid exposure to situations where drugs might be present), and *L*eave (leave the situation).

One key to producing an effective resistance strategy is to plan ahead. Alberts and colleagues (1991) found that individuals who were more motivated to resist drugs were more likely to plan their resistance behaviors before actually being subjected to an offer. Moreover, the extent to which individuals needed to plan subsequently was related to how effective their messages were. This observation is consistent with Dillard's GPA Model of compliance messages and suggests that waiting until a drug offer is actually made to develop an *ad hoc* strategy on the spot makes fashioning an effective resistance message more difficult.

SUMMARY

This chapter focused on the production and resistance of interpersonal influence messages. Using Dillard's theory of Goals, Plans, and Action, we first discussed the nature of social influence goals. Dillard asserts that primary goals (e.g., asking for a favor) define the nature of the influence attempt, while secondary goals serve to limit a source's options in message generation. Plans are produced in an effort to reach goals, and their complexity can be an important aspect of them, for better or worse. Research indicates that, while complex plans are more complete, they are also more difficult to present—particularly when the message source proves particularly uncooperative. Message presentation also depends upon the goals and plans previously developed, including the impressions that the message source wants to leave with his or her target(s).

We also discussed the research on resisting compliance messages. In this section, we focused primarily on studies dealing with refusing offers of alcohol and other drugs. The same primary and secondary goals outlined by Dillard (1990a) can be invoked in resistance situations as well. In this case, however, the primary goal is resistance while the secondary goals (particularly identity and relationship management) limit the number of viable resistance strategies. M. A. Miller and colleagues (2000) reported that while initial drug offers were simple and direct (e.g., "Wanna beer?"), subsequent offers following a refusal could well become more complex. Refusing the more complex counteroffers required a more complete and convincing explanation of why the offer was being refused. The more successful explanations included claiming a nonuser identity (e.g., "I'm not the sort of person who does that") and noting one's concern about potential consequences (e.g., fearing the highly unpredictable side effects or getting into trouble). The interactions involving offers, counteroffers, and refusals highlight the importance of the established relationship between the person offering the drugs and the person refusing them.

NOTES

1. This discussion of competing forces (both pro and con) over compliance can also be cast in terms of goals, as discussed earlier. In Dillard's (Dillard et al., 1989) terms, the primary goal in the smoking pot example would be to resist compliance (i.e., to *not* smoke pot), and the secondary resistance goals would likely be relational (i.e., maintain a positive relationship) and identity-related (i.e., maintain your identify as a non-drug user).

2. While offers can involve tobacco, alcohol, or other drugs, we will use the generic term *drug* from this point forward.

3. The observation that the second drug offer normally entails more overt social pressure than the first is consistent with what Hample and Dallinger (1998) call the "rebuff phenomenon": "When an initial persuasive effort is rebuffed, follow-up persuasive messages are ruder, more aggressive, and more forceful than the first one" (p. 305; see also Dillard et al., 2002).

CHAPTER 13

Persuasive Communication Campaigns

LOOKING AHEAD . . . This chapter discusses the role of persuasion theory in health promotion and political campaigns. It is beyond the scope of this book to provide a detailed overview of the research literature on persuasion campaigns. Indeed, many volumes have already been written on this subject (see, for example, Pfau & Parrott, 1993, and Rice & Atkin, 2013). Instead of providing a comprehensive review of the literature, this concluding chapter focuses on three distinct approaches to communication campaigns and examines the theory and methods underpinning each approach.

We begin this chapter with a discussion of some persuasive communication campaigns that have employed the various persuasion theories described earlier. We also examine the importance of personalizing persuasive appeals by using both the mass media and interpersonal modes of communication. Following this discussion, we describe certain campaigns predicated on Social Cognitive Theory (Akers, Krohn, Lanza-Kaduci, & Radosevich, 1979; Bandura, 1977, 1986) and review how that theory has been used to study behavior change in adolescents. We end with a discussion of how Inoculation Theory (McGuire, 1964) has been used to promote resistance to persuasion in political and anti-smoking campaigns.

PERSUASIVE COMMUNICATION CAMPAIGNS

Simons, Morreale, and Gronbeck (2001) define *persuasive communication campaigns* as "organized sustained attempts at influencing groups or masses of people through a series of messages" (p. 211). Barack Obama's 2008 and 2012 presidential campaigns represent recent examples of successful political campaigns; however, mass media campaigns are not always effective. While Barack Obama's campaigns produced substantial electoral college majorities for him, nonetheless hundreds of millions of dollars were spent on advertising campaigns for candidates—Democratic and Republican alike—who *lost* their elections (Dooling, 2012).

Health promotion campaigns have also found mass media-based campaigns to be an attractive avenue of persuasion. Anti-smoking, AIDS education, and driver safety campaigns routinely involve the heavy use of mass media to disseminate informational and motivational messages. The concept of a "designated driver" and the slogan "Friends don't let friends drive drunk" have become etched in memory owing to our repeated exposure to them over many years. Finally, of course, advertisers universally use persuasive communication campaigns to build brand awareness and loyalty for their clients' products and services.

While the mass media have become a staple of both health and political campaigns, it is often difficult to ascertain the effectiveness of specific persuasive messages in political campaigns. For example, Ross Perot's 1992 campaign for the presidency involved relatively few personal appearances or speeches before live audiences. Instead, he relied on television newscasts, appearances on talk shows, and paid commercial announcements to explain his economic proposals to American voters. Although Perot garnered nearly 19% of the national popular vote as a third-party candidate, it is difficult to determine how effective his media campaign truly was. Did he receive 19% of the popular vote *because* of his campaign messaging, or were disgruntled voters in the midst of a recession simply voicing displeasure with the establishment candidates from the Republican and Democratic parties? Indeed, the unique characteristics of every political campaign—ranging from the credibility of the candidates, the mood of the electorate, social and economic conditions, and the absence of a control or comparison group—make it difficult to empirically determine the effectiveness of political media campaigns.

In contrast, many health-related communication campaigns have been designed by communication scholars and health care professionals and subsequent studies have examined the effects of various message strategies. These studies have utilized appropriate control and comparison groups to permit unambiguous findings about the campaigns' effectiveness. Consequently, there is a sizable body of research on the effects of media campaigns on attitude and behavior change as they relate to health care topics and outcomes.

Stages of Persuasive Campaigns

Much of the persuasion research reviewed in this book has focused on persuasive appeals that involve a single message or short sequence of messages (like the *foot-in-the-door and door-in-the-face* techniques) that are intended to produce immediate effects. The short-term nature of these appeals is markedly different from the sustained efforts of communication campaigns. Successful communication campaigns typically represent structured sequences of messages developed from theories of communication or social psychology that are designed to generate particular outcomes. Throughout this book, we have described a number of theories that have been used extensively in health promotion campaigns, including the Theory of Reasoned Action (treated in Chapter 3), the Health Belief Model, the Protection Motivation Theory, and the Extended Parallel Processing Model (all treated in Chapter 8).

Persuasive communication campaigns that apply these theories typically involve developing and sending a series of messages over time that are designed to realize certain specific persuasive goals. These goals (and the messages designed to achieve them) may change over time, suggesting that persuasive communication campaigns go through a number of identifiable stages. The number and nature of these stages, however, likely depend on the type of campaign under consideration, such that a typology that works in one context won't necessarily work in another (Larson, 2001; Trent & Friedenberg, 2008).

The groundwork for Barack Obama's 2008 presidential campaign began when he gave the keynote speech at the 2004 Democratic National Convention. It was there that he first introduced himself to the country and began the long process of building name recognition. During its early stages, the unofficial Obama campaign was focused on creating awareness through informational messages including position papers, his book *The Audacity of Hope,* and media interviews. By early 2008, the now formalized campaign was focused on motivating his most ardent supporters to make campaign contributions and vote in the primaries. Later, during the general election, the campaign focused on reinforcing the attitudes of supporters and persuading undecided voters to vote for Barack Obama.

Similarly, health promotion campaigns typically involve several stages. For example, a campaign to promote healthy diet and exercise among college students might begin with a communication of the problem and the need for change. After creating awareness, the diet and exercise campaign might provide recommendations and incentives for students to adopt a healthy lifestyle. Once the adoption process was under way, the campaign might then focus on messages reinforcing the commitment to a healthier lifestyle. Thus, while there might be important differences between health and political campaigns, both types typically involve several stages that are designed to achieve specific goals that change over time.

Effectiveness of Mass Media Health Campaigns

Snyder and LaCroix (2013) define media campaigns as organized mass media activity that is directed at a target group for a specific period of time to achieve a stated goal (p. 113). Media campaigns can readily be distinguished from personal appeals that rely on one-on-one or small group interactions to achieve a particular goal.

During the past three decades, considerable research has been conducted to assess the overall effectiveness of mass media campaigns in promoting health-related behaviors (for a review, see Rice & Atkin, 2013). Given the complexity of the multiple tasks involved—including generating awareness about the problem, creating perceptions of self-efficacy, motivating targets to adopt a specific set of health recommendations, and accurately measuring health behaviors—evidence that many campaigns have generated only modest results should come as little surprise. Indeed, Snyder and LaCroix (2013) conducted a meta-analytic review of the health campaign literature that produced highly sobering findings, very small effect sizes among varied across media campaigns focused on reducing alcohol consumption (average $r = .11$ for adults, .07 for youths), smoking prevention and cessation (.03), HIV/STD prevention through condom use (.11), mammography screenings for breast cancer (.03), and healthy nutrition (.20 for reduced fat consumption, .13 for fruit and vegetable consumption).

Overall, these findings suggest that mass media campaigns have had only modest success. Pfau (2003) notes, however, that while "most health campaigns are flawed in design and execution," small effect sizes can actually reflect robust findings, given the "arduous task of altering established behaviors" (p. 448). In this regard, small effect sizes can be substantively important when considering the effects of health promotion campaigns involving a very large number of message receivers. Under these circumstances, even a small percentage change means that a lot of people have been influenced.

One of the primary limitations of traditional health communication campaigns is that they rely on single theories that are applied to large groups of people and ignore important differences among target audiences. Weinstein, Rothman, & Sutton (1998) classified many of the most common health behavior theories—including the Theory of Reasoned Action (Fishbein & Ajzen, 1975); the Theory of Planned Behavior (Ajzen & Madden,

1986), the Health Belief Model (Janz & Becker, 1984), the Protection Motivation Theory (Maddux & Rogers, 1983), and the Subjective Expected Utility Model (Ronis, 1992)—as *continuum theories* whose approach is to identify variables that influence action and then combine those variables in a predictive equation. Weinstein and colleagues (1998) note that "when applied to a particular individual, the value generated by the equation indicates the probability that a person will act" (p. 291). Essentially, this notion seems to assume that everyone is alike and that everyone will respond to the message in pretty much the same way.

Bandura (2000) has criticized this "one-size-fits-all" approach by emphasizing that many campaigns are ineffective because they fail to *customize* their messages based upon the target audience's particular characteristics. Hawkins and colleagues (Hawkins, Kreuter, Resnicow, Fishbein, & Dijkstra, 2008) defined *customization* as the amount of audience segmentation utilized in creating messages. Although the degree of personalization could create a broad continuum with many gradations, research typically considers three types of messages (e.g., Kreuter et al., 1999).

First, *general or mass appeals* have very little customization because little or no audience segmentation is performed. In these cases, the same message is disseminated to and received by a large audience. For example, a high school principal might send an email message to every graduating senior to encourage him or her to spend extra time studying for final exams.

Second, *group targeted* messages involve a moderate degree of audience segmentation. In this case, appeals are modified to match the experiences, attitudes, and motives of people in a particular group, usually defined by at least one demographic variable (e.g., age or sex or medical condition; Kreuter et al., 1999). Extending the high school example, a principal might send a targeted message to students in a particular class (like chemistry or business), encouraging them to study for their exam (given that it had proved particularly difficult in the past).

Third, *individually tailored* messages require a high degree of audience segmentation, as they are personalized to match the individual receiver's unique experiences, attitudes, and motives. Extending the high school testing example a bit further, a principal might send email messages to specific students who had worked hard to improve their grades and were currently awaiting word on their financial aid applications for college—again, to urge them to study even harder for their exams.

Are You *Ready* to Change?

Targeting and tailoring persuasive messages are important because there are important differences among message receivers. One important difference is the extent to which receivers *want to change*. Weinstein et al. (1998) recognized that people differ in their readiness for change—cognitively, emotionally, and behaviorally—and in how *quickly* they move from one stage of readiness to another. Two different phase models—the Transtheoretical Model of Behavior Change (Prochaska, DiClemente, & Norcross, 1992) and the Precaution Adoption Process Model (Weinstein, 1988)—distinguish between people who have not yet decided to change their behavior, those who have decided to change but have not yet done so, and those who are already changing (Weinstein et al., 1998, p. 292). Prochaska and colleagues (1992) initially developed a five-stage model for recovery from addictive behaviors. The first stage is *precontemplation,* or where the person has not considered changing the addictive (or other problematic) behavior. At the second stage, *contemplation,* the person becomes aware that a problem exists and begins thinking about addressing it (but doesn't actually do anything about it). In the third step, *preparation,* the individual develops an intention to take action to change his or her behavior. In the fourth stage, *action,* the individual takes concrete steps to change the behavior. Finally, in the fifth stage, *maintenance,* steps are taken to reinforce the change and prevent a relapse back to the original problematic behavior.[1]

Applied to the promotion of health behaviors or to political campaigns, these models suggest that a persuasive campaign's messaging should be tailored to the particular stage in the change sequence that the target occupies. Messages that appeal to persons in one stage of the change process are unlikely to be equally persuasive for those in other stages. For example, a message on the health benefits of smoking cessation may be best designed to convince a smoker in the *precontemplation* stage to think about quitting smoking, but it is unlikely to have much incremental persuasive effect for someone in the *preparation* stage who has already *decided* to quit smoking but has yet to take any concrete action.

Research conducted by Ockene, Ockene, and Kristeller (1988) provides evidence for the importance of tailoring message interventions to the receivers' stages of change. The researchers developed an intensive smoking cessation campaign focused on moving receivers to the action and maintenance stages of change. Their results indicated that the campaign was much more effective for smokers in the action and preparation stages than for those in the precontemplation and contemplation stages. Twenty-two percent of the smokers who were in the *precontemplation* stage when the program began were not smoking 6 months later; 43% of those who were in the *contemplation* stage were not smoking 6 months later; and 76% of those who were in the *action* stage when the program was administered were not smoking 6 months later (Ockene et al., 1988). These findings provide clear support for the supposition that the patient's stage of acceptance had a significant impact on the relative persuasiveness of the action- and maintenance-focused messages in the smoking cessation program.

Cho and Salmon (2006) applied the Transtheoretical Model and the Extended Parallel Processing Model to the study of fear appeals. Kim Witte's EPPM (1992, 1994; see Chapter 8) posits that fear appeals can have unintended effects (what she called fear control outcomes) when the perceived threat is stronger than the perceived efficacy. This is important because Cho and Salmon (2006) hypothesized that one of the things that happens as people progress from the precontemplation stage through the maintenance stage is that perceptions of both self-efficacy and response efficacy increase. In short, people believe more strongly that they can quit smoking and that doing so will reduce their chances of being stricken with cancer and other smoking-related diseases in the future.

Because the EPPM posits that high-threat messages are likely more effective when people have perceptions of self-efficacy, Cho and Salmon (2006) hypothesized that high-threat messages would be most effective for targets in the later stages of change and less effective for those who were in the early stages of the change process. Specifically, the two researchers tested these hypotheses in a study of fear appeals promoting the use of sunscreen to prevent skin cancer. They examined the effect of the messages on people in the precontemplation, contemplation, and action stages of cutting back on tanning themselves. The findings were consistent with both the Transtheoretical Model and the EPPM. After exposure to a high-threat message, people in the *precontemplative* stage reported less favorable attitudes and less intention to change behavior than people in the *contemplative* stage who, in turn, expressed less favorable attitudes and intention to change than people in the *action* stages. In other words, people in the earlier stages of the change process were more likely to reject than accept the fear appeal. In contrast, those in the later stages of change were more likely to adopt the message recommendations.

The most obvious and direct implication of this body of research is the apparent need for one to assess the given target's relative readiness for change based on the stage and then tailor the persuasive messages and interventions accordingly (Prochaska et al., 1992, p. 1110). Persuasive campaigns that fail to consider audience members' stages of change and then *customize* their message strategies accordingly are likely to produce disappointing results. Indeed, this lack of specificity in many persuasive campaigns may account for the relatively small persuasive effects observed.[2]

Tailored Message Appeals

In addition to differences among persuasive targets and their readiness for accepting behavior change, and designing messages that correspond with these stages of change, campaign experts have recognized the importance of *tailoring* persuasive appeals to the specific individual characteristics of the target audience. Bandura (2000) criticized persuasive communication campaigns as "costly, cumbersome, and minimally effective" (p. 316) because they ignore that the people being targeted differ on a wide variety of factors like personal needs, risk factors, and current health status. Even among people who are all at the same stage of change (i.e., contemplation), there are likely other important differences among them that will affect the persuasiveness of a message appeal.

If persuasive campaigns rely on a uniform set of messages to appeal to a mass audience, or even a targeted group at the same stage of change (e.g., contemplation), they are essentially adopting the "one-size-fits-all" perspective that Bandura (2000) criticized. Put simply, a single set of messages cannot effectively resonate equally effectively with all members of a diverse audience. What is needed instead are persuasive campaigns where messages can be varied to fit the audience's unique situation and needs.

DeBusk and colleagues (1994) discuss just such a program. They focused on helping hospital patients recover from their heart attack. While still in the hospital, participants were given detailed training on how to change their diet, develop an exercise program, and reduce their weight and cholesterol levels. Using a computer-based system, DeBusk et al. allowed their participants to focus on the particular outcomes they felt were important and to set their own short-term attainable goals. The participants kept in contact with a single program administrator, who then provided them with detailed feedback on the outcomes that they had chosen and "individually-tailored guides for self-directed change" (Bandura, 2000, p. 316). Results of the DeBusk and colleagues (1994) study indicated that participants in the individualized promotion program had more positive health outcomes than participants in the control condition (who received only the typical physician-based care). Specifically, the former group members were more likely to have stopped smoking, had lower cholesterol levels, and had more efficient heart functioning than the latter ones in the control group.

One major advantage of the individualized program is that patients self-manage their recovery from major illness. "The self-management approach, therefore, serves as a generic model that can be adapted to different chronic diseases" (Bandura, 2000, p. 324). Informing patients about the benefits of health-related behaviors and allowing them to choose which behaviors to focus on helps to provide the motivation and self-efficacy needed for significant behavior change. Bandura (2000) provides several examples of focused persuasive communication campaigns that have been successfully implemented.

Summarizing the Tailored-Messages Literature

Two meta-analytic reviews have produced somewhat inconsistent findings. The first one, undertaken by Snyder and LaCroix (2013), reviewed the literature focused on examining the effectiveness of mass media, interpersonal, and the combination of mass media and interpersonal interventions in promoting a wide variety of health behaviors. Their meta-analysis revealed that mass media campaigns were most effective for certain topics (HIV/STD prevention, mammography), while a combination of mass media and customized interpersonal appeals were most persuasive for other topics (e.g., youth substance abuse prevention, adult alcohol abuse, nutrition, and smoking cessation). The finding that mass media messages are sometimes more effective than the combination of mass media plus interpersonal appeals is inconsistent with Bandura's (2000) critique of one-size-fits-all approaches. Snyder and LaCroix (2013) noted that the examination of mass media or interpersonal messages to promote health behaviors should take into account the proper match between goals, necessary content, and the cost of a campaign.

Similarly, Lustria and colleagues (2013) performed a meta-analytic review of studies assessing the effectiveness of personally tailored health behavior interventions. The health intervention studies that were included in their review used a computer algorithm that tailored message appeals, delivered the intervention content over the Internet by using emails and websites, and evaluated at least one health behavior. Lustria and colleagues found that personally tailored web-based interventions had a significantly greater effect on health behavior outcomes than nontailored web-based interventions. Moreover, the effectiveness of these interventions persisted, with no observable decay effects over time (p. 1056).

The inconsistent findings from these two meta-analyses suggest that much work still remains to be done to more fully understand the circumstances under which personally tailored messages are more effective than less precisely targeted ones aimed at a larger group (and the theoretical mechanisms that would account for the differences).

In recent years, the use of mass media and tailored messages has also become a staple of political campaigns. In 2012, both President Obama and Mitt Romney used a combination of mass media messages and microtargeting strategies by creating individually tailored messages to appeal to individual voters. In these days of unlimited PAC donations, some candidates appear to have concluded that a barrage of advertising messages that blanket the airways for months before election day may help to introduce and define their candidacy. Nonetheless, many scholars remain convinced that personalized appeals are an important key to motivating voting behavior (McCoy, 2012).

BOX 13.1. Microtargeting in Political Campaigns

Consumers have known for some time that companies like Amazon, Google, and Facebook collect, use, and sell personal information about them to companies for marketing purposes. Purchase a book from Amazon and you will receive immediate online recommendations of other books you might like. Use Google to search for a place to hang out during spring break and you will soon see pop-up ads for cruise companies and resorts. Not surprisingly, the practice of targeting advertisements to people with particular interests has rapidly spread to political campaigns.

In 2008, Barack Obama gained a considerable advantage through the use of such social media platforms as Facebook to communicate directly with voters, gather information, and raise money through millions of small donations. By the time of the 2012 elections, advances in social media and computer technology had enabled campaigns to suddenly rely heavily on microtargeting.

For years, political campaigns used public voting records to make decisions about persuasive activities. Armed with information about party affiliation and voting history, canvassers would knock on doors in neighborhoods where there was the greatest opportunity for success. Information that one resident on a block is a regular voter and a registered Republican, for example, while her neighbor is a sporadic voter and a registered Democrat enables campaigns to make decisions about which voters to target in an effort to encourage early voting.

Microtargeting takes this process of targeting messages based on potential voters' salient characteristics to a much higher level of sophistication. While microtargeting played a relatively small role prior to 2008, by 2012 both presidential campaigns were investing heavily in computer programs designed to mine information from many sources to learn more about individual voters. Once the infrastructure is established, analysts identify trends and calibrate messages to appeal to individual voters. If the Obama campaign learned that a particular voter in Ohio was a pro-life Catholic union member, it would leave him off email blasts related to abortion rights and develop messages emphasizing Obama's role in saving the auto industry through the federal government's quick action on bankruptcy proceedings and needed financial aid (Murphy, 2012).

Political marketing companies nowadays develop toolkits that enable candidates to use the social media to send video messages and advertisements to people with specific interests and characteristics. These microtargeting strategies are now a common feature of national political campaigns (for reviews, see Brennan, 2012; Gavett, 2012; Murphy, 2012). These efforts are akin to the personalized persuasive message appeals described in the literature on both health care and political persuasion campaigns.

Thus far, we have focused on the level of customization in campaign messages and have summarized the research on the effectiveness of broad-based appeals—that is, those that are targeted at groups of message receivers who share similar characteristics—as well as messages that are tailored to the personal experiences of individual message receivers. Largely absent from this discussion has been a focus on theoretical perspectives that may guide the development and implementation of persuasive campaigns.

In previous chapters we described a number of theoretical perspectives that have been effectively applied to persuasive campaigns, including the Elaboration Likelihood Model (Chapter 5), the Health Belief Model (Chapter 8), and the Extended Parallel Processing Model (Chapter 8). Two theoretical perspectives, Social Cognitive Theory and Inoculation Theory, that also have been used effectively in communication campaigns have yet to be discussed. Thus, the next section of this chapter describes the use of Social Cognitive Theory to promote health and safety initiatives in adolescents, and the final section examines the use of Inoculation Theory in preparing people to resist persuasive appeals.

SOCIAL COGNITIVE THEORY

Although its application has proved very effective in persuasive contexts, Social Cognitive Theory (Bandura, 1977, 1986, 2011) was developed as a general model of behavior acquisition (initially called Social Learning Theory) and has expanded into a more general theory of human functioning (Bandura, 2001). Social learning remains an important component of the theory, and, as a consequence, remains an important model from which to develop persuasive communication campaigns (Bandura, 2000, 2011).

Social Cognitive Theory has been particularly relevant to the study of mass media social influence. As Bandura (1977) pointed out, "An influential source of social learning is the abundant and varied symbolic modeling provided by television, films, and other visual media" (p. 39). This modeling can have positive or negative consequences. For example, there are those who argue that media depictions of violence produce aggressive behavior (see, e.g., Gunter, 1994). On the positive side, Social Cognitive Theory has provided the conceptual foundation for many health-related communication campaigns.

We begin the discussion of this theory by describing its major assumptions. Then, we examine tests of the theory and describe persuasive campaigns in which it has been effectively applied.

Social Learning

Before discussing this theory's applicability to social influence campaigns, we should understand its fundamental assumptions and its predictions about learning behavior. Many early learning theories posited that behavior acquisition or change in an individual is a function of the positive reinforcement provided when a desired behavior is produced as well as punishments provided following undesirable behavior (e.g., Skinner, 1938). Given this perspective, humans and animals learn behavior by pairing performance of a particular behavior with the outcomes (i.e., rewards or punishments) that it generates. For example, when parents teach their children to read, they routinely provide verbal praise when a word or letter is properly pronounced. When a word, phrase, or sound is incorrectly pronounced, the error is noted and assistance is provided to help the child pronounce it correctly. Over time, the child learns the correct pronunciation because it has been associated with positive reinforcement. This learning process takes time and occurs "over a number of 'trials' in which the link between the stimuli and the response to be learned is reinforced" (DeFleur & Ball-Rokeach, 1989, p. 216).

Social Cognitive Theory (Bandura, 1977, 1986) differs from early learning theories in that it emphasizes the capacity of humans to also learn through *observation* instead of strictly through one's own trial and error. Observational learning is vital for both development and survival. Because mistakes can produce costly—or even fatal—consequences, the prospects for survival would be slim indeed if one could learn only by suffering the consequences of trial and error. For this reason, one does not teach children to swim, adolescents to drive automobiles, and novice medical students to perform surgery by having them discover the appropriate behavior through the consequences of their successes and failures. The more costly and hazardous the possible mistakes, the heavier the reliance on observational learning from competent examples (Bandura, 1977, p. 12).

In addition, some behaviors cannot be learned through trial and error alone. For example, adults and older children, who constantly provide a model for children to mimic, facilitate a child's language acquisition and development. In other cases, observational learning provides the benefit of experience that cannot be acquired through trial and error. For example, high-risk activities such as skydiving and bungee jumping may not allow participants to recover from an error. In this regard, Social Cognitive Theory is ideal for persuasive campaigns that promote resistance to high-risk behaviors such as drug use and drunk driving.

Social Cognitive Theory and Social Influence

The fundamental assumption of Social Cognitive Theory is that by observing others, an individual forms an idea of how new behaviors are performed as well as how those new behaviors are rewarded or punished. On later occasions, this information serves as a guide for the observer's own behavior (Bandura, 1977, p. 22). Observing the positive and negative consequences of a model's behavior serves several functions in the social cognitive process.[3] First, this observation provides information about the consequences that are associated with particular behaviors. Thus, the *information function* allows people to develop and test hypotheses about which responses are most appropriate and most likely to be rewarded in particular situations. Second, observation of a model's behavior serves a *motivation function* by establishing a value (either positive or negative) for the behavior and an incentive (or disincentive) to enact it. Finally, observation serves a *reinforcement function* by strengthening the connection between behaviors and outcomes that have already been learned (Bandura, 1977, p. 17). Observational learning is effective to the extent that it causes people to anticipate the consequences of a particular behavior and establishes an incentive for learners to receive the positive consequences of behavior and a disincentive to avoid the negative ones.

There are several stages of effective observational learning in mass media contexts. First, a target person *observes* a model engaging in a particular behavior. Second, the observer *identifies* with the model. Third, the observer *realizes* that the observed behavior will produce a desired result. Fourth, the observer *remembers* the actions of the model and *reproduces* the relevant behavior in appropriate situations. Fifth, the modeled behavior is actually *reinforced*. Reinforcement increases the probability that the behavior will be repeated (DeFleur & Ball-Rokeach, 1989, pp. 216–217).

Consistent with these stages of modeling, Bandura (1977) identified several factors that affect the extent to which people learn behavior through observation. For example, the rate and amount of observational learning is determined in part by the nature of the modeled behaviors: the more complex the behavior, the less likely it will be modeled effectively. For example, while it may be relatively easy for adolescents to model drug resistance behavior by viewing such behavior on an instructional video, it is much more difficult for them to learn to drive by watching a parent engage in the behavior. In this regard, applications of Social Cognitive Theory in persuasion campaigns often include a skills training component.

Many campaigns based on Social Cognitive Theory that involve developing new skills highlight the importance of self-efficacy in observational learning. We addressed self-efficacy in our discussion of fear appeals in Chapter 8. Fear appeal theorists borrowed Bandura's concept of self-efficacy because they found it useful in explaining the cognitive processing of fear appeals (e.g., Rogers, 1983; Witte, 1992). Bandura (2000) defined *self-efficacy* as "beliefs in one's capabilities to organise and execute the courses of action required to promote given levels of attainment" (p. 300).

For example, when applied to safe-sex behaviors, a person with high self-efficacy is more likely to talk to his or her sexual partners about engaging in safe-sex practices and acts assertively in behavior that leads to condom usage. On the other hand, individuals with low self-efficacy regarding safe-sex behaviors are unlikely to successfully persuade their partner to use a condom if their partner objects to doing so (Perloff, 2001). Consistent with this view, researchers have found that skills training is an essential component of effective drug resistance campaigns targeted at adolescents (M. A. Miller et al., 2000; Rohrbach, Graham, Hansen, Flay, & Johnson, 1987). While self-efficacy generally focuses on behavior, it might also involve focusing on an individual's motivations, thoughts, or feelings (Bandura, 2000).

In addition to observing and learning to perform a desired behavior, *differential reinforcement* serves to motivate people to enact the behavior they have learned. Differential reinforcement occurs when models are rewarded for performing desired behaviors and when they are punished or left unrewarded for performing undesired behaviors. Over time, observers learn to match the performance of desired behaviors with the positive reinforcements and undesired behaviors with less favorable outcomes. This matching process motivates observers to enact desired behaviors once they have been acquired. Bandura (1977, p. 37) argued that the anticipated benefits of a particular behavior can strengthen what has been learned observationally by motivating people to rehearse modeled behavior that they value highly.

Supporting Evidence

Research has repeatedly found that children and adults acquire attitudes, emotional responses, and new styles of conduct through film and TV modeling (Bandura, 1973, 1977, 2000; Liebert, Neale, & Davidson, 1973). As previous examples indicate, the Social Cognitive Model has been applied to investigations of adolescent drinking and driving (DiBlasio, 1986, 1987) and adolescent sexual behavior (DiBlasio & Benda, 1990), among other topics (Bandura, 2000). Based on a Social Cognitive Model of deviant behavior (Akers et al., 1979), DiBlasio (1986) argued that "social behavior is understood through studying the impact of differential association with adults and peers, internalization of group norms (normative definitions), modeling, and the combination of positive and negative reinforcement (differential reinforcement)" (p. 175).

Akers and his colleagues (1979) examined the role of five theoretical factors in the social learning process. *Differential association* is defined as the respective levels of approval from adults and peers that a particular behavior generates. For example, a college student who rides with someone driving under the influence of alcohol might receive a different approval level from his peers than from his parents.

Group norms reflect community (or peer) social standards and laws concerning people's behavior as well as the person's willingness to obey them. In the context of drinking and driving, group norms reflect the attitudes of one's friends, family, coworkers, and the wider community toward these behaviors.

Combined differential reinforcement reflects the perceived rewards versus costs of engaging in a particular behavior. Adolescents may perceive that drinking and driving is convenient and one way to gain acceptance from peers, but these benefits might be offset by the consequences of an accident or anticipated feelings of guilt. When perceived rewards outweigh anticipated costs, the behavior is more likely to be performed, and vice versa.

Differential social reinforcement reflects the social praise and negative reactions of others. For adolescent drivers, praise from parents and peers for avoiding DUI infractions combined with the negative reactions of peers and parents to DUI offenses serves to reinforce adolescents' decisions to abstain from drinking and driving.

Finally, *modeling* occurs by observing others who either engage in or abstain from a particular behavior. Because parents serve as important role models for their children, adolescents who watch their parents drive after drinking may be inclined to model that errant behavior. In addition, sports and music personalities who participate in DUI prevention campaigns may also serve as positive role models for adolescents.

A consistent pattern of findings has emerged from the many investigations of this model's predictive powers (DiBlasio, 1986, 1987; DiBlasio & Benda, 1990; see Table 13.1). For example, in a study of adolescent drinking and driving, DiBlasio (1986) found that all five of the theoretical factors in Akers and colleagues' (1979) Social Learning Model were significantly related to driving under the influence or riding with others who are doing so. Combined, these five theoretical factors accounted for more than half of adolescent decisions regarding driving under the influence and riding with drivers who were under the influence. A subsequent study of adolescent sexual behavior (DiBlasio & Benda, 1990) produced similar results. In this study, four of the five theoretical factors were employed, and each was significantly related to sexual activity. Combined, these four factors accounted for 40% of the variance in the frequency of adolescent sexual intercourse.

These results clearly indicate that the constructs developed from Social Cognitive Theory accurately depict the forces that influence behavioral intentions. Moreover, DiBlasio (1986) concluded that these findings were consistent with prior studies that found one's peer group was the most

TABLE 13.1. Multiple Correlation Coefficients for the Theoretical Factors in the Social Learning Model

| | Adolescent behavior | | |
| | Study 1 | | Study 2 |
Theoretical predictors	DUI	Riding	Sex
1. Differential association	.66	.62	.54
2. Group norms	.52	.50	.41
3. Combined differential reinforcement	.44	.33	.50
4. Differential social reinforcement	.35	.30	NA
5. Modeling	.37	.44	.28
Total variance explained by theoretical factors	.56	.52	.40

Note. DUI = driving under the influence of alcohol; Riding = riding with a person operating a vehicle under the influence of alcohol; Sex = sexual intercourse; Study 1 = DiBlasio (1986); Study 2 = DiBlasio and Benda (1990); NA = not available.

influential group in the lives of adolescents (Alexander & Campbell, 1966; Jessor & Jessor, 1977); that reinforcement is an important determinant of behavior (Bandura, 1969; Wodarski & Bagarozzi, 1979); and that observation of adult and peer models contributes to driving under the influence and riding with drivers under the influence (DiBlasio, 1986, p. 186). Findings from these studies provide strong evidence of social learning and its significant influence on behavior. Unlike learning by doing, which requires repeated experience by individuals, social learning occurs by observing others and recognizing the positive and negative reinforcements associated with their behavior (Bandura, 1977).

Application of Social Cognitive Theory

The success of these models suggests that Social Cognitive Theory provides an excellent foundation for persuasion campaigns targeted at adolescents. Rather than focusing on each theoretical predictor variable, research projects have attempted to determine the effectiveness of an overall program based on Social Cognitive Theory.

As we have noted, one important problem that adolescents experience is peer pressure to smoke. Adolescent smoking is a social phenomenon. More than one-half of cigarettes smoked by adolescents are smoked in the presence of another teen or an adult (Biglan, McConnell, Severson, Bavry, & Ary, 1984). Over the years, a number of persuasion campaigns have been implemented to promote resistance to smoking. For the most part, these campaigns rely on school-based educational programs and mass media

(Flay, 1986, 1987). Given the social nature of adolescent smoking and the importance of peer pressure, group norms, and social reinforcement in the aforementioned studies, Social Cognitive Theory has served as a foundation for many smoking prevention campaigns.

One campaign tested the effectiveness of a refusal-skills training program for over 1,500 junior high and high school students. Mirroring the essential elements of Social Cognitive Theory, this program included instruction on specific skills for refusing cigarettes, the modeling of effective refusals, behavior rehearsal, teacher and peer reinforcement for refusal behavior, and practice (Biglan et al., 1987, p. 618). Videotaped presentations were used extensively to provide instruction on refusal skills and examples of effective refusals. Nine months after the intervention, adolescent smokers who participated in the refusal-skills training program reported significantly less smoking and had significantly lower biological readings of smoking (carbon monoxide in saliva) than students in the control condition.

However, interestingly, students who were originally *nonsmokers* and who received the refusal-skills training reported significantly higher levels of smoking on the posttest than nonsmokers in the control condition. Yet, the biochemical measures revealed no significant differences between these groups. This finding underscores the importance of targeted persuasive messages for people in specified stages of change (described earlier in this chapter). Clearly, the refusal-skills training for nonsmokers had an unintended consequence, namely, it caused them to report that they were smoking more even though the biological measures suggested otherwise. That is, the intervention caused unintended consequences for nonsmokers because the training was designed for smokers.

Despite this finding, the overall results of this investigation indicate that a refusal-skills training program consistent with Social Cognitive Theory was effective in reducing smoking among adolescents. Other skills training programs have proved equally effective in promoting long-term resistance to smoking among adolescents (Leupker, Johnson, Murray, & Pechacek, 1983; Schinke & Gilchrist, 1984). In addition, Domel and colleagues (1993) reported on the effectiveness of a program based on Social Cognitive Theory that was designed for fourth- and fifth-grade students to consume more fruits and vegetables. The program proved effective for increasing consumption of fruits but not vegetables.

Research has demonstrated the powerful impact that learning theories can have when applied to advertising and other mass media campaigns. Social Cognitive Theory underscores the human capacity to learn through observation and describes how people acquire integrated patterns of behavior without having to develop them gradually through tedious trial and error (Bandura, 1977, p. 12). However, some behaviors, such as communicative strategies for refusing drugs, alcohol, and cigarettes, are sufficiently complex that they can only be acquired through modeling and rehearsal. Taken together, the findings from these studies suggest that communication campaigns that combine modeling peer group behavior, communication skills training, the rehearsal of acquired skills, and reinforcement are effective in promoting behavior change.

While Social Cognitive Theory focuses on the learning and reinforcement of new behaviors, Inoculation Theory (McGuire, 1964) has been applied to promote resistance to persuasive appeals in political and health care contexts. The final section of this chapter describes Inoculation Theory and how it has been employed as a strategy for resisting persuasion.

INOCULATION THEORY

During the early 1960s, William McGuire developed a program of research that investigated resistance to persuasive messages. He was interested in understanding the psychological and cognitive processes that affect a person's willingness and motivation to resist arguments that attack widely held beliefs. McGuire called these types of beliefs *cultural truisms*, or beliefs that are thought to be true among a vast majority of members of a particular culture (e.g., "You should brush your teeth at least twice a day" and "Mental illness is not contagious"). Cultural truisms are interesting to study because they are rarely challenged or given much thought.

A Biological Metaphor

McGuire (1961a, 1961b, 1964, 1999) described a technique for inducing resistance to persuasive attacks against cultural truisms. Inoculation Theory posits that promoting resistance to persuasion is analogous to inoculating the body against a virus. When people are inoculated against a virus, such as smallpox or the flu, the vaccine they receive contains a weak dosage of the virus itself. In response to the inoculation, the body's immune system creates antibodies to fight the virus. If the body's immune system is functioning properly, the initial attack of the weak virus leaves the body better prepared to attack stronger, naturally occurring, infections from the same virus strain.

Applied in persuasive situations, the inoculation metaphor suggests that, because cultural truisms are widely believed, they are rarely scrutinized or given much attention. Such beliefs are often vulnerable to persuasive attacks because people "have had little motivation or practice in developing supporting arguments to bolster [them] or in preparing refutations for the unsuspected counterarguments" (McGuire & Papageorgis, 1961,

p. 327). McGuire's inoculation technique was designed to prepare people to resist attacks against cultural truisms. Analogous to the way in which a vaccine works, inoculation against persuasive arguments involves presenting people with weak arguments against a cultural belief and allowing receivers to develop stronger arguments to refute these attacks. McGuire and Papageorgis (1961) proposed that "the 'supportive therapy' approach of pre-exposing a person to arguments in support of [a] belief has less immunizing effectiveness than the 'inoculation' procedure of pre-exposing them to weakened, defense stimulating forms of the counterarguments" (p. 327). Presumably, after receiving weak counterarguments and the opportunity to construct a defense against them, people are better prepared and more motivated to counterargue with future stronger attacks on these cultural truisms.

Persuasive Inoculation

The basic procedure for inoculating people against persuasive attacks involves providing them with a message containing weak arguments that attacks a particular belief. People are then asked to generate arguments that refute the arguments contained in the attack message. Sometimes inoculation procedures involve presenting people with the refutations (passive refutation) instead of asking them to generate their own refutations (active refutation). For example, if you wanted to inoculate schoolchildren against persuasive appeals to try drugs, you might present them with a series of weak arguments supporting drug use and then ask them to write an essay (active refutation) refuting the arguments advocating drug use that they had just heard. You could also inoculate students by presenting them with a weak message advocating drug use and then ask them to read a second message that refuted the arguments advocating drug use (passive refutation).

Once the inoculation procedure has been performed, people who have been inoculated should be less susceptible to future attacks on their beliefs than people who did not experience inoculation. To test the effectiveness of this technique, researchers usually conduct an experiment in which an inoculation treatment (an attack message on the cultural truism followed by a refutation message) is presented to people in the experimental group, while people in the control condition receive a message supportive of the cultural truism (or no message at all). After some time has passed, people in the experimental and control groups are exposed to a message containing stronger arguments that attack their beliefs about the issue in question. Following this second attack message, the attitudes or beliefs of experimental and control group participants are measured. If the attitudes or beliefs about the issue in question are more favorable among the experimental group than among the control group, then the inoculation treatment is

---

BOX 13.2. Refutational Arguments in the Courtroom

Many attorneys are reluctant to use refutation arguments during opening statements and closing arguments because they fear that such arguments will lend credence to the opposition's case and ultimately undermine the credibility of their own arguments. However, Jim routinely encourages attorneys to use such arguments, because they can help accomplish three goals. First, refutation arguments encourage jurors to counter-argue positions advocated by opposing counsel and prepare jurors to be effective advocates for the preferred position during deliberations. Second (and consistent with our discussion of credibility assessment in Chapter 6), jurors want to know that attorneys have fairly considered the issues in the case and that they are not withholding key information in their presentation of the evidence. Jurors are critical of attorneys whenever they conclude that one has withheld important information from them. In other words, jurors expect that attorneys will discuss all of the relevant issues, and a failure to do so diminishes their credibility. Third, if the refutation arguments are part of the plaintiff's opening statement, they effectively preview the position that will be advocated by the defense counsel during the case. Previewing the opposing side's strongest arguments diminishes the novelty of those arguments when they are presented by opposing counsel. Thus, the use of refutation arguments prepares jurors to become effective advocates, enhances the credibility of the attorney, and diminishes the novelty of the opposing side's presentation.

---

deemed effective for promoting resistance to a persuasive attack. Extending the example of promoting resistance to drugs, if children who receive the inoculation treatment are better able to resist subsequent invitations to use drugs than children who do not receive the inoculation treatment, we can conclude that the inoculation treatment was effective.

Supporting Evidence

In an initial test of this technique, McGuire and Papageorgis (1961) examined beliefs about a number of cultural truisms such as "Everyone should brush his teeth after every meal if possible" and "The effects of penicillin have been, almost without exception, of great benefit to mankind." For one of the statements, participants read or generated a message supporting the belief (supportive message condition). For a second statement, participants read a weak attack against the belief statement and then were asked to read (passive refutation condition) or write (active refutation condition) a message that refuted the attack on their belief.

Two days after these initial treatments, participants read essays that attacked the cultural truisms they had defended earlier. After reading the stronger attack essays, participants indicated the extent to which they felt the truism was true or false. Findings revealed that the inoculation treatment was more effective than producing a supportive message in promoting resistance to persuasion. People who received the supportive message treatment followed by the persuasive attack were less certain about whether the cultural truism was true or false. However, those who received the inoculation treatment were more resistant to the subsequent persuasive attack and indicated greater agreement that the cultural truism in question was true.

In addition, McGuire and Papageorgis (1961) compared active and passive refutation inoculation procedures. Students who read the refutation statement were more resistant to subsequent persuasive attacks than those who generated their own refutation arguments. This finding may have occurred because students were not able to develop rebuttals that were as strong as the arguments provided by the experimenter (McGuire, 1999).

That passive refutation is superior to active refutation is also consistent with our discussion of "filling in the blanks" in Chapter 7. In that chapter, we argued that leaving parts of the message implicit for recipients to "fill in" (e.g., with implicit conclusions or warrants) was a relatively ineffective strategy. McGuire and Papageorgis's (1961) results were consistent with this hypothesis because people who were asked to develop their own counterarguments were less resistant to persuasion than participants who read the passive refutation message. In this sense, McGuire's biological metaphor breaks down, because it does not appear that providing a weak attack message *naturally* provides receivers with the ammunition to counter future attacks.

McGuire and Papageorgis (1961) found that, in addition to promoting resistance to attacks against the cultural belief in question, inoculation procedures also enhanced persuasion resistance for other, related, beliefs. More recently, Inoculation Theory has been employed to strengthen attitudes and promote resistance to persuasion against beliefs that are not culturally accepted (Pfau, 1995; see Compton, 2013, for a review of this literature).

However, inoculation treatments appear to be less effective for controversial topics than they are for cultural truisms (D. J. O'Keefe, 1990). Pfau (1992) argued that one reason why traditional inoculation studies have proved more effective than recent investigations involving more controversial topics is that traditional inoculation studies involved the use of *threat,* or the forewarning against an impending challenge to existing attitudes (Pfau, Van Bockern, & Kang, 1992). According to Pfau (1992, 1995), threat is required for successful inoculation (see also McGuire, 1999). Pfau, Kenski, Nitz, and Sorenson (1990) argued that "inoculation promotes resistance through the use of the impending attack, *employed in conjunction with* refutational preemption. The warning of an impending attack is designed to threaten the individual, triggering the motivation to bolster arguments supporting attitudes" (p. 28).

Applications of Inoculation Theory

Although most investigations of Inoculation Theory have been conducted in laboratory environments, inoculation treatments have recently become a central component in many persuasive campaigns. Extending the analysis that threat is an essential feature of effective inoculation treatments, Pfau and his colleagues revitalized interest in Inoculation Theory, after it lay dormant for nearly a quarter-century, by examining the effectiveness of inoculation treatments in political campaigns (Pfau & M. Burgoon, 1988; Pfau & Kenski, 1990; Pfau et al., 1990), comparative advertising (Pfau, 1992), and campaigns designed to prevent smoking among adolescents (Pfau et al., 1992). In this section we examine how Inoculation Theory has been employed successfully in political and public health campaigns (see also Compton, 2013).

Inoculation against Political Attacks

Recent political campaigns for national, state, and local offices have become increasingly negative. Political campaigns must provide reasons for voting for a particular candidate, but they must also present reasons for voting against the opponent. As a result, negative campaigns, or attack politics, have become an essential feature of many campaign operations (Devlin, 2001). Pfau and Kenski (1990) offer several reasons for their increased use. First, negative messages can be more influential than supportive messages, are cheaper to produce, and can be effectively aired on radio (a low-cost medium), and are often viewed as a counterbalance to the weight of incumbency.

The rapid growth of attack politics has sent candidates and campaign coordinators scrambling for effective defenses. Inoculation techniques can provide a valuable strategy for defending against hostile political advertising. Inoculation messages in these contexts have two essential components. First, as previously discussed, they must contain a warning that an opponent is likely to launch a persuasive attack. The threat of an impending attack serves to motivate receivers to defend against the attack. Second, inoculation messages must contain a preemptive refutation. That is, they must respond in advance to counterarguments that an opponent is likely to produce. Thus, effective inoculation pretreatments warn of an impending threat, motivating receivers to develop arguments to bolster their position against subsequent attacks (Pfau & Kenski, 1990, p. 75) and provide counterargument ammunition.

BOX 13.3. Preemptive Refutation in Political Campaigns

The 2008 presidential campaign provided an excellent example of preemptive refutation. On his radio show Rush Limbaugh accused Barack Obama of playing the race card and played the following clip from Barack Obama to support his position:

> What they're going to try to do is make you scared of me. You know, he—oh, he's not patriotic enough, he's got a funny name—you know—he doesn't look like all those other presidents on those dollar bills, you know. He's risky. That's the argument. ("Obama Plays the Race Card," 2008)

Although not framed in terms of Inoculation Theory, Obama's statement was a clear example of a preemptive argument. Barack Obama warned his audience about how others would characterize him and then encouraged the audience to dismiss the characterization.

Two studies provide evidence of the effectiveness of inoculation techniques in political campaigns. Pfau and colleagues (1990) performed a study of attitudes toward candidates Bush and Dukakis in the 1988 presidential campaign that involved directly mailing political campaign messages and measuring voters' candidate preferences and voting intentions. Three experimental conditions were created. The *inoculation condition* consisted of individuals who received an inoculation message in the mail several days after responding to a telephone survey about their candidate preferences. These messages warned that potentially persuasive attacks on their candidate were likely to occur (threat component) and provided a rebuttal to the attacks (refutation component).

People in the *inoculation-plus-reinforcement condition* responded to the telephone survey, received an inoculation message (containing both the threat and preemptive refutation components), and a week later received another mailing that reinforced their candidate preference. Finally, people in the *post hoc-refutation condition* responded to the telephone survey and later received a message that attacked the candidate whom they supported. A week later, these people were mailed a message that refuted the attacks made against their candidate.

Several days after the reinforcement and *post hoc* refutations were mailed, researchers conducted interviews in the homes of the research participants. During these interviews, people in the inoculation and inoculation-plus-reinforcement conditions were presented with a message that attacked their candidate's position. Following this, participants completed a survey of their attitudes toward the candidate and indicated their likelihood of voting for that candidate. People in the *post hoc* refutation condition had already received the attack message in the mail. These participants simply completed the attitude and voting preference survey.

Although party affiliation and treatment conditions interacted to affect posttest attitude and voting intentions, the general pattern of findings indicated strong support for the inoculation techniques. The effects for people with weak party affiliations were somewhat mixed, but the effects among people who clearly identified with one of the two political parties and among those with no party affiliation were consistently clear: the inoculation and inoculation-plus-reinforcement treatments were superior in deflecting the influence of an attack message to the *post hoc* refutation treatment (Pfau et al., 1990).

A similar study found additional evidence for the effectiveness of inoculation treatments. Studying a campaign for a U.S. Senate seat, Pfau and M. Burgoon (1988) found that inoculation treatments increased resistance to attitude change following a persuasive attack. In discussing the implications of their findings, they concluded that "inoculation deflects the persuasiveness of subsequent political attacks in a number of ways: undermining the potential influence of the source of political attacks, deflecting the specific content of political attacks, and reducing the likelihood that political attacks will influence receiver voting intention" (pp. 105–106).

Inoculation against Smoking

Based on the success of these earlier studies, Pfau and colleagues (1992) endeavored to study inoculation's effectiveness in an adolescent smoking prevention program. Students in seventh-grade health education classes were exposed to a videotaped message that was designed to help them resist peer pressure to smoke. This is a particularly important group to target, because students generally leave elementary school with negative attitudes toward smoking and smokers. However, this negative view tends to erode through the junior high school years. Indeed, it is precisely during these years when many long-term smokers develop the habit. Thus, inoculation theory seems an obvious choice for preventing attitude slippage among the junior high school age group.

As a consequence, Pfau and colleagues (1992) expected seventh-grade students who were exposed to the typical inoculation series of messages to exhibit more negative attitudes toward smoking and be more likely to resist smoking initiation as compared to students in the control condition. They were also interested in the extent to which self-esteem (a person's positive, neutral, or negative view of him- or herself) influenced the effectiveness of the inoculation messages. Self-esteem is important because of peer pressure's significant role in smoking onset. Individuals with low self-esteem are likely to be particularly susceptible to peer pressure and may be most helped by inoculation.

Over 1,000 seventh-grade students were randomly assigned to either inoculation or control conditions. Students in the inoculation condition watched a video presentation that included a threat component warning students of oncoming peer pressure to get them to smoke; inoculation messages that challenged anti-smoking attitudes (e.g., "Smoking is cool"; Pfau et al., 1992, p. 219); and, third, direct refutations of the attacking arguments. This study did not include a subsequent attack message, because the researchers expected such messages to occur naturally in the form of peer pressure.

Four dependent variables (attitudes toward smoking, attitudes toward smokers, likelihood of smoking, and chance of resisting smoking) were measured both 19 and 33 weeks following exposure to the message. These same variables had also been measured 1 month *before* message exposure to obtain baseline levels of attitudes and likely behaviors.

Pfau and colleagues' (1992) results indicated that the students reported negative attitudes toward smoking and few behavioral intentions to smoke at the beginning of the school year. These attitudes and intentions, however, eroded across the school year. Inoculation helped to slow this erosion, but only among low-self-esteem participants. Low-self-esteem participants in the inoculation condition exhibited more negative attitudes following message exposure as compared to low-self-esteem participants in the control condition. Inoculation had no impact on moderate- and high-self-esteem participants. It bears mentioning that these inoculation effects were observed following exposure to a single treatment and were not part of a communication campaign per se.

Summarizing Inoculation Findings

Early investigations of Inoculation Theory conducted by McGuire and colleagues (McGuire, 1961a, 1961b, 1964; McGuire & Papageorgis, 1961) occurred in controlled laboratory settings and focused on cultural truisms. Inoculation treatments have also been used successfully to promote resistance to persuasive political ads. Through studies involving political, marketing, and public health campaigns, Pfau and his colleagues (Pfau, 1992; Pfau & Burgoon, 1988; Pfau & Kenski, 1990; Pfau et al., 1990) demonstrated that inoculation treatments that warn of an impending persuasive attack motivate receivers to resist a subsequent persuasive appeal.

The breadth of this theory is evident in the variety of mass media persuasive campaigns that have effectively employed inoculation treatments. Inoculation can be a useful technique for preserving a previously established attitude about a particular candidate, product, or idea. This suggests that inoculation will be put to best use in the legitimization, participation, and penetration campaign stages. Pfau and colleagues (1992) attempted to legitimize nonsmoking attitudes and behaviors. The early stages of the "just say 'No'" campaigns performed a similar function by attempting to portray *not* taking drugs as "cool." Along similar lines, an important part of those campaigns was to accurately communicate to students how few of their peers engage in binge drinking (e.g., Lederman & Stewart, 2005). Such information can perform an inoculation focus, as it provides handy information that counters messages claiming that everyone is doing it.

Along a similar line, a nonsmoking campaign can be designed to work at the participation stage. As Pfau and colleagues (1992) found, students generally leave elementary school with negative attitudes toward smoking. Inoculation campaigns such as those reported by Pfau and colleagues are attempts to keep adolescents at the participation stage (where they refrain from smoking). However, the effectiveness of these single-message interventions can diminish over time.

In the political arena, inoculation strategies merge at the crossroads of two competing persuasive communication campaigns (one for the candidate and one for the opponent). For example, in recent political campaigns, it has been an effective strategy for both positive and negative campaign messages. A prospective voter with an established attitude is likely to have that attitude challenged by the opponent's negative ads. A forewarning of the threat and providing counterarguments are likely to be effective means for maintaining voters' support.

It is important to point out that inoculation message strategies do not have to provide the actual attack message in order to work. In several contexts (as in the Pfau et al. [1992] study on smoking), the attack messages occur naturally (e.g., seeing peers smoke and being asked to smoke). While persuaders may not be able to predict the specific nature of an attack message, they should be able to predict what issues or positions might be attacked.

Inoculation works because it arms individuals with counterarguments to fend off future persuasive attacks. There are times, however, when warning of an impending attack and providing individuals with possible counterarguments is not enough. Sometimes people also need practice in using the arguments they have been provided as well as those of others who also share their attitudes. For example, M. A. Miller and colleagues (2000) found that students were more effective in resisting offers to use drugs when they had an opportunity to discuss and rehearse different resistance strategies with others of a like mind.

SUMMARY

This chapter examined several models of social influence that have been effectively applied in mass media campaigns. We began by discussing research on these campaigns and highlighted the importance of customizing messages to specific characteristics of the target audience. For many issues, the combination of mass media and interpersonal messages has allowed campaigns to differentiate the general and personalized appeals, thereby enhancing their persuasiveness.

Social Cognitive Theory embodies a general approach to persuasion and human functioning that is derived from observational learning. By observing the rewards and punishments that others receive for their behavior, people learn vicariously how to enact socially desirable behaviors. For adolescents, who are particularly sensitive to peer and role model influences, Social Cognitive Theory explains behavior acquisition and change particularly well. Capitalizing on the influence of peer and adult models is one strategy for developing programs to promote prosocial behavior in adolescents.

Research on Inoculation Theory documents the effectiveness of this technique in promoting resistance to persuasion. Field experiments have confirmed the success of this method in building resistance to attack messages in both political and health promotion campaigns.

NOTES

1. The model proposed by Weinstein and colleagues (1998) describes seven specific stages but we will spare you those details because the two models are otherwise quite similar.
2. This problem exists for both persuasive campaigns and one-shot persuasive appeals.
3. A *model,* in this context, is another person observed performing the behavior. It could be a family member, a valued friend, or a TV, movie, or sports star. The more positively valued the model, the more likely that social learning will occur.

Epilogue

It has been more than two decades since the first edition of this book was published, and during that time there have been significant developments in the study of persuasion. Though we are not certain that we have our finger on the pulse of the field, there are a number of observations that struck us as we prepared the final revisions to this edition. Many of these are forward-looking and reflect our view of where the field is headed.

We can safely say that, after decades of a strong push toward cognitive processing models of persuasion, the field is starting to see a renewed focus on affective responses and the role of emotional influences in persuasion. Much work remains to be done in this regard, but we expect that the marginalization of affect is nearing an end and that tomorrow's scholars will rightly emphasize the importance of affective and cognitive factors in their ongoing research.

The eventual impact of the new social media is difficult to envision with certainty, but there is little doubt that they amount to a game changer in the way the individuals, campaigns, and corporations attempt to influence one another. The Internet is the great equalizer, and its ready accessibility to literally billions of people has already resulted in the Establishment's loss of control over social and political agendas that corporations, the news media, and the political elite once enjoyed exclusively. We think that the continuing emergence of robust social media platforms will make it possible for persuasion campaigns to microtarget message receivers in a truly cost-effective way. Within the next few years, we anticipate that personalized messages will assume a central role in advertising, health promotion, and political campaigns. As the cost of collecting and analyzing information about individual targets decreases, there will be a corresponding increase in the use of personalized persuasive appeals.

Given the role of consumer-generated messages in response to news events (e.g., Internet websites and blog commentary) and advertising messages, traditional message sources are losing control over the persuasion process. Secondary and tertiary messages generated by targets of the original message will make it more difficult to exercise control over the content and tone of persuasive appeals. Future research will look at the interaction between the messages created by advertising agencies (and the like) and those generated by consumers (perhaps in response) and how the two mutually shape future persuasion campaigns.

We are somewhat disappointed by the increasing resort to complexity in many models of persuasion, with an explosion in the number of mediating and moderating variables in our theories (many times without any cost–benefit analysis as to their utility). We anticipate that scholars will increasingly require evidence of enhanced predictive utility before allowing substantive "improvements" to a model or theory in the future.

Perhaps the most encouraging development since *Persuasive Communication*'s first edition was published 23 years ago has been the growing focus on applied communication research and the continuing transition from laboratory to field research settings. While basic research will continue to play a significant role in the development of persuasion theory, we anticipate burgeoning growth in applied research conducted in field settings.

References

Ajzen, I. (1985). From intentions to actions: A theory of planned behavior. In J. Kuhland & J. Beckman (Eds.), *Action-control: From cognitions to behavior* (pp. 11–39). Heidelberg, Germany: Springer.

Ajzen, I., & Fishbein, M. (1977). Attitude behavior relations: A theoretical analysis and review of empirical research. *Psychological Bulletin, 84*, 888–918.

Ajzen, I., & Fishbein, M. (1980). *Understanding attitudes and predicting social behavior.* Englewood Cliffs, NJ: Prentice-Hall.

Ajzen, I., & Madden, T. J. (1986). Prediction of goal-directed behavior: Attitudes, intentions, and perceived behavioral control. *Journal of Experimental Social Psychology, 22*, 453–474.

Akers, R. L., Krohn, M. D., Lanza-Kaduci, L., & Radosevich, M. (1979). Social learning and deviant behavior: A specific test of a general theory. *American Sociological Review, 44*, 636–655.

Albarracín, D., Johnson, B. T., Fishbein, M., & Muellerleile, P. A. (2001). Theories of reasoned action and planned behavior as models of condom use: A meta-analysis. *Psychological Bulletin, 127*, 142–161.

Alberts, J. K., Hecht, M. L., Miller-Rassulo, M., & Krizek, R. L. (1992). The communicative process of drug resistance among high school students. *Adolescence, 27*, 203–226.

Alberts, J. K., Miller-Rassulo, M. A., & Hecht, M. L. (1991). A typology of drug resistance strategies. *Journal of Applied Communication Research, 19*, 129–151.

Alexander, N. C., & Campbell, E. Q. (1966). Peer influence on alcohol drinking. *Journal of Studies on Alcohol, 28*, 444–453.

Allen, M. (1991). Meta-analysis comparing the persuasiveness of one-sided and two-sided messages. *Western Journal of Speech Communication, 55*, 390–404.

Allen, M. (1993). Determining the persuasiveness of message sidedness: A prudent note about utilizing research summaries. *Western Journal of Communication, 57*, 98–103.

Allen, M. (1998). Comparing the persuasive effectiveness of one- and two-sided messages. In M. Allen & R. W. Preiss (Eds.), *Persuasion: Advances through meta-analysis* (pp. 89–98). Cresskill, NY: Hampton Press.

Allen, M., Hale, J., Mongeau, P., Berkowitz-Stafford, S., Stafford, S., Shanahan, W., et al. (1990). Testing a model of message sidedness: Three replications. *Communication Monographs, 57*, 274–291.

Allen, M., Mabry, E. A., Banski, M., Stoneman, M., & Carter, P. (1990). A thoughtful appraisal of measuring cognition using the Role Category Questionnaire. *Communication Reports, 3*, 49–57.

Allen, M., & Preiss, R. W. (1997). Comparing the persuasiveness of narrative and statistical evidence using meta-analysis. *Communication Research Reports, 14*, 125–131.

Allen, M., & Stiff, J. B. (1989). Testing three models for the sleeper effect. *Western Journal of Speech Communication, 53*, 411–426.

Allport, G. W. (1935). Attitudes. In C. Murchison (Ed.), *A handbook of social psychology* (pp. 798–844). Worcester, MA: Clark University Press.

Andersen, P. A., & Guerrero, L. K. (Eds.). (1998). *Handbook of communication and emotion: Research, theory, applications, and contexts.* San Diego, CA: Academic Press.

Anderson, N. H. (1959). Test of a model for opinion change. *Journal of Abnormal and Social Psychology, 59*, 371–381.

Anderson, N. H. (1971). Integration theory and attitude change. *Psychological Review, 78*, 171–206.

Anderson, N. H. (1981). *Foundations of information integration theory.* San Diego, CA: Academic Press.

Anderson, N. H., & Hovland, C. (1957). The representation of order effects in communication research. In C. Hovland (Ed.), *The order of presentation in persuasion* (pp. 158–169). New Haven, CT: Yale University Press.

Andreoli, V., & Worchel, S. (1978). Effects of media, communicator, and message position on attitude change. *Public Opinion Quarterly, 42*, 59–70.

Andrews, K. R., Boster, F. J., & Carpenter, C. J. (2013). Persuading in the small group context. In J. P. Dillard & L. Shen (Eds.), *The SAGE handbook of persuasion: Developments in theory and practice* (2nd ed., pp. 354–370). Thousand Oaks, CA: Sage.

Applegate, J. L. (1982). The impact of construct system development on communication and impression formation in persuasive contexts. *Communication Monographs, 49*, 277–289.

Aristotle. (1960). *The rhetoric of Aristotle* (L. Cooper, Trans.). Englewood Cliffs, NJ: Prentice-Hall. (Original translation published 1932)

Armitage, C. J., & Conner, M. (1999). Distinguishing perceptions of control from self-efficacy: Predicting consumption of a low fat diet using the theory of planned behavior. *Journal of Applied Social Psychology, 29*, 72–90.

Armitage, C. J., & Conner, M. (2001). Efficacy of the theory of planned behaviour: A meta-analytic review. *British Journal of Social Psychology, 40*(4), 471–499.

Aronson, E. (1968). Dissonance theory: Progress and problems. In R. P. Abelson, E. Aronson, W. J. McGuire, T. M. Newcomb, M. J. Rosenberg & P.

H. Tannenbaum (Eds.), *Theories of cognitive consistency: A sourcebook* (pp. 5–27). Chicago: Rand McNally.

Aronson, E. (1992). The return of the repressed: Dissonance theory makes a comeback. *Psychological Inquiry, 3,* 303–311.

Aronson, E. (1999). *The social animal* (8th ed.). New York: Worth.

Aronson, E., Turner, J. A., & Carlsmith, J. M. (1963). Communicator credibility and communication discrepancy determinants of opinion change. *Journal of Abnormal and Social Psychology, 67,* 31–36.

Asch, S. E. (1955). Opinions and social pressures. *Scientific American, 193,* 31–35.

Asch, S. E. (1956). Studies of independence and conformity: A minority of one against a unanimous majority. *Psychological Monographs, 70*(9, Whole No. 416).

Atkin, C. K., & Rice, R. E. (2013). Theory and principles of public communication campaigns. In R. E. Rice & C. K. Atkin (Eds.), *Public Communication Campaigns* (4th ed., pp. 3–18). Los Angeles: Sage.

Axsom, D., Yates, S., & Chaiken, S. (1987). Audience response as a heuristic cue in persuasion. *Journal of Personality and Social Psychology, 53,* 30–40.

Bacon, S. J. (1974). Arousal and the range of cue utilization. *Journal of Experimental Psychology, 102,* 81–87.

Banas, J. A., & Rains, S. A. (2010). A meta-analysis of research on inoculation theory. *Communication Monographs, 77,* 281–311.

Bandura, A. (1969). *Principles of behavior modification.* New York: Holt, Rinehart & Winston.

Bandura, A. (1973). *Aggression: A social learning analysis.* Englewood Cliffs, NJ: Prentice-Hall.

Bandura, A. (1977). *Social learning theory.* Englewood Cliffs, NJ: Prentice-Hall.

Bandura, A. (1982). Self-efficacy mechanism in human agency. *American Psychologist, 37,* 122–147.

Bandura, A. (1986). *Social foundations of thought and action: A social cognitive theory.* Englewood Cliffs, NJ: Prentice-Hall.

Bandura, A. (2000). Health promotion from the perspective of social cognitive theory. In P. Norman, C. Abraham, & M. Conner (Eds.), *Understanding and changing health behavior: From health beliefs to self-regulation* (pp. 299–339). Amsterdam, The Netherlands: Harwood Academic.

Bandura, A. (2001). Social cognitive theory of mass communication. *Media Psychology, 3,* 265–299.

Bandura, A. (2011). The social and policy impact of social cognitive theory. In M. M. Mark, S. I. Donaldson, & B. Campbell (Eds.), *Social psychology and evaluation* (pp. 33–70). New York: Guilford Press.

Bandura, A., Adams, N. E., Hardy, A. B., & Howells, G. N. (1980). Tests of the generality of self-efficacy theory. *Cognitive Therapy and Research, 4,* 39–66.

Bargh, J. A., & Pratto, E. (1986). Individual construct accessibility and perceptual selection. *Journal of Experimental Social Psychology, 22,* 293–311.

Baron, P. H., Baron, R. S., & Roper, G. (1974). External validity and the risky shift: Empirical limits and theoretical implications. *Journal of Personality and Social Psychology, 30,* 95–103.

Bartsch, K., Wright, J. C., & Estes, D. (2010). Young children's persuasion in everyday conversation: Tactics and attunement to others' mental states. *Social Development, 19*, 394–416.

Basil, D. Z., Ridgway, N. M., & Basil, M. D. (2006). Guilt Appeals: The mediating effect of responsibility. *Psychology and Marketing, 23*, 1035–1054.

Baumeister, R. F., Stillwell, A. M., & Heatherton, T. F. (1994). Guilt: An interpersonal approach. *Psychological Bulletin, 115*, 243–267.

Baumhart, R. (1968). *An honest profit: What businessmen say about ethics in business*. New York: Holt, Rinehart & Winston.

Baxter, L., & Montgomery, B. M. (1996). *Relating: Dialogues and dialectics*. New York: Guilford Press.

Beaman, A. L., Cole, C. M., Preston, M., Klentz, B., & Steblay, N. M. (1983). Fifteen years of foot-in-the-door research: A meta-analysis. *Personality and Social Psychology Bulletin, 9*, 181–196.

Beatty, M. (1987). Erroneous assumptions underlying Burleson's critique. *Communication Quarterly, 35*, 329–333.

Beatty, M., & Payne, S. (1984). Loquacity and quantity of constructs as predictors of social perspective taking. *Communication Quarterly, 32*, 207–210.

Beatty, M., & Payne, S. (1985). Is construct differentiation loquacity?: A motivational perspective. *Human Communication Research, 11*, 605–612.

Beck, K. H., & Frankel, A. (1981). A conceptualization of threat communications and protective health behavior. *Social Psychology Quarterly, 44*, 204–217.

Becker, B. J. (1986). Influence again: An examination of reviews and studies of gender differences in social influence. In J. S. Hyde & M. C. Linn (Eds.), *The psychology of gender: Advances through meta-analysis* (pp. 178–209). Baltimore: Johns Hopkins University Press.

Becker, M. H. (1974). *The health belief model and personal health behavior*. Thorofare, NJ: Slack.

Becker, S. L. (1963). Research on emotional and logical proofs. *Southern Speech Journal, 28*, 198–207.

Bem, D. J. (1965). An experimental analysis of self-persuasion. *Journal of Experimental Social Psychology, 1*, 199–218.

Bem, D. J. (1967). Self-perception: An alternative interpretation of cognitive dissonance phenomena. *Psychological Review, 74*, 183–200.

Bem, D. J. (1972). Self-perception theory. In L. Berkowitz (Ed.), *Advances in experimental social psychology* (Vol. 6, pp. 1–62). New York: Academic Press.

Benoit, W. L. (2007). *Communication in political campaign*s. New York: Peter Lang.

Berger, A. A. (1995). *Essentials of mass communication theory*. London: Sage.

Berger, C. R. (1997). *Planning strategic interaction: Attaining goals through communicative action*. Mahwah, NJ: Erlbaum.

Berger, C. R., Karol, S. H., & Jordan, J. M. (1989). When a lot of knowledge is a dangerous thing: The debilitating effects of plan complexity on verbal fluency. *Human Communication Research, 16*, 91–119.

Berger, J. M., & Cornelius, T. (2003). Rising the price of agreement: Public commitment and the lowball compliance procedure. *Journal of Applied Social Psychology, 33*, 923–934.

Berlo, D. K. (1960). *The process of communication: An introduction to theory and practice*. New York: Holt, Rinehart & Winston.

Berlo, D. K., Lemert, J. B., & Mertz, R. J. (1969). Dimensions for evaluating the acceptability of message sources. *Public Opinion Quarterly, 33*, 563–576.

Berscheid, E. (1966). Opinion change and communicator–communicatee similarity and dissimilarity. *Journal of Personality and Social Psychology, 4*, 670–680.

Berscheid, E., & Walster, E. (1974). Physical attractiveness. In L. Berkowitz (Ed.), *Advances in experimental social psychology* (Vol. 7, pp. 157–215). San Diego, CA: Academic Press.

Berthon, P. R., Pitt, L. F., Plangger, K., & Shapiro, D. (2012). Marketing meets Web 2.0, social media, and creative consumers: Implications for international marketing strategy. *Business Horizons, 55*, 261–271.

Besson, A. L., Roloff, M. E., & Paulson, G. D. (1998). Preserving face in refusal situations. *Communication Research, 25*, 183–199.

Bettinghaus, E. P., & Cody, M. J. (1987). *Persuasive communication*. New York: Holt, Rinehart & Winston.

Bettinghaus, E. P., Miller, G. R., & Steinfatt, T. M. (1970). Source evaluation, syllogistic content, and judgments of logical validity by high- and low-dogmatic persons. *Journal of Personality and Social Psychology, 16*, 238–244.

Biglan, A., Glasgow, R., Ary, D., Thompson, R., Severson, H., Lichtenstein, E., et al. (1987). How generalizable are the effects of smoking prevention programs?: Refusal skills, training, and parent messages in a teacher-administered program. *Journal of Behavioral Medicine, 10*, 613–628.

Biglan, A., McConnell, S., Severson, H. H., Bavry, J., & Ary, D. (1984). A situational analysis of adolescent smoking. *Journal of Behavioral Medicine, 7*, 109–114.

Bingham, S. G., & Burleson, B. R. (1989). Multiple effects of messages with multiple goals: Some perceived outcomes of responses to sexual harassment. *Human Communication Research, 16*, 184–216.

Bochner, S., & Insko, C. A. (1966). Communicator discrepancy, source credibility, and opinion change. *Journal of Personality and Social Psychology, 4*, 614–621.

Booth-Butterfield, S., & Gutowski, C. (1993). Message modality and source credibility can interact to affect argument processing. *Communication Quarterly, 41*, 77–89.

Boster, F. J. (1990). Group argument, social pressure, and the making of group decisions. In J. A. Anderson (Ed.), *Communication yearbook 13* (pp. 303–312). Newbury Park, CA: Sage.

Boster, F. J., Fryrear, J. E., Mongeau, P. A., & Hunter, J. E. (1982). An unequal speaking linear discrepancy model: Implications for the polarity shift. In M. Burgoon (Ed.), *Communication yearbook 6* (pp. 395–418). Beverly Hills, CA: Sage.

Boster, F. J., & Hunter, J. E. (1978). *The effect of dimensions of Machiavellianism on compliance-gaining message selection*. Unpublished manuscript, Department of Communication, Arizona State University, Tempe, AZ.

Boster, F. J., & Mayer, M. E. (1984). Choice shifts: Argument qualities or social comparisons? In R. N. Bostrom (Ed.), *Communication yearbook 8* (pp. 393–410). Beverly Hills, CA: Sage.

Boster, F. J., Mayer, M. E., Hunter, J. E., & Hale, J. L. (1980). Expanding the persuasive arguments explanation of the polarity shift: A linear discrepancy model. In D. Nimmo (Ed.), *Communication yearbook 4* (pp. 165–176). New Brunswick, NJ: Transaction Books.

Boster, F. J., & Mongeau, P. A. (1984). Fear-arousing persuasive messages. In R. N. Bostrom (Ed.), *Communication yearbook 8* (pp. 330–375). Beverly Hills, CA: Sage.

Boster, F. J., & Stiff, J. B. (1984). Compliance gaining message selection behavior. *Human Communication Research, 10*, 539–556.

Boster, F. J., Stiff, J. B., & Reynolds, R. A. (1985). Do persons respond differently to inductively-derived and deductively-derived lists of compliance gaining messages?: A reply to Wiseman and Schenck-Hamlin. *Western Journal of Speech Communication, 49*, 177–187.

Braverman, J. (2008). Testimonials versus informational persuasive messages: The moderating effect of delivery mode and personal involvement. *Communication Research, 35*, 666–694.

Brehm, J. W. (1966). *A theory of psychological reactance.* New York: Academic Press.

Brehm, J. W. (2007). A brief history of dissonance theory. *Social and Personality Psychology Compass, 1*, 381–391.

Brehm, J. W., & Cohen, A. R. (1962). *Explorations in cognitive dissonance.* New York: Wiley.

Brennan, A. (2012, November 5). *Microtargeting: How campaigns know you better than you know yourself.* CNN.com.

Brock, T. (1965). Communicator–recipient similarity and decision change. *Journal of Personality and Social Psychology, 1*, 650–654.

Brown, P., & Levinson, S. C. (1987). *Politeness: Some universals in language usage.* Cambridge, UK: Cambridge University Press.

Brown, R., & Gilman, A. (1989). Politeness theory and Shakespeare's four major tragedies. *Language in Society, 18*, 159–212.

Buller, D. B. (1986). Distraction during persuasive communication: A meta-analytic review. *Communication Monographs, 53*, 91–114.

Burger, J. M. (1986). Increasing compliance by improving the deal: The that's not all technique. *Journal of Personality and Social Psychology, 51*, 277–283.

Burger, J. M. (1999). The foot-in-the-door compliance procedure: A multiple-process analysis and review. *Personality and Social Psychology Review, 3*, 303–325.

Burger, J. M., & Cornelius, T. (2003). Raising the price of agreement: Public commitment and the lowball compliance procedure. *Journal of Applied Social Psychology, 33*(5), 923–934.

Burgoon, J. K., Burgoon, M., Miller, G. R., & Sunnafrank, M. (1981). Learning theory approaches to persuasion. *Human Communication Research, 7*, 161–179.

Burgoon, J. K., Stacks, D. W., & Burch, S. A. (1982). The role of rewards and violations of distancing expectations in achieving influence in small groups. *Communication, 11*, 114–128.

Burgoon, M. (1989). Messages and persuasive effects. In J. J. Bradac (Ed.), *Message effects in communication science* (pp. 129–164). Newbury Park, CA: Sage.

Burgoon, M., & Burgoon, J. K. (1975). Message strategies in influence attempts. In G. J. Hanneman & W. J. McEwen (Eds.), *Communication and behavior* (pp. 149–165). Reading, MA: Addison-Wesley.

Burgoon, M., Cohen, M., Miller, M. D., & Montgomery, C. L. (1978). An empirical test of a model of resistance to persuasion. *Human Communication Research, 5*, 27–39.

Burgoon, M., & Klingle, R. S. (1998). Gender differences in being influential and/or influenced: A challenge to prior explanations. In D. J. Canary & K. Dindia (Eds.), *Sex differences and similarities in communication: Critical essays and empirical investigations of sex and gender in interaction* (pp. 257–285). Mahwah, NJ: Erlbaum.

Burleson, B., Applegate, J., & Newwirth, C. (1981). Is cognitive complexity loquacity?: A reply to Powers, Jordan, and Street. *Human Communication Research, 7*, 212–215.

Burleson, B., Waltman, M., & Samter, W. (1987). More evidence that cognitive complexity is not loquacity: A reply to Beatty and Payne. *Communication Quarterly, 35*, 317–328.

Campbell, C., Pitt, L., Parent, M., & Berthon, P. (2011). Understanding consumer conversations around ads in a Web 2.0 world. *Journal of Advertising, 40*, 87–102.

Campbell, D. T., & Stanley, J. C. (1966). *Experimental and quasi-experimental designs for research.* Chicago: Rand McNally.

Canary, D. J., Brossmann, B. G., & Seibold, D. R. (1987). Argument structures in decision-making groups. *Southern Speech Communication Journal, 53*, 18–37.

Canary, D. J., & Dindia, K. (Eds.). (1998). *Sex differences and similarities in communication: Critical essays and empirical investigations of sex and gender in interaction.* Mahwah, NJ: Erlbaum.

Canary, D. J., & Hause, K. S. (1993). Is there any reason to research sex differences in communication? *Communication Quarterly, 41*, 129–144.

Card, N. A. (2012). *Applied meta-analysis for social science research.* New York: Guilford Press.

Carli, L. L. (2001). Gender and social influence. *Journal of Social Issues, 57*, 725–741.

Carpenter, C. J. (2012). A meta-analysis and an experiment investigating the effects of speaker disfluency on persuasion. *Western Journal of Communication, 76*, 552–569.

Carpenter, C. J., Boster, F. J., & Andrews, K. R. (2013). Functional attitude theory. In J. P. Dillard & L. Shen (Eds.), *The SAGE handbook of persuasion: Developments in theory and practice* (2nd ed., pp. 104–119). Los Angeles: Sage.

Caughlin, J. P. (2010). A multiple goals theory of personal relationships: Conceptual integration and program overview. *Journal of Social and Personal Relationships, 27*, 824–848.

Caughlin, J. P., Brashers, D. E., Ramey, M. E., Kosenko, K. A., Donovan-Kicken, E., & Bute, J. J. (2008). The message design logics of responses to HIV disclosures. *Human Communication Research, 34*, 655–684.

Chaiken, S. (1979). Communicator physical attractiveness and persuasion. *Journal of Personality and Social Psychology, 37,* 1387–1397.

Chaiken, S. (1980). Heuristic versus systematic information processing and the use of source versus message cues in persuasion. *Journal of Personality and Social Psychology, 39,* 752–766.

Chaiken, S. (1986). Physical appearance and social influence. In C. P. Herman, M. P. Zanna, & E. T. Higgins (Eds.), *Physical appearance, stigma, and social behavior: The Ontario Symposium* (Vol. 3, pp. 143–177). Hillsdale, NJ: Erlbaum.

Chaiken, S. (1987). The heuristic model of persuasion. In M. P. Zanna, J. M. Olson, & C. P. Herman (Eds.), *Social influence: The Ontario Symposium* (Vol. 5, pp. 3–39). Hillsdale, NJ: Erlbaum.

Chaiken, S., Duckworth, K. L., & Darke, P. (1999). When parsimony fails. *Psychological Inquiry, 10,* 118–123.

Chaiken, S., & Eagly, A. H. (1976). Communicator modality as a determinant of message persuasiveness and message comprehensibility. *Journal of Personality and Social Psychology, 34,* 606–614.

Chaiken, S., & Eagly, A. H. (1983). Communication modality as a determinant of persuasion: The role of communicator salience. *Journal of Personality and Social Psychology, 45,* 241–256.

Chaiken, S., & Ledgerwood, A. (2012). A theory of heuristic and systematic message processing. In P. A. M. Van Lange, A. W. Kruglanski, & E. T. Higgins (Eds.) *The handbook of theories of social psychology* (Vol. 1, pp. 224–245). London: Sage.

Chaiken, S., Liberman, A., & Eagly, A. H. (1989). Heuristic and systematic information processing within and beyond the persuasion context. In J. S. Uleman & J. A. Bargh (Eds.), *Unintended thought* (pp. 212–252). New York: Guilford Press.

Chapanis, N. P., & Chapanis, A. (1964). Cognitive dissonance theory: Five years later. *Psychological Bulletin, 61,* 1–22.

Chang, Y., Yu, H., & Lu, H. (2015). Persuasive messages, popularity cohesion, and message diffusion in social media marketing. *Journal of Business Research, 68,* 777–782.

Chen, S., & Chaiken, S. (1999). The heuristic–systematic model in its broader context. In S. Chaiken & Y. Trope (Eds.), *Dual-process theories in social psychology* (pp. 73–96). New York: Guilford Press.

Cho, H., & Salmon, C. T. (2006). Fear appeals for individuals in different stages of change: Intended and unintended effects and implications on public health campaigns. *Health Communication, 20,* 91–99.

Cialdini, R. B. (2009). *Influence: Science and practice* (5th ed.). Boston: Pearson.

Cialdini, R. B., Cacioppo, J. T., Bassett, R., & Miller, J. A. (1978). Low-ball procedure for producing compliance: Commitment then cost. *Journal of Personality and Social Psychology, 36,* 463–476.

Cialdini, R. B., & Goldstein, N. J. (2004). Social influence: Compliance and conformity. *Annual Review of Psychology, 55,* 591–621.

Cialdini, R. B., Levy, A., Herman, C. P., & Evenbeck, S. (1973). Attitudinal politics: The strategy of moderation. *Journal of Personality and Social Psychology, 25,* 100–108.

Cialdini, R. B., Levy, A., Herman, C. P., Kozlowski, L. T., & Petty, R. E. (1976). Elastic shifts of opinion: Determinants of direction and durability. *Journal of Personality and Social Psychology, 34*, 663–672.

Cialdini, R. B., & Petty, R. E. (1981). Anticipatory opinion effects. In R. E. Petty, T. M. Ostrom, & T. C. Brock (Eds.), *Cognitive responses in persuasion* (pp. 217–235). Hillsdale, NJ: Erlbaum.

Cialdini, R. B., & Schroeder, D. A. (1976). Increasing compliance by legitimizing paltry contributions: When even a penny helps. *Journal of Personality and Social Psychology, 34*, 599–604.

Cialdini, R. B., Trost, M. R., & Newsome, J. T. (1995). Preference for consistency: The development of a valid measure and the discovery of surprising behavioral implications. *Journal of Personality and Social Psychology, 69*, 318–328.

Cialdini, R. B., Vincent, J. E., Lewis, S. K., Catalan, J., Wheeler, D., & Darby, B. L. (1975). Reciprocal concessions procedure for inducing compliance: The door-in-the-face technique. *Journal of Personality and Social Psychology, 31*, 206–215.

Clark, R. A. (1979). The impact of self interest and desire for liking on the selection of communicative strategies. *Communication Monographs, 46*, 257–273.

Clark, R. A., & Delia, J. G. (1979). Topoi and rhetorical competence. *Quarterly Journal of Speech, 65*, 187–206.

Clarkson, J. J., Tormala, Z. L., & Leone, C. (2011). A self-validation perspective on the mere thought effect. *Journal of Experimental Social Psychology, 47*, 449–454.

Clary, E. G., & Snyder, M. (1992). Persuasive communications strategies for recruiting volunteers. In D. R. Young, R. M. Hollister, & V. A. Hodgkinson (Eds.), *Governing, leading, and managing nonprofit organizations: New insights from research and practice* (pp. 121–137). San Francisco: Jossey-Bass.

Cody, M. J., Canary, D. J., & Smith, S. W. (1994). Compliance-gaining goals: An inductive analysis of actors' and goal types, strategies, and successes. In J. A. Daly & J. M. Wiemann (Eds.), *Strategic interpersonal communication* (pp. 33–90). Hillsdale, NJ: Erlbaum.

Cody, M. J., & McLaughlin, M. L. (1985). The situation as construct in interpersonal communication research. In M. Knapp & G. R. Miller (Eds.), *Handbook of interpersonal communication* (pp. 263–312). Beverly Hills, CA: Sage.

Cohen, A., Stotland, E., & Wolfe, D. (1955). An experimental investigation of need for cognition. *Journal of Abnormal and Social Psychology, 51*, 291–294.

Cohen, J. R., Brehm, J. W., & Fleming, W. H. (1958). Attitude change and justification for compliance. *Journal of Abnormal and Social Psychology, 56*, 276–278.

Cohen, M. R. (1949). *Studies in philosophy and science.* New York: Holt.

Compton, J. (2013). Inoculation theory. In J. P. Dillard & L. Shen (Eds.), *The SAGE handbook of persuasion: Developments in theory and practice* (2nd ed., pp. 220–236). Thousand Oaks, CA: Sage.

Compton, J., & Pfau, M. (2009). Spreading inoculation: Inoculation, resistance to influence, and word-of-mouth communication. *Communication Theory, 19*, 9–28.

Condon, S. (2011, April 21). *Poll: One in four Americans think Obama was not born in U.S.* CBS News Political Hotsheet.

Conner, M., & Armitage, C. J. (1998). Extending the theory of planned behaviour: A review and avenues for further research. *Journal of Applied Social Psychology, 28,* 1429–1464.

Cook, D. T., & Campbell, D. T. (1979). *Quasi-experimentation: Design and analysis issues for field settings.* Chicago: Rand McNally.

Cooke, R., & French, D. P. (2008). How well do the theory of reasoned action and theory of planned behaviour predict intentions and attendance at screening programmes?: A meta-analysis. *Psychology and Health, 23,* 745–765.

Cooper, J. (2007). *Cognitive dissonance: Fifty years of a classic theory.* London: Sage.

Cooper, J. (2012). Cognitive dissonance theory. In P. A. M. Van Lange, A. W. Kruglanski, & E. T. Higgins (Eds.), *The handbook of theories of social psychology* (Vol. 1, pp. 377–397). London: Sage.

Cooper, J., & Fazio, R. H. (1984). A new look at dissonance theory. In L. Berkowitz (Ed.), *Advances in experimental social psychology* (Vol. 17, pp. 229–266). New York: Academic Press.

Cooper, J., Zanna, M. P., & Taves, P. A. (1978). Arousal as a necessary condition for attitude change following induced compliance. *Journal of Personality and Social Psychology, 36,* 1101–1106.

Cooper-Thomas, H., & Anderson, N. (2002). Newcomer adjustment: The relationship between organizational socialization tactics, information acquisition and attitudes. *Journal of Occupational and Organizational Psychology, 75,* 423–437.

Corey, S. M. (1937). Professed attitudes and actual behavior. *Journal of Educational Psychology, 28,* 271–280.

Cotte, J., Coulter, R. A., & Moore, M. (2005). Enhancing or disrupting guilt: The role of ad credibility and perceived manipulative intent. *Journal of Business Research, 58,* 361– 368.

Coulter, R. H., & Pinto, M. B. (1995). Guilt appeals in advertising: What are their effects? *Journal of Applied Psychology, 80,* 697–705.

Crabtree, S. (2010, July 1). *NRA: Kagan a threat to gun rights.* The Hill. Available at *www.thehill.com/homenews/senate/106753–nra-blasts-kagan-as-threat-to-gun-rights.*

Crano, W. D. (2006). Reading the tea leaves in models that seek to integrate implicit and explicit measures and cognitions: Is this the future of social psychology? *Psychological Inquiry, 17,* 217–223.

Crano, W. D., & Prislin, R. (Eds.). (2008). *Attitudes and attitude change.* New York: Psychology Press.

Cronkhite, G., & Liska, J. (1976). A critique of factor analytic approaches to the study of credibility. *Communication Monographs, 43,* 91–107.

Cronkhite, G., & Liska, J. (1980). The judgment of communicator acceptability. In M. E. Roloff & G. R. Miller (Eds.), *Persuasion: New directions in theory and research* (pp. 101–139). Beverly Hills, CA: Sage.

Croyle, D. T., & Cooper, J. (1983). Dissonance arousal: Physiological evidence. *Journal of Personality and Social Psychology, 45,* 782–791.

Davis, J. H., Kerr, N. L., Atkin, R. S., Holt, R., & Meek, D. (1975). The decision processes of 6– and 12–person mock juries assigned unanimous and two-thirds majority rules. *Journal of Personality and Social Psychology, 32*, 1–14.

DeBono, K. G. (2000). Attitude functions and consumer psychology: Understanding perceptions of product quality. In G. R. Maio & J. M. Olson (Eds.), *Why we evaluate: Functions of attitudes* (pp. 195–221). Mahwah, NJ: Erlbaum.

DeBono, K. G., Ruggeri, D., & Foster, A. (1997). Unpublished raw data.

DeBusk, R. G., Miller, N. H., Superko, H. R., Dennis, C. A., Thomas, R. J., Lew, H. T., et al. (1994). A case-management system for coronary risk factor modification after acute myocardial infarction. *Annals of Internal Medicine, 120*, 721–729.

DeFleur, M. L., & Ball-Rokeach, S. (1989). *Theories of mass communication.* New York: Longman.

de Hoog, N., Stroebe, W., & de Wit, J. B. F. (2005). The impact of fear appeals on processing and acceptance of action recommendations. *Personality and Social Psychology Bulletin, 31*, 24–33.

de Hoog, N., Stroebe, W., & de Wit, J. B. F. (2007). The impact of vulnerability to and severity of a health risk on processing and acceptance of fear-arousing communications: A meta-analysis. *Review of General Psychology, 11*, 258–285.

Delia, J. G., & Crockett, W. H. (1973). Social schemas, cognitive complexity, and the learning of social structures. *Journal of Personality, 41*, 413–429.

Delia, J. G., Kline, S. L., & Burleson, B. R. (1979). The development of persuasive communication strategies in kindergartners through twelfth graders. *Communication Monographs, 46*, 274–281.

Delia, J. G., & O'Keefe, B. J. (1979). Constructivism: The development of communication in children. In E. Wartella (Ed.), *Children communicating* (pp. 157–185). Beverly Hills, CA: Sage.

Deutsch, M., & Gerard, H. B. (1955). A study of normative and informational social influence upon individual judgment. *Journal of Abnormal and Social Psychology, 51*, 629–636.

Devlin, L. P. (2001). Contrasts in presidential campaign commercials of 2000. *American Behavioral Scientist, 44*, 2338–2369.

DiBlasio, E. A. (1986). Drinking adolescents on the roads. *Journal of Youth and Adolescence, 15*, 173–188.

DiBlasio, E. A. (1987). Predriving riders and drinking drivers. *Journal of Studies on Alcohol, 49*, 11–15.

DiBlasio, E. A., & Benda, B. B. (1990). Adolescent sexual behavior: Multivariate analysis of a social learning model. *Journal of Adolescent Research, 5*, 449–466.

Dillard, J. P. (1988). Compliance gaining message selection: What is our dependent variable? *Communication Monographs, 55*, 162–183.

Dillard, J. P. (1989). Types of influence goals in personal relationships. *Journal of Social and Personal Relationships, 6*, 293–308.

Dillard, J. P. (1990a). A goal-driven model of interpersonal influence. In J. P. Dillard (Ed.), *Seeking compliance: The production of interpersonal influence messages* (pp. 41–56). Scottsdale, AZ: Gorsuch-Scarisbrick.

Dillard, J. P. (1990b). Self-inference and the foot-in-the-door technique. *Human Communication Research, 16*, 422–447.

Dillard, J. P. (1991). The current status of research on sequential-request compliance techniques. *Personality and Social Psychology Bulletin, 17*, 283–288.

Dillard, J. P. (1994). Rethinking the study of fear appeals: An emotional perspective. *Communication Theory, 4*, 295–323.

Dillard, J. P. (1998). Foreword: The role of affect in communication, biology, and social relationships. In P. A. Andersen & L. K. Guerrero (Eds.), *Handbook of communication and emotion: Research, theory, applications, and contexts* (pp. xvii–xxxii). San Diego, CA: Academic Press.

Dillard, J. P., Anderson, J. W., & Knobloch, L. K. (2002). Interpersonal influence. In M. Knapp & J. Daly (Eds.), *Handbook of interpersonal communication* (3rd ed., pp. 425–474). Thousand Oaks, CA: Sage.

Dillard, J. P., Hunter, J. E., & Burgoon, M. (1984). Sequential-request persuasive strategies: Meta-analysis of foot-in-the-door and door-in-the-face. *Human Communication Research, 10*, 461–488.

Dillard, J. P., & Knobloch, L. K. (2011). Interpersonal influence. In M. L. Knapp & J. A. Daly (Eds.), *The SAGE handbook of interpersonal communication* (4th ed., pp. 398–421). Thousand Oaks, CA: Sage.

Dillard, J. P., & Meijnders, A. (2002). Persuasion and the structure of affect. In J. P. Dillard & M. W. Pfau (Eds.), *The SAGE handbook of persuasion: Developments in theory and practice* (pp. 309–327). Thousand Oaks, CA: Sage.

Dillard, J. P., Plotnick, C. A., Godbold, L. C., Freimuth, V. S., & Edgar, T. (1996). The multiple affective outcomes of AIDS PSAs: Fear appeals do more than scare people. *Communication Research, 23*, 44–72.

Dillard, J. P., & Seo, K. (2013). Affect and persuasion. In J. P. Dillard & L. Shen (Eds.), *The SAGE handbook of persuasion: Developments in theory and practice* (2nd ed., pp. 150–166). Thousand Oaks, CA: Sage.

Dillard, J. P., Segrin, C., & Hardin, J. M. (1989). Primary and secondary goals in the production of interpersonal influence messages. *Communication Monographs, 56*, 19–38.

Dillard, J. P., Wilson, S. R., Tusing, K. J., & Kinney, T. A. (1997). Politeness judgments in personal relationships. *Journal of Language and Social Psychology, 16*, 297–325.

Dion, K., Baron, R., & Miller, N. (1970). Why do groups make riskier decisions than individuals? In L. Berkowitz (Ed.), *Group processes* (pp. 227–299). New York: Academic Press.

Dion, K., Berscheid, E., & Walster, E. (1972). What is beautiful is good. *Journal of Personality and Social Psychology, 24*, 285–290.

Domel, S. B., Baranowski, T., Davis, H., Thompson, W. O., Leonard, S. B., Riley, P., et al. (1993). Development and evaluation of a school intervention to increase fruit and vegetable consumption among 4th and 5th grade students. *Journal of Nutrition Education, 25*, 345–349.

Dooling, W. (2012, November 13). *The "Biggest Loser" of the 2012 Election: Karl Rove.* Center for Media and Democracy's PR Watch. Available at *www.prwatch.org/news/2012/11/11854/biggest-loser-2012-election-karl-rove.*

Dulany, D. E. (1961). Hypotheses and habits in verbal "operant conditioning." *Journal of Abnormal and Social Psychology, 63*, 251–263.

Dulany, D. E. (1968). Awareness, rules, and propositional control: A confrontation with S–R behavior theory. In D. Horton & T. Dixon (Eds.), *Verbal behavior and S–R behavior theory* (pp. 340–387). Englewood Cliffs, NJ: Prentice-Hall.

Dutta, S., & Fraser, M. (2008, November 19). Barack Obama and the Facebook Election. *U.S. News and World Report.* Available at *www.usnews.com/opinion/articles/2008/11/19/barack-obama-and-the-facebook-election.*

Eagly, A. H. (1974). Comprehensibility of persuasive arguments as a determinant of opinion change. *Journal of Personality and Social Psychology, 29*, 758–773.

Eagly, A. H. (1978). Sex differences in influenceability. *Psychological Bulletin, 85*, 86–116.

Eagly, A. H., Ashmore, R. D., Makhijani, M. G., & Longo, L. C. (1991). What is beautiful is good, but . . . : A meta-analytic review of research on the physical attractiveness stereotype. *Psychological Bulletin, 110*, 109–128.

Eagly, A. H., & Carli, L. L. (1981). Sex of researchers and sex-typed communications as determinants of sex differences in influenceability: A meta-analysis of social influence studies. *Psychological Bulletin, 90*, 1–20.

Eagly, A. H., & Chaiken, S. (1976). Why would anyone say that?: Causal attribution of statements about the Watergate scandal. *Sociometry, 39*, 236–243.

Eagly, A. H., & Chaiken, S. (1993). *The psychology of attitudes.* Fort Worth, TX: Harcourt Brace Jovanovich.

Eagly, A. H., & Chaiken, S. (2007). The advantages of an inclusive definition of attitude. *Social Cognition, 25*, 582–602.

Eagly, A. H., Chaiken, S., & Wood, W. (1981). An attribution analysis of persuasion. In J. H. Harvey, W. J. Ickes, & R. E. Kidd (Eds.), *New directions in attribution research* (Vol. 3, pp. 37–62). Hillsdale, NJ: Erlbaum.

Eagly, A. H., & Warren, R. (1976). Intelligence, comprehension, and opinion change. *Journal of Personality, 44*, 226–242.

Eagly, A. H., Wood, W., & Chaiken, S. (1978). Causal inferences about communicators and their effect on opinion change. *Journal of Personality and Social Psychology, 36*, 424–435.

Edwards, K. (1990). The interplay of affect and cognition in attitude formation and change. *Journal of Personality and Social Psychology, 59*, 202–216.

Edwards, W. (1961). Behavioral decision theory. *Annual Review of Psychology, 12*, 473–498.

Ellis, A. M., Bauer, T. N., & Erdogan, B. (2014). New-employee organizational socialization. In J. E. Grusec & P. D. Hastings (Eds.), *Handbook of socialization: Theory and research* (2nd ed., pp. 301–322). New York: Guilford Press.

Fazio, R. H. (1987). Self-perception theory: A current perspective. In M. P. Zanna, J. M. Olson, & C. P. Herman (Eds.), *Social influence: The Ontario Symposium* (Vol. 5, pp. 129–150). Hillsdale, NJ: Erlbaum.

Fazio, R. H., Chen, J., McDonel, E. C., & Sherman, S. J. (1982). Attitude accessibility, attitude–behavior consistency, and the strength of the object–evaluation association. *Journal of Experimental Social Psychology, 18*, 339–357.

Fazio, R. H., Sanbonmatsu, D. M., Powell, M. C., & Kardes, F. R. (1986). On the automatic activation of attitudes. *Journal of Personality and Social Psychology, 50*, 229–238.

Fazio, R. H., & Williams, C. J. (1986). Attitude accessibility as a moderator of the attitude–perception and attitude–behavior relations: An investigation of the

1984 presidential election. *Journal of Personality and Social Psychology, 51,* 505–514.

Fazio, R. H., & Zanna, M. P. (1981). Direct experience and attitude–behavior consistency. In L. Berkowitz (Ed.), *Advances in experimental social psychology* (Vol. 14, pp. 161–202). New York: Academic Press.

Fazio, R. H., Zanna, M. P., & Cooper, J. (1977). Dissonance and self-perception: An interactive view of each theory's proper domain of application. *Journal of Experimental Social Psychology, 13,* 464–479.

Feeley, T. H., Anker, A. E., & Aloe, A. M. (2012). The door-in-the-face persuasive message strategy: A meta-analysis of the first 35 years. *Communication Monographs, 79,* 316–343.

Fehr, B., & Russell, J. A. (1984). Concept of emotion viewed from a prototype perspective. *Journal of Experimental Psychology, 113,* 464–484.

Fern, E. E., Monroe, K. B., & Avila, R. A. (1986). Effectiveness of multiple request strategies: A synthesis of research results. *Journal of Marketing Research, 23,* 144–152.

Festinger, L. (1953). An analysis of compliant behavior. In M. Sherif & M. O. Wilson (Eds.), *Group relations at the crossroads* (pp. 232–256). New York: Harper & Brothers.

Festinger, L. (1954). A theory of social comparison processes. *Human Relations, 7,* 117–140.

Festinger, L. (1957). *A theory of cognitive dissonance.* Stanford, CA: Stanford University Press.

Festinger, L. (1964). Behavioral support for opinion change. *Public Opinion Quarterly, 28,* 404–417.

Festinger, L., & Carlsmith, J. M. (1959). Cognitive consequences of forced compliance. *Journal of Abnormal and Social Psychology, 58,* 203–210.

Festinger, L., & Maccoby, N. (1964). On resistance to persuasive communication. *Journal of Abnormal and Social Psychology, 68,* 359–366.

Fink, E. L., & Cai, D. A. (2013). Discrepancy models of belief change. In J. P. Dillard & L. Shen, *The SAGE handbook of persuasion: Developments in theory and practice* (2nd ed., pp. 84–103). Thousand Oaks, CA: Sage.

Fink, E. L., Kaplowitz, S. A., & Bauer, C. L. (1983). Positional discrepancy, psychological discrepancy, and attitude change: Experimental tests of some mathematical models. *Communication Monographs, 50,* 413–430.

Fishbein, M. (Ed.). (1967). *Readings in attitude theory and measurement.* New York: Wiley.

Fishbein, M., & Ajzen, I. (1975). *Belief, attitude, intention, and behavior.* Reading, MA: Addison-Wesley.

Fishbein, M., & Ajzen, I. (1980). Predicting and understanding consumer behavior: Attitude behavior correspondence. In I. Ajzen & M. Fishbein (Eds.), *Understanding attitudes and predicting social behavior* (pp. 148–172). Englewood Cliffs, NJ: Prentice-Hall.

Fishbein, M., & Ajzen, I. (2010). *Predicting and changing behavior: The reasoned action approach.* New York: Psychology Press.

Fisher, R. A. (1935). *The design of experiments.* New York: Hafner Press.

Fiske, S. T., & Taylor, S. E. (1991). *Social cognition* (2nd ed.). New York: McGraw-Hill.

Flay, B. R. (1986). Mass media linkages with school-based programs for drug abuse prevention. *Journal of School Health, 56,* 402–406.

Flay, B. R. (1987). Mass media and smoking cessation: A critical review. *American Journal of Public Health, 77,* 153–160.

Fointiat, V., Morisot, V., & Pakuszewski, M. (2008). Effects of past transgressions in an induced hypocrisy paradigm. *Psychological Reports, 103,* 625–633.

Folkes, V. S. (1982). Communicating the reasons for social rejection. *Journal of Experimental Social Psychology, 18,* 235–252.

Forsyth, D. R. (2010). *Group dynamics* (5th ed.). Belmont, CA: Wadsworth.

Francik, E. P., & Clark, H. H. (1985). How to make requests that overcome obstacles to compliance. *Journal of Memory and Language, 24,* 560–568.

Freedman, J. L., & Fraser, S. (1966). Compliance without pressure: The foot-in-the-door technique. *Journal of Personality and Social Psychology, 4,* 195–202.

Freedman, J. L., & Sears, D. O. (1965). Selective exposure. In L. Berkowitz (Ed.), *Advances in experimental social psychology* (Vol. 2, pp. 58–98). New York: Academic Press.

French, J. P. R., Jr., & Raven, B. (1960). The bases of social power. In D. Cartwright & A. Zander (Eds.), *Group dynamics* (pp. 607–623). New York: Harper & Row.

Galanter, M. (1999). *Cults: Faith, healing, and coercion* (2nd ed.). New York: Oxford University Press.

Gallup, G. H. (1977). *The Gallup Poll: Public opinion 72–77.* Wilmington, DE: Scholarly Resources.

Gallup Organization. (2011). *For first time, majority of Americans favor legal gay marriage: Republicans and older Americans remain opposed.* Retrieved from *www.gallup.com/poll/147662/first-time-majority-americans-favor-legal-gay-marriage.aspx.*

Gass, R. H., & Seiter, J. S. (1999). *Persuasion, social influence, and compliance gaining.* Boston: Allyn & Bacon.

Gavett, G. (2012, November 2). *Electing a president in a microtargeted world.* Harvard Business Review. HBR.org.

Gawronski, B. (2007). Editorial: Attitudes can be measured! But what is an attitude? *Social Cognition, 25,* 573–581.

Gawronski, B., & Bodenhausen, G. V. (2007). Unraveling the processes underlying evaluation: Attitudes from the perspective of the APE model. *Social Cognition, 25,* 687–717.

Geller, E. S. (1989). Using television to promote safety belt use. In R. E. Rice & C. K. Atkin (Eds.), *Public communication campaigns* (pp. 201–203). Newbury Park, CA: Sage.

German, K. M., Gronbeck, B. E., Ehninger, D., & Monroe, A. H. (2013). *Principles of public speaking* (18th ed.). Boston: Allyn & Bacon.

Glass, G. V., McGaw, B., & Smith, M. L. (1981). *Meta-analysis in social research.* Beverly Hills, CA: Sage.

Goethals, G. R., & Nelson, R. E. (1973). Similarity in the influence process: The belief–value distinction. *Journal of Personality and Social Psychology, 25,* 117–122.

Goldfarb, L., Gerrard, M., Gibbons, E. X., & Plante, T. (1988). Attitudes toward sex, arousal, and the retention of contraceptive information. *Journal of Personality and Social Psychology, 55,* 634–641.

Gorassini, D. R., & Olson, J. M. (1995). Does self-perception change explain the foot-in-the-door effect? *Journal of Personality and Social Psychology, 69,* 91–105.

Gould, S. J. (1983). *Hen's teeth and horse's toes.* New York: Norton.

Gouldner, A. W. (1960). The norm of reciprocity: A preliminary statement. *American Sociological Review, 25,* 161–178.

Grabe, M. E., Kamhawi, R., & Yegiyan, N. (2009). Informing citizens: How people with different education levels process television, newspaper, and web news. *Journal of Broadcasting and Electronic Media, 53,* 90–111.

Gray, J. (1992). *Men are from Mars, women are from Venus: A practical guide for improving communication and getting what you want in your relationships.* New York: HarperCollins.

Greene, K., & Brinn, L. S. (2003). Messages influencing college women's tanning bed use statistical versus narrative evidence format and a self-assessment to increase perceived susceptibility. *Journal of Health Communication, 8,* 443–461.

Greenwald, A. G. (1975). On the inconclusiveness of "crucial" cognitive tests of dissonance vs. self-perception theories. *Journal of Experimental and Social Psychology, 11,* 490–499.

Greenwald, A. G. (1989). Why are attitudes important? In A. R. Pratkanis, S. J. Breckler, & A. G. Greenwald (Eds.), *Attitude structure and function* (pp. 1–10). Hillsdale, NJ: Erlbaum.

Greenwald, A. G., Brock, T. C., & Ostrom, T. M. (1968). *Psychological foundations of attitudes.* New York: Academic Press.

Greenwald, A. G., & Ronis, D. L. (1978). Twenty years of cognitive dissonance: Case study of the evolution of a theory. *Psychological Review, 85,* 53–57.

Groh, D. R., Jason, L. A., & Keys, C. B. (2008). Social network variables in Alcoholics Anonymous: A literature review. *Clinical Psychology Review, 28,* 430–450.

Gruder, C., Cook, T., Hennigan, K., Flay, B., Alessis, C., & Halamaj, J. (1978). Empirical tests of the absolute sleeper effect predicted from the discounting cue hypothesis. *Journal of Personality and Social Psychology, 36,* 1061–1074.

Guadagno, R., & Cialdini, R. B. (2010). Preference for consistency and social influence: A review of current research findings. *Social Influence, 5,* 152–163.

Guerrero, L. K., Andersen, P. A., & Trost, M. R. (1998). Communication and emotion: Basic concepts and approaches. In P. A. Andersen & L. K. Guerrero (Eds.), *Handbook of communication and emotion: Research, theory, applications, and contexts* (pp. 5–27). San Diego, CA: Academic Press.

Gunter, G. (1994). The question of media violence. In J. Bryant & D. Zillman (Eds.), *Media effects: Advances in theory and research* (pp. 163–211). Hillsdale, NJ: Erlbaum.

Haaland, G. A., & Venkatesen, M. (1968). Resistance to persuasive communications: An examination of the distraction hypothesis. *Journal of Personality and Social Psychology, 9,* 167–170.

Hagger, M. S., Chatzisarantis, N. L. D., & Biddle, S. J. H. (2002). A meta-analytic review of the theories of reasoned action and planned behavior in physical activity: Predictive validity and the contribution of additional variables. *Journal of Sport and Exercise Psychology, 24,* 3–32.

Hahn, U., Harris, A. J. L., & Corner, A. (2009). Argument content and argument source: An exploration. *Informal Logic, 29,* 337–367.

Hale, J., Mongeau, P. A., & Thomas, R. M. (1991). Cognitive processing of one- and two-sided persuasive messages. *Western Journal of Speech Communication, 55,* 380–389.

Hall, J. A., & La France, B. H. (2007). Attitudes and communication of homophobia in fraternities: Separating the impact of social adjustment function from hetero-identity concern. *Communication Quarterly, 55,* 39–60.

Hample, D. (1977). Testing a model of value argument and evidence. *Communication Monographs, 44,* 106–120.

Hample, D. (1978). Predicting immediate belief change and adherence to argument claims. *Communication Monographs, 45,* 219–228.

Hample, D. (1979). Predicting belief change using a cognitive theory of argument and evidence. *Communication Monographs, 46,* 142–151.

Hample, D., & Dallinger, J. M. (1987). Cognitive editing of argument strategies. *Human Communication Research, 14,* 123–144.

Hample, D., & Dallinger, J. M. (1998). On the etiology of the rebuff phenomenon: Why are persuasive messages less polite after rebuffs? *Communication Studies, 49,* 305–321.

Harkins, S. G., & Petty, R. E. (1981). The multiple source effect in persuasion: The effects of distraction. *Personality and Social Psychology Bulletin, 7,* 627–635.

Harmon-Jones, E. (2002). A cognitive dissonance theory perspective on persuasion. In J. P. Dillard & M. Pfau (Eds.), *The SAGE handbook of persuasion: Developments in theory and practice* (pp. 99–116). Thousand Oaks, CA: Sage.

Harmon-Jones, E., Amodio, D. M., & Harmon-Jones, C. (2009). Action-based model of dissonance: A review. In M. P. Zanna (Ed.), *Advances in experimental social psychology* (Vol. 41, pp. 119–166). Burlington: VT: Academic Press.

Harmon-Jones, E., & Mills, J. (Eds.). (1999). *Cognitive dissonance: Progress on a pivotal theory in social psychology.* Washington, DC: American Psychological Association.

Harrington, N. G. (1995). The effects of college students' alcohol resistance strategies. *Health Communication, 7,* 371–391.

Hart, W., Albarracín, D., Eagly, A. H., Brechan, I., Lindberg, M., & Merrill, L. (2009). Feeling validated versus being correct: A meta-analysis of selective exposure to information. *Psychological Bulletin, 135,* 555–588.

Hatfield, E., & Sprecher, S. (1986). *Mirror, mirror . . . : The importance of looks in everyday life.* Albany: State University of New York Press.

Hawkins, R. P., Kreuter, M., Resnicow, K., Fishbein, M., & Dijkstra, A. (2008). Understanding tailoring in communicating about health. *Health Education Research, 23,* 454–466.

Hecht, M. L., Corman, S. R., & Miller-Rassulo, M. (1993). An evaluation of the Drug Resistance Project: A comparison of film versus live performance media. *Health Communication, 5,* 75–88.

Hecht, M., Trost, M. R., Bator, R. J., & MacKinnon, D. (1997). Ethnicity and sex similarities and differences in drug resistance. *Journal of Applied Communication Research, 25,* 75–97.

Heider, E. (1946). Attitudes and cognitive organization. *Journal of Psychology, 21,* 107–112.

Herek, G. W. (1984a). Attitudes toward lesbians and gay men: A factor analytic study. *Journal of Homosexuality, 10,* 39–51.

Herek, G. W. (1984b). Beyond "homophobia": A social psychological perspective on attitudes toward lesbians and gay men. *Journal of Homosexuality, 10,* 2–17.

Herek, G. W. (1987). Can functions be measured?: A new perspective on the functional approach to attitudes. *Social Psychology Quarterly, 50,* 285–303.

Herek, G. W. (1988). Heterosexuals' attitudes toward lesbians and gay men: Correlates and gender differences. *Journal of Sex Research, 25,* 451–477.

Herek, G. M. (2000). The social construction of attitudes: Functional consensus and divergence in the U.S. public's reactions to AIDS. In G. R. Maio & J. M. Olson (Eds.), *Why we evaluate: Functions of attitudes* (pp. 325–364). Mahwah, NJ: Erlbaum.

Herek, G. M. (2009). Hate crimes and stigma-related experiences among sexual minority adults in the United States. *Journal of Interpersonal Violence, 24,* 54–74.

Hewgill, M. A., & Miller, G. R. (1965). Source credibility and response to fear-arousing communications. *Speech Monographs, 32,* 95–101.

Higgins, E. T. (1996). Knowledge activation: Accessibility, applicability, and salience. In E. T. Higgins & A. W. Kruglanski (Eds.), *Social psychology: Handbook of basic principles* (pp. 133–168). New York: Guilford Press.

Higgins, E. T. (2012). Accessibility theory. In P. A. M. Van Lange, A. W. Kruglanski, & E. T. Higgins (Eds.), *The handbook of theories of social psychology* (Vol. 1, pp. 75–96). London: Sage.

Higgins, E. T., King, G. A., & Mavin, G. H. (1982). Individual construct accessibility and subjective impressions and recall. *Journal of Personality and Social Psychology, 43,* 35–47.

Hill, D. B., & Willoughby, B. L. (2005). The development and validation of the genderism and transphobia scale. *Sex Roles, 53,* 531–544.

Hong-Youl, H., Joby, J., Swinder, J., & Siva, M. (2011). The effects of advertising spending on brand loyalty in services. *European Journal of Marketing, 45,* 673–691.

Hovland, C. I., Janis, I. L., & Kelley, H. H. (1953). *Communication and persuasion.* New Haven, CT: Yale University Press.

Hovland, C., Lumsdaine, A., & Sheffield, E. (1949). *Experiments in mass communication.* Princeton, NJ: Princeton University Press.

Hovland, C. I., & Pritzker, H. A. (1957). Extent of opinion change as a function of amount of change advocated. *Journal of Abnormal and Social Psychology, 54,* 257–261.

Hovland, C., & Weiss, W. (1951). The influence of source credibility on communication effectiveness. *Public Opinion Quarterly, 15,* 635–650.

Hullett, C. R. (2004). Using functional theory to promote sexually transmitted disease testing. *Communication Research, 31,* 363–396.

Hullett, C. R. (2006). Using functional theory to promote HIV testing: The impact of value-expressive messages, uncertainty, and fear. *Health Communication, 20*, 57–67.

Hullett, C. R., & Boster, F. J. (2001). Matching messages to the values underlying value-expressive and social-adjustive attitudes: Reconciling an old theory with a contemporary measurement approach. *Communication Monographs, 68*, 133–153.

Hunter, J. E., Danes, J. E., & Cohen, S. H. (1984). *Mathematical models of attitude change: Change in single attitudes and cognitive structure.* New York: Academic Press.

Hunter, J. E., & Schmidt, F. L. (1990). *Methods of meta-analysis: Correcting error and bias in research findings.* Newbury Park, CA: Sage.

Hunter, J. E., Schmidt, F. L., & Jackson, G. B. (1982). *Meta-analysis: Cumulating research findings across studies.* Beverly Hills, CA: Sage.

Ifert, D. E. (2000). Resistance to interpersonal requests: A summary and critique of recent research. In M. Roloff (Ed.), *Communication yearbook 23* (pp. 125–161). Thousand Oaks, CA: Sage.

Ifert, D. E., & Roloff, M. E. (1994). Anticipated obstacles to compliance: Predicting their presence and expression. *Communication Studies, 45*, 120–130.

Insko, C. A. (1967). *Theories of attitude change.* New York: Appleton Century Crofts.

Insko, C. A., Turnbull, W., & Yandell, B. (1974). Facilitative and inhibiting effects of distraction on attitude change. *Sociometry, 37*, 508–528.

International Cultic Studies Association. (2012). *Prevalence.* Retrieved from *http://icsahome.com/infoserv_respond/info_researchers.asp?ID=49607.*

Isenberg, D. J. (1986). Group polarization: A critical review and meta-analysis. *Journal of Personality and Social Psychology, 50*, 1141–1151.

Izard, C. E. (1977). *Human emotions.* New York: Plenum.

Jackall, R., & Hirota, J. M. (2000). *Image makers: Advertising, public relations, and the ethos of advocacy.* Chicago: University of Chicago Press.

Jackson, S., & Allen, M. (1987, May). *Meta-analysis of the effectiveness of one-sided and two-sided argumentation.* Paper presented at the annual meeting of the International Communication Association, Montreal, Canada.

Janis, I. L. (1967). Effects of fear arousal on attitude change: Recent developments in theory and research. In L. Berkowitz (Ed.), *Advances in experimental social psychology* (Vol. 3, pp. 166–224). New York: Academic Press.

Janis, I. L., & Feshbach, S. (1953). Effects of fear arousing communications. *Journal of Abnormal and Social Psychology, 48*, 78–92.

Janis, I. L., & Frick, E. (1943). The relationship between attitudes toward conclusions and errors in judging logical validity of syllogisms. *Journal of Experimental Psychology, 33*, 73–77.

Janis, I. L., Kaye, D., & Kirschner, P. (1965). Facilitating effects of "eating-while-reading" on responsiveness to persuasive communications. *Journal of Personality and Social Psychology, 1*, 181–186.

Janis, I. L., & King, B. T. (1954). The influence of role-playing on opinion change. *Journal of Abnormal and Social Psychology, 49*, 211–218.

Janz, N. K., & Becker, M. H. (1984). The health belief model: A decade later. *Health Education Quarterly, 11*, 1–47.

Jeong, S., & Hwang, Y. (2012). Does multitasking increase or decrease persuasion? Effects of multitasking on comprehension and counterarguing. *Journal of Communication, 62,* 571–587.

Jessor, R., & Jessor, S. L., (1977). *Problem behavior and psychosocial development: A longitudinal study of youth.* New York: Academic Press.

Jimenez, M., & Yang, K. C. C. (2008). How guilt level affects green advertising effectiveness? *Journal of Creative Communications, 3,* 231–254.

Johnson, B. T., & Eagly, A. H. (1989). Effects of involvement on persuasion: A meta-analysis. *Psychological Bulletin, 106,* 290–314.

Johnson, B. T., & Eagly, A. H. (1990). Involvement and persuasion: Types, traditions, and the evidence. *Psychological Bulletin, 107,* 375–384.

Kahneman, D. (1973). *Attention and effort.* Englewood Cliffs, NJ: Prentice-Hall.

Kahneman, D., & Frederick, S. (2002). Representativeness revisited: Attribute substitution in intuitive judgment. In T. Gilovich, D. Griffin, & D. Kahneman (Eds.), *Heuristics and biases: The psychology of intuitive judgment* (pp. 49–81). New York: Cambridge University Press.

Kahneman, D., & Tversky, A. (1973). On the psychology of prediction. *Psychological Review, 80,* 237–251.

Kaid, L. L., & Bystrom, D. G. (Eds.). (1999). *The electronic election: Perspectives on the 1996 campaign communication.* Mahwah, NJ: Erlbaum.

Katz, A. H. (1993). *Self-help in America: A social movement perspective.* New York: Twayne.

Katz, D. (1960). The functional approach to the study of attitudes. *Public Opinion Quarterly, 24,* 163–204.

Kellermann, K. (1980). The concept of evidence: A critical review. *Journal of the American Forensics Association, 16,* 159–172.

Kellermann, K. (2004). A goal-directed approach to gaining compliance: Relating differences among goals to differences in behaviors. *Communication Research, 31,* 397–445.

Kellermann, K., & Cole, T. (1994). Classifying compliance-gaining messages: Taxonomic disorder and strategic confusion. *Communication Theory, 4,* 3–60.

Kelley, H. H. (1952). Two functions of reference groups. In G. E. Swanson, T. M. Newcomb, & E. L. Hartley (Eds.), *Readings in social psychology* (2nd ed., pp. 410–414). New York: Holt.

Kelley, H. H. (1967). Attribution theory in social psychology. In D. Levine (Ed.), *Nebraska Symposium on Motivation* (Vol. 15, pp. 192–238). Lincoln: University of Nebraska Press.

Kelley, H. H., & Thibaut, J. W. (1978). *Interpersonal relationships.* New York: Wiley.

Kelman, H. C. (1958). Compliance, identification, and internalization: Three processes of attitude change. *Journal of Conflict Resolution, 2,* 51–60.

Kelman, H. C. (1961). Processes of opinion change. *Public Opinion Quarterly, 25,* 57–78.

Kelman, H., & Hovland, C. (1953). Reinstatement of the communicator in delayed measurement of opinion change. *Journal of Abnormal and Social Psychology, 48,* 327–335.

Kerlinger, F. N., & Lee, H. B. (2000). *Foundations of behavioral research* (4th ed.). Fort Worth, TX: Harcourt Brace.

Kiesler, C. A. (1971). *The psychology of commitment: Experiments linking behavior to belief.* San Diego, CA: Academic Press.

Kiesler, C. A., Collins, C. A., & Miller, N. (1983). *Attitude change: A critical analysis of theoretical approaches.* Malabar, FL: Krieger. (Original work published 1969)

Kim, M. S., & Hunter, J. E. (1993a). Attitude–behavior relationships: A meta-analysis of attitude relevance and topic. *Journal of Communication, 43,* 101–142.

Kim, M. S., & Hunter, J. E. (1993b). Relationships among attitudes, behavioral intentions, and behaviors: A meta-analysis. *Communication Research, 20,* 331–364.

King, B. T., & Janis, I. L. (1956). Comparison of the effects of improvised versus nonimprovised role playing in producing opinion changes. *Human Relations, 9,* 177–186.

Knoblach-Westerwick, S., & Sarge, M. (2015). Impacts of exemplification and efficacy as characteristics of an online weight-loss message on selective exposure and subsequent weight-loss behavior. *Communication Research, 4,* 547–568.

Kogan, N., & Wallach, M. A. (1967). Risky-shift phenomenon in small decision-making groups: A test of the information exchange hypothesis. *Journal of Experimental Social Psychology, 6,* 467–471.

Kokkinaki, F., & Lunt, P. (1997). The relationship between involvement, attitude accessibility, and attitude–behavior consistency. *British Journal of Social Psychology, 36,* 497–509.

Kopfman, J. E., Smith, S. W., Yun, J. K., & Hodges, A. (1998). Affective and cognitive reaction to narrative versus statistical evidence in organ donation messages. *Journal of Applied Communication Research, 26,* 279–300.

Kreuter, M. W., Strecher, V., & Glassman, B. (1999). One size does not fit all: The case for tailoring print materials. *Annals of Behavioral Medicine, 21,* 276–283.

Kruglanski, A. W., Erbs, H.-P., Pierro, A., Mannetti, L., & Chun, W. Y. (2006). On parametric continuities in the world of binary either ors. *Psychological Inquiry, 17,* 153–165.

Kruglanski, A. W., & Thompson, E. P. (1999). Persuasion by a single route: A view from the unimodel. *Psychological Inquiry, 10,* 83–109.

Kumkale, G. T., & Albarracín, D. (2004). The sleeper effect in persuasion: A meta-analytic review. *Psychological Bulletin, 130,* 143–172.

Kumkale, G. T., Albarracín, D., & Seignourel, P. J. (2010). The effects of source credibility in the presence or absence of prior attitudes: Implications for the design of persuasive communication campaigns. *Journal of Applied Social Psychology, 40,* 1325–1356.

Kupor, D., & Tormala, Z. (2015). Persuasion, interrupted: The effect of momentary interruptions on message processing and persuasion. *Journal of Consumer Research, 42,* 300–315.

Lamm, H., & Myers, D. G. (1978). Group-induced polarization of attitudes and behavior. In L. Berkowitz (Ed.), *Advances in experimental social psychology* (Vol. 11, pp. 145–195). New York: Academic Press.

LaPiere, R. T. (1934). Attitudes versus actions. *Social Forces, 13,* 230–237.

Larson, C. U. (2001). *Persuasion: Reception and responsibility* (9th ed.). Belmont, CA: Wadsworth.

Latané, B., & Darley, J. M. (1968). Group inhibition of bystander intervention in emergencies. *Journal of Personality and Social Psychology, 10*, 215–221.

Latané, B., & Darley, J. M. (1970). *The unresponsive bystander: Why doesn't he help?* New York: Appleton-Century-Crofts.

Latané, B., & Rodin, J. (1969). A lady in distress: Inhibiting effects of friends and strangers on bystander intervention. *Journal of Experimental Social Psychology, 5*, 189–202.

Laughlin, P. R. (2011). Social choice theory, social decision scheme theory, and group decision-making. *Group Processes and Intergroup Relations, 14*, 63–79.

Lavine, H. (1999). Types of evidence and routes to persuasion: The unimodel versus dual-process models. *Psychological Inquiry, 10*, 141–144.

Lavine, H., & Snyder, M. (2000). Cognitive processing and the functional matching effect in persuasion: Studies of personality and political behavior. In G. R. Maio & J. M. Olson (Eds.), *Why we evaluate: Functions of attitudes* (pp. 97–131). Mahwah, NJ: Erlbaum.

Lederman, L. C., & Stewart, L. (2005). *Changing the culture of college drinking: A socially-situated health communication campaign.* New York: Hampton Press.

Lee, C., & Green, R. T. (1991). A cross-cultural examination of the Fishbein behavioral intention model. *Journal of International Business Studies, 22*, 289–305.

Lenihan, K. J. (1965). *Perceived climates as a barrier to housing desegregation.* Unpublished manuscript, Columbia University, Bureau of Applied Social Research, New York.

Leone, C. (1994). Opportunity for thought and differences in the need for cognition: A person by situation analysis of self-generated attitude change. *Personality and Individual Differences, 17*, 571–574.

Leupker, R. V., Johnson, C. A., Murray, D. M., & Pechacek, T. E. (1983). Prevention of cigarette smoking: Three-year follow-up of an education program for youth. *Journal of Behavioral Medicine, 6*, 53–62.

Leventhal, H. (1970). Findings and theory in the study of fear communications. In L. Berkowitz (Ed.), *Advances in experimental social psychology* (Vol. 5, pp. 119–186). New York: Academic Press.

Levin, K. D., Nichols, D. R., & Johnson, B. T. (2000). Involvement and persuasion: Attitude functions for the motivated processor. In G. R. Maio & J. M. Olson (Eds.), *Why we evaluate: Functions of attitudes* (pp. 163–194). Mahwah, NJ: Erlbaum.

Lewin, K. (1935). *A dynamic theory of personality.* New York: McGraw-Hill.

Lewis, I. M., Watson, B. C., Tay, R. S., & White, K. M. (2007). The role of fear appeals in improving driver safety: A review of the effectiveness of fear-arousing (threat) appeals in road safety advertising. *International Journal of Behavioral and Consultation Therapy, 3*(2), 203–222.

Liebert, R. M., Neale, J. M., & Davidson, E. S. (1973). *The early window: Effects of television on children and youth.* New York: Pergamon Press.

Luchok, J. A., & McCroskey, J. C. (1978). The effect of quality of evidence on attitude change and source credibility. *Southern Speech Communication Journal, 43*, 371–383.

Lumsdaine, A. A., & Janis, I. L. (1953). Resistance to "counter-propaganda" produced by one-sided and two-sided "propaganda" presentations. *Public Opinion Quarterly, 17,* 311–318.

Lustria, M. L., Noar, S. M., Cortese, J., Van Stee, S. K., Glueckauf, R. L., & Lee, J. (2013). A meta-analysis of web-delivered tailored health behavior change interventions. *Journal of Health Communication, 18,* 1039–1069.

MacHovec, E. J. (1989). *Cults and personality.* Springfield, IL: Thomas.

Madden, T. J., Ellen, P. S., & Ajzen, I. (1992). A comparison of the theory of planned behavior and the theory of reasoned action. *Personality and Social Psychology Bulletin, 18,* 3–9.

Maddux, J. E., & Rogers, R. W. (1983). Protection motivation and self-efficacy: A revised theory of fear appeals and attitude change. *Journal of Experimental Social Psychology, 19,* 469–479.

Maio, G. R., & Olson, J. M. (2000a). Preface. In G. R. Maio & J. M. Olson (Eds.), *Why we evaluate: Functions of attitudes* (pp. vii–xi). Mahwah, NJ: Erlbaum.

Maio, G. R., & Olson, J. M. (Eds.). (2000b). *Why we evaluate: Functions of attitudes.* Mahwah, NJ: Erlbaum.

Mandler, G. (1984). *Mind and body: Psychology of emotion and stress.* New York: Norton.

Marshall, L. J. (2000). Toward a life-span perspective on the study of message production. *Communication Theory, 10,* 188–199.

Marwell, G., & Schmitt, D. R. (1967). Dimensions of compliance-gaining behavior: An empirical analysis. *Sociometry, 30,* 350–364.

Mayer, M. E. (1986). Explaining the choice shift: A comparison of competing effects-coded models. In M. L. McLaughlin (Ed.), *Communication yearbook 9* (pp. 297–314). Beverly Hills, CA: Sage.

McCoy, T. (2012, April 10). The creepiness factor: How Obama and Romney are getting to know you. *The Atlantic.* Available at *www.theatlantic.com/politics/archive/2012/04/the-creepiness-factor-how-obama-and-romney-are-getting-to-know-you/255499.*

McCroskey, J. C. (1966). Scales for the measurement of ethos. *Speech Monographs, 33,* 65–72.

McCroskey, J. C. (1967a). Experimental studies of the effects of ethos and evidence in persuasive communication (Doctoral dissertation, Pennsylvania State University, State College, PA, 1966). *Dissertation Abstracts International, 27,* 3630A.

McCroskey, J. C. (1967b). The effects of evidence in persuasive communication. *Western Speech, 31,* 189–199.

McCroskey, J. C. (1969). A summary of experimental research on the effects of evidence in persuasive communication. *Quarterly Journal of Speech, 55,* 169–176.

McCroskey, J. C. (1970). The effects of evidence as an inhibitor of counter-persuasion. *Communications Monographs, 37,* 188–194.

McCroskey, J. C., & Dunham, R. E. (1966). Ethos: A confounding element in communication research. *Communication Monographs, 33,* 464–466.

McCroskey, J. C., & Teven, J. J. (1999). Goodwill: A reexamination of the construct and its measurement. *Communication Monographs, 66,* 90–103.

McGuire, W. J. (1960). A syllogistic analysis of cognitive relationships. In C. I. Hovland & M. J. Rosenberg (Eds.), *Attitude organization and change: An analysis of consistency among attitude components* (pp. 65–111). New Haven, CT: Yale University Press.

McGuire, W. J. (1961a). The effectiveness of supportive and refutational defenses in immunizing and restoring beliefs against persuasion. *Sociometry, 24,* 184–197.

McGuire, W. J. (1961b). Persistence of resistance to persuasion induced by various types of persuasive defenses. *Journal of Abnormal and Social Psychology, 64,* 241–248.

McGuire, W. J. (1964). Inducing resistance to persuasion: Some contemporary approaches. In L. Berkowitz (Ed.), *Advances in experimental social psychology* (Vol. 1, pp. 191–229). New York: Academic Press.

McGuire, W. J. (1966). Attitudes and opinions. *Annual Review of Psychology, 17,* 475–514.

McGuire, W. J. (1968). Personality and attitude change: An information processing theory. In A. G. Greenwald, T. C. Brock, & T. M. Ostrom (Eds.), *Psychological foundations of attitudes* (pp. 171–196). New York: Academic Press.

McGuire, W. J. (1969). The nature of attitudes and attitude change. In G. Lindzey & E. Aronson (Eds.), *Handbook of social psychology* (Vol. 3, pp. 136–314). Reading, MA: Addison-Wesley.

McGuire, W. J. (1999). *Constructing social psychology: Creative and critical processes.* Cambridge, UK: Cambridge University Press.

McGuire, W. J., & Papageorgis, D. (1961). The relative efficacy of various types of prior belief-defense in producing immunity against persuasion. *Journal of Abnormal and Social Psychology, 62,* 327–337.

McLaughlin, M. L., Cody, M. J., & Robey, C. S. (1980). Situational influences on the selection of strategies to resist compliance-gaining attempts. *Human Communication Research, 7,* 14–36.

McMillan, S. J., & Downes, E. J. (2000). Defining interactivity: A qualitative identification of key dimensions. *New Media and Society, 2,* 157–179.

Metts, S., Cupach, W. R., & Imahori, T. T. (1992). Perceptions of sexual compliance resisting messages in three types of cross-sex relationships. *Western Journal of Communication, 56,* 1–17.

Meyers, R. A. (1989). Persuasive arguments theory: A test of assumptions. *Human Communication Research, 15,* 357–381.

Meyers, R. A., Brashers, D. E., & Hanner, J. (2000). Majority–minority influence: Identifying argumentative patterns and predicting argument-outcome links. *Journal of Communication, 50,* 3–30.

Meyers, R. A., & Seibold, D. R. (1990). Perspectives on group argument: A critical review of persuasive arguments theory and an alternative structurational view. In J. A. Anderson (Ed.), *Communication yearbook 13* (pp. 268–302). Newbury Park, CA: Sage.

Millar, M. (2002). Effects of a guilt induction and guilt reduction on door in the face. *Communication Research, 29,* 666–680.

Millar, M. G., & Millar, K. U. (1990). Attitude change as a function of attitude type and argument type. *Journal of Personality and Social Psychology, 59,* 217–228.

Miller, G. R. (1963). Studies in the use of fear appeals: A summary and analysis. *Central States Speech Journal, 14*, 117–125.

Miller, G. R. (1967). A crucial problem in attitude research. *Quarterly Journal of Speech, 53*, 235–240.

Miller, G. R. (1973). Counterattitudinal advocacy: A current appraisal. In C. D. Mortensen & K. K. Sereno (Eds.), *Advances in communication research* (pp. 105–152). New York: Harper & Row.

Miller, G. R. (1980). On being persuaded: Some basic distinctions. In M. E. Roloff & G. R. Miller (Eds.), *Persuasion: New directions in theory and research* (pp. 11–28). Beverly Hills, CA: Sage.

Miller, G. R., Boster, E. J., Roloff, M., & Seibold, D. (1977). Compliance-gaining message strategies: A typology and some findings concerning effects of situational differences. *Communication Monographs, 44*, 37–51.

Miller, G. R., Boster, F., Roloff, M., & Seibold, D. (1987). MBRS rekindled: Some thoughts on compliance gaining in interpersonal settings. In M. E. Roloff & G. R. Miller (Eds.), *Interpersonal processes: New directions in communication research* (pp. 89–116). Newbury Park, CA: Sage.

Miller, G. R., & Burgoon, M. (1978). Persuasion research: Review and commentary. In B. D. Ruben (Ed.), *Communication yearbook 12* (pp. 29–47). New Brunswick, NJ: Transaction Books.

Miller, K. I. (2005). *Communication theories: Perspectives, processes, and contexts* (2nd ed.). New York: McGraw-Hill.

Miller, M. A., Alberts, J. K., Hecht, M. L., Trost, M. R., & Krizek, R. L. (2000). *Adolescent relationships and drug use.* Mahwah, NJ: Erlbaum.

Miller, N. (1965). Involvement and dogmatism as inhibitors of attitude change. *Journal of Experimental Social Psychology, 1*, 121–132.

Miller, N., & Pederson, W. C. (1999). Assessing process distinctiveness. *Psychological Inquiry, 10*, 150–156.

Mischel, W. (1968). *Personality and assessment.* New York: Wiley.

Mongeau, P. A. (2013). Fear appeals. In J. P. Dillard & L. Shen (Eds.), *The SAGE handbook of persuasion: Developments in theory and practice* (2nd ed., pp. 184–199). Thousand Oaks, CA: Sage.

Mongeau, P. A., Hale, J. L., & Alles, M. (1994). An experimental investigation of accounts and attributions following sexual infidelity. *Communication Monographs, 61*, 326–344.

Mongeau, P. A., & Stiff, J. B. (1993). Specifying causal relationships in the elaboration likelihood model. *Communication Theory, 3*, 65–72.

Moscovici, S., Lage, E., & Naffrechoux, M. (1969). Influence of a consistent minority on the responses of a majority in a color perception test. *Sociometry, 32*, 365–380.

Murphy, T. (2012, September–October). Inside the Obama campaign's hard drive: Obama's tech guru and his microtargeting wiz kids are building a new kind of Chicago machine. Can they help the president hold on to the Oval Office? *Mother Jones.* Motherjones.com.

Nabi, R. L. (2002). Discrete emotions and persuasion. In J. P. Dillard & M. Pfau (Eds.), *The SAGE handbook of persuasion: Developments in theory and practice* (pp. 289–308). Thousand Oaks, CA: Sage.

Nabi, R. L. (2010). The case for emphasizing discrete emotions in communication research. *Communication Monographs, 77*, 153–159.

Newcomb, T. M. (1953). An approach to the study of communicative acts. *Psychological Review, 60*, 393–404.

Newcomb, T. M., Turner, R. H., & Converse, P. E. (1965). *Social psychology*. New York: Holt, Rinehart & Winston.

Obama plays the race card. (2008, July 31). *The Rush Limbaugh Show*. Available at *www.rushlimbaugh.com/daily/2008/07/31/obama_plays_the_race_card*.

Ockene, J., Ockene, I., & Kristeller, J. (1988). *The coronary artery smoking intervention study*. Worcester, MA: National Heart Lung Blood Institute.

Okazaki, S., & Taylor, C. (2015). Social media and international advertising: Theoretical challenges and future directions. *International Marketing Review, 30*, 56–71.

O'Keefe, B. J. (1988). The logic of message design: Individual differences in reasoning about communication. *Communication Monographs, 55*, 80–103.

O'Keefe, B. J. (1990). The logic of regulative communication: Understanding the logic of message designs. In J. P. Dillard (Ed.), *Seeking compliance: The production of interpersonal influence messages* (pp. 87–106). Scottsdale, AZ: Gorsuch-Scarisbrick.

O'Keefe, B. J., & Delia, J. G. (1978). Construct comprehensiveness and cognitive complexity. *Perceptual and Motor Skills, 46*, 548–550.

O'Keefe, B. J., Lambert, B. L., & Lambert, C. A. (1997). Conflict and communication in a research and development unit. In B. D. Sypher (Ed.), *Case studies in organizational communication 2: Perspectives on contemporary worklife* (pp. 31–52). New York: Guilford Press.

O'Keefe, B. J., & McCornack, S. A. (1987). Message design logic and message goal structure: Effects on perceptions of message quality in regulative communication situations. *Human Communication Research, 14*, 68–92.

O'Keefe, B. J., & Shepherd, G. J. (1987). The pursuit of multiple objectives in face-to-face persuasive interactions: Effects of construct differentiation on message organization. *Communication Monographs, 54*, 396–419.

O'Keefe, D. J. (1987). The persuasive effects of delaying identification of high- and low-credibility communicators: A meta-analytic review. *Central States Communication Journal, 38*, 64–72.

O'Keefe, D. J. (1990). *Persuasion: Theory and research*. Newbury Park, CA: Sage.

O'Keefe, D. J. (1993). The persuasive effects of message sidedness variations: A cautionary note concerning Allen's (1991) meta-analysis. *Western Journal of Communication, 57*, 87–97.

O'Keefe, D. J. (1997). Standpoint explicitness and persuasive effect: A meta-analytic review of the effects of varying conclusion articulation in persuasive messages. *Argumentation and Advocacy, 34*, 1–12.

O'Keefe, D. J. (1998). Justification explicitness and persuasive effect: A meta-analytic review of the effects of varying support articulation in persuasive messages. *Argumentation and Advocacy, 35*, 61–75.

O'Keefe, D. J. (2000). Guilt and social influence. In M. Roloff (Ed.), *Communication yearbook 23* (pp. 67–101). Thousand Oaks, CA: Sage.

O'Keefe, D. J. (2002). Guilt as a mechanism of persuasion. In J. P. Dillard & M. W.

Pfau (Eds.), *The SAGE handbook of persuasion: Developments in theory and practice* (2nd ed., pp. 329–344). Thousand Oaks, CA: Sage.

O'Keefe, D. J. (2013). The elaboration likelihood model. In J. P. Dillard & L. Shen (Eds.), *The SAGE handbook of persuasion: Developments in theory and practice* (2nd ed., pp. 137–149). Thousand Oaks, CA: Sage.

O'Keefe, D. J. (2015). *Persuasion: Theory and research* (3rd ed.). Los Angeles: Sage.

O'Keefe, D. J., & Delia, J. D. (1981). Construct differentiation and the relationship of attitudes and behavioral intentions. *Communication Monographs, 48,* 146–157.

O'Keefe, D. J., & Figgé, M. (1997). A guilt-based explanation of the door-in-the-face influence strategy. *Human Communication Research, 24,* 64–81.

O'Keefe, D. J., & Hale, S. L. (1998). The door-in-the-face influence strategy: A random effects meta-analytic review. In M. Roloff (Ed.), *Communication yearbook 21* (pp. 1–33). Thousand Oaks, CA: Sage.

O'Keefe, D. J., & Hale, S. L. (2001). An odds-ratio-based meta-analysis on the door-in-the-face influence strategy. *Communication Reports, 14,* 31–38.

Oskamp, S., & Schultz, P. W. (2005). *Attitudes and opinions* (3rd ed.). Mahwah, NJ: Erlbaum.

Osterhouse, R. A., & Brock, T. C. (1970). Distraction increases yielding to propaganda by inhibiting counterarguing. *Journal of Personality and Social Psychology, 15,* 344–358.

Pascual, A., & Gueguen, N. (2005). Foot-in-the-door and door-in-the-face: A comparative meta-analytic study. *Psychological Reports, 96,* 122–128.

Patch, M. A. (1988). Differential perception of source legitimacy in sequential request strategies. *Journal of Social Psychology, 128,* 817–823.

Perez, E. (2015, April 23). How ISIS is luring so many Americans to join its ranks. CNN. Available at *cnn.com/2015/04/22/politics/isis-recruits-american-arrests.*

Perloff, R. M. (2001). *Persuading people to have safer sex: Applications of social science to the AIDS crisis.* Mahwah, NJ: Erlbaum.

Perloff, R. M., & Brock, T. C. (1980). " . . . And thinking makes it so": Cognitive responses to persuasion. In M. E. Roloff & G. R. Miller (Eds.), *Persuasion: New directions in theory and research* (pp. 67–99). Beverly Hills, CA: Sage.

Petty, R. E., & Briñol, P. (2006). Understanding social judgment: Multiple systems and processes. *Psychological Inquiry, 17,* 217–223.

Petty, R. E., & Briñol, P. (2012). The elaboration likelihood model. In P. A. M. Van Lange, A. W. Kruglanski, & E. T. Higgins (Eds.), *The handbook of theories of social psychology* (pp. 246–266). London: Sage.

Petty, R. E., Briñol, P., Loersch, C., & McCaslin, M. J. (2009). The need for cognition. In M. R. Leary & R. H. Hoyle (Eds.), *Handbook of individual differences in social behavior* (pp. 318–329). New York: Guilford Press.

Petty, R. E., Briñol, P., & Tormala, Z. L. (2002). Thought confidence as a determinant of persuasion: The self-validation hypothesis. *Journal of Personality and Social Psychology, 82,* 722–741.

Petty, R. E., Briñol, P., Tormala, Z. L., & Wegener, D. T. (2007). The role of metacognition in social judgment. In E. T. Higgins & A. W. Kruglanski (Eds.),

Social psychology: A handbook of basic principles (2nd ed., pp. 254–284). New York: Guilford Press.

Petty, R. E., & Cacioppo, J. T. (1981). *Attitudes and persuasion: Classic and contemporary approaches.* Dubuque, IA: Brown.

Petty, R. E., & Cacioppo, J. T. (1986). *Communication and persuasion: Central and peripheral routes to attitude change.* New York: Springer-Verlag.

Petty, R. E., & Cacioppo, J. T. (1990). Involvement vs. persuasion: Tradition vs. integration. *Psychological Bulletin, 107,* 367–374.

Petty, R. E., Cacioppo, J. T., & Goldman, R. (1981). Personal involvement as a determinant of argument-based persuasion. *Journal of Personality and Social Psychology, 41,* 847–855.

Petty, R. E., Kasmer, J. E., Haugtvedt, C. P., & Cacioppo, J. T. (1987). Source and message factors in persuasion: A reply to Stiff's critique of the elaboration likelihood model. *Communication Monographs, 54,* 233–249.

Petty, R. E., Ostrom, T. M., & Brock, T. C. (1981). *Cognitive responses in persuasion.* Hillsdale, NJ: Erlbaum.

Petty, R. E., & Wegener, D. T. (1998). Attitude change: Multiple roles for persuasion variables. In D. Gilbert, S. Fiske, & G. Lindzey (Eds.), *Handbook of social psychology* (4th ed., pp. 323–390). New York: McGraw-Hill.

Petty, R. E., & Wegener, D. T. (1999). The elaboration likelihood model: Current status and controversies. In S. Chaiken & Y. Trope (Eds.), *Dual-process theories in social psychology* (pp. 41–72). New York: Guilford Press.

Petty, R. E., Wegener, D. T., Fabrigar, L. R., Priester, J. R., & Cacioppo, J. T. (1994). Conceptual and methodological issues in the elaboration likelihood model of persuasion: A reply to the Michigan State critics. *Communication Theory, 3,* 336–363.

Petty, R. E., Wells, G. L., & Brock, T. C. (1976). Distraction can enhance or reduce yielding to propaganda: Thought disruption versus effort justification. *Journal of Personality and Social Psychology, 34,* 874–888.

Petty, R. E., Wheeler, S. C., & Bizer, G. Y. (1999). Is there one persuasion process or more?: Lumping versus splitting in attitude change theories. *Psychological Inquiry, 10,* 156–163.

Petty, R. E., Wheeler, S. C., & Bizer, G. Y. (2000). Attitude functions and persuasion: An elaboration likelihood approach to matched versus mismatched messages. In G. R. Maio & J. M. Olson (Eds.), *Why we evaluate: Functions of attitudes* (pp. 133–162). Mahwah, NJ: Erlbaum.

Petty, R. E., Wheeler, S. C., & Tormala, Z. L. (2003). Persuasion and attitude change. In T. Millon & M. J. Lerner (Eds.), *Handbook of psychology* (Vol. 3, 2nd ed., pp. 353–382). Hoboken, NJ: Wiley.

Pew Research Center. (2011, October 5). *GOP candidates hardly household names.* Pew Research Center for People & the Press, pp. 1–6.

Pfau, M. (1992). The potential of inoculation in promoting resistance to the effectiveness of comparative advertising messages. *Communication Quarterly, 40,* 26–44.

Pfau, M. (1995). Designing messages for behavioral inoculation. In E. Maibach & R. L. Parrott (Eds.), *Designing health messages: Approaches from communication theory and public health practice* (pp. 99–113). Thousand Oaks, CA: Sage.

Pfau, M. (2003). Persuasive communication [Review of the book *Persuasive Communication* (2nd ed.) by J. S. Stiff & P. A. Mongeau]. *Journal of Language and Social Psychology, 22*, 446–449.

Pfau, M., & Burgoon, M. (1988). Inoculation in political communication. *Human Communication Research, 15*, 91–111.

Pfau, M., & Kenski, H. C. (1990). *Attack politics: Strategy and defense.* New York: Praeger.

Pfau, M., Kenski, H. C., Nitz, M., & Sorenson, J. (1990). Efficacy of inoculation strategies in promoting resistance to political attack messages: Application to direct mail. *Communication Monographs, 57*, 25–43.

Pfau, M., & Parrott, R. (1993). *Persuasive communication campaigns.* Boston: Allyn & Bacon.

Pfau, M., Van Bockern, S., & Kang, J. G. (1992). Use of inoculation to promote resistance to smoking initiation among adolescents. *Communication Monographs, 59*, 213–230.

Pitt, L., Berthon, P., Watson, R., & Zinkhan, G. (2002). The Internet and the birth of real consumer power. *Business Horizons, 45*, 7–14.

Pornpitakpan, C. (2004). The persuasiveness of source credibility: A critical review of five decades' evidence. *Journal of Applied Social Psychology, 34*, 243–281.

Portnoy, D. B., Scott-Sheldon, L. A., Johnson, B. T., & Carey, M. P. (2008). Computer-delivered interventions for health promotion and behavioral risk reduction: A meta-analysis of 75 randomized controlled trials, 1988–2007. *Preventive Medicine, 47*, 3–16.

Powell, M. C., & Fazio, R. H. (1984). Attitude accessibility as a function of repeated attitude expression. *Personality and Social Psychology Bulletin, 10*, 139–148.

Powers, W., Jordan, W., & Street, R. (1979). Language indices in the measurement of cognitive complexity: Is complexity loquacity? *Human Communication Research, 6*, 69–73.

Pratkanis, A. R., Greenwald, A. G., Leippe, M. R., & Baumgardner, M. H. (1988). In search of reliable persuasion effects: III. The sleeper effect is dead. Long live the sleeper effect. *Journal of Personality and Social Psychology, 54*, 203–218.

Prochaska, J. O., DiClemente, C. C., & Norcross, J. C. (1992). In search of how people change: Applications to addictive behaviors. *American Psychologist, 47*, 1102–1114.

Rawlings, E. I. (1970). Reactive guilt and anticipatory guilt in altruistic behavior. In J. R. Macaulay & L. Berkowitz (Eds.), *Altruism and helping behavior* (pp. 163–177). New York: Academic Press.

Regan, D. T., & Fazio, R. H. (1977). On the consistency between attitudes and behavior: Look to the method of attitude formation. *Journal of Experimental Social Psychology, 13*, 28–45.

Reimer, T., Mata, R., & Stoecklin, M. (2004). The use of heuristics in persuasion: Deriving cues on source expertise from argument quality. *Current Research in Social Psychology, 10*, 69–83.

Reinard, J. C. (1988). The empirical study of the persuasive effects of evidence: The status after fifty years of research. *Human Communication Research, 15*, 3–59.

Reynolds, R. A., & Burgoon, M. (1983). Belief processing, reasoning, and evidence.

In R. Bostrom (Ed.), *Communication yearbook 7* (pp. 83–104). Beverly Hills, CA: Sage.

Reynolds, R. A., & Reynolds, J. L. (2002). Evidence. In J. P. Dillard & M. Pfau (Eds.), *The SAGE handbook of persuasion: Developments in theory and practice* (pp. 427–444). Thousand Oaks, CA: Sage.

Rhine, R. J., & Severance, L. J. (1970). Ego-involvement, discrepancy, source credibility, and attitude change. *Journal of Personality and Social Psychology, 16,* 175–190.

Rice, R., & Atkin, C. K. (2013). *Public communication campaigns.* Los Angeles: Sage.

Ridgeway, C. L. (1981). Nonconformity, competence and influence in groups: A test of two theories. *American Sociological Review, 46,* 33347.

Rieh, S. Y., & Danielson, D. R. (2007). Credibility: A multidisciplinary framework. *Annual review of information science and technology, 41,* 307–364.

Rogers, R. W. (1975). A protection motivation theory of fear appeals and attitude change. *Journal of Psychology, 91,* 93–114.

Rogers, R. W. (1983). Cognitive and physiological processes in fear appeals and attitude change: A revised theory of protection motivation. In J. Cacioppo & R. Petty (Eds.), *Social psychophysiology* (pp. 153–176). New York: Guilford Press.

Rohrbach, L. A., Graham, J. W., Hansen, W. B., Flay, B. R., & Johnson, C. A. (1987). Evaluation of resistance skills training using multitrait–multimethod role play skill assessment. *Health Education Research, 2,* 401–407.

Rokeach, M. (1968). *Beliefs, attitudes and values: A theory of organization and change.* San Francisco: Jossey-Bass.

Ronis, D. L. (1992). Conditional health threats: Health beliefs, decisions, and behaviors among adults. *Health Psychology, 11,* 127–134.

Rosenthal, R. (1991). *Meta-analytic procedures for social science research* (rev. ed.). Newbury Park, CA: Sage.

Roskos-Ewoldsen, D. R., Apran-Ralstin, L., & St. Pierre, J. (2002). Attitude accessibility and persuasion: The quick and the strong. In J. P. Dillard & M. W. Pfau (Eds.), *The persuasion handbook: Developments in theory and practice* (pp. 39–61). Thousand Oaks, CA: Sage.

Roskos-Ewoldsen, D. R., & Monahan, J. L. (Eds.). (2007). *Communication and social cognition: Theories and methods.* Mahwah, NJ: Erlbaum.

Rostker, B. D., Hosek, S. D., & Vaiana, M. E. (2011). *Gays in the military: Eventually, new facts conquer old taboos (RAND Review,* Vol. 35, pp. 1–4). Santa Monica, CA: RAND Corporation. Available at *www.rand.org/pubs/corporate_pubs/CP22-2011-04.*

Rule, B. G., Bisanz, G. L., & Kohn, M. (1985). Anatomy of a persuasion schema: Targets, goals, and strategies. *Journal of Personality and Social Psychology, 48,* 1127–1140.

Sabee, C. M., & Wilson, S. R. (2005). Students' primary goals, attributions, and facework during conversations about disappointing grades. *Communication Education, 54,* 185–204.

Sadler, O., & Tesser, A. (1973). Some effects of salience and time upon interpersonal hostility and attraction during social isolation. *Sociometry, 36,* 99–112.

Samp, J. A., & Solomon, D. H. (1998). Communicative responses to problematic events: I. The variety and facets of goals. *Communication Research, 25,* 66–95.

Sandberg, T., & Conner, M., (2008). Anticipated regret as an additional predictor in the theory of planned behaviour: A meta-analysis. *British Journal of Social Psychology, 47,* 589–606.

San Miguel, C. L., & Millham, J. (1976). The role of cognitive and situational variables in aggression toward homosexuals. *Journal of Homosexuality, 1,* 11–27.

Sarnoff, D. (1960). Reaction formation and cynicism. *Journal of Personality, 28,* 129–143.

Schachter, S., & Singer, J. E. (1962). Cognitive, social, and physiological determinants of emotional state. *Psychological Review, 65,* 121–128.

Schinke, S. P., & Gilchrist, L. D. (1984). Preventing cigarette smoking with youth. *Journal of Primary Prevention, 5,* 48–56.

Schrader, D. C., & Dillard, J. P. (1998). Goal structures and interpersonal influence. *Communication Studies, 49,* 276–293.

Schwartz, M. (2011, November 28). Pre-occupied: The origins and future of Occupy Wall Street. *The New Yorker.* Retrieved from *www.newyorker.com.*

Schwarz, N. (2007). Attitude construction: Evaluation in context. *Social Cognition, 25,* 638–656.

Seibold, D. R., Cantrill, J. G., & Meyers, R. A. (1985). Communication and interpersonal influence. In M. L. Knapp & G. R. Miller (Eds.), *Handbook of interpersonal communication* (pp. 551–611). Beverly Hills, CA: Sage.

Shadish, W. R., Cook, T. D., & Campbell, D. T. (2002). *Experimental and quasi-experimental designs for generalized causal inference.* Boston: Houghton Mifflin Harcourt.

Shen, L., & Bigsby, E. (2013). The effects of message features: Content, structure, and style. In J. P. Dillard & L. Shen (Eds.), *The SAGE handbook of persuasion: Developments in theory and practice* (2nd ed., pp. 20–35). Thousand Oaks, CA: Sage.

Sherif, C. W., Sherif, M., & Nebergall, R. E. (1965). *Attitude and attitude change.* Philadelphia: Saunders.

Sherif, M., & Hovland, C. I. (1961). *Social judgment: Assimilation and contrast effects in communication and attitude change.* New Haven, CT: Yale University Press.

Sherif, M., & Sherif, C. W. (1956). *An outline of social psychology.* New York: Harper & Row.

Sherif, M., & Sherif, C. W. (1967). Attitude as the individual's own categories: The social judgment–involvement approach to attitude and attitude change. In C. W. Sherif & M. Sherif (Eds.), *Attitude, ego-involvement, and change* (pp. 105–139). New York: Wiley.

Sillars, A. L. (1980). The stranger and the spouse as target persons for compliance-gaining strategies: A subjective expected utility model. *Human Communication Research, 6,* 265–279.

Simons, H. W., Berkowitz, N. N., & Moyer, R. J. (1970). Similarity, credibility, and attitude change: A review and a theory. *Psychological Bulletin, 73,* 1–16.

Simons, H. W., Morreale, J., & Gronbeck, B. (2001). *Persuasion in society.* Thousand Oaks, CA: Sage.

Sivacek, J., & Crano, W. D. (1982). Vested interest as a moderator of attitude-behavior consistency. *Journal of Personality and Social Psychology, 43,* 210–221.

Skinner, B. F. (1938). *The behavior of organisms: An experimental analysis.* Englewood Cliffs, NJ: Prentice-Hall.

Smith, M. B., Bruner, J. S., & White, R. W. (1956). *Opinions and personality.* New York: Wiley.

Snyder, L. B., & LaCroix, J. M. (2013). How effective are mediated health campaigns? In R. E. Rice & C. K. Atkin (Eds.), *Public communication campaigns* (pp. 113–129). Thousand Oaks, CA: Sage.

Snyder, M. (1986). *Public appearances/private realities: The psychology of self-monitoring.* New York: Freeman.

Snyder, M., & DeBono, K. (1985). Appeals to image and claims about quality: Understanding the psychology of advertising. *Journal of Personality and Social Psychology, 49,* 586–597.

Staats, C. K., & Staats, A. W. (1957). Meaning established by classical conditioning. *Journal of Experimental Psychology, 54,* 74–80.

Stahelski, A., & Patch, M. E. (1993). The effect of the compliance strategy choice upon perception of power. *Journal of Social Psychology, 133,* 693–698.

Steyn, P., Ewing, M., Ven Heerden, G., Pitt, L., & Windisch, L. (2015). From whence it came: Understanding source effects in consumer-generated advertising. *International Journal of Advertising, 30,* 133–160.

Stiff, J. B. (1986). Cognitive processing of persuasive message cues: A meta-analytic review of the effects of supporting information on attitudes. *Communication Monographs, 53,* 75–89.

Stiff, J. B., & Boster, F. J. (1987). Cognitive processing: Additional thoughts and a reply to Petty, Kasmer, Haugtvedt, and Cacioppo. *Communication Monographs, 54,* 250–256.

Stone, J., Aronson, E., Crain, A. L., Winslow, M. P., & Fried, C. B. (1994). Inducing hypocrisy as a means of encouraging young adults to use condoms. *Personality and Social Psychology Bulletin, 20,* 116–128.

Stone, J., & Fernandez, N. C. (2008). To practice what we preach: The use of hypocrisy and cognitive dissonance to motivate behavior change. *Social and Personality Psychology Compass 2,* 1024–1051.

Stoner, J. A. E. (1968). Risky and cautious shifts in group decisions: The influence of widely held values. *Journal of Experimental Social Psychology, 4,* 442–459.

Strack, F. (1999). Beyond dual-process models: Toward a flexible regulation system. *Psychological Inquiry, 10,* 166–169.

Strahan, E. J., & Zanna, M. P. (1999). Content versus process: If there is independence, can there still be two levels of information processing? *Psychological Inquiry, 10,* 170–172.

Stroebe, W. (1999). The return of the one-track mind. *Psychological Inquiry, 10,* 173–176.

Sun, L. H., & Kliff, S. (2012, February 7). Komen vice president resigns as details emerge on Planned Parenthood debate. *The Washington Post*. Retreived from *www.washingtonpost.com*.

Sutton, S. R. (1982). Fear-arousing communications: A critical examination of theory and research. In J. R. Eiser (Ed.), *Social psychology and behavioral medicine* (pp. 303–337). London: Wiley.

Sutton, S. R., & Eiser, J. R. (1984). The effect of fear-arousing communications on cigarette smoking: An expectancy-value approach. *Journal of Behavioral Medicine, 7*, 13–33.

Szabo, E. A., & Pfau, M. (2002). Nuances in inoculation: Theory and application. In J. P. Dillard & M. W. Pfau (Eds.), *The SAGE handbook of persuasion: Developments in theory and practice* (pp. 233–258). Thousand Oaks, CA: Sage.

Tannenbaum, P. H. (1953). *Attitudes toward source and concept as factors in attitude change through communications*. Unpublished doctoral dissertation, Institute for Communications Research, University of Illinois, Urbana.

Tellis, G. J. (1987). *Advertising, exposure, loyalty, and brand purchase: A two-stage model of choice* (Report No. 87–105). Cambridge, MA: Marketing Science Institute.

Tesser, A. (1978). Self-generated attitude change. In L. Berkowitz (Ed.), *Advances in experimental social psychology* (Vol. 11, pp. 289–338). New York: Academic Press.

Tesser, A., & Conlee, M. C. (1975). Some effects of time and thought on attitude polarization. *Journal of Personality and Social Psychology, 31*, 262–270.

Tesser, A., Martin, L., & Mendolia, M. (1995). The impact of thought on attitude extremity and attitude–behavior consistency. In R. E. Petty & J. A. Krosnick (Eds.), *Attitude strength: Antecedents and consequences* (pp. 73–92). Mahwah, NJ: Erlbaum.

Thompson, E. P., Kruglanski, A. W., & Spiegel, S. (2000). Attitude as knowledge structures and persuasion as a specific case of subjective knowledge acquisition. In G. R. Maio & J. M. Olson (Eds.), *Why we evaluate: Functions of attitudes* (pp. 59–94). Mahwah, NJ: Erlbaum.

Thurstone, L. L. (1928). Attitudes can be measured. *American Journal of Sociology, 33*, 529–544.

Thurstone, L. L. (1931). The measurement of social attitudes. *Journal of Abnormal and Social Psychology, 26*, 249–269.

Tiedens, L. Z., & Linton, S. (2001). Judgment under emotional certainty and uncertainty: The effects of specific emotions on information processing. *Journal of Personality and Social Psychology, 81*, 973–988.

Tormala, Z. L., Briñol, P., & Petty, R. E. (2007). Multiple roles for source credibility under high elaboration: It's all in the timing. *Social Cognition, 25*, 536–552.

Toulmin, S. (1964). *The uses of argument*. Cambridge, UK: Cambridge University Press.

Trafimow, D. (2000). A theory of attitudes, subjective norms, and private versus collective self-concepts. In D. J. Terry & M. A. Hogg (Eds.), *Attitudes, behaviors, and social context: The role of norms and group membership* (pp. 47–65). Mahwah, NJ: Erlbaum.

Trafimow, D., Clayton, K. D., Sheeran, P., Darwish, A.-F., & Brown, J. (2010). How do people form behavioral intentions when others have the power to determine social consequences? *The Journal of General Psychology, 137*, 287–309.

Trafimow, D., & Finlay, K. A. (1996). The importance of subjective norms for a minority of people: Between-subjects and within-subjects analyses. *Personality and Social Psychology Bulletin, 22*, 820–828.

Trafimow, D., & Fishbein, M. (1994). The moderating effect of behavior type on the subjective norm–behavior relationship. *Journal of Social Psychology, 134*, 755–763.

Trampe, D., Stapel, D. A., Siero, F. W., & Mulder, H. (2010). Beauty as a tool: The effect of model attractiveness, product relevance, and elaboration likelihood on advertising effectiveness. *Psychology and Marketing, 27*, 1101–1121.

Trent, J. S., & Friedenberg, R. V. (2008). *Political campaign communication: Principles and practices* (6th ed.). Lanham, MD: Rowman & Littlefield.

Triandis, H. C. (1971). *Attitudes and attitude change*. New York: Wiley.

Trost, M. R., Langan, E. J., & Kellar-Guenther, Y. (1999). Not everyone listens when you "just say no": Drug resistance in relational context. *Journal of Applied Communication Research, 27*, 120–138.

Turner, M. M., Tamborini, R., Limon, M. S., & Zuckerman-Hyman, C. (2007). The moderators and mediators of door-in-the-face requests: Is it a negotiation or a helping experience? *Communication Monographs, 74*, 333–356.

Tusing, K. J., & Dillard, J. P. (2000). The psychological reality of the door-in-the-face: It's helping, not bargaining. *Journal of Language and Social Psychology, 19*, 5–25.

Tversky, A., & Kahneman, D. (1974). Judgment under uncertainty: Heuristics and biases. *Science, 185*, 1124–1134.

Tversky, A., & Kahneman, D. (1982). Judgments of and by representativeness. In D. Kahneman, P. Slovic, & A. Tversky (Eds.), *Judgment under uncertainty: Heuristics and biases* (pp. 163–178). Cambridge, UK: Cambridge University Press.

Tybout, A., Sternthal, B., & Calder, B. J. (1983). Information availability as a determinant of multiple request effectiveness. *Journal of Marketing Research, 20*, 280–290.

Vangelisti, A. L., Daly, J. A., & Rudnick, J. R. (1991). Making people feel guilt in conversation: Techniques and correlates. *Human Communication Research, 18*, 3–39.

Vangelisti, A. L., & Sprague, R. J. (1998). Guilt and hurt: Similarities, distinctions, and conversational strategies. In P. A. Andersen & L. K. Guerrero (Eds.), *Handbook of communication and emotion: Research, theory, applications, and contexts* (pp. 124–154). San Diego, CA: Academic Press.

Vinokur, A., & Burnstein, E. (1974). Effects of partially shared persuasive arguments on group-induced shifts: A group problem-solving approach. *Journal of Personality and Social Psychology, 29*, 305–315.

Vohs, J. L., & Garrett, R. L. (1968). Resistance to persuasion: An integrative framework. *Public Opinion Quarterly, 32*, 445–452.

Watson, J. D. (1968). *The double helix: A personal account of the discovery of the structure of DNA*. New York: Atheneum.

Webb, T. L., Joseph, J., Yardley, L., & Michie, S. (2010). Using the internet to promote health behavior change: A systematic review and meta-analysis of the impact of theoretical basis, use of behavior change techniques, and mode of delivery on efficacy. *Journal of Medical Internet Research, 12*(1).

Wegener, D. T., & Claypool, H. M. (1999). The elaboration continuum by any other name does not smell as sweet. *Psychological Inquiry, 10*, 176–181.

Weinstein, N. D. (1988). The precaution adoption process. *Health Psychology, 7*, 355–386.

Weinstein, N. D., Rothman, A. J., & Sutton, S. R. (1998). Stage theories of health behavior: Conceptual and methodological issues. *Health Psychology, 17*, 290–299.

Wheatley, J. J., & Oshikawa, S. (1970). The relationship between anxiety and positive and negative advertising appeals. *Journal of Marketing Research, 7*, 85–89.

Whittaker, J. O. (1967). Resolution of the communication discrepancy issue in attitude change. In C. W. Sherif & M. Sherif (Eds.), *Attitude, ego-involvement, and change* (pp. 159–177). New York: Wiley.

Whittaker, J. O., & Meade, R. D. (1967). Sex of the communicator as a variable in source credibility. *Journal of Social Psychology, 72*, 27–34.

Wicker, A. W. (1969). Attitudes versus actions: The relationship of verbal and overt behavioral responses to attitude objects. *Journal of Social Issues, 25*, 41–78.

Wicklund, R. A., & Brehm, J. W. (1976). *Perspectives on cognitive dissonance*. Hillsdale, NJ: Erlbaum.

Williams, K. D., & Williams, K. B. (1989). Impact of source strength on two compliance techniques. *Basic and Applied Social Psychology, 10*, 149–159.

Wilson, J. D. (1992, September 14). Gays under fire. *Newsweek*, pp. 35–40.

Wilson, S. R. (1990). Development and test of a cognitive rules model of interaction goals. *Communications Monographs, 57*, 81–103.

Wilson, S. R. (1997). Developing theories of persuasive message production. In J. O. Greene (Ed.), *Message production: Advances in communication theory* (pp. 15–43). Mahwah, NJ: Erlbaum.

Wilson, S. R. (2002). *Seeking and resisting compliance: Why people say what they do when trying to influence others*. Thousand Oaks, CA: Sage.

Wilson, S. R. (2010). Seeking and resisting compliance. In C. R. Berger, M. E. Roloff, & D. Roskos-Ewoldsen (Eds.), *The handbook of communication science* (2nd ed., pp. 219–235). Thousand Oaks, CA: Sage.

Wilson, S. R., Aleman, C. G., & Leatham, G. B. (1998). Identity implications of influence goals: A revised analysis of face-threatening acts and application to seeking compliance with same-sex friends. *Human Communication Research, 25*, 64–96.

Wilson, S. R., Cruz, M. G., Marshall, L. J., & Rao, N. (1993). An attributional analysis of compliance-gaining interactions. *Communication Monographs, 60*, 1–22.

Wilson, S. R., & Feng, H. (2007). Interaction goals and message production:

Conceptual and methodological developments. In D. R. Roskos-Ewoldsen & J. L. Monahan (Eds.), *Communication and social cognition: Theories and methods* (pp. 71–96). Mahwah, NJ: Erlbaum.

Wiseman, R. L., & Schenck-Hamlin, W. (1981). A multidimensional scaling validation of an inductively-derived set of compliance-gaining strategies. *Communication Monographs, 48*, 251–270.

Witte, K. (1992). Putting the fear back into fear appeals: The extended parallel process model. *Communication Monographs, 59*, 329–349.

Witte, K. (1994). Fear control and danger control: A test of the extended parallel process model (EPPM). *Communication Monographs, 61*, 113–134.

Witte, K., & Allen, M. (2000). A meta-analysis of fear appeals: Implications for effective public health campaigns. *Health Education and Behavior, 27*, 591–615.

Wodarski, J., & Bagarozzi, D. (1979). *Behavioral social work*. New York: Human Sciences Press.

Wolman, D. (2013, April 16). Facebook, Twitter, help the Arab Spring bloom. *Wired*. Retrieved from *www.wired.com*.

Wood, J. T. (2011). *Gendered lives: Communication, gender, and culture*. Belmont, CA: Wadsworth.

Wood, W., & Eagly, A. H. (1981). Stages in the analysis of persuasive messages: The role of causal attributions and message comprehension. *Journal of Personality and Social Psychology, 40*, 246–259.

Woodall, W. G., & Burgoon, J. K. (1981). The effects of nonverbal synchrony on message comprehension and persuasiveness. *Journal of Nonverbal Behavior, 5*, 207–223.

Worchel, S., Andreoli, V., & Eason, J. (1975). Is the medium the message?: A study of the effects of media, communicator, and message characteristics on attitude change. *Journal of Applied Social Psychology, 5*, 157–172.

Wyer, R. S. (1970). The quantitative prediction of belief and opinion change: A further test of a subjective probability model. *Journal of Personality and Social Psychology, 16*, 559–570.

Wyer, R. S. (2006). Three models of information processing: An evaluation and conceptual integration. *Psychological Inquiry, 17*, 185–255.

Wyer, R. S., & Goldberg, L. (1970). A probabilistic analysis of the relationships among beliefs and attitudes. *Psychological Review, 77*, 100–120.

Wyer, R. S., & Srull, T. K. (1981). Category accessibility: Some theoretical and empirical issues concerning the processing of social stimulus information. In E. T. Higgins, C. P. Herman, & M. P. Zanna (Eds.), *Social cognition: The Ontario Symposium* (Vol. 1, pp. 161–197). Hillsdale, NJ: Erlbaum.

Ybarra, O., & Trafimow, D. (1998). How priming the private self or collective self affects the relative weights of attitudes and subjective norms. *Personality and Social Psychology Bulletin, 24*, 362–370.

Yzer, M. (2012). The integrative model of behavioral prediction as a tool for designing health messages. In H. Cho (Ed.), *Health Communication Message Design* (pp. 21–40). Los Angeles: Sage.

Yzer, M. (2013). Reasoned action theory: Persuasion as belief-based behavior change. In J. P. Dillard & L. Shen (Eds.), *The SAGE handbook of persuasion: Developments in theory and practice* (2nd ed., pp. 120–136). Thousand Oaks, CA: Sage.

Zanna, M. P., & Cooper, J. (1974). Dissonance and the pill: An attributional approach to studying the arousal properties of dissonance. *Journal of Personality and Social Psychology, 29,* 703–709.

Zanna, M. P., & Rempel, J. K. (1988). Attitudes: A new look at an old concept. In D. Bar-Tal & A. W. Kruglanski (Eds.), *The social psychology of knowledge* (pp. 315–334). Cambridge, UK: Cambridge University Press.

Zebregs, S., van den Putte, B., Neijens, P., and de Graaf, A. (2015). The differential impact of statistical and narrative evidence on beliefs, attitude, and intention: A meta-analysis. *Health Communication, 30,* 282–289.

Zimbardo, P. G. (1960). Involvement and communication discrepancy as determinants of opinion conformity. *Journal of Abnormal and Social Psychology, 60,* 86–94.

Zimbardo, P. G., & Ebbesen, E. B. (1970). Experimental modification of the relationship between effort, attitude, and behavior. *Journal of Personality and Social Psychology, 16,* 207–213.

Index